Abandoned Children
of the Italian Renaissance

The Johns Hopkins University Studies in
Historical and Political Science

123rd series (2005)

Abandoned Children
of the Italian Renaissance

Orphan Care in Florence and Bologna

Nicholas Terpstra

The Johns Hopkins University Press
Baltimore

This book has been brought to publication with the generous
assistance of the Lila Acheson Wallace–Reader's Digest Publications
Subsidy at Villa I Tatti.

The Johns Hopkins University Press
2715 North Charles Street
Baltimore, Maryland 21218-4363
www.press.jhu.edu

Library of Congress Cataloging-in-Publication Data

Terpstra, Nicholas.
    Abandoned children of the Italian Renaissance : orphan care in
Florence and Bologna / Nicholas Terpstra.
        p.   cm. — (The Johns Hopkins University studies in historical and
political science ; 123rd ser.)
    Includes bibliographical references and index.
    ISBN 0-8018-8184-6 (hardcover : alk. paper)
        1. Orphanages—Italy—Florence—History—16th century.
    2. Orphanages—Italy—Florence—History—17th century.
    3. Orphanages—Italy—Bologna—History—16th century.
    4. Orphanages—Italy—Bologna—History—17th century. I. Title.
II. Series.
        HV1190.T47 2006
        362.73'2—dc22   2005003707

A catalog record for this book is available from the British Library.

For Nigel, Christopher, and Alison

Contents

Tables, Graphs, and Figures

Figures

Acknowledgments

This study began with wider ambitions in a narrower field. Having set out to write a book on the full range of charitable institutions founded in sixteenth-century Bologna, I was diverted to Florence by a fellowship from the Harvard Center for Italian Renaissance Studies (Villa I Tatti). I Tatti proved to be more than just diverting—though thanks to an animated group of Fellows in 1994–95, it certainly was that—and my first thanks are to then-director Walter Kaiser and the community of Fellows and staff who made up that incomparable center. They facilitated my entry into Florence's archives and history, and have proven unfailingly generous and personally supportive in the years since. Having initially intended never to work on the city by the Arno, I was surprised by how congenial and stimulating it could be. A number of colleagues whom I first met in that year have made subsequent returns to Florence all the more welcome, and I would like to thank in particular Sabine Eiche, Allen Grieco and Sara Matthews-Grieco, and John Law.

What became a comparative study still had roots firmly planted in Bologna. Mauro Carboni has been instrumental in helping those roots dig deeper into Bolognese soil. Mary Posthuma, herself adopted into Bologna and ever its passionate advocate, has been the most generous and spirited of friends.

A number of people contributed significantly to the project in various stages, including research assistants Elizabeth Bernhardt, Roisin Cossar, Petra Fisher, Jamie Smith, and Jenea Tallentire. Edwin Bezzina, Sheila Das, and Sandra Parmegiani were instrumental in moving the work forward, and frequently reminded me that what may eventually end up as data on a page or a statistic in a table starts with a very human story about vulnerable boys and girls. Peter Thompson offered critical professional help when the tables seemed in danger of collapsing. Sabine Eiche secured the photos, and Byron Moldofsky and Jane Davie of the Cartography Office at the University of Toronto prepared the maps of Florence and Bologna.

The Social Sciences and Humanities Research Council of Canada provided the first funding for this study, and has continued to support it generously. The Andrew Mellon Foundation offered the fellowship that allowed me to spend the year at Villa I Tatti. AMS Services gave funds for more focused research into health conditions and medicines in the conservatories, and the Renaissance Society of America awarded a Senior Scholar Grant to enable work in the Archivio di Stato in Florence. The University of Toronto has supported this research through a number of small grants and with a larger Connaught Research Grant. I am grateful to these agencies for making this research possible. With the text finished, Villa I Tatti continued its generosity with a Lila Acheson Wallace Reader's Digest Publications Subsidy that allowed it to be illustrated with contemporary images. I would like to thank Director Joseph Connors and the Publications Committee for their support.

Some parts of this book appeared previously in an earlier form and are used here with permission of the publishers. The articles were "Making a Living, Making a Life: Work in the Orphanages of Florence and Bologna," *Sixteenth Century Journal* 31, no. 4 (2000): 1063–79; "Competing Views of the State and Social Welfare: The Medici Dukes, the Bigallo Magistrates, and Local Hospitals in Sixteenth Century Tuscany," *Renaissance Quarterly* 54, no. 4 (2001): 1319–55; and "Mothers, Sisters, and Daughters: Girls and Conservatory Guardianship in late Renaissance Florence," *Renaissance Studies* 17, no. 2 (2003): 201–29.

There are four people for whom this study of abandonment has not been a scholarly abstraction. There may be some irony in the fact that the research for it required me to regularly spend weeks or months away from home; if so, they have very graciously avoided mentioning it. Angela has supported it at every stage and through all difficulties. To her I owe more than thanks can repay. There were times when Nigel, Christopher, and Alison came along for the work, and times when they were left behind. If in compensation they have sometimes adopted a mocking stance of distance toward the Italian Renaissance—with Nigel dismissing it as "the Las Vegas of Classical Rome"—they have never exercised that distance toward their too-frequently absent father. For that I am very grateful, and to them I dedicate this book.

Abandoned Children
of the Italian Renaissance

Down and Out and *Off* the Streets

Sheltering Renaissance Children

Renaissance cities swarmed with children. As many as half of those who walked their streets or lived in their crowded homes were under 15 years old, and perhaps one-third were under 8. In modern societies percentages this high trigger violence, vandalism, and anxiety about a self-indulgent, youth-oriented consumer culture. Renaissance adults were concerned too. They may not have wrung their hands and fretted about their youth as obsessively as people do today, but they complained in familiar ways that young people lacked morals, discipline, and respect for their elders. They worried about sex and violence becoming a way of life for children without adult supervision. And they wondered what to do with all those children.

By and large, Renaissance parents pushed their children quickly toward adulthood. This frequently involved forcing them out of the house and into work and marriage. Children moved into the homes of others for days, weeks, or years at a time, some to apprentice with a master, others to serve in the kitchen and at table. This might happen as early as age 8 or 10, and would almost certainly have happened by the later teen years, when a child might return to her or his parents' home only as a visitor. This might strike us as heartless, and it once struck some historians as evidence that Renaissance adults could not have cared much for children or, for that matter, family.[1] Yet nothing could be further from the truth. In pushing their offspring out of the house, Renaissance parents were sending them into larger families who would help shelter, feed, educate, and raise the children better than any single set of parents could. These larger families might be related by blood or marriage, but frequently were not. They were created by choice and circumstance, occupation and neighborhood. People freely used the language of family to strengthen social ties—honorary brothers and sisters weren't found only in monasteries and convents, but also in guilds, in political assemblies, and in the lay religious groups known as confraternities that helped organize much of people's day-to-day worship and charitable activity.

Most people could identify a wide range of these surrogate mothers, fathers, brothers, and sisters in their social life. The long list began with the "milk parents," consisting of one's wet nurse and her husband. It continued with "godparents," those adults called in to provide spiritual instruction and practical benefits in equal measure. It even extended to the friends that young boys ran around with as well as the co-workers they sweated with before they were even 10 years old. All these were kin, and the older you grew, the more extensive your web of kin became. Although people were free with the language of family, they were strict with its obligations. Charity began at home, but the walls of that home expanded outward to incorporate many others. When you needed them, they should be there for you, and the more brothers and sisters you could gather into your home, the more secure you would be if illness hit, or unemployment, or death. People now claim that you can't choose your family, but in the Renaissance you could—and would be foolish not to. Some even found in their deliberately constructed family a welcome alternative to the incessant demands and claustrophobia of their blood family, or from the pressures to conform from neighbors and business associates. Whatever the reasons, you constructed a family quite deliberately, and this was what responsible parents were building when they sent their preadolescent children out to live with others.

Did it work? The language of kinship was egalitarian, and some groups such as guilds and confraternities aimed to preserve the fiction that within their constructed family, rich and poor could meet as brothers without distinction. But this was still a society more accustomed to thinking vertically than horizontally. The successful brother or sister was the one who recognized the richer and more powerful fathers and mothers in the group and deferred accordingly. Similarly, the language of kinship could be highly inclusive, but it was spoken most enthusiastically by the middling range of artisans, merchants, and professionals who were the active agents in the local economy. They had first used this language in the thirteenth century, when they needed solidarity to seize political control of towns and cities from nobles, magnates, and clergy. By the fifteenth and sixteenth centuries, they were banding together against the larger numbers of day laborers and working poor who filled the city streets. By that time, however, the language of kinship had become so common a part of the political discourse that even the merchants' and professionals' traditional opponents appealed to it to justify expanding their authority. Local oligarchs practiced tight and effective kinship, and nobles and monarchs gladly assumed the title, role, and powers of the father of the social family and head of the body politic. By the sixteenth century, the language of kinship was heard everywhere, but social kinship itself was less egalitarian and more exclusive than either the rhetoric implied or history taught.

We can move quickly from the child-crowded streets of the Renaissance city to the family-rich terms of Renaissance political science because family and kinship framed people's experience and view of the world. But to understand the strengths and tensions, the definitions and contradictions, we need to look at what happened when families broke down. And they did frequently. The extended webs of kinship that men and women wove as they moved into adulthood and parenthood were aimed at easing the devastating effects of poverty and death, and in most cases did. Yet some families still disintegrated after the death of one parent or both, threatening to cast children on the street. When plague or famine hit, the results were catastrophic. The Bolognese jurist Alessandro Stiatici, who had witnessed the devastating plague of the mid-1520s, painted a harrowing picture:

> Many poor men and women died of hunger . . . leaving their children of both sexes abandoned and stripped of every means of subsistence. These, having no home at all, slept under the porticoes, or like beasts in holes and caverns, or at night in the trash heaps and dung hills. By day they were seen going around the city all foul, filthy, and smelly, their faces and limbs lean and gaunt, looking as though they had stepped out of the grave. It was a horrifying thing. Something miserable to see, but even more to hear their cries and moans day and night, wailing like injured animals. Some went to sleep at night close to the fires of the night watchmen, or at the kitchen of the city council, so as not to die of cold, being nearly naked. In getting closer to the fire, they burned the few rags that they had. While a few were

picked up, many of these boys and girls found themselves on the streets, fed and helped only by charitable people and servants of God.[2]

This book looks at how people like Stiatici tried a new approach to get these children off the streets. The institutional homes they created filled the gap that yawned when kin failed, but it is telling that the homes themselves were still organized around kinship: staff and wards were to consider each other parents and siblings. Some administrators even saw themselves as the fathers and mothers of the dozens of children under their care, arranging work and marriages for their wards as they would for their own children. In other instances they saw their responsibility as strictly short-term, returning the girls and boys to their blood kin as soon as possible. Yet through the course of the century while family rhetoric remained strong, some orphanages took on more of the features of workshops and factories, particularly for the textile trade. This was not necessarily a contradiction, since much preindustrial production took place within small family workshops. But by the end of the sixteenth century, the larger orphanages could count many dozens of wards. If their work was to be done efficiently, it had to be organized more strictly than was the case in a home workshop operated by a married couple with a few of their own children, perhaps a brother or cousin, and a traveling journeyman. From the sixteenth into the seventeenth centuries, orphanages for children from lower social ranks slowly transformed into the large-scale factories, pushed by their needs, their numbers, and opportunities in textile industries that valued small hands, low wages, and a captive labor force. By the eighteenth century, orphanage factories could be found across Europe from Leiden to Venice to Lyon, organized on an ever larger scale by governments when it became clear that the private kin-based charities that had founded them could no longer cope. Kin-language and kin-organization were overwhelmed by the economic demands and rational organization of these workhouses, though they never quite died. They remained potent through the eighteenth century in the secret associations of traveling journeymen, and then reemerged in the nineteenth century as the chosen language and automatic bond of unions and fraternal organizations that fought to restore some justice and humanity to the industrial workplace.

But this is to look far ahead. This book concentrates on the sixteenth and early seventeenth centuries, and investigates how orphanages emerged out of a host of needs, expectations, resources, and opportunities. Charity drove the earliest founders, and they had many models to draw on when they aimed to act as kin to children whose "real" family had failed due to death or poverty. I trace the gradual evolution of common forms, the slow construction of networks of homes in a couple of Italian cities, and the dawning realization that the cost of care could be borne in some part by those being cared for. There was nothing deliberate or inevitable about this evolution. While some orphanages evolved into factories, others became schools or convents. And while the children worked more and more, their governors frequently found employment opportunities for them beyond factories and fabrics.

Orphanages emerged out of the disintegration of the family. Yet families had faced disintegration before these orphanages existed, and even afterward only a proportion of orphaned and abandoned children could enter through their doors. Before focusing on the new orphanages, we need to look at the circumstances of orphaning and abandonment, and then at some of the ways that Renaissance society had kept these children off the street before institutional orphanages appeared.

Orphaned and Abandoned

Renaissance families dealt constantly with death. Within a few years of marriage, most young couples faced the death of their parents and, more tragically, the deaths of their children. Few parents could escape the deaths of one or more of their children, and if some aimed to compensate by having more children, the strategy did not keep them far ahead of the scythe. The Florentine merchant Gregorio Dati fathered twenty-eight children with five mothers from the time he was 29 until age 69, but only eight remained alive when the last was born in 1431, and Dati buried most of the rest while they were still young. High death rates offset high birth rates, with the result that few households had more than two or three children in them at any one time.[3]

Death hit most often in the first days or weeks of life, but could take also children who were old enough to be starting school, entering apprenticeships, or preparing to leave the home and strike out on their own. Though conditions varied across Europe and between town and country, as many as 20 to 40 percent died before their first birthday and 50 percent before their tenth. In Florence, which kept a series of Books of the Dead, fully half of those dying from 1385 to 1430 were children, and during plagues they died at twice the rate of adults. Worms, diarrhea, and smallpox killed most of them, though as David Herlihy and Christiane Klapisch-Zuber pointed out, these were often the diagnostic face of simple malnutrition, contaminated water, and haphazard sanitation, problems faced primarily by the poor.[4]

A Renaissance family's first encounter with death was likely the death of a child. But the death of the mother or father might not be far behind. The worst case was the deaths of both parents within a short period, a tragedy usually triggered by plagues, which regularly swept back and forth through cities in both their episodic and epidemic forms, taking away a good part of the population each time. Even outside of periods of epidemic, two of five Florentines died of plague, with young children particularly vulnerable. Gregorio Dati's family battled plague through the summer of 1420, twice moving to different houses in search of healthier quarters. In five short weeks, Dati buried a manservant, a slave, and five daughters.[5] The toll was so high, devastating families, neighborhoods, and social groups, that all the usual kin-based resources for helping each other and particularly for sheltering children were strained to the breaking point. Almost all of the orphanages in this book were founded in wake of plague epidemics.

Whether due to plague, miscarriage, or accident, the death of a mother or father could create conditions that forced the surviving parent to disperse the children. Women were more likely than men to live into old age, but they faced the gravest threats during their childbearing years. A contemporary French proverb held that "a pregnant woman has one foot in the grave," and possibly 20 percent of women died in childbirth or through complications that could extend their suffering for weeks afterward. Some historians believe that the percentage was likely even higher. Recall that half of all children might die by age 10, and yet that half the population of cities was typically made up of children, and you realize that Renaissance women were frequently pregnant, and as a result, often in danger. Three of Gregorio Dati's four wives succumbed in or through childbirth.[6] Widowers frequently remarried, and the stepmother ensured that the household would remain intact, but some men cited their wife's death as the reason why they could no longer care for all of their children and had to abandon one or more.

The deaths of children and mothers brought grief, but it was more often the death of a father that caused the family to collapse. The widow might have little income and few resources beyond her dowry, and her parents and siblings could pressure her to remarry, particularly if she was in her 20s or younger. Taking on a new husband most often meant leaving her children behind. They were considered the "property" and responsibility of her late husband's line, and of no concern to her new spouse, who was under no obligation to take them into his home. Gregorio Dati's third wife, Ginevra, had an 8-month-old son from her first marriage to Tommaso Brancacci, but in his *libro di ricordo*, Dati neither mentions his name nor writes of what happened to him when the 21-year-old Ginevra married the 41-year-old Gregorio.

Italian women in the fifteenth and sixteenth centuries married men eight to fifteen years older than themselves, and the higher up the social scale the broader the age gap yawned. By the end of the fifteenth century, women were contracting their first marriages at age 21 and men at age 29. Their ancestors a hundred years before had married a good five or six years younger, and among the upper classes marriage for girls at 15 or 16 was still the norm.[7]

Richer husbands were older, poorer husbands were less healthy. Regardless of social class, young women marrying older men faced the very real prospect that they would be widows before their children were fully grown. In 1427, 14 percent of Florentine households were headed by widows, not a surprising statistic when we consider that a quarter of all women at the time *were* widows. Women headed 17.6 percent of households by 1552, and 25 percent by 1632, and most of these were widows too. By age 40, 18 percent of Quattrocento Florentine women were widowed, and by age 50, almost 45 percent were.[8] The younger and wealthier among them faced enormous pressures to remarry. Christiane Klapisch-Zuber notes that, judging by the diaries kept by more prosperous families, "two-thirds of the women who became widows before 20 found a new husband, one-third of those widowed between 20 and 29, but only 11 percent of those widowed between 30 and 39—when their numbers grow." Wealthy women were the most likely to marry a far older man, and hence the most likely to be widowed early, yet they were the least likely to head a household.[9]

A woman widowed at age 50 could likely live out her years with an adult child, but younger widows faced more complicated prospects. Most widows had the right to recover their dowries and return to their natal homes (the *tornata*). While their parents, siblings, or more distant blood kin were obligated to shelter them until death, some saw this as a convenient opportunity to employ the young woman in their alliance-building strategies, and so arranged a second marriage for her.[10] This required prompt return of the dowry, something which so strained the resources of the widow's in-laws that many husbands loaded their wills with incentives for wives who remained in the family home and penalties for those who left. A widow who remained loyal to her dead husband's family could often count on more generous allowances, life tenancies on property, and the return of her dowry with interest. A widow who bolted—and some young ones did so almost as soon as their dead husbands were in the ground—could count on nothing more than the return of the dowry. While her natal family wanted to use the dowry to remarry the young widow, her late husband's clan were loathe to withdraw it from their own holdings, and in any event counted on it as the allowance that would offset the costs of raising the now-fatherless children. The mother's dowry came out of the children's inheritance. Diaries and memoirs complain of the "cruel mother," whose lust, greed, and self-centeredness led her to abandon and impoverish her own children, but in fact it was more often obedience to her father or brothers that drove a young widow to remarry. One Florentine memoirist, Giovanni Morelli, complained bitterly of having been "abandoned" by his "cruel" widowed mother because she remarried when he was only 3. Yet Giovanni lived in her household with his stepfather until he was a teenager. She was not cruel for having removed her affections from her son, but for having removed her dowry from his inheritance. Klapisch-Zuber notes that "abandonment was economic as much as affective, and what abandoned children complained of explicitly was the financial implications of their mother's remarriage."[11]

These convoluted marital politics were played out at the higher social levels, but two legal obligations resonated on down the social scale when widows remarried. On one hand, Roman law and local custom held that their new husbands were under no obligation to bring another man's offspring into their households (and were frequently discouraged from doing so as it could play havoc with any children of their own from a previous marriage). On the other hand, the dead father's own blood relatives were obligated to take the children on as part of his personal legacy and their family's collective property and lineage. From what we know of wealthier families whose members penned diaries and saved notarial contracts, this obligation was usually honored, either by taking the children into another household within the family or by boarding them with others for a fee, all under the watchful eye of a guardian. In some instances, these families even arranged a deal with the widow and her second husband, formally appointing them the children's guardians and even reimbursing them for their costs in raising the children. This allowed the remarrying widows to bring their own children into their second marriages, as Giovanni Morelli's mother did. There were nonetheless many poorer families who bore the same obligations in law, but who had nowhere near the resources, and who may have lost contact with parents and siblings if the couple had moved to a new city in search of work. Children from these poorer families were in the worst circumstance, since they had no right to a stepfather's attention and no guarantee of an uncle's care.[12]

Death was not the only wrecker of families. Poverty, plague, famine, and un-employment left some parents unable to care for their children. Local studies in London, Madrid, Limoges, and northern Italy demonstrate that when bread prices rose, more and more children were abandoned at the foundling homes and orphanages. Parents intended or promised to reclaim them when conditions improved, but frequently this proved impossible, or the child died in the over-crowded home.[13] Sometimes fathers simply disappeared. Fathers might aban-don their families in order to escape unhappy marriages, since divorce was vir-tually impossible to obtain. Like Martin Guerre in sixteenth-century France, they might simply slip away in order to escape family pressures and explore opportunities elsewhere, intending to return at some point in the future. Crim-inal activities caught up to other fathers, and if they did not manage to flee jus-tice, they might instead endure months in prison, years in the galleys, or a rela-tively quick trip to the scaffold—all of these were reasons given by mothers who found themselves left with more children than they could manage.

Orphaned and abandoned children whose families had fractured and collapsed would end up on the street unless kin, neighbors, or civic officials found a place for them. The painting of *Our Lady of Succour* from the Florentine church of S. Spirito (Figure I.1) graphically depicts their fear of the devil's reach. The boys would join street gangs and survive on theft and extortion. The girls would almost certainly become prostitutes. What options did they have to ensure that these children would have the adult *governo* necessary to keep them from these fates?

Sheltering Orphaned and Abandoned Children

The shelter found for orphaned and abandoned children before the sixteenth century was almost always small scale, like the home of a poor woman who took in a few wards for money, or the workshop of a guild master who acted as a fos-ter father to his apprentices. Failing that, shelter came in institutions that had a general charitable and religious purpose, like hospitals or convents. Most were organized by kin of one sort or another, though some larger cities like Florence and Bologna established civic magistracies to look after the interests of children in this situation.

Dealing with a prestatistical era, we cannot put comparative percentages on these options open for children affected by the breakup of their families. And while we look at the variety of shelters that stood in for family and that became the models in one way or another for institutional orphanages, we should never

Figure I.1. Master of the Johnson Nativity, *Our Lady of Succour* (showing the devil attacking a child), ca. 1450 (Church of S. Spirito, Florence)

forget that the great majority of these children were simply absorbed without a trace into households of grandparents, uncles, aunts, and siblings. These blood relatives had the most direct and powerful obligations to their destitute kin. They might take the children into their own homes, but they might also steer the children into apprenticeships or domestic service, the very forms of fostering that the children's own parents may have intended for them.

If blood ran thin, was water—specifically the water of baptism—thicker? The first spiritual kin relations for all European Christians were the godparents who had brought the infant to the baptismal font within days or weeks of his or her birth. Godparents were primarily expected to look to their godchildren's spiritual health and education through prayer and catechizing, but were also to take on physical care if the parents were unable or absent. They were popularly expected to look to the child's practical advantage as well—helping find work, housing, or a mate when the time came. There are no systematic studies of godparenthood in Italy, but those for contemporary England suggest that godparents played only a small role in their godchildren's lives after the baptismal ceremony, and that few stepped in as foster parents when the necessity arose. For all the rhetoric surrounding this spiritual kinship bond, it seems to have had little traceable effect when children were orphaned or abandoned. Gregorio Dati recorded the godparents of only about half of his children, and typically recruited between one and three people, though on one occasion he had the standard bearers of all but two of Florence's militia companies. Dati's boys typically received businessmen and colleagues as godparents, while girls received friars, a neighbor, and "the blind woman," who was clearly recruited more for the prayers she could offer than for her ability to raise the child in the event that Dati died. It is entirely possible that some of these godparents arranged for legal guardians or foster parents when their wards were orphaned, but we have no clear evidence.[14]

Guild and confraternity members were also spiritual kin, and seem to have put more efforts into rescuing the children of their deceased brothers and sisters. Some of Renaissance Florence's estimated thirty-five hospitals were small shelters with a few beds operated by guilds primarily for the benefit of members and relatives who might be old, sick, or poor; S. Giovanni Decollato was run by and for the porters, S. Onofrio by dyers, and S. Trinità by the shoemakers. In Venice, members of the major confraternities, called Scuole Grande, knew that after they died, their dependents could be assigned quarters in confraternal housing. Both confraternities and guilds frequently offered dowries to set the daughters of their dead members on a new life, and in Bologna, the confraternity of S. Maria Maddalena guaranteed that needy boys of deceased members would have first call on any spaces that came available in the S. Onofrio orphanage that the confraternity operated.[15]

With or without the death of a father, a child's apprenticeship was much like fostering. Up to half of boys and perhaps a third of all girls left the parental home to spend a few years as an apprentice or domestic servant in the homes of others, and the percentages moved higher with orphaned children of both sexes. Twenty-two percent of apprenticeship contracts in Florence's Wool Guild in the sixteenth century were with girls, and of these, 70 percent had lost their fathers and had been enrolled by mothers or other relations. Girls tended to have longer apprenticeships than boys: in five-year contracts, the ratio was 80 boys to 20 girls, in those of 6 years it became 60:40, and in those of 7 years and more, it moved to 20:80. The extra years represent apprenticeships that started before the usual age of 12. In one extreme case, Bernardo di Monticelli took on 3-year-old orphaned Nannina di Jacopo for a 14-year apprenticeship, and received use of her legacy in the meantime in recognition of the cost of raising her. As Luciano Marcello notes, this contract was really a "form of adoption" that wasn't at all rare in the case of very young orphaned children.[16]

What did this apprenticeship-fostering mean for orphans? In 1419, the year he gained the commission to design Florence's new foundling home, the Ospedale degli Innocenti, Filippo Brunelleschi fostered and then apprenticed a young orphan Antonio Cavalcanti.[17] The 7-year-old boy had the nickname "Il Buggiano" from his home village 40 kilometers northwest of Florence. Brunelleschi's father owned some land in Buggiano, and it was likely a web of connections anchored in that small village that directed Il Buggiano to Brunelleschi's home and shop. The boy trained with and eventually worked alongside Filippo, sculpting significant marble pieces for the master's two other major Florentine commissions, the cathedral and the church of S. Lorenzo. Brunelleschi never married, and was master, employer, and father to the orphan. This gave the two much to argue about, and they fell out when Buggiano was in his early 20s and growing increasingly frustrated by Filippo's unwillingness to pay him for his work. The young man's sculptures were good enough to win him independent commissions, but he felt that Brunelleschi was still treating him as a child. Buggiano stole some jewels as payment, and fled to Naples to set up shop there. Brunelleschi wasn't willing to let either the jewels or Buggiano go, and it is a sign of his determination that he appealed to the highest authorities for help. Pope Eugenius IV was then residing in Florence, and he intervened with the queen of Naples, who returned Buggiano to Florence. We might expect Brunelleschi's response to be a harsh one, but in fact the confrontation seems to have triggered a reconciliation. Filippo named Buggiano his heir soon afterward, and the two continued to lived together until Brunelleschi died 12 years later at age 69.

One hundred years later, the Venetian Antonio di Leonardo Capello dal Banco wrote in his will that he had taken a child from the Venetian foundling home of the Pietà as his *fio di anima*. He named him Bonaventura, and lodged him with a Sier Zorzi, agent of a Filippo Capello who, judging by the name, may have been a relative. Antonio Capello paid the Zorzi family for Bonaventura's maintenance, and also for his apprenticeship in the Zorzi goldsmith shop on the Rialto. In a few years Bonaventura would be 18 and, if his benefactor were no longer alive, the trustees were to pay off Zorzi and give the orphan boy some clothing and some funds set aside in trust. Bonaventura would be independent and, while Antonio begged his relatives the trustees to consider him as their responsibility, there was no question of formal adoption, of naming Bonaventura an heir, or of bringing him into the Capello home. A late-sixteenth-century confessor's manual recommended that priests impose this kind of individualized care for orphans as a penance on those who were wealthy enough to afford it, but it is hard to get a sense of how common such arm's-length fostering was.[18]

Filippo's relationship with Buggiano, Antonio's with Bonaventura, and Bernardo's with 3-year-old Nannina demonstrate some of the paradoxes of substitute family life in the Renaissance. Their relationships look to us very much like modern-day fostering or adoption, and we might be tempted to use the terms. Yet Renaissance families shied away from this terminology, and by the late fifteenth and early sixteenth centuries, some European legal codes began making adoption illegal or difficult, forcing parents through loopholes if they wished to contract it. The issues were economic and moral, and vexed wealthier families and legal theorists more than they did those of the middle and lower social ranges. According to its detractors, the adoptive child was a thief. Anything he inherited from his adoptive parents was stolen from their extended family line, which had accumulated property over generations and had maintained it within the line through careful marriages, gifts, and legacies. His adoptive parents were more rightly the custodians than the owners of family property, and their misplaced sentiments should not be allowed to undermine a long-standing family strategy aimed at increasing collective wealth generation after generation. On this line of reasoning, it would be unnecessary and redundant for a paternal relative to formally adopt an orphaned or abandoned child because she or he was already in the family. But adoption that brought an outsider into the family undermined proper patriarchal authority and family solidarity, encouraged illegitimacy, could lead to unintentional incest, and challenged the fundamental belief that blood alone bound families together. Looming behind these alarmist fears was the image of the anonymous and likely illegitimate orphan who had emerged out of the foundling home to wreak havoc on the domestic hearth. The image stirred upper-class lawmakers into action, and so forced adoptive parents into finding ingenious ways around one of the most common restrictions, the ban on letting adopted children (and illegitimate children generally) inherit property. It was sometimes enough to preempt inheritance disputes by donating property through a simple gift *inter vivos* (i.e., between living persons) that was registered with a notary, but there was no guarantee that uncles, cousins, or relatives twice removed might not hire lawyers to get the family property back into the blood line.[19]

But a paradox has two sides. We should remember that while Renaissance society fought legal adoption with an intensity and line of reasoning that may puzzle us, many families—and even unmarried individuals like Filippo Brunelleschi—regularly took others' children into their households and raised them as though they were their own, with an ease that we also cannot imagine. The family was legally closed, but practically open. Many Renaissance families divorced emotive relations from property transfers, and counted more on the kinship ties they could create than on the property they could accumulate. The bulk of families could not hope to transfer more than some tools, household furniture, and clothing from one generation to the next and so legal property transfer was an abstract point. Their indifference to this abstract legality began with marriages undertaken without benefit of ecclesiastical ceremony or legal contract. So-called free or clandestine marriages were recognized popularly by symbols of exchange, by processions and communal meals, and above all by the simple act of living together publicly for an extended period of time. So while we recognize the legal restrictions on fostering and adoption, we should also remember that many people conducted their family lives below the legal radar (the cause of extraordinary complications when they decided to go to court for one domestic reason or another), and that real family ties were sometimes created in spite of legal restrictions or, like the artists who adopted the names of their famous masters, in a free adaptation of convention. Paradoxically, people constructed their families so freely and broadly, that many felt little need to formalize this in law. This would change in the coming centuries.

As we move farther out from the family circle, arrangements for sheltering orphaned and abandoned children become more impersonal—organized by guardians who may not know the children, contracted with professional care providers for a fee, or carried out in institutions that may also have had their eyes on the fee, or may even have had their eyes on the child. But we need to be

careful about our assumptions here, because what may look like impersonal care
on the surface sometimes turns out to have hidden or indirect kin connections.
For instance, many of the guardians who arranged for paid care or apprenticeships may have been godparents, guild brothers, or *confratelli*, but either were
not identified as such in documents or made their arrangements without leaving
a documentary record.

One guardian that did leave records consistently was the city government,
which sometimes took on legal guardianship of orphaned minors. Bologna's
podestà had appointed tutors from at least 1267, and in 1393 Florence established
a five-man *Magistrato dei pupilli et adulti* to formalize guardianship practices that
civic officials had been taking on for at least twenty-five years, often at the request
of families themselves. Tutors and Pupilli officials stepped in when fathers had
died intestate, or when the guardians appointed by fathers were fighting, dishonest, or negligent, or if the family wanted an outside body to oversee the
actions of family guardians. The officials inventoried and administered the ward's
property, appointed foster parents and guardians, saw to education if that was
required, arranged apprenticeships and marriages, and generally looked out for
the orphan's interest until he or she came of age (25 for girls and 18 for boys),
married, or entered a religious house.[20] Bolognese officials had to render accounts annually to the ward's relatives and the *podestà*, and from 1454 these were
to be passed on to the Camera degli Atti and kept in the communal archive. Florence was initially reluctant to take on guardianship, but once it granted itself
legal powers to borrow money from the wards' estates, the government's attitude changed. This conflict of interest meant that relatives had to keep a close
eye on the Pupilli's activities. In 1397, Caterina di Giovanni Gherardini, widow
of Bartolomeo di Ser Spinello, complained to Florence's Signoria that when her
husband died leaving their 18-month-old son Giovanni as his sole heir, she had
petitioned the Commune to appoint administrators for the estate who would
collect the large number of debts owing and manage the properties. Their management demonstrated the worst-case scenario: the administrators had failed to
collect on debts, they had failed to appeal excessive taxes and forced loans, and
their mismanagement had driven down the value of the estate by one-quarter,
or 36,000 florins. The Signoria agreed to Caterina's request for a formal investigation of Giovanni's records in the office of the Pupilli, though it is not clear
if they reduced his tax assessment.[21]

Caterina demonstrates the active mother who calls in the civic magistrates to
administer the estate, but still keeps an eye on things as an informal guardian.

This was a job that by law and custom fell to her late husband's family, but in later centuries maternal and paternal families frequently cooperated in managing such estates. As Giulia Calvi found in her study of 150 cases from 1580 to 1750, the Pupilli itself appointed remarried mothers and stepfathers as the ward's caregivers in 45 percent of cases. Mothers were actually favored since under Roman law they were unable to inherit from their children, and so they would not be tempted to endanger or defraud the child, as male relatives could and did. "There was thus a possibility of reconstituting a family unit around the new couple, who could keep with them, besides the children of the new husband's previous marriages (that, of course, was obvious), those of the widow's first marriage too." The balance of cases were entrusted either to paternal family (18%), or to other caregivers who offered care for a fee.[22] What other caregivers could Bologna's tutors or Florence's Pupilli magistrates draw on?

Their preference, and the preference of other kin who had the obligation and the funds to care for wards, but who lacked the space or inclination to take the orphan into their own households, was to entrust the child to communities of women. This might take the form of an agreement with an established convent of nuns. Many Florentine convents took girls in temporarily as boarders in an arrangement called *serbanza*. The girls might be orphans, but they could equally be young women whose fathers were simply out of town on business. Sharon Strocchia has shown how *serbanza* became popular from the early fifteenth century as concerns about plague, sexual honor, and marriage loomed larger in Florentine civil discourse.[23] It was challenged and even outlawed by religious reformers in the early sixteenth century, who thought that the presence of young lay girls was bad for the morals and morale of the nuns. Yet *serbanza* carried on because it was convenient, reliable, and cheap for families, and because it was a valuable source of income for the convents. In the early fifteenth century, girls entered at about age 7 to 9, and stayed one to three years for a fee—10 to 14 florins annually—that tax officials had estimated as a fair cost of living. By century's end, the fee had risen somewhat and the length of stay had extended to five to ten years. Almost all Florentine convents except the strictly Observant houses took girls on *serbanza*, and many had four or five at a time; the poorer the house, the more it relied on this as a source of income. Some even took in a larger contingent when they faced particularly expensive repairs. Families and guardians decided on one or another house based in part on its reputation for security, for piety, for the quality of education it offered wards, or for the quality of food it put on the table. A larger factor was the presence of family members among the nuns in the house, particularly the sisters or aunts of an orphan's late father. *Serbanza* could thereby reinforce kin ties, and in Florence this frequently took on a political dimension as well. Each girl was assigned a nun-mentor, perhaps her relative in the home, who would train her in spiritual disciplines and domestic arts. This intense mentorship resembled the training that novice nuns received, but *serbanza* was not meant to be an extended novitiate; most girls left the convent to get married, and very few became nuns.[24]

Serbanza assumed a relatively open convent that maintained relations with lay society. One of the challenges faced by the nuns was training their wards for lives as wives and mothers. Religious reformers who promoted tight enclosure couldn't decide whether this was immoral or a contradiction, but they did succeed in curtailing the practice by the mid-sixteenth century. But not all communities of religious women were formally structured as convents. Italian widows sometimes banded together in loose communities to share living expenses and carry out charitable works. These households of *bizzoche* and *pinzochere* might only last for the lifetime of their founding members, though some eventually affiliated with religious orders as tertiaries. The widows could capitalize on their experience as wives and mothers to offer shelter and domestic training to orphans for a fee. Florence's first conservatory was essentially the work of a widow, Leonarda Barducci Ginori who, assisted by her daughters Caterina and Maria, funneled needy girls to a residence where they came under the care of a trio of widows headed by Mona Nanina. In some cases, individual widows offered the same service for two or three orphans at a time. As we will see below, Bologna's S. Croce conservatory began when the philanthropist Bonifacio dalle Balle hired the widow Lucrezia Seghandina to shelter a few children in her home. One child led to two, then four, and soon dalle Balle transferred Seghandina and the girls to larger quarters. As the number of children grew beyond Seghandina's ability to manage, dalle Balle transferred the girls to a community of four female tertiaries, and eventually recast it as a conservatory like the others in Bologna.[25]

These forms of fostering blurred the lines between institutional and noninstitutional care: the nuns and widows fit groups of children into the rhythms of the convent or household, but they never took in more than a few at a time, and the care they offered was relatively individualized. Moreover, the child's kin kept up regular contact and eventually took the child back in or arranged the marriage, apprenticeship, or other work that would launch her or him on an independent life. It was the return to lay life that separated this kind of care from oblation, another form of fostering carried out in convents and monasteries that was superficially similar but that had different results. We can consider it here briefly. The practice of parents dedicating their young children as oblates to a monastery or convent emerged in Western Europe in the late fifth century and peaked in the thirteenth. Most oblates cut their ties with lay life and their families before age 10 and became monks or nuns by late adolescence. Religious reformers were always fearful of the possibility of sexual ties between young and old in the religious house, and many oblates were ill-suited—or at least ill-disposed—to the contemplative life, and could be very disruptive. The practice declined significantly by the fourteenth century, at least for boys. Yet it did not die out altogether as a form of fostering or abandonment: Desiderius Erasmus (1466–1536), illegitimate son of a priest and a doctor's daughter, was sent by his guardians to the Augustinian monastery at Steyn when his parents died; at this point, he was 21 years old and a veteran of a series of boarding schools. Ulrich von Hutten (1488–1523), who would later become Erasmus's more stridently schismatic counterpart in the early stages of the Reformation, was abandoned to the monastery at Fulda by a father who saw little hope for his survival. Perhaps not surprisingly, both men railed at the monasteries and thought that forced confinement in them was tantamount to a prison sentence.[26]

A more institutionalized and thoroughly lay form of care that guardians could turn to took place in the hospitals that were found in every town and city. These places were not just for the sick; hospitals offered hospitality. They provided care in accordance with the demands of Christian charity and to those categories of the needy that the Gospels identified as most deserving: widows, orphans, pilgrims, the hungry, the sick, and the dying. Guilds and confraternities might run hospitals for their own members, and in Florence there was also a number that had been opened thanks to the legacy of a pious benefactor who sometimes installed his family in perpetuity as the governors, caregivers, and even the beneficiaries of his testamentary charity; almost all kin-organized hospitals assumed that charity began at home with one's own. Beyond this were the large civic hospitals like Siena's S. Maria della Scala which, from its late-eleventh-century origins as a pilgrims' shelter, grew to the point where, by the fifteenth century, it was that city-state's largest landholder, most important economic agent, and the occupant of a vast extended complex of buildings that stepped down the hillside opposite the cathedral. In small towns or large hospitals, the various classes of needy might be mixed together under one roof and possibly in one bed, but from the fifteenth century Italian hospitals moved toward greater specialization, frequently under pressure from civic authorities who wanted better care for all their citizens. Separate rooms were desirable, and separate buildings optimal. This was particularly the case for the foundlings who, usually in the middle of the night, were laid in fonts posted just by the main door and off the ground to keep them safe from roaming and hungry animals.

This is not the place to summarize the vast body of literature that over the past few decades has brought to light the details of infant abandonment in Renaissance Italy. Through a host of local studies we know how many infants were abandoned, of what gender and at what age, and sometimes from what locale. We know that most were illegitimate, the offspring of slaves and servants who had been assaulted in the homes where they worked—by employers or owners, by household friends or guests, by fellow workers. We know how these children were cared for, from their early transit to wet nurses to their eventual return to hospital-homes where they received some education before being sent out as teenage apprentices or servants. And we know that even for a time when people expected that one-third of children might die before their first birthday, these hospitals had staggering death rates, the consequence of overcrowding, malnutrition, and disease.[27]

Among the foundling homes established in Renaissance Italy, one of the first and most famous was Florence's Ospedale degli Innocenti. Planned from 1419 and opened in 1445, it is as famous for Filippo Brunelleschi's elegant building as for the thousands of children who passed through its turntable—the innovation that eventually replaced the raised font. Though funded and run initially by the Silk Guild, which Florence had first appointed to be in charge of foundlings in 1294, the Innocenti eventually came under closer civic control and became a model for similar institutions elsewhere in Italy. Bologna's Ospedale dei SS. Pietro e Procolo—colloquially known as the "Esposti" (exposed) or more vulgarly as the "Bastardini"—began construction in 1500 on a building that had the kind of prominent location and portico that many associated with the Innocenti.[28]

Large hospitals like S. Maria della Scala and foundling homes like the Innocenti and Bastardini sheltered hundreds of orphans and abandoned children, and were the most immediate inspiration for the orphanages that this book examines. Yet they differed in three key respects. Children entered as infants, often only hours old. They were largely illegitimate. They had been dropped off anonymously, and as such had been cut off from connections with their parents' blood and spiritual kin. Foundling homes began in the fourteenth and fifteenth centuries to rescue infants who might otherwise be abandoned in church doorways, thrown into nearby rivers, or left to die in garbage heaps. As we will see,

the orphanages that emerged a hundred years later were more deliberately selective, taking in only children who were older, who were preferably legitimate,
and who might yet have some network of kin relations into which they could be
reinserted by late adolescence. They were far smaller, and offered far better living conditions. The differences between foundling homes and orphanages were
significant enough that guardians like Florence's Pupilli magistrates and Bologna's tutors seldom sent their wards to lodge at the former.

The orphanages of the sixteenth century were to some extent a refinement of
the foundling homes of the fifteenth, with concerns about class and citizenship
creating somewhat more comfortable homes for these legitimate children of
respectable parents. Yet these initial differences faded over time under the pressures of numbers and costs. Distinct in their origins, foundling homes and orphanages came to resemble each other by the eighteenth and nineteenth centuries, with both sharing the grim characteristics that we associate with the
institutions from *Oliver Twist*. That said, Italian foundling homes in the industrial age exceeded even the lachrymose descriptions of a Charles Dickens. By the
1830s, 10 percent of all Tuscan infants, but a staggering 38 percent of all infants
born in the capital city of Florence were regularly abandoned to foundling
homes. Married parents began joining unmarried women in the trek to the Innocenti turntable once they realized that their infant might get better care and perhaps education, a job, or a dowry. In 1451 the Innocenti foundlings had represented 4.8 percent of Florentine baptisms. This almost doubled to 8.9 percent
by 1465, doubled again to 21.9 percent by 1531, and then shot to 37.3 percent
by the crisis year of 1552. These are spikes pushed by famine and plague, but by
the later eighteenth century, the Innocenti regularly cared for one-third of all
Florentine infants. Whatever their parents' hopes, most foundlings got little
more than baptism. Overcrowding pushed the death rate up precipitously, with
60 to 70 percent dying before their first birthday. Perhaps the worst case was
Modica in Sicily, where 1,459 infants were abandoned between 1873 and 1883;
three survived. One observer in Salerno claimed that these homes were "the
tomb of the foundlings."[29] If this was where it ended, where did it all begin?

The Test Cases: Florence and Bologna

This study will compare the networks of orphanages that developed in two
cities in the course of the sixteenth century: Florence and Bologna. Both had

populations that ranged between 60,000 and 75,000 through the course of the century, and both experienced the plagues and famines that drove those numbers down on a regular basis. Both were economically prosperous, with a rapidly expanding silk industry growing beside more traditional textile trades and banking, but both also suffered the cyclical movements of these industries that could halt the looms and throw hundreds or thousands out of work and into poverty. Both drew in large numbers of workers from their surrounding hinterlands whose deaths often left their families stranded in a strange city far from kin. Both were culturally sophisticated and internationally connected. Florence was a center for the arts and humanities that drew writers, thinkers, and artists from across Italy. Bologna was the home of Europe's oldest university that attracted students from across the Continent for professional studies in law and medicine. As a result, both cities had sophisticated governing elites who were conversant with political and social developments elsewhere in Italy and Europe. Both had dozens of active and sometimes very wealthy confraternities whose members shaped local civic religious life and charitable activity. In both cities, these confraternities worked closely with civic authorities, and often served as the agents that organized and delivered social welfare on the city's behalf and with its money. Both had major hospitals that dated back to the twelfth and thirteenth centuries, and were well known for the advanced level of charitable care offered in them. Both had civic governments that were ready to experiment with ways of making the plethora of large and small hospitals more effective by imposing forms of rationalization and specialization. Both made significant changes and additions to their networks of institutional charities in the 1550s, opening new homes and devising new forms of administration that combined private and civic funding, and that reached new categories of poor children. Both found that this expanded network began to strain and break under the accelerating cycle of plagues and famines that hit in the 1590s.

In short, Florence and Bologna were both wealthy, progressive, and innovative cities. Propelled by a combination of religious, economic, and political motivations, both fashioned new systems of poor relief out of older models and institutions and resources and traditions. Yet there were also significant differences, above all in political structure. Florence was the capital of an independent state. Small groups of powerful families had controlled its republican government through the fifteenth century, and continued to exercise control after the defeat of the last republic in 1530 and the installation of the Medici as dukes.

They assumed that this would continue when 17-year-old Cosimo de Medici, son of the illegitimate Medici mercenary Giovanni delle Bande Nere, was drafted onto the ducal throne in 1537, but they were soon disappointed. Duke Cosimo turned out to be a gifted survivalist and the architect of one of the most effective centralizing governments of the sixteenth century. Ducal Tuscany was a prototype of absolutist government, and given its more compact scale and lack of serious internal religious, cultural, and linguistic distinctions, it demonstrated a more effective absolutism than those larger European states, like France, to which the term is usually applied. Yet it was also effective because Duke Cosimo I knew how to negotiate with the families, institutions, and towns within his state, adapting dictate and compromise as situations required. His reforms to Florence's welfare system, and his determination that this should be more tightly controlled by his appointees and should more generously serve the whole of the territorial state, profoundly shaped the direction of charitable institutions generally, and orphanages in particular.

Bologna was not an independent state, but the second city of the papal state. Though the fifteenth century a faction within its oligarchy had coalesced around one family, the Bentivoglio, and had worked with them toward de facto autonomy. They were successful to a point, because Bologna was strategically located and was able to develop strong links with other cities that wanted to influence peninsular politics, Milan in particular. The Bentivoglio party monopolized political power and tapped into the city's tax revenues so successfully that it alienated many other leading families and clashed with a series of popes. They survived one major conspiracy and the advance of Cesare Borgia, but eventually found their match in Pope Julius II. The Bentivoglio fled without a fight before his entry to the city in November 1506, but Julius II's subsequent efforts to subdue the city proved too harsh, and it fell to Pope Leo X to devise the governing structure that lasted to the end of the ancien régime. Leo established a senate of forty (increased to fifty in 1590) members drawn from leading families, believing rightly that this brought all the traditional faction leaders and families into one governing chamber. Senate decisions had to be approved by the papal legate and vice versa. Members served for life, and some seats tended to become family possessions. The senate itself became a closed oligarchy whose members guarded Bologna's privileges and their own prerogatives very closely. Early on, they worked to rationalize the network of Bologna's charitable institutions and to complete it with a workhouse that opened in 1563 as the keystone of a broad set of poor relief services that arched over the city. Unlike Duke Cosimo I in

Florence, they aimed to restrict these services to the citizens of the city rather than to residents of the outlying hinterland.

Their histories gave the two cities different relations with the institutional Church. Florence was always much closer to the institutions and hierarchy of the Catholic Church. It had little to fear and much to profit, particularly when its bankers lent money to popes and its leading families controlled lucrative curial positions like the depository general. Authors from Boccaccio to Machiavelli freely lampooned clergy, but in their confraternities and their personal relations ordinary Florentines demonstrated loyalty to and confidence in the clergy. They had particularly close relations with religious houses and their charismatic leaders; the Dominican friar Savonarola was popular locally, and retained a determined following long after his ashes had floated down the Arno. Florentine charities often had closer relations with both religious houses and secular clergy, and indeed as we will see, some of the conservatories opened in the sixteenth century metamorphosed into convents by the seventeenth.

Bologna's relations with the institutional Church were always marked by political conflict, and the continuation of this conflict over centuries had bred anticlericalism more deeply into the bone. There were no charismatic religious leaders like Savonarola based in the city, and the Dominicans (associated with papal authority as the agents of the Inquisition) could not find here the popular following they enjoyed in Florence—Bolognese preferred to follow the Franciscans, who frequently seemed to get into trouble with Rome. The city's main agents of civic-religious culture were its confraternities rather than its clergy. Even after the senatorial oligarchs realized that their personal futures were best served through cooperation with the papal hierarchy, they aimed to keep the city's charitable institutions in confraternity hands and thus outside the purview of the papal legate and archbishop. As just one example, through the 1580s the founders of Bologna's dowry fund fought to avoid juridical designation as a so-called *luogo pio*, or pious institution, because after the Council of Trent bishops had the authority to conduct pastoral visits of *luoghi pii*, to review their accounts, and to appoint clerics to their boards. Though ecclesiastics challenged its autonomy repeatedly, and in spite of a papal charter, the Monte del Matrimonio successfully protected its status as a lay institution governed by its own statutes to the end of the ancien régime.[30]

The sixteenth century was a critical time across Europe for the development of civic welfare systems that were more comprehensive in scope, more selective in service, and more ambitious in what they aimed to achieve both for the poor and for the city itself. Where individuals had always woven personal safety nets through a multitude of intersecting and overlapping kinship ties, cities now aimed to weave larger nets that could rescue and redeem the poor while simultaneously directing their energies to the needs of the urban community. The threads in these larger nets included local charitable traditions and institutions like the hospitals, active lay bodies like the confraternities, expanding state bureaucracies, new financial institutions like charitable pawn shops offering cheap loans to the poor, new industries like silk, and religious reform movements that emphasized redeeming the poor. The resulting welfare bureaucracies of the sixteenth century were hybrids—both political and private, lay and clerical, secular and religious, domestic and institutional. They were built on the material resources of the past, represented by hospital and confraternity legacies, supplemented by the potential earnings of the present, reflected in the work carried out by those whom the new institutions served and the tax revenues that governments funneled into them. It was once common to attribute these developments to the Protestant Reformation, and for good reason. Protestantism was an intellectual and political revolution. It did away with those elements of Catholic theology that promoted charity as a means of getting into heaven. It drew poor relief into its vision of a government-organized and lay-directed church that expropriated the resources of former monasteries, convents, parishes, and confraternities, and used the funds to underwrite worship, education, and social services more generally. But if Protestantism was an overt revolution that reshaped northern Europe, Catholicism underwent its own revolutions that changed the delivery of welfare in much the same way. Catholic reform movements promoted an aggressively activist piety that used charity to save body and soul. And Catholic governments proved no less eager than Protestants to try and control or at least employ the resources of charitable and clerical institutions. The Spanish Catholic humanist Juan Luis Vives codified the ideas embraced by Protestant and Catholic governments alike in his *De Subventione Pauperum* (1526), a book that circulated widely throughout Europe in various translations. The book drew on some experiments and inspired others, and many cities kept one eye on the expanding literature and another on the multiplying practical models as they altered their welfare systems through the sixteenth century.[31]

This study focuses on Florence and Bologna because, in an era when *all* welfare reform happened at the civic level, they were at the forefront of change in at least three ways. First, they led other cities in the number, type, and organization of shelters for needy poor generally, and children in particular. Bologna opened one of the first specialized orphanages in Europe, and the first specialized paupers' workhouse in Italy. Florence had pioneered a century earlier with its Innocenti foundling home. More to the point, while other European cities experimented with single homes for one category of poor or another that might be established by philantropists, confraternities, political leaders, or churchmen, Florence and Bologna forged ahead with deliberately integrated *networks* of homes that wove such individual efforts into a coordinated web of care. Second, these two cities demonstrated two very different approaches to the practical problem of running a network, and their differences would become models for government welfare bureaucracies in early modern Europe. In Bologna, large bodies of volunteers ran smaller homes that were hybrids of the small medieval hospital and the specialized shelter. There were fewer paid staff, and administrators had more day-to-day contact with the children and more personal involvement in bringing them in and eventually seeing them out. In Florence, small councils of administrators ran large homes with the help of paid staff in what was more definitely a prototype for modern government. Administrators had closer relations with their political masters than with their juvenile wards, and their push for efficiency and economy became a push toward the ever larger homes and factory-style workshops that multiplied across Europe. Third, the differences between Florentine and Bolognese welfare bureaucracies and institutions were rooted at least in part in the emerging political distinction between the two cities, and offered distinct lessons to cities on one side or another of the gap that yawned as early modern territorial states began to emerge and consolidate. A few cities followed Florence and became the capitals of these territorial states, retaining political influence and expanding their boundaries. Many more cities were, like Bologna, forced under umbrella of such states, and looked for ways to stem the erosion of their traditional autonomy. The Bolognese built their coherent network of interlocking specialized institutions as much to shore up the local authority of a political elite that now functioned under the wing and in the shadow of the papal state, as to offer better care to select groups of citizens. They focused more directly on the economic and demographic needs of the city itself, and worked far more deliberately to return the poor to an active role in it. Florence's institutions were agents of the state's expansion and fringe benefits for subject communities, and as such were open to a broader range of poor drawn from the whole of Tuscany. They were initially less organized and innovative because Florence's system of hospitals had long been adequate for its needs, and it typically took a serious crisis to bring change. Moreover, in spite of a magistracy established for the purpose in 1542, Florence took longer to achieve the ordered and rational network that Bologna quickly developed. The early dukes were ambivalent and wanted to be sure that the magistrates running such a network would not undermine their own authority and patronage. On a different level, the Florentines generally were also ambivalent, and took far longer to embrace the *idea* of a lay religious network of charitable orphanages, particularly for girls. Some of its homes turned into convents, and under the pressure of numbers, the remaining institutions more quickly degenerated into the large and grim welfare institutions that we associate with later centuries.

In societies accustomed to distinguishing between worthy and unworthy poor, orphaned and abandoned children were universally recognized as the most vulnerable and needy of the poor. Yet few universals remained as cities worked out the details of how to help them. As we investigate how Florence and Bologna came to care for these children, we will see what difference gender, class, and citizenship made. We will also see that, given the political and bureaucratic differences just noted, the accidents of geography could result in quite different experiences for children in one city or the other. While these homes demonstrate the best charitable care that cities could muster for their most deserving poor, they also show us how demographic, economic, and social pressures gradually reshaped that care over the course of the sixteenth century. Chapter 1 will review how the two cities developed their networks of homes in response to the demographic crises, famines, and plagues of the sixteenth and early seventeenth centuries (particularly the 1520s, 1540s–50s, and 1590s). Chapter 2 will consider who entered the homes and how they got in. Chapters 3 and 4 will look at how girls and boys respectively experienced life in the homes. Chapter 5 will shift attention to the adults who ran the homes, looking at how the two cities ran their homes differently, and then at how women ran homes differently from men. Chapter 6 will look at how and when children left their homes, and where they ended up once the doors opened for them.

Note on terminology: The shelters for orphaned and abandoned children that this book deals with were generally called only *ospedale* or *casa* in the Renaissance because those were the institutions and terms that contemporaries were familiar with. For convenience and clarity, I will refer to shelters for boys as orphanages and shelters for girls as conservatories, though strictly speaking these terms only came in to use later. We can call the children themselves orphans even though many still had one surviving parent (most often the mother) because contemporaries used the words *orfano* or *orfanello* to designate a fatherless child.

Note on dating: Until 1751, Florentines calculated the new year from 25 March. Dates in this volume have been adjusted such that the new year begins on 1 January.

Opening a Home

Famine grew in Bologna, such that you couldn't find anything to live on, and in every part of the city one heard cries and laments . . . the Senate commanded the Captains of the Gates not to let in any people from the countryside. These were so desperate, that in order not to die from hunger they ate the roots of plants, and made bread from grass roots, crushed grape skins, and nut shells . . . they collected the blood of cattle and the skins of eels and ate them . . . It happened that many girls, forgetting themselves in hunger, went around in public to ask at the doors for alms for the love of God. Some citizens, fearful of God and for the honor of these girls, quickly came and led them to the hospital of S. Giobbe, and dressed them all in gray. They laid no obligations on them other than that they pray to God at certain hours, and then work, and these citizens gave the girls something to eat. They were later conducted to S. Vitale, where there was a house, and they called them the girls of Santa Marta . . . Many poor and young boys were also brought to the hospitals, and helped so that they would not die of hunger.[1]

The priest Ghirardacci's account is shot through with the chaos of famine. Young women forget themselves in desperation, throwing aside the reserve that their now-dead parents had taught them, and roaming from door to door in search of something to eat. Some citizens hear of this and rush to intercept them, less afraid of the girls' literal death from hunger than their potential social death from public begging. Possibly cursing themselves for having allowed the situation to degenerate to this point, they hurry the girls to the newly opened charitable hospital of S. Giobbe. Since it shields and cures the victims of syphilis, it offers more secretive and protective enclosure than any other hospital in the city. Who could pause to appreciate the irony of its becoming a shelter to protect the sexual honor of adolescent girls? The Bolognese citizens who hustle the girls into the shelter have no leisure for irony. More to the point, they have no clear model to follow when gathering these orphaned and abandoned girls, no priority beyond getting them off the dangerous and endangering streets. They are breaking new ground, because nothing like this has been tried before in Italy or even beyond the Alps. They turn the *abbandonate* into ersatz nuns, clothing them in identical habits, asking them to pray the canonical hours, finding a bit of work to keep the girls occupied, sharing the responsibility of keeping the girls fed, and, no doubt, wondering what to do next.

Gradually a conservatory takes shape through this welter of improvisations and makeshifts that begins in the autumn of 1505. The backdrop of chaotic famine shifts by the end of the next year to become the backdrop of disordered politics as the Bentivoglio family that had controlled the city for decades flees in the advance of Pope Julius II, who is intent on exercising the papacy's claims over Bologna to the fullest. The family and their supporters had progressively tightened their grip on Bologna's charities over the previous decade as one of many strategies of expanding their power, and it is by no means clear what direction these charities will now take. No one expects the Bentivoglio to sit idly in exile, so local politics are increasingly provisional, suspicious, and fearful, and cast their shadow on local charity.

Through this period, the number of individuals and groups claiming a stake in the girls' welfare expands. Among these is the Compagnia dei Poveri Vergognosi (the Company of the Shamefaced Poor), a charitable confraternity that discretely gathers and distributes alms for distressed gentlefolk who would be shamed by public begging. The Poveri Vergognosi are represented by someone whose name is among the first to be associated with the girls, Carlo Duosi. This exclusive brotherhood numbered in its ranks some traditional opponents of the Bentivoglio, but Duosi's own politics are unclear. The confraternity running the Ospedale di S. Giobbe also claims an interest in the girls, as does a third, more loosely organized group made up most likely of some of the original citizens who had aided the girls and who appointed legal representatives to look after their interests. Cooperation among these three groups sometimes becomes testy over the decades that follow.

The girls themselves, so far as we can tell, live largely day to day: praying, possibly doing piecework for the silk trade, and moving from one temporary shelter to another as their guardians improvise their care. The series of homes was all in the eastern end of the city, near the Ospedale di S. Giobbe, the old Porta Ravennate market, and the emerging Jewish quarter, and frequently in the shadow of Bologna's landmark two towers, the leaning Garisenda and the towering Asinelli. Perhaps after a few too many ribald jokes had been made about housing virgin girls in the company of syphilitic men, they left S. Giobbe for a house on nearby Via S. Vitale, a major street skirting the Bentivoglio neighborhood. From there it was on to other borrowed rooms in the same district. In 1515 this decade of moving came to an end when the girls' legal guardian, Carlo Antonio Rubini, likely acting as the agent for the informal group of sponsors, bought a home. They were back on Via S. Vitale but a little closer to the city center. They were now popularly called the "girls of S. Marta," suggesting that they were expected to be practical and domestic, if not necessarily married. Their care was guaranteed by the Compagnia dei Poveri Vergognosi and the Ospedale di S. Giobbe. Should the informal group represented by Rubini ever fall apart, the charitable confraternities of S. Giobbe (run by families of the Bentivoglio faction) and the Poveri Vergognosi (with a heavier representation of anti-Bentivoleschi) would gain title to the house and share responsibility for its girls.[2]

As the girls grew older their ambivalent status became more troubling to their guardians. Some had reached the age of marriage, but those who had been 13 or 14 when the citizens first swept them off the street in 1505 would have long passed it by the time they could move as the "girls of S. Marta" into their home on Via S. Vitale. Some would have returned to their extended families in the years since that catastrophic famine, and others might have found their way out through marriages arranged by these families or other guardians. There are no documents to tell us. Yet many girls remained, and they weren't girls in anything but the strictly legal sense of being unmarried dependents. Having spent another decade in the social limbo between convent and community, some of these women were persuaded that their best option would be to become actual nuns in a proper convent of their own. Steps in this direction had already been taken when Cardinal Bishop Lorenzo Campeggi threw a group of nuns out of their convent of Santa Maria delle Pugliole on grounds of overdue reform. In March 1526, thirty-two of the girls walked out of the door of their conservatory on Via S. Vitale and followed in procession behind five nuns drawn from Bologna's leading convent, Corpus Domini, to the recently vacated cloister. This they renamed S. Bernardino e S. Marta, in memory both of the prominent fifteenth-century preacher who had stayed at the convent on his first visit to Bologna and of their own saintly protector S. Marta. These thirty-two took the habit and rule of the Poor Clares.[3]

Far from settling matters, their departure only set the stage for yet another upheaval. The new nuns and their guardian Rubini seem to have assumed that the girls remaining in S. Marta would find their exits through vows of matrimony, leaving the eventually vacant house on S. Vitale to be folded into the convent's patrimony. Yet as the thirty-two were processing out the front door, a new contingent of abandoned girls was being ushered in the back door by another confraternity, the Compagnia di S. Maria della Castità. Its origins and rights were unclear, but by 25 May 1526, this confraternity compensated the newly formed nuns of S. Bernardino e S. Marta, and became the proprietor of the home and the sponsor of its expanded community of abandoned girls. There seems to have been more than a little strong-arm pressure on the part of the upper-class members of S. Maria della Castità, who planned to restrict entry to the poor daughters of Bolognese citizens. However, shaped by expedients, uncertainties, and the competing visions of three confraternities, S. Marta had by 1526 an identity as *a* place for abandoned girls. More to the point, it had walls, a roof, and beds.

Although Rubini and representatives of the Poveri Vergognosi and S. Giobbe all signed an agreement, enough dissatisfaction and loopholes remained to keep the nuns and the *abbandonate* fighting for years over who had rights to the building, the conservatory's early legacies, and even its title of S. Marta.[4] And enough uncertainty remained that both the original informal group of guardians and the successor confraternity of S. Maria della Castità—by all appearances a hastily cobbled-together brotherhood—soon faded from the scene, leaving the Poveri Vergognosi to pick up the pieces. It exercised its control in 1554 by writing the first set of statutes to govern the activities of the girls, of the nuns who supervised their day-to-day care, and of the lay men and women who oversaw the operation and integrated it into the Poveri Vergognosi's expanding activities. Almost fifty years after those first girls, "forgetting themselves in hunger," had hit Bologna's streets, a clearly governed system for their care had emerged.

The home that became the Conservatory of S. Marta was many things to many people over its first five decades. Few of them would have known what a conservatory was or could be and, judging by the departure of thirty-two in 1526, not all would have thought that a lay-directed shelter that steered abandoned girls into marriage or work was even a good thing. Not all homes had so improvised and unsettled a start. Particularly as the century progressed, governments, lay-people, or clergy starting a home in cities like Bologna or Florence tried to lay the groundwork well in advance. They secured quarters, financing, and supporters before the doors even opened. Working directly or indirectly, they imposed overhauls and consolidations to streamline administration, focus care, and put these institutions under closer political oversight. Existing homes became ready models both for what to follow and for what to avoid. New homes adopted their statutes with modifications that reflected new circumstances or old lessons learned about fraud, incompetence, or exploitation. Those who ran established homes in both cities lent their experience and sometimes resurrected their hopes in the new places. Yet best-laid plans often went astray. No matter how well-planned, each home had to improvise in the face of the famines, plagues, political trials, and economic dislocation that reared up suddenly and pushed both plans and experience to the limit. Almost all homes had to revise their ambitions and their statutes within a matter of decades—or at least to write these if that hadn't already been done.

This chapter reviews the opening months and years of the homes that emerge in Bologna and Florence from the early sixteenth through the early seventeenth centuries, focusing on how social and political circumstances shaped a network of institutional support for orphaned and abandoned boys and girls in each city. Individually and in their networks, they became templates for the homes established across the Continent in later decades. While gender was the most critical category distinguishing one home from the other, social class was not far behind. Class determined the size of homes, the quality of care offered in them, and even the likelihood that their wards would exit from them into adult lives as spouses, servants, artisans, or clergy. Where records allow, we will look more closely at a few homes in order to convey the experience from the point of view of both the organizers and the organized—that is, those adults who desperately sought to provide a home, and those children who sought, equally desperately, to survive in them.

Building a Network: Bologna

The deft coup of 1526 that saw the confraternity of S. Maria della Castità steal the home of S. Marta out from under its departing girls and their puzzled guardians was not an isolated act, but part of a larger shakeup of Bolognese *ospedali* driven by the series of famines and plagues that shook northern Italy from 1525 to 1527. There is no direct evidence that the older girls of S. Marta had to move in order to make space for the younger *abbandonate* thrown up by the new disaster, but certainly this famine and plague forced Bologna's charitable *ospedali* to open their doors to more needy children than they had seen before. They also had to be prepared to give them more than simply meals and a bed for a few days; these children needed a home and a future. This would require more coordinated planning, and through the 1520s and 1530s, Bologna's political and religious leadership responded by framing the first elements of a synchronized system of care specifically for abandoned children—or at least those from the more worthy ranks in society.

S. Marta had spaces for some three dozen girls, but this was nowhere near enough. The issue was less one of space than of class. Civic officials had opened the old monastery of S. Gregorio about a kilometer outside the Porta Maggiore gate at some point in the early years of the century, and a 1534 alms-gathering permit notes that over two hundred poor girls called it home.[5] But this was a home for the daughters of laborers or small artisans; few considered S. Gregorio an appropriate shelter for girls whose fathers had been shopkeepers, guild members, or professionals. In order to meet this socially specific need, one of Bologna's larger pilgrims' hostels was pressed into service by the late 1520s. The hostel and shrine of S. Maria del Baraccano at the southeast corner of the city wall by the S. Stefano city gate were significant centers on the local civic religious map. Under Bentivoglio sponsorship in the fifteenth century, the latter's miracles had acquired a particularly political cast, with the Virgin conveniently springing into extraordinary defensive action at times when the leading family was under threat.[6] Julius II had supported the shrine and its elite confraternity after expelling the Bentivoglio in 1506 and 1512, and, thanks to subsequent formal visits by Leo X and Clement VII, it retained its high standing. Papal officials and half the city's ruling senate were on its membership list. This group decided in 1528 to open the doors to abandoned and orphaned girls whose parents had been Bolognese citizens. Approximately eighty were admitted, their care entrusted to a five-man blue-ribbon commission that included the papal legate and representatives drawn from Bologna's foundling home, the Ospedale degli Esposti, and from other charitable *ospedali*.[7] It was a far cry from either the ragtag group that had improvised S. Marta, or the open door that characterized S. Gregorio. Armed with a papal brief and the support of Bologna's political bodies, the new commission won the right to order all of the city's confraternities and *ospedali* to submit statements of their resources and income, which would be taxed to support the poor generally and the girls of S. Maria del Baraccano in particular. Two years later, the pope granted the legate the authority to tax monasteries and other *luoghi pii* (pious institutions) for the same purpose.[8]

The scale of the problems generated by the famine and plague of the 1520s pushed Bologna's governors to lay more obligations on the hitherto largely independent confraternally run *ospedali*. The pilgrims' hostel of S. Francesco temporarily sheltered girls from 1530 until the worst of the problems subsided, but there was as yet no shelter for boys. This was addressed in the same year, when the *gonfaloniere di giustizia* Filippo Guastavillani ordered the men of the confraternity of S. Bartolomeo di Reno to admit orphaned and abandoned boys into their hostel by the Reno canal, just north of the city center.[9] At first glance, the choice was an odd one, since the hostel was far smaller than either S. Maria del Baraccano or S. Francesco. Yet it was adjacent to the rapidly expanding silk district and was run largely by middling-ranked guild masters and artisans who could integrate the fatherless boys into the world of work; some may have already been doing this individually in their own shops. But demand was greater than they thought. The first boys admitted took the small number of beds in the hostel. As more and more arrived, picked up off the streets by zealous citizens, they occupied the confraternity's equally small oratory and eventually every free space available. Crowding ever more tightly as the heat of summer bore down, many of the weakened boys fell ill and died. *Confratelli* realized that they would have to expand their quarters with a dormitory, refectory, and church. Construction on this complex began, largely at the confraternity's own expense, in 1536.[10]

As the brothers of S. Bartolomeo di Reno sought ways to build a larger home for their boys, civic, ecclesiastical, and confraternal officials turned their attention to the equally vexing problem of finding funds to build a future for abandoned girls. Levies on *ospedali*, monasteries, and confraternities could put food on the table, but a clearer sense was growing in the city that more permanent homes—whether domestic or cloistered—would have to be found for the girls. For that dowries would be necessary. In a remarkable public effort, civic and

guild officials in 1535 established a dowry fund under the auspices of the charitable pawn bank, the Monte di Pietà. Guilds, confraternities, and individuals had
long subsidized dowries for the daughters of deceased members of their particular family, locality, or corporate body. This new effort was a public fund established in part by formal subscription and serving the needs of girls in particular
homes.

There was a dual symbolism in the public subscription: the homes of S. Marta,
S. Maria del Baraccano, and S. Gregorio each received funds from twelve donors
and, apart from one guild, each of the twelve was a woman. The list provides a
snapshot of the social constituency of each home: S. Marta and S. Gregorio had
larger numbers of widows and guild families among their subscribers than did
S. Maria del Baraccano. All drew dowries from a number of single women. Most
dowries were for 100 lire—a standard dowry locally for artisanal girls—though
the eight dowries of 50 lire pledged for S. Gregorio are a sign of the lower rank
of that hostel's girls.[11] The Monte di Pietà banked the funds, and disbursements
were the work of a three-man commission made up of the heads of the Bologna's
Dominican, Benedictine, and Observant Franciscan (male) religious houses; the
commission could recall any dowries that it thought were spent in loose or lux-
urious living. With resources for only a small number of girls, and no guarantee
of future income, this fund was a small step indeed. Yet it was the first clear sign
that Bologna's elite was looking beyond the models of either temporary shelter
or ersatz convent, and was seeking ways of reintegrating its girls into Bolognese
society as wives and mothers.

With these developments Bologna had, by the mid-1530s, a reasonably coherent network of homes for orphaned and abandoned children. About three
hundred girls could find shelter in one of three homes that was now dedicated
to their care. These were distinguished roughly according to social rank, supported by confraternities acting individually or in tandem, secured by papal
authorization, and funded by public levies. They were clearly seen as a network:
when Sylvio Guidotti, one of the architects of the 1528 relief plan and the 1535
dowry scheme, died in 1536, local chronicler Giacomo Rinieri eulogized him as
"a devout man, and one of those who governed the hospitals, that is, the girls of
Baraccano, and of S. Marta, and of S. Gregorio."[12] The experience of individuals like Guidotti ensured that the lessons of S. Marta's early years would inform
the newer homes and help at least some girls exit them as wives or nuns. The
network expanded when S. Bartolomeo di Reno opened its doors to orphaned
and abandoned boys, again by public decree and with some public subsidy. It is

hard to tell how many it sheltered at this point, though later in the century a hundred boys made their home in its newly built dormitory. Yet the fact that it existed at all was a clear sign that the Bolognese felt that not all abandoned boys would find shelter with relatives, and that these should not be left to make their homes in the street. The two shelters of S. Maria del Baraccano and S. Bartolomeo di Reno were at the heart of Bologna's emerging network. Their frequent pairing in private wills and public documents demonstrates that many Bolognese saw them as complementary institutions that demonstrated the city's charitable care for orphaned and abandoned children. Alongside these institutions, an indeterminate number of children of both sexes who had been abandoned as foundlings lived at the Ospedale degli Esposti. As was the case with the majority of contemporary foundling homes in Italy, most of these children were girls, and most were illegitimate.[13] In short, by mid-century over four hundred children in this city of 55,000 made their home in one of the charitable *ospedali* scattered throughout the city.

It was not enough. If the plagues of the 1520s triggered the opening of homes and the roughly coordinated system of care for children that brought together ecclesiastical, civic, confraternal, and private efforts, the famines of the 1540s and 1550s pushed demand up to a new level. Chronicler Giacomo Rinieri recorded the city's efforts to placate God, open local purses, and stretch meager resources. Already in 1535, the races normally held on the feast days of S. Rafelo, S. Pietro, S. Petronio, and S. Martino were canceled and the prize moneys donated to the cash-strapped and overrun Ospedale degli Esposti. In 1539 the city government threatened to throw the poor out of the city, following the kind of assessment of needs proposed thirteen years earlier by Juan Luis Vives to the magistrates of Bruges. In April and May officials began a parish-by-parish census of those poor men and women who had lived in the city for less than ten years. These were the "foreign" poor whose eviction would free up food and alms for the "genuine'" Bolognese. Many suspected that they were also frauds— young, fit, and shiftless. Yet when the standard-bearer of justice Giorgio Manzoli and the city's twelve elders (*anziani*) went out with their banners and robes of office in November to begin the expulsion from just two parishes, they were confronted with families—men, women, and babes in arms, all wailing for mercy. The officials lost heart and canceled the expulsion.

Drought continued pushing the price of bread beyond the means of many, until by April 1540, Bologna's bulk measure of grain, the corbe, cost 13 lire, almost three times its price only a year before when the famine began. At this point, a form of typhus began cutting through the hungry city. Locals called it the "male de la pelara," or the "scalding sickness": fevers, lesions, and death took both high and low, and among the names in Rinieri's long list of notable victims we find Carlo Poeta, another of the architects of the 1528 relief system. Authorities now mandated processions every Sunday to gather alms, but one after another of these failed to generate more than handful of change, even as they escalated to a grand gathering of all the confraternities, guilds, and regular and secular clergy on 17 May.[14]

As *confratelli*, artisans, and priests took off their processional robes and emptied their rattling alms boxes, they began thinking of the more direct actions that would be necessary when famine and plague hit again. The result over the next fifteen years was a series of changes that brought new coherence and order to the still relatively loose collection of charitable institutions serving the poor children who were the first victims of these crises. Existing homes merged, new institutions opened, and administrative statutes were written and revised. Through all these changes we can get a clearer sense of which children the Bolognese thought deserved help, and what kind of help they needed. Provisions for children were part of the city's broader efforts to try and come to grips with everescalating poverty. In 1548 the senate and legate revisited the failed effort to expel beggars made a decade earlier. They endorsed a comprehensive plan for relief that would systematically weed out fraudulent, vagrant, "unworthy," and foreign (now more generously defined as those resident less than a year) beggars. A bureaucracy of visitors, censuses, and punishments would rationalize the city's charitable resources and distribute these through more tightly controlled neighborhood distribution centers in the main mendicant churches. A large residential hostel for the poor would avoid the tear-filled chaos of the aborted expulsion of 1539. After some revisions, the city began implementing the sweeping plan in 1550.[15]

The beggars' hostel was the keystone of this system, and after a number of false starts it opened in 1563, occupying the same monastery of S. Gregorio outside the Porta Maggiore gate that had been used earlier as a conservatory for girls of the lower social orders. Where had these girls gone? They may well have gone out the back door and returned in the front in some strange echo of the events at S. Marta some decades before. In 1547, S. Maria del Baraccano had assumed administration of the S. Gregorio conservatory. Formal union with its down-market counterpart came in 1553, over the objections of one-third of the elite confraternity's members. While S. Maria del Baraccano then increased its intake by about twenty-five girls, this represented little more than 12 percent of the girls who called S. Gregorio home. Indeed, as the union was taking effect, the Baraccano *confratelli* rewrote their administrative statutes to establish more clearly the restrictions of class, citizenship, and honor for entry to their conservatory. Girls falling outside these restrictions presumably remained in the S. Gregorio shelter, and within a decade they received new administrators over them and new poor at their side in the dormitories, refectory, and workshop. On 18 April 1563, Bologna's worthy, local, but homeless poor were herded into the cathedral courtyard to begin their formal procession to S. Gregorio, newly styled the Ospedale dei Mendicanti. Over eight hundred poor marched in this inaugural procession, more than two-thirds of them women and children, and some of these no doubt girls and young women already living there who had not been deemed fit for entry into S. Maria del Baraccano. Bologna's Ospedale dei Mendicanti marked the first time an Italian city experimented with putting the poor behind bars. Although not an orphanage or conservatory per se, it shaped the subsequent development of the city's network of surrogate homes by absorbing much of the demand for shelter by lower-class and indigent poor. This freed the other homes to be far more selective, far smaller, and far more generous in their treatment of their children. As we will see, the situation was very different in Florence.

The best index of the system's success was an apparent reduction in demand for new shelters. In spite of continuing dearth and S. Maria del Baraccano's reduction in spaces, only one new home opened in mid-century. Brothers of the Confraternity of S. Maria Maddalena, who had begun meeting in 1512 and had moved around periodically since then, had finally gained their own quarters in 1532. The derelict hostel of S. Onofrio in via Mascarella, just east of the cattle market, still bore traces of the elaborate frescoes painted by Cristoforo da Bologna when it had opened almost two hundred years earlier to serve members of a Spanish religious order as they passed through Bologna on their way to and from Rome. The confraternity immediately undertook badly needed repairs.[16] *Confratelli* patrolled the streets by night, offering food and some rudimentary education in guild crafts (*arti*) to the homeless children there, and soon began bringing the boys back to the underutilized hostel for shelter. By 1557, they had received permission to turn S. Onofrio into an orphanage, provided some beds were still available for traveling Spanish clerics. Adapting the new statutes of S. Bartolomeo di Reno and the more selective methods of S. Marta, they began sheltering a dozen or so boys of somewhat higher rank than S. Bartolomeo and utilizing them in public—and profitable—funerary rituals. Renovations to the dormitory began immediately.[17]

As Bologna's civic system of poor relief was taking shape through the 1550s, orphanages and conservatories had to decide more explicitly what part they were to play in it. Scraping by on good will and improvisation gave way to a flurry of consolidations, administrative overhauls, and the first efforts to write statutes for the homes. S. Bartolomeo di Reno began this with statutes drafted in 1550, shortly before it absorbed, through union, the properties of an *ospedale* outside the city walls and assumed, through aggregation, the spiritual benefits of Rome's orphanage of S. Maria della Visitazione. All these actions consolidated its identity as Bologna's main orphanage for boys, a status that citizens recognized with a spike of donations and legacies through the decade.[18] S. Maria del Baraccano wrote statutes in 1553, and the Compagnia dei Poveri Vergognosi did the same in 1554, shortly after they had absorbed S. Gregorio and S. Marta, respectively.[19] S. Onofrio wrote its statutes within three years of opening, though its six-man drafting committee cribbed heavily from S. Bartolomeo.[20] Carefully worded sections on administration, fiscal responsibility, and the duties of resident staff hint at sad experiences with fraud, abuse, and mismanagement; resident wardens were not above inviting friends and family members in to feed at the orphans' tables. Equally careful sections lay out complicated processes for nominating, reviewing, interviewing, and voting on children who sought entrance to the home (or whose parents sought it). These suggest that zealous *confratelli* and wardens had hitherto enrolled children on a more haphazard basis. Boys and girls had won space through the intervention of pushy *confratelli*, the bribing of a cooperative warden, or the luck of appearing at the door when an older teen was leaving for good.

Because the homes had moved beyond being simple temporary shelters, the promise of education, work, and a dowry made entrance to them that much more attractive, and more *confratelli* and civic officials wanted to share in the opportunities and challenges of patronage. Statute clauses underlined the civic nature of the homes, which drew their volunteer officers from among the ranks of the politically active and the economically influential. Each confraternal charity aimed to recruit its highest official, the rector, from Bologna's senate, giving the city's chief legislative body a clear supervisory and coordinating role while leaving the confraternities with responsibility for financing and administration. With senators cycling through various homes as rectors, and members of other leading families joining the confraternities that ran the homes, the patricians could coordinate a wide range of charitable institutions in the backrooms of the Palazzo Communale and in the drawing rooms of Bologna's palaces, without any single governing body setting the rules or picking up the tab.[21] They worked together to restrict access to the conservatories and orphanages to the children of local citizens. All the statutes lay out complicated processes of nomination and review to prevent entry by children who were sick, morally suspect, or socially dispensable. These rules were frequently pushed aside by sheer demand and by the politics of patronage, but their appearance in all the statutes shows that the homes shared in that desire to distinguish worthy and unworthy, local and vagrant, responsible and dispensable poor that we find in all charitable reform of the period. Moreover, although the homes remained independent of each other, there was the clear sense of a local cooperative network under local political control. When it came time to launch the Opera dei Mendicanti itself, Pope Pius IV's brief neatly indicated the broader scale and cohesive organization of that network by specifically ordering that the Mendicanti's adminstration be patterned on those of the foundling home of the Esposti, the Opera dei Poveri Vergognosi, the orphanages of S. Bartolomeo di Reno and S. Maria del Baraccano, and the syphilitics' hostel of S. Giobbe. All were under the control of ennobled confraternities, all were recently outfitted with new statutes, and all were participants in the semiofficial network of confraternal institutions that comprised Bologna's civic welfare system.[22]

The sheer size of the Ospedale dei Mendicanti—it expanded in 1567 to allow separation of men from the women and children, and over the next few decades regularly housed between 1,000 and 1,700 poor—meant that the system of supports for abandoned children established in the 1550s was adequate until once again a combination of famine and plague ratcheted demand up to a new level in the late 1580s and 1590s.[23] One new home emerged in the intervening period, but it was an anomaly in being the work of a pious individual with a particular group of children in mind. In time, it too was co-opted and adapted to the demands of the broader welfare system. Yet it deserves attention here as an example of the tortuous—and sometimes litigious—route from private charity to semipublic institution.

Bonifacio dalle Balle was the youngest of three sons born into a merchant family with deep roots in Bologna.[24] He later wrote of having a "badly spent" (*mal spesa*) youth: no cares, no morals, no wife, and a daughter Anna born to a servant and later put in a convent.[25] Shaken by a deep conversion experience in his early 30s, dalle Balle adopted a path tried by many Catholics in those decades of unrest and reform. We could call it a personal lay vocation: not attracted to the religious orders, he nonetheless framed a life along the lines of the regulars, never marrying, voluntarily leaving his business, studying intently, and devoting his life to charitable work and teaching, particularly with girls and women. Although no Protestant, he was one of those reformed and reforming early modern Catholics, both men and women, who fell between the stools, and whose actions and writings display scant regard for the intermediary role of saints, hierarchy, and clerics generally. Instead, he penned sermons and tracts, copied spiritual works, and wrote a few sometimes contradictory autobiographical fragments that cast his life and work as a morality tale. Dalle Balle professed a determination to "work in the world for the greater glory of God and to establish a current of love between the creation and the Creator." His intensely Christocentric piety may be one reason why his shelter, alone of all those established in Bologna, was not dedicated to either the Virgin Mary or one of the saints, but pointed to the crucified Christ.[26]

What became the conservatory of S. Croce began around 1583. Dalle Balle later penned a few dramatic autobiographical accounts of these years, and while they are not entirely consistent, they show what moved him. In one account, dalle Balle is walking down a street at night behind a young prostitute and her client, and hears her sigh, "Who will deliver me from this life?" In another, he encounters a 12-year-old girl holding off a gang of boys with a stick, tracks down her mother, and, after numerous visits, gets her consent to put the girl with a good woman named Anna. In yet another, he simply picks a little abandoned girl Dorotea off the street and pays a widow Lucrezia Seghandina 7 lire a month to take care of her.[27] Dalle Balle kept in touch with Dorotea and could note two decades later that she had married and was still living. Soon he brought another girl, Lodovica, to live with Mona Seghandina, and then another, and another, until Seghandina ran out of space in her house. Dalle Balle transferred them all to a larger house by the city wall by 1583 or 1584, and then across town to another place on Via della Lame a couple of years later. There were dozen girls in Seghandina's care by this time, but it is not clear what they might have done, if anything. Like the early girls at S. Marta, this group seems to have spent considerable time in spiritual training: Seghandina accompanied the girls to church, and dalle Balle may have preached to them some of the sermons that appear in his hand in the conservatory's archives. Although not enclosed as such, Seghandina was forbidden to tell outsiders anything of the work, and if asked about the girls' sponsor, was to lie and say that it was a foreigner.[28]

Why the secrecy, the dissimulation, and the spiritual training? The girls were the daughters of prostitutes, and secrecy was perhaps the best means of avoiding the questions of honor and dishonor that would swirl around the unmarried dalle Balle's close, albeit arm's length, association with their daughters. Word got out all the same, however, since dalle Balle's efforts to spread the financial liability led him to seek the help of his brothers; of Alfonso Paleotti, nephew and eventual successor of Archbishop Gabrielle Paleotti; and of the local Capuchins and Franciscan tertiaries. The brothers amicably divided the family property, Paleotti promised and occasionally paid a subsidy of 50 scudi (or 200 lire bolognese), and the Capuchins offered spiritual association. The Franciscan tertiaries, whom dalle Balle joined in 1585, became both his salvation and his downfall. In 1592, the tertiaries agreed to dalle Balle's proposal that they turn over to the use of his girls a defunct hostel and some revenue-bearing properties, in return for a share in the governance of what would become a more formal conservatory: four tertiaries would join with dalle Balle in running the place, though there were as yet no statutes to tell them how. Some Franciscan tertiary sisters in the hostel would become the girls' resident guardians in place of the overwhelmed Mona Seghandina.[29]

The five moved quickly. Within half a year, they had sold all the property in order to buy more suitable quarters on Via S. Mamolo near the city gate of the same name at the south end of the city. Although approved by the ecclesiastical authorities, some of the tertiary sisters resisted the sale and refused to leave. Local police eventually chased them out, but the sale was then challenged by the conventual Franciscans, who claimed that they were the rightful overseers of the tertiaries and that, since they hadn't been consulted on the sale, it was invalid. The problem was resolved in 1598 by leaving control of the new properties with the tertiaries, and granting use to S. Croce. By this point, some forty girls were sheltered in S. Croce. Or barely so. A report by the abbot of S. Giovanni in Monte claimed that they had no bread, no wood, and little wine; their most notable possession was a debt of 3,000 lire. Even the baker took them to court for unpaid bills.[30] Dalle Balle had sunk his life and fortune into the conservatory, and was determined to retain control, but with troubles escalating more powerful parties moved into play, adopting techniques that had proven useful in charitable confraternities over the previous century. These rivals joined the body of tertiaries in 1605, shortly before Archbishop Paleotti ordered that statutes finally be writ-ten for S. Croce.[31] A whisper campaign to discredit dalle Balle now swung into high gear, helped in part by the fact that he lived in a separate apartment within the conservatory, an irregular arrangement which even his supporters found awk-ward. He survived charges of immorality and poor administration leveled in the archiepiscopal curia in 1607, but missed a critical meeting in January 1609 when the statutes he had written were up for approval. These reflected his vision for the home as a safe shelter for the spiritual refashioning of girls from the margins of society, and had already been approved by Archbishop Paleotti. In his absence, the meeting quickly became a review of dalle Balle himself, with officials claim-ing that he was contrary, scornful of his colleagues and superiors, and a bad exam-ple for others. The group voted unanimously to throw him out and then set about writing a second set of statutes animated by a very different vision. These cast S. Croce unambiguously as a workhouse and school, removing the emphasis on shelter for the vulnerable daughters of prostitutes, and putting it under the kind of politically connected administration found in Bologna's other orphanages and conservatories. Paleotti obligingly signed these statutes as well.[32] Although dalle Balle was eventually restored to the home and remained active in S. Croce until his death three years later, it soon became a conservatory remarkably different from the one he had envisioned but very similar to the Bolognese model.

Dalle Balle's difficulties in keeping S. Croce going in its early years were due in part to the escalating cycles of famine in 1588–89, 1590, and 1593–94, which cut Bologna's population from 72,000 in 1587 to 59,000 by 1595. At the same time, protective legislation against the import of silk in 1589 had hindered an industry that built a significant part of its profits on finishing imported raw ma-terials. Employment collapsed as weavers left the city. These two developments forced almost 1,700 Bolognese to seek help at the Ospedale dei Mendicanti, but it too had seen the collapse of revenues and was threatening to turn the poor out and close its doors. As crisis threatened the institutional network that had been laid out in the 1520s and expanded in the 1550s, civic and ecclesiastical officials reached desperately to expand it.[33] They approached the confraternity of S. Gia-como with the request that it shelter boys in its hostel next to the Church of S. Giacomo, once a center of Bentivoglio patronage. Some fiscal and legal priv-ileges sweetened the deal, and the confraternity took in thirty boys temporarily in 1590, deciding the next year to make the arrangement permanent. Apart from their lessons, the boys spent time and earned money participating in funerals, of which there was no shortage in that decade. Their confraternal sponsors established a subgroup to run the orphanage and this soon became the base from which more recently recruited patrician members gained control of the operation and integrated it into the established network of Bolognese homes.[34]

The final home established in this period was a hybrid of these types. It reflected the pious charity of a group of gentlewomen, the influence of Catholic Reformation currents in the form of a Jesuit promoter and facilitator, and integration into the local network through the inevitable entry of Bolognese patrician men into its governing council. Known variously as S. Giuseppe or S. Gioseffo, it opened in 1606 as the only conservatory established and run by women. They clearly wanted to serve needs that existing homes failed to meet and, to some extent, exacerbated. Navigating the complicated nomination, scrutiny, and approval processes for the homes of S. Maria del Baraccano, S. Marta, and even the lower-ranked S. Croce could take months. Some confraternities carefully weeded through the fraudulent applications of and for girls who weren't in desperate straits, but who were attracted by the conservatory dowry funds. Other homes exchanged their own entrance procedures for the financial and political support of high-born patrons by allowing them to nominate girls. The net result was the same: prompt help for truly needy abandoned girls was harder and harder to come by.

In order to regain this much-needed assistance, the women establishing S. Giuseppe set five critical departures from local practice: quick review and prompt acceptance, short-term stays, a preference for older girls, no dowries, and guarantors who would take the girls after a stipulated period of time.[35] This last provision was the key that would make the others work, and what made it all the more radical was that the women themselves served as the guarantors. The system favored those families in temporary difficulty that required only short-term accommodation for their daughters or nieces. It decidedly did not help those from the lowest ranks of society, since the doors were shut to any girls who had either begged or spent time in the Ospedale dei Mendicanti.

Twelve women began the home, working with the Jesuit Giorgio Giustiniani and supported by the archbishop. They initially rented quarters until with the help of supporters they were able to buy some houses of their own just inside the Porta Castiglione at the southern city wall.[36] The women initially ran the home very differently from those found elsewhere in Bologna, but after men joined the administration in 1631, S. Giuseppe came to operate more like its companion institutions in the city, with perhaps a greater emphasis on taking in paying customers.[37] As such, it eventually looked more like a boarding school and less like the prompt short-term shelter that its original promoters had envisioned.

Building a Network: Florence

Florence's extensive network of *ospedali* was initially far more effective in keeping good children off of bad streets. Founded by families, guilds, and confraternities from the eleventh century, and thereafter periodically merged, closed, consolidated, subsidized, or looted by communal governments, these *ospedali* ranged from rooms with a couple of beds scattered through the city's neighborhoods, to major institutions like S. Maria Nuova a few blocks north of the cathedral in the city's center, one of the largest, wealthiest, and, by some measures, most progressive institutions in Italy if not Europe. Though communal and ducal governments frequently interfered to nominate officials, merge institutions, or audit accounts, these were largely proprietorial institutions, in that control rested at least in part in the hands of the family or corporation that had founded it. For all its size and civic importance, S. Maria Nuova continued to have as rector a descendant of Folco Portinari, who had founded it in 1288.[38] Family friends, clients, or servants, or the surviving kin of dead guild or confraternity members found shelter in these *ospedali*. Uncoordinated and vulnerable to institutional and familial fraud, this informal network nonetheless carried Florence through the worst of those famines and plagues of the mid-1520s that stretched and broke similar networks elsewhere in Europe. Its local success in that rough decade is all the more remarkable in that the desperate measures of Florence's last republic from 1527 to 1530 included a systematic looting of *ospedale* coffers and the demolition of any suburban investment properties that could shelter the guns or troops of the besieging Spanish armies. Ironically, the network gained its cohesion through those difficult years thanks to the dedication of those followers of Savonarola whose dream of a charitable Christian republic was in some measure responsible for bringing the Spanish troops to besiege the city.[39]

Florentines fit their conservatories and orphanages into existing *ospedali*, but didn't follow Bologna's example and draft or compel an existing confraternity to devote its quarters, staff, membership, and resources to running the charity. The new institutions for children moved around various derelict former convents, *ospedale* buildings, and rented houses, but these buildings were essentially empty and unstaffed. All these shelters eventually developed administrative confraternities or congregations that elected officials, collected money, and found jobs and husbands for their adolescent charges, but only after the fact. Most originated as the work of a few individuals who were driven by charitable conviction, clerical prodding, or political mandate. An early effort by Cosimo I to devise a rational, state-supervised poor relief system for the whole territory had child care as its foundation and a beggars' hostel as its keystone, but was effectively abandoned by the duke when he saw the broader political ambitions of its promoters.[40] As a result, the informal network of homes found in Bologna—distinguished by class and gender and coordinated through senatorial rectors, cross-memberships by patrician families in administrative Larga confraternities, and the discrete conversations of gentlemen and gentlewomen in the city's palaces—evolved differently in Florence. The government—in this instance, Duke Cosimo I (1537–74) and his sons and successors Francesco I (1574–87) and Ferdinando I (1587–1609)—was more involved in ordering shelters opened or closed and in assigning quarters, but less involved in the ongoing task of running or coordinating the homes. A class hierarchy emerged all the same, together with some coordination of efforts. In the case of boys, this was a moot point. They all entered a single state-sponsored institution called the Ospedale degli Abbandonati. For girls, coordination took the far looser form of a somewhat shadowy confraternity, the Compagnia di S. Maria Vergine, whose members were involved in some way or other in the start of all but one of the six conservatories established in Florence by the end of the century.

Florence's traditional network of care weathered the plagues and population collapse of 1522–23 and 1526–28, and even the siege that ended the republic of 1527–30. Yet it frayed in the serious famine of 1539–40 and began coming apart in the even more critical decade of the 1550s. Famine hit in 1551 and then annually from 1554 through 1557. A 1552 census recorded 59,000 inhabitants in the city, a far cry from the 80,000 who had lived there in 1520, and the effects of these deaths on families were critical. From 1530 to 1540, the foundling home of the Innocenti took in 5,400 children, with 1,000 of these in 1539 alone; this was equivalent to 38.9 percent of all babies baptized in the city in that troubled year, double the percentage reached earlier in the decade.[41] Moreover, in 1554 Cosimo I launched the war against Siena that absorbed Florentine finances until 1559, costing 2 million scudi before it was done. This was money drained from the pockets of citizens, the hands of the poor, and the patrimonies of charitable institutions.[42] As the demographic and subsistence crises deepened through these decades, Florence launched an institutional response that was similar to Bologna's. Within two years of the 1539–40 famine, two complementary shelters—one for girls and one for boys—had opened under a combination of private philanthropy and government fiat. Pressure built for a broader reform of civic welfare, involving a consolidation of charitable resources, surveys of the poor, and discipline of able-bodied beggars similar to that seen in Bologna's Ospedale dei Mendicanti. After a few bold moves, Duke Cosimo I backtracked, and Florentines responded to immediate needs by opening a further three conservatories through the 1550s, each serving a different social group.

The complementary pair of institutions that opened in the immediate aftermath of the famine of 1539–40 emerged under radically different circumstances, but combined their efforts until Cosimo I curbed their cooperation. Lionarda Barducci Ginori led a group of Florentine gentlewomen in establishing the first distinct conservatory in 1541, a shelter that Florentines came to call the Ospedale delle Povere Fanciulle Abbandonate. Ginori was from a family that had been associated with the Savonarolan movement from the beginning, and she recruited like-minded volunteers to help her in running the home. Sharon Strocchia notes that religious reformers had been aiming to eliminate convent guardianship of lay girls for decades, and Ginori's new shelter offered an alternative as the opportunities for *serbanza* dried up.[43] With her volunteers, she found girls on the streets or by referral, and brought them to the old pilgrims' *ospedale* of S. Niccolò dei Fantoni at Piazza S. Felice opposite the modern-day Pitti Palace, where they came under the care of a trio of women headed by the resident warden, Mona Nanina. S. Niccolò was run by the Compagnia di S. Maria del Bigallo under the terms of a legacy given by Lapo Fantoni almost two hundred years earlier. Typical of such donors, Fantoni was as prescriptive as he was generous. Only female pilgrims could share spaces in one of the ten beds he had funded, and for no more than three days at that; if they had any male companions, these presumably slept in the Osteria della Buca next door.[44] With its reputation as a safe shelter for women only, the S. Niccolò hostel was a natural place to bring vulnerable girls; Ginori, moreover, may have secured it through a family connection on the Compagnia del Bigallo.[45] It is not clear if her abandoned girls took all of the space meant for pilgrims or if some of these continued coming, as happened in a few other hostel-cum-conservatories opened later in the century. With few extant records, it is difficult to determine how many girls were helped, from what class, for how long, or on what models. What is clear is that

Ginori made it her vocation, drawing her daughters Caterina and Maria into the work over the next decade, and leaving a small farm to the conservatory on her death in 1549.

Less than a year after Ginori's Ospedale delle Abbandonate began taking in vulnerable adolescent girls, the Ospedale degli Poveri Fanciulli Abbandonati opened as Florence's first distinct orphanage for young boys. It was the first step of a broader review and consolidation of poor relief that Cosimo I formally launched two weeks later on 17 March 1542.[46] The Ospedale degli Abbandonati was the main charge and beneficiary of a new magistracy, the Buonomini Sopra i Poveri Mendicanti, whose five members (twelve by August) were to inventory the possessions, reform the administrations, and appropriate the excess revenues of over two hundred charitable *ospedali* in the dominion, funneling these into shelters for beggar children and adults in the capital. Cosimo I moved in the next half year to underwrite this social work by suppressing the Compagnia di S. Maria del Bigallo, and transferring its assets, testamentary responsibilities, and name over to the magistracy.[47]

The Compagnia del Bigallo was one of Florence's oldest (est. 1244) and wealthiest confraternities. Centuries of legators had endowed it with a host of small shelters and hostels like S. Niccolò dei Fantoni just noted above. Some of these took in abandoned children, and Bigallo's reputation in this area had expanded after 1425, when the communal government forced it to merge with another old and wealthy confraternity, the Compagnia della Misericordia. The Misericordia had built prominent quarters at the corner of Piazza S. Giovanni opposite the cathedral, complete with a corner loggia where Florentines had abandoned their children before the *ospedali* of S. Maria della Scala, S. Gallo, and particularly the Innocenti took in foundlings in the fifteenth century. On the outside of the building, a large fourteenth-century fresco depicted the Misericordia captains entrusting young children to mothers, some of whom may have been adopting, others possibly reclaiming children whom they had abandoned temporarily out of necessity. While the union of the Misericordia and Bigallo was reversed by 1489, the Bigallo retained the building and inherited the reputation—the Misericordia shifted its efforts toward care for the sick and dying. Apart from its considerable assets, Cosimo I clearly wanted to transfer the Misericordia-Bigallo's reputation for child care over to his new magistracy-orphanage.[48] Florentines continued abandoning children under the loggia, to the dismay of the Bigallo magistrates, who for decades kept a woman lodged in the apartment above the loggia to take these children in before they died of hunger or exposure.[49]

These *abbandonati* didn't stay in the residence appended to the impressive quarters on Piazza S. Giovanni, but a few blocks north in the old Ospedale Broccardi. The Broccardi had a similar high-profile location on Via S. Gallo, Florence's main street leading north from the city center to the Porta S. Gallo (modern-day Piazza della Libertà) and, beyond that, over the Appenines as the Via Bolognese. Such thoroughfares usually had a cluster of pilgrims' hostels and infirmaries serving travelers, some of them adapted over time to other purposes. When searching for a home for its syphilitics' infirmary, Florence had settled on S. Maria della Trinità just down the street. Pilgrims had also stayed at the Ospedale Broccardi, established by Pietro Broccardi in a legacy to the Arte di Calimara in 1402, and meant by him to complement the large infirmary called the Ospedale Bonifazio located next door.[50] At Cosimo I's behest, the guild consuls ceded the Broccardi to the orphans, but they seem to have stripped it bare of all but a few beds and tables before leaving. Apart from the quantities of bread, wine, and oil that had to be bought to get the kitchen going, the resident warden Sandro Cechi had to buy a big kettle, some small pots, bowls, knives, cups, other utensils, and tablecloths.

As the boys began coming in through the spring months, Cechi busied himself refitting the Ospedale degli Abbandonati, storing up wood, bringing in barrels of wine and large flasks of oil, purchasing notebooks in which to keep the accounts, paying a trio of boys 12 soldi to move a couple of beds in, and then spending 5 lire for sheets. Carpenters built four small lockable alms boxes for pairs of boys to bring around in their collection drives through Florentine streets and churches, and Cechi matched this with a couple of heavy canvas bags for collecting bread and vegetables. A brass plaque went up on the outside of the building, and locks went into its doors. Some of the boys coming in to the Ospedale degli Abbandonati may have had their own sets of clothing, but Cechi also bought large quantities of cloth, sending some to the tailor Ambrogio Baldesi for shirts, and the rest to another tailor Schalabrino to turn into vests that would mark all the boys as recipients of Florentine charity; later the orphanage would dress its wards in uniform brown tunics. Cechi purchased straw hats for the boys, presumably to shelter them as they went through the city looking for alms. These would later be replaced with brown cloth caps matching the tunic. Few poor boys had shoes, so the orphanage adopted a traditional charitable practice of providing these for their incoming wards.[51]

But that was in the future. After working hard for a few months to open the orphanage, the Buonomini sopra i Poveri Mendicanti threw a party on the eve of the feast day of S. Giovanni Battista (24 June). Almost a hundred poor diners, possibly the boys, the staff, and the workmen and artisans who had helped transform the old Broccardi hostel, sat down to eat their *piatanzine*, the traditional pauper's allowance of meat and drink, at long tables decked with cloths; their overseers dined separately on cuttlefish.[52] The day was rich with symbolism. With the support of the Medici, who aimed to associate themselves more closely with the cult of the patron saint, Florentines had been expanding their S. Giovanni Battista feast day celebrations over the course of the sixteenth century. So many parades, races, games, and displays of wealth had to be fit in that activities sometimes began three or four days before the feast itself. The meal at the Ospedale degli Abbandonati was but one part of a celebration that was almost certainly marked by a public procession in the evening in which the boys with their magistrate-sponsors issued out of the *ospedale* and down Via S. Gallo to Piazza S. Giovanni and the Duomo. They carried *secodelle* (small faggots of kindling) to help light the bonfires that burned across the city in celebration that night, a legacy of the festival's origin as the Roman solstice festival of Fors Fortuna. Processions on the evening before S. Giovanni Battista had traditionally been colorful, vibrant, and noisy affairs featuring guilds, representatives of the *gonfaloni* (Florence's sixteen administrative districts), and confraternities. Yet through the later fifteenth century, Lorenzo il Magnifico had steadily tightened the screws on all of these competing centers of craft, neighborhood, or religious identity and authority, to the point where, if they processed at all it was only in their immediate localities. The Medici dukes followed his example, and aimed to ensure that bigger processions across different neighborhoods served them more particularly.[53]

The sight of the berobed Buonomini with perhaps a hundred young uniformed *abbandonati* passing through the streets advertised Cosimo I's direct paternal care for the city's helpless children. Or at least some of them. While a foundling home like the Innocenti was bursting at the seams with all the infants dropped anonymously at its door, the new Ospedale degli Abbandonati was deliberately selective. Innocenti wards, whether children, youths, or adult women, were predominantly illegitimate and often of no clear rank. With their uniform shirts and vests and, more particularly the hats and shoes that were critical markers of status, the Abbandonati boys were clearly not destitute *sottoposti* (day laborers), but the heirs of artisans, merchants, and others of middling rank who had fallen on hard times. As they marched, some of the boys carried alms boxes, others bore the fifty signs depicting *caritas* that the painter Giovan Battista del

Verrochio had been commissioned to produce for them, and yet others the twenty-five newly purchased *ciotole*, special dishes used by the poor to beg for drinks.[54]

Cosimo I gained his propaganda points at remarkably modest cost to himself. Almost half of the money raised for this work over its first few months had come from the magistracy and its individual members. The balance came from alms boxes that the boys carried around to the cathedral and to the churches of S. Maria Novella, S. Croce, and especially the Annunziata, where newly married couples or women experiencing difficulty in conception came to say prayers and give offerings. This was the first place that the boys went with their alms boxes, and they made sure to be there on the feast of the Annunciation, scarcely three weeks after the orphanage opened, when the church would be full of people eager to give the coins that would secure them the prayers of these well-scrubbed uniformed orphans.[55] With their tunics and hats, their paintings, and their alms boxes, the Abbandonati boys became familiar sights on the streets and in the markets of Florence. As they raised more of the orphanage's income in the years that followed, individual donations trailed off. Cosimo I finally coughed up 300 lire early the next year, but did more for the Abbandonati financially in November 1542, when he used his authority to grant it the holdings, resources, and name of the Compagnia del Bigallo, and when he added a rider to this legislation granting it one-third of the fines generated by a recent law against blasphemy.[56]

Lionarda Ginori's Ospedale delle Abbandonate was never formally part of the Buonomini's mandate, but in those early years the ambitious magistrates (now styled the *capitani del Bigallo*) sought to extend their authority as broadly as possible over all classes of the poor. Immediately after the celebrations on the feast of S. Giovanni Battista, the magistracy's president, Angelo Marzi de'Medici, bishop of Assisi, sent some flour and money to Ginori, the first of a string of gifts ranging from wine and flour to mattresses, cloth, and alms for dowries. The Bigallo captains subsequently wrote the care of abandoned girls into their draft statutes, and gave periodic subsidies to the conservatory. When Cosimo expropriated and ceded Bigallo holdings to the magistracy, it became the landlord of Ginori's conservatory. Though never large enough to keep the Abbandonate running, these gifts and links helped cement relations between the two homes.[57] Yet the gifts were always entered in the Abbandonate's account book as gifts to Ginori or to individual girls rather than to her home, and when she died in 1550, Cosimo I ordered that the conservatory be closed.[58]

It's doubtful that it was. It would have been an odd choice at a critical time:

over 20 percent of baptized infants were being abandoned annually by the end of this decade, with almost nine hundred children pushed through the Innocenti's open door in 1551 alone.[59] Mona Nanina, the Abbandonate's resident warden, appealed to the grand duke for use of a small farm that Ginori had left for the work or, failing that, for one of the Bigallo's houses. While she framed this as a request for a form of pension after ten years of honorable service, she also requested funds to keep the girls' shelter going. Ginori's daughters Catherina (herself now a widow) and Maria also wrote to the duke, asking that individual vulnerable girls be sheltered with Mona Nanina in the home that their mother had founded. In 1549 they wrote of encountering on the streets two teenage girls who had fled home to escape being abused by their father. Later it was a 15-year-old girl, Agnola, who needed someplace to shelter temporarily until her father could care for her. Still later it was the case of Agnoletta who, with her 7- and 9-year-old daughters, had lived with her father Lorenzo "il Candela" after being abandoned by her own husband six years before. The family had scraped by for a few years, but now Lorenzo was too old and sick to carry on with his work as a carpenter, while Agnola, nursing a broken arm, could not care for him or for her daughters. Catherina Ginori Tedaldi pleaded with Cosimo that these girls needed someplace to guard their safety and salvage what honor they could, and asked that they be accepted "nel monasterio di detta M.Leonarda" their mother. The duke's secretary Lelio Torelli passed all these requests on to the Bigallo magistrates, who clearly were continuing to provide some kind of shelter to abandoned and vulnerable girls under the care of Mona Nanina.[60]

While it's doubtful that Ginori's Ospedale delle Abbandonate really closed, documentary lacunae make it difficult to trace the transition to an institution that inherited its name, its work, and a site in its neighborhood.[61] On 1 March 1552, Cosimo I gave a license to the new "Hospedale povere Fanciulle Abbandonate," operating under the title and protection of S. Maria Vergine. Five girls had entered its rented quarters in the old Ospedale de Bini by S. Felice in Piazza the day before, and a sixth arrived on the day of Cosimo's license. Two days later, with Cosimo's approval firmly in hand, the group behind the home formally adopted its statutes and, like the home, soon came to be known as the Compagnia di S. Maria Vergine.[62] These notaries, doctors, priests, and gentlemen had already been hard at work for months lining up the donors who would keep the girls fed and clothed until they could begin earning their own keep through piecework for textile merchants. Francesco Rosati provided 12 staia of grain, 6 barrels of wine, and 42 lire, Michele di Lorenzo Dilnica gave 30 lire and promised to send mattresses and bedding, while Francesco di Mattio Ughetti offered the use of a house in Borgo S. Niccolò and promised to leave it as a legacy. Valuable as these one-time donations were, the new Ospedale di Fanciulle Abbandonate di S. Maria Vergine relied more on pledges. These ranged from generous donors like Donato Canbini, who promised and delivered 12 staia of grain and 4 barrels of wine annually, to the more modest cloth shearer Lorinzo di Tommaso, who faithfully gave 3 lire annually over the next few years. The first set of donations, totaling lire 1,019.10 together with 24 staia of wheat, 10 barrels of wine, and the use of a house, had been registered two months before the home opened, suggesting that its backers had been at work long before that.[63]

Donations and pledges undoubtedly helped convince the perennially cost-conscious Cosimo I to support the conservatory, but more immediate pressure played on the duke in the form of his wife, Eleonora of Toledo, who was concerned with the fate of worthy girls made vulnerable by their parents' poverty or death. The duchess gave alms periodically to the new Casa di S. Maria Vergine, bought a farm that had been donated to it, and eventually included a 200 scudo legacy in her will. But it was more closely and publicly in her eye and under her care. Had she wanted to, she could walk across the street to the conservatory from the house she had just bought from the Pitti family, and which her husband was remodeling into the ducal palace. Eleonora channeled her involvement in S. Maria Vergine indirectly through her courtiers, most notably Francesco d'Astudiglio, a Spanish priest and doctor who was one of the founders of the Compagnia and Casa of S. Maria Vergine. Don Francesco was a generous donor in his own right and on behalf of the duchess, and one of the witnesses to her will.[64]

The Casa di S. Maria Vergine was not for the poor. Its sponsors anticipated gathering only about eighteen girls at a time, but in its first four years eighty-eight girls called it home for some period of time. The girls no doubt benefited from living across the street from the new ducal palace, but space was tight all the same, and in 1557 they transferred to larger quarters in the old S. Marco monastery just outside the S. Gallo gate. This put them much closer to the Ospedale degli Abbandonati, but living outside the city walls on the opposite side of town put a serious dent in the girls' abilities to go around shops, markets, homes, and churches gathering alms. Eight months later they returned to the cramped rooms, but generous neighbors around the Bini Ospedale began looking for another option. It came soon enough in the form of the convent of the Ceppo, located along the Arno just east of the church of S. Croce. The girls moved there in 1564, and over time their conservatory came to be known colloquially as the Ceppo.

The Compagnia di S. Maria Vergine focused its efforts on keeping its own house in order, but as Rosalia Manno Tolu has demonstrated, some of its members were involved in establishing and running the two other conservatories opened in Florence in the 1550s and, for that matter, in every other home established later in the century.[65] Lacking the Bigallo's formal mandate in care for poor children (and with no apparent links to that magistracy), its thirty members (forty from 1584) nonetheless helped secure a dramatic increase in the number of spaces for vulnerable girls in a set of institutions that were distinguished, as in Bologna, by size and class. And as in Bologna, this confraternity achieved a discrete behind-the-scenes coordination and creative cross-fertilization of administrators, clerics, and *confratelli* between institutions that gave Florence a more synchronized network of care than may appear to be the case at first sight. Some members, like Carlo di Francesco Portinari, brought the benefit of their experience with other Florentine *ospedali*, while others, like the priest Antonio Cattani da Milano, actually served in a number of the conservatories at different times.

The largest of the new Florentine conservatories was the Casa della Pietà, opened in late 1554 or early 1555 as the work of a group of pious women headed by Margherita di Carlo Borromei and Marietta Gondi and assisted by Antonio Cattani da Milano. Don Antonio Cattani was both a member of the Compagnia di S. Maria Vergine and the first chaplain and confessor of the girls in its Casa. He later became the Pietà's first chaplain and confessor and, by some accounts, had earlier helped Lionora Ginori run her conservatory.[66] The Bigallo magistrates may have lent the benefit of their experience if not of their resources; Borromei, Gondi, and Don Antonio rented the Ospedale di S. Maria dell'Umiltà in Borgo Ognissanti from the Bigallo, and soon complained to Cosimo I about the high rents they had to pay for what was really just a couple of houses.[67] The founders followed the example of the Compagnia di S. Maria Vergine and made up for the lack of an endowment by securing numerous gifts and annual pledges in advance from supporters drawn from all classes of Florentine society. Necessity drove this form of funding, but it was also a canny way of keeping Medici hands out of the home's purse, a problem that was becoming ever more acute for Florentine charities like the Innocenti and the Monte di Pietà as the ducal family dipped into their endowments and income in order to fund everything from paintings to dowries to the war against Siena.[68]

Male professionals, gentlemen, clerics, and guild masters had paid for the few and relatively exclusive beds of S. Maria Vergine, but it was a gathering number of women—widows, married and unmarried women of better families, and even female domestics—who pledged to maintain the large number of beds in the Pietà. From September 1554 Borromei and Gondi went around Florence collecting pledges from all they knew. They intensified their efforts by the end of December and formally opened the Pietà a couple of days before Christmas, perhaps in an effort to stir up a greater sense of urgency, since the first girls weren't registered in the home until a month later. It worked. Almost every day thereafter, two or three or five more women enrolled in the Compagnia della Pietà, until there were 149 members ready to support the conservatory when the first girls are recorded as coming in at the end of January. Recruitment never let up: a year later the number of sponsors had risen to 270, and by the end of 1558, 320 supporters—almost entirely women—were giving donations to keep the conservatory going. These were not wealthy women. While S. Maria Vergine's patrons reckoned their pledges in bushels of grain, barrels of wine, and healthy sums of lire, most Pietà pledges were less than a scudo or a florin. Only eighteen of the first year's 270 donors gave more than a scudo, and the frequency of standard amounts like lire 1.5 or 2.10 suggests that Borromei, Gondi, and other fundraisers proposed small set amounts that were within the means of large numbers of Florentine women. They approached women of every rank: one of Gondi's servants, Lucrezia da Signa, pledged lire 3.10 annually, and consistently gave about twice that amount.[69] This support was critical. While the Pietà girls would soon enough have to earn their keep through textile piecework, donations put food on the table in the critical first year. The Pietà governors spent over 4,800 lire—almost 80 percent of total expenses—through 1555 for bread, wine, and oil, and it was alms and pledges that paid these bakers and merchants.[70]

As we will see in chapter 5, many Savonarolan families supported the Pietà, and the women's way of running the home had all the hallmarks of the Savonarolan approach to charity, though Rosalia Monno Tolu argues that they put their anti-Medici politics aside in order to meet the acute needs of the moment.[71] Did they feel betrayed or disappointed by the small size and selective procedures of the Medici-supported Casa di S. Maria Vergine, or by their exclusion from its confraternity and administration? Certainly the Pietà was notable among all of Florence's conservatories for having the most open administration and admission procedures; in this it was comparable to Bologna's S. Giuseppe, which was also the work of a group of women. Unlike S. Giuseppe, however, the Pietà opened its doors in the midst of a plague that swept in and took some girls almost as soon as they arrived.

Scribes began entering the girls' names in the Pietà's *Libro Segreto* on 25 January 1555. Fifty-two names are entered for that day. While some of these may actually have entered a few days or weeks earlier, the atmosphere was one of desperate chaos nonetheless. The old pilgrims' hostel rented from the Bigallo had about eighteen beds, and even if a few more could be fit into rooms and corridors, the girls were sleeping three or more to a bed.[72] This was a common enough practice, but some of those crowding in were already clearly very sick, and in such close quarters illness spread rapidly. Five died within a month, and another seven a month later; one 10-year-old girl was turned around and sent on to S. Maria Nuova, where she died almost immediately. Of the 147 girls enrolled through December 1555, twenty-nine died before year's end, with those under 12 being particularly vulnerable. It never let up; seventy-four of that first year's wards had died by the end of 1559, more than left the home through marriage, a return to family, or flight.[73]

Adding to the confusion, Margherita Borromei died on the eve of the Pietà's opening. Marietta Gondi quickly stepped in as the mother prioress, and ended up overseeing admissions, directing administration, and recruiting patrons for the next twenty-five years. She worked together with a resident prioress, and with Andrea di Benedetto Biliotti, 66 years old and a member of the Compagnia di S. Maria Vergine, who kept the accounts for alms and piecework and oversaw expenses. In August they hired a widow, Mona Betta, to teach the girls weaving. Betta came to live in the Pietà with her 7-year-old daughter, but the arrangement collapsed six months later when Betta fell ill and had to leave. A group of priests came in to teach Christian Doctrine, but these soon gave way to a confraternity (whose members also collected alms for the home), and eventually to the Carmelite sisters of S. Maria Angeli, who were also in the Savonarolan camp. Don Antonio Cattani had become the Carmelite's resident confessor by August 1555, and by 1557, the Pietà girls were regularly crossing the Arno to get to the Carmelite convent in Borgo S. Frediano on the other side, where they learned the Office and singing (*canto ecclesiastico*). When Don Antonio died, the Carmelites turned to Fra Alessandro Capocchi, a Dominican friar of S. Maria Novella who was one of the key figures keeping the memory and legacy of Savonarola alive through those years. Before long Capocchi was also visiting the conservatory's quarters in Borgo Ogni Santi and seeing for himself how cramped these were.[74] Ambitious, active, and well-connected, Capocchi worked to change the home's focus and organization before the women of the Compagnia della Pietà soured on him and fired him.[75]

The third home that Florentines established in the 1550s was S. Niccolò, which opened in 1556 after Cosimo I urged the magistracy of the Otto di Guardia e Balia to offer some shelter to those girls who, without parents and guardians, were being assaulted in Florence's streets, shops, and stalls. The Otto prosecuted criminal cases, and had taken over investigating and trying sexual assault against women and children in 1542. It punished rapes on a sliding scale linked to the victim's class: violating a virgin, married woman, or honorable widow merited a 500 lire fine, a servant girl 25 lire, and a prostitute nothing.[76] The new home sheltered mainly girls from families new to Florence, and eventually even took in a few daughters of prostitutes. The Otto appointed Francesco Rosati, a commissioner of the Stinche prison, to implement Cosimo's charge. At the Stinche, Rosati made sure that prisoners had mattresses, meals, and spiritual counselors. More significantly for this assignment, he was also a founding member of the Compagnia di S. Maria Vergine.[77] He located a shelter for the girls in Borgo S. Niccolò in the Oltrarno, perhaps at least temporarily in the home that his *confratello*, Francesco di Mattio Ughetti, had given to S. Maria Vergine a few years before. Rosati soon found the girls a more permanent location in the former Ospedale di S. Lorenzo by the S. Niccolò gate. About eighty girls sheltered in the home at any one time. Many came from towns outside of Florence, and some stayed only temporarily before being sent out on domestic service contracts to homes and shops in the city. S. Niccolò had resident staff, but the Otto di Guardia had apparently not found colleagues who could help Rosati in overseeing accounts, entrances, exits, jobs, and other work necessary to provide for the girls. He clearly found it onerous, appealing at least twice to Cosimo to give him some assistance since he was old, infirm, and couldn't carry on by himself. In 1564, the duke finally consented and ordered the Compagnia di S. Maria Vergine to take S. Niccolò under its wing. The confraternity complied by annually electing five of its members to a subcommittee overseeing S. Niccolò, but otherwise kept the two conservatories separate until 1620, when it moved S. Niccolò's girls across the river into its own quarters in the Ceppo.[78]

By the end of the 1550s, Florence had a network of homes that hadn't existed two decades before to shelter its orphaned and abandoned children. About a hundred boys lived in the Ospedale degli Abbandonati under the care of the magistracy of the Bigallo, whose members were appointed by Cosimo I and whose actions were referred to, if not always closely scrutinized by, the duke.

Possibly twenty girls drawn from worthy families lived in the Casa di S. Maria Vergine, a further eighty of somewhat lower rank in the S. Niccolò, and possibly 160 of yet lower status in the Conservatorio della Pietà. The network to some extent augmented the work of the Ospedale degli Innocenti, but with possibly a thousand residents, that overcrowded foundling home far overshadowed these more selective shelters. While S. Maria Vergine and the Pietà had their own governing confraternities, and S. Niccolò's administration was apparently left in the hands of a few overworked individuals, all three homes shared a connection to the Compagnia di S. Maria Vergine and, through it, to the duchess Eleonora of Toledo. Articulated in distinct institutions that preserved differences of social rank, relying on semiautonomous confraternities for fundraising and administration, linked indirectly to the ruling family, and operating on a makeshift basis in the absence of any clearly stated overarching policy, the Florentine network at mid-century had all the hallmarks of the early modern social welfare bureaucracy.

This network survived unchanged through the following three decades, in spite of recurring famines. The Bigallo magistrates periodically asked the Medici dukes for expansions of their powers to include greater control over conservatories and over the poor generally, and held up Bologna's Opera dei Mendicanti as a model, getting a handwritten draft of the latter's first statute revisions in 1573, and going so far in one instance as to print up an example of the kind of beggar's permit that they had in mind.[79] Cosimo and his sons stonewalled, and changes on the scale of those found in Bologna did not come until 1619–20 and the opening of Florence's Ospedale dei Mendicanti. The lack of a beggars' workhouse to absorb vulnerable girls of lower status put particular strains on the Pietà conservatory.

As in Bologna, the next two additions to the network came through the initiative of an individual activist Catholic in the 1580s and government responses to the famine of 1590–91. In 1558, Vittorio dell'Ancisa, son of a minor civic official, joined the youth confraternity of the Archangel Raphael, where he came under the influence of its Savonarolan *padre spirituale* Fra Santi di Cino Cini of S. Marco. After a decade of worshipping with and filling various elected posts in the confraternity, he joined Fra Cini's Congregazione di Carità, a group dedicated to charity and prayer in the traditions of Archbishop Antoninus and Savonarola. A year later, dell'Ancisa took minor orders. A priest by 1571, he served as confessor of the girls of the Casa di S. Maria Vergine from 1573 to 75 before heading off to Rome to work with Philip Neri.[80] Dell'Ancisa returned to Florence in 1584 after the death of his brother, and used his inheritance to establish an Ospedale della Carità that would take some poor men and women off the streets. The shelter opened in 1588, when Grand Duke Ferdinand I granted dell'Ancisa the former Ospedale del Porcellana in Via della Scala west of Piazza S. Maria Novella. Following Fra Cini's example, dell'Ancisa drew friends and followers into a Congregatione della Carità to help in running—and paying for—the paupers' hostel. As famine worsened through the coming year, some members of the Buonomini di S. Martino, the equivalent in Florence of Bologna's Opera dei Poveri Vergognosi, approached dell'Ancisa with a request to help an 18-year-old girl from a worthy family whom they feared would turn to prostitution if she wasn't taken into a secure shelter. He cooperated, and the Buonomini returned the next day with three more girls.[81]

The paupers' hostel was at a turning point, and not all those involved in it wanted to make the turn. For a few years it continued to shelter paupers, but these were increasingly out of place. The girls brought by the Buonomini di S. Martino were from the ranks of the "shamefaced poor," with a few having high-born and even noble connections although some were illegitimate. Over the years following, the Buonomini gave monthly subsidies of flour, Grand Duke Ferdinand and Duchess Cristina gave alms periodically, and other high-born families offered dowries or paid monthly fees to keep particular girls in place. The Ospedale della Carità was coming to be seen as an appropriate place where well-born families could lodge their orphaned adolescent nieces and cousins before marriages or convents could be arranged for them. These were the girls who had traditionally found shelter in convents in the past, under the arrangement known as *serbanza*.[82] The resident female wardens who had cared for the paupers were soon deemed not fit to take care of these better girls and, after some disagreements, were replaced by a widow and some of her female relations. The poor men who still had to come to get meals at the *ospedale* were also deemed to be inappropriate visitors, and were moved out in 1595, as was the male Congregatione della Carità that had fed them. A female Congregation was to assume its duties, but it is not clear whether or how long this group functioned. As we will see in chapter 5, the women resisted dell'Ancisa's directions in anything but purely spiritual matters, and seem to have had different ideas for the shelter. The situation became tense, but it was a battle the women could not win. The modern historian of the home discretely notes that the controversies became so violent in this period that dell'Ancisa had to take shelter in a convent for a few days to avoid being beaten up, and Archbishop Alessandro de'Medici had to intervene directly to bring contrary voices into line.[83]

As with Bologna's S. Croce conservatory, the intense controversy over control and direction of the home may have made it impossible to put formal statutes in place. Dell'Ancisa made some moves to write them, but all that remained on his desk when he died in 1598 were a few rough notes. They confirm that he wanted the conservatory to be for well-born and well-educated girls. While some well-born men and women would oversee it, final control would lay with dell'Ancisa who, for all his qualities, was not quite so well-born. Was dell'Ancisa trying to promote these changes or, like Bonifacio dalle Balle in Bologna, was he trying to prevent other more powerful individuals from completely hijacking the Casa della Carità? It is hard to tell. The Carità had clearly become his life's work and, like dalle Balle, dell'Ancisa penned numerous sermons and spiritual texts for the girls. His own passing made a moot point out of the question of control, and turned his fragmentary statutes into something of a dead letter. The aims of groups now involved gave the home a direction and momentum that would be hard to alter. As we will see, dell'Ancisa's successors steered the Ospedale della Carità through a series of changes until by 1627 it was a convent under the archbishop's authority.[84]

The first moves to turn the Ospedale della Carità from a paupers' hostel into a conservatory had been forced by the dearth of the late 1580s. As shortages deepened into the famine of 1590–91, Florence's sixth conservatory, S. Caterina, opened as one part of a desperate effort to head off disaster. Grand Duke Ferdinand followed many other Italian rulers in scouting out grain supplies across Europe, subsidizing large imports from the Baltic, and distributing these through the magistracy of the Abbondanza to communities around Tuscany. Prices were still so high that these communities had to borrow from the pawn bank of the Monte di Pietà in order to buy the grain. Starving poor flocked to the capital to beg, borrow, or steal a meal. Ferdinand bowed to pressure and allowed Florence to expel most "foreign" beggars—even though most were also his subjects. Once outside the city gates, they didn't have far to go. Those fit for it were put to work building the Belvedere Fortress that crowned the hill above the ducal palace, and others were sheltered in a couple of old *ospedali* in Florence's suburbs. Males went to the old monastery of S. Marcho Vecchio outside the Porta S. Gallo, the kind of catch-all institutional building outside many cities' walls (Bologna's S. Gregorio was a similar place) that officials resorted to

in times of need. The girls of the Casa di S. Maria Vergine had sheltered at
S. Marco briefly in 1557, and it had more recently been used as a quarantine
house where goods suspected of being infused with pestilential vapors could be
aired out and fumigated before being brought into the city. Women and children were put in the Ospedale di S. Onofrio, run by the Company of Dyers,
immediately west of the Fortezza del Basso.[85] Sheltered at night, these poor
women and children roamed around by day scraping together what they could
for survival by begging, petty theft, and prostitution.

This was Florence's first experiment with a beggars' hostel, but characteris-
tically Grand Duke Ferdinand refused to entrust the work to the magistracy of
the Bigallo, which had been clamoring for the responsibility for almost fifty years
and which had sent him a long memo on the matter in May 1588.[86] Instead, he
entrusted both shelters to a gentleman, Giovanni Battista Botti, whose brother
Matteo was a familiar figure in a series of important state magistracies. Botti soon
recognized that a shelter in the shadow of a barracks was no place to protect beggar girls from prostitution. Sharing his concerns with Archbishop Alessandro
de'Medici, he enlisted the help of two other well-connected gentlemen who were
members of powerful and wealthy military-religious orders. Girolamo di Antonio Michelozzi was a cavalier of the Order of S. Stefano, established by Cosimo
I in 1562, and friar Giulio Zanchini was a member of the Knights of Malta.
Michelozzi provided, among other things, the critical personal connection to the
Compagnia di S. Maria Vergine. The trio initially thought only of following
Grand Duke Ferdinand's cautious mandate and sheltering the girls until the
worst of the famine had passed; three years ought to be sufficient, they thought.
They rented three houses at Porta alla Croce at the eastern city wall by the current Piazza Beccaria and, on the inspiration of an image found on the walls there,
gave it the name S. Caterina. This account of the origin of the name, given in
its first statutes, seems more pious trope (i.e., the saint finding her followers
rather than vice versa) than reality. Daniella Lombardi notes that the cult of
S. Catherine framed particularly as the patron saint of adolescent girls expanded
in the sixteenth and seventeenth centuries when the pressures and family strategies related to dowry and marriage were forcing many girls into convents and
conservatories, many of which took on the saint's name in a sad and ironic twist.[87]
On St. Bartholomew's Day (24 August) 1591, Botti, Michelozzi, and Zanchini
staged a procession of girls from the S. Onofrio *ospedale* east through the city to
this new home, which workmen were already busy transforming into a secure
conservatory. Bars were fitted into the windows and new locks into the doors,

some walls were rebuilt, a mattress maker delivered bedding, and firewood was brought in to prepare for the winter. And food. Aware that the already inflated bread prices would only rise through winter and spring, the trio immediately began stockpiling large quantities of grain. It was a costly business, and Botti himself gave 600 florins necessary to cover the first two months' expenses, the bulk of it going into grain purchases.[88]

Botti and his colleagues drew others into the work as soon as possible. The Dominican friars of S. Marco provided a priest to hear confessions and say Mass as they did for the girls of the Pietà. A widow, Alexandra Dragonari, came to live in the home as the prioress. Two businessmen joined as *provveditori* to handle purchases and accounts, and report to the trio's weekly Thursday meetings. A year later, Botti followed his convictions into the Theatine Order, but he continued to be active on S. Caterina's behalf, most notably a few years later when he approached Grand Duke Ferdinand appealing for new quarters. The homes at Porta alla Croce were fine when scouted out and renovated in the summer and fall of 1591, but had proven damp and unhealthy for the girls in the winters that followed. The grand duke offered the conservatory use of the Ospedale Broccardi in Via S. Gallo north of the city center, home until then of the abandoned boys under the Bigallo's care, and big enough to take in S. Caterina's eighty *abbandonate*. About 180 boys had lived there in conditions so cramped and difficult, that when the plague and famine hit in 1591, many of them—reputedly half—had died in a mere six months. The surviving boys moved a few blocks west to a former convent, also called S. Caterina, bought by the Bigallo captains.[89] S. Caterina's girls reversed their procession of a few years before and moved into a neighborhood that was already well known for its enclosed women: seven convents lined Via S. Gallo, others dotted the sidestreets, and the Pietà conservatory was just a few blocks away.[90]

Their move was the clearest sign that the original calculation of a three-year temporary shelter had been set aside by the trio and the grand duke alike. But what was the S. Caterina conservatory to become? It was much like the Conservatorio della Pietà, roughly the same size and sheltering girls who were far below the status of those enrolled in the S. Maria Vergine and Carità conservatories and even below those of S. Niccolò in the Oltrarno. Both were places of last resort, where girls who had little chance of marriage or convent, and who couldn't seem to last long even on domestic service contracts, went to live out their lives working at various kinds of textile piecework. S. Caterina had few sponsors to underwrite its monthly food bill and few funds to help its girls establish themselves in society. Girolamo Michelozzi had left a small legacy to fund an annual dowry when he died in 1594, but it generated only 100 lire annually, barely enough to help even one of the eighty *abbandonate* find a future in marriage or the convent. Even the foundling home of the Innocenti offered its wards dowries of 300 lire by this point.[91]

Finally, in 1615 the confraternity-magistracy of the Bigallo won its long argument with the dukes and gained permission to build the Convento per le Povere Fanciulle Derelitte to house forty girls, complementing its Ospedale degli Abbandonati. As if to underscore the point, it built the new conservatory adjacent to the orphanage.[92] It drew on the Pietà for models and practical help, recruiting as its resident prioresses two women who had entered the Pietà conservatory as children and had lived there for decades.[93] Thus the Bigallo gained by the end of our period the clear responsibility for abandoned children of both sexes that it had sought from the beginning—even though this did not extend to authority over Florence's other conservatories. The Bigallo magistrates seem to have assumed that it was only a matter of time, and their confidence, or at least their lobbying, went beyond letters to the grand dukes and incorporated even the artwork they commissioned for their offices on Piazza S. Giovanni.

Around 1570, Carlo Portelli produced two paintings for the Bigallo. The smaller one, a pendant (Figure 1.1), shows Charity in the guise of a young woman embracing one infant while nursing another at her breast, as a third at her feet contemplates an urn; all these infants are males. From the shadows at her back, a young boy in the Ospedale degli Abbandonati's rough brown uniform and cloth hat looks out; his eyes and those of the nursing infant are the only ones that engage the viewer. Portelli's larger painting of *Madonna in Heaven with Angels Adored by Two Children* (Figure 1.2) depicts Mary in the center of the canvas with two children kneeling in prayer at her feet. A barefoot boy dressed in the same brown uniform turns his back to the viewer in order to face the Virgin. Yet Mary's gaze is not directed to him, but turns to fix on a girl at her left, dressed in an equivalent uniform and with a white head covering and a Rosary. No Florentine girls wore that uniform in 1570.[94] The girl's eyes turn to the distant heavens in the conventional attitude of prayer, but her folded hands may well be directed to the grand duke, a plea that those like her may come under the protective care of the Bigallo magistrates. Mary's appreciative gaze validates this secular prayer, but the sons of Cosimo and Eleonora were no more likely to put girls under the Bigallo's care than their parents had been. Francesco I quite explicitly ruled this out a few years after the painting was completed.[95] It took

Figure 1.1. Carlo Portelli, *Charity* (personified as woman with an orphan boy), ca. 1570 (Museo del Bigallo, Florence)

the next generation to accept that shift, by which point broader circumstances made it more trouble than the Bigallo magistrates had anticipated. Poor harvests from 1617 to 1621, typhoid outbreaks in 1619–20 and again in 1630, together with the onset of a serious depression in the textile industry meant that the Bigallo's Fanciulle Derelitte conservatory was overwhelmed almost from the

Figure 1.2. Carlo Portelli, *Madonna in Heaven with Angels Adored by Two Children,* ca. 1570 (Museo del Bigallo, Florence)

time it opened. As Lombardi notes, even though it had promoted silk spinning, the Fanciulle Derelitte's financial difficulties forced it to restrict and sometimes suspend admissions.[96]

Over the course of the fifteenth and sixteenth centuries, both Bologna and Florence devised ambitious networks of institutional care for orphaned and abandoned girls and boys. Florence had opened a specialized foundling home in 1445, and Bologna had followed suit five decades later. Now Bologna began with specialized orphanages and conservatories in the 1510s and 1520s, and Florence followed its example in the 1540s. In both cases, they were pioneering with specialized shelters that would soon be imitated across Italy and Europe. By the end of the 1610s, both cities could care for approximately 1,800 to 2,000 children in a series of shelters ranging from foundling homes and workhouses to more selective orphanages and conservatories. Gender and class shaped the size and quality of care in each particular home, while local charitable traditions and significant political changes shaped the home-by-home articulation of city's evolving network and helped determine just how selective the orphanages and conservatories could be. Each city's network grew out of some combination of private charitable initiative, government fiat, and clerical encouragement, and each came in time to be coordinated—sometimes loosely—by confraternities and government bodies working together.

But this was background. In the foreground, recurring crises of plague and famine were the catalysts that had brought new homes into being and disrupted the careful arrangements in existing ones. Three bouts had been particularly critical, triggering three stages in the development of each city's network of orphanages. The first for Bologna was that of the mid-1520s into the early 1530s, while for Florence it was the early 1540s. Both shared in the devastation of the 1550s and that of the late 1580s and early 1590s. In the first stage, each city framed a provisional network with complementary homes for boys and for girls. Each expanded and refined this network with new homes, administrative consolidations, and the prospect of more comprehensive systems of poor relief in the second stage. Each made minor expansions (but no fundamental reforms) in the third.

By the end of the 1610s, these networks had combinations of large and small institutions serving different social groups. As Figures 1.3 and 1.4 show, they were distributed across the two cities. Bologna's network centered on the companion institutions of S. Maria del Baraccano and S. Bartolomeo di Reno, each

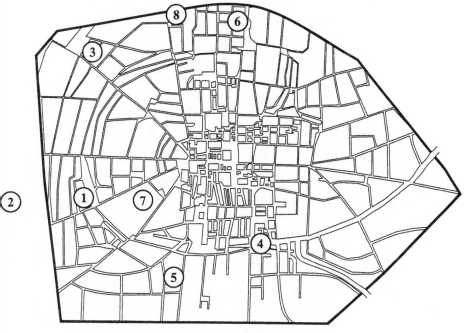

Figure 1.3. Map of Bologna, giving location of homes. **1.** *S. Marta.* **2.** *S. Gregorio* (later Ospedale dei Mendicanti). **3.** *S. Maria del Baraccano.* **4.** *S. Bartolomeo di Reno.* **5.** *S. Onofrio.* **6.** *S. Croce.* **7.** *S. Giacomo.* **8.** *S. Giuseppe.*

serving roughly 75 to 100 children from solid artisanal families, with S. Giacomo (30–40) and S. Onofrio (15–25) serving boys of somewhat higher status, and S. Marta (30–40) and S. Giuseppe (15–25) serving girls of higher status. S. Croce (30–40) was for girls of lower status. At this system's base were the 2 institutions that, while not orphanages or conservatories, absorbed enough poor children to allow the others to be so selective: the Ospedale dei Mendicanti, with 1,000 and sometimes up to 1,500 very poor and infirm, and the foundling home of the Esposti, with perhaps 400 children of all ages. Florence's network similarly centered on 2 companion institutions serving artisanal families, though these were themselves unions of 2 distinct homes. The Ceppo, which combined S. Maria Vergine and S. Niccolò, gathered about 75 girls, while the Bigallo's Ospedale degli Abbandonati sheltered 100 to 150 boys and its Ospedale delle Fanciulle Derelitte housed 40 girls. The Ospedale della Carità served Florentine girls of a higher status, while the Pietà and S. Caterina (150 each) assisted those at the bottom of the social scale; these latter institutions gathered the poorer and more

Figure 1.4. Map of Florence, giving location of homes. **1.** *Ospedale delle Abbandonate* of Lionora Ginori (former S. Niccolò dei Fantoni). **2.** *S. Maria della Vergine* (former Ospedale Bini—to 1564). **3.** *S. Maria della Vergine* (former Convento del Ceppo—from 1564; joined by *S. Niccolò* in 1620). **4.** *Ospedale degli Abbandonati* (former Ospedale Broccardi—to 1594) *S. Caterina* (from 1594). **5.** *Ospedale degli Abbandonati* (former Convento S. Caterina—from 1594); joined by *Convento per le Povere Fanciulle Derelitte* in 1615. **6.** *S. Niccolò* (former Ospedale S. Lorenzo—to 1620). **7.** *Casa della Pietà* (Ospedale S. Maria dell Umiltà—to 1568). **8.** *Casa della Pietà* (from 1568). **9.** *Casa della Carità* (former Ospedale Porcellana). **10.** *S. Caterina* (1591–94).

infirm children who otherwise would have gone to an Ospedale dei Mendicanti. At the base of Florence's network was the institution whose larger size and reputation overshadowed the rest: the Ospedale degli Innocenti where, if we extrapolate from a 1579 report, many were no longer even children. Of 1,220 staff and children resident that year, 968 were females; 733 of these were of marriageable age, and 223 were over age 40.[97]

For all its informality, each city's network assumed a local charitable culture that all individual homes had to fit into. This culture was defined less by any formal policy than by the conversations and connections, and the convictions and ambitions of those who populated the network as administrators, confessors, and donors. Both Bonifacio dale Balle in Bologna and Vittorio dell'Ancisa in Florence found out how difficult it was to maintain a home that was distinct from the local type. Each struggled to run a home that reflected a distinct and individual vision, and in neither case did that vision last long beyond the founder's death. The women behind Florence's Pietà and Bologna's S. Giuseppe found much the same thing when men moved in and subtly reshaped the institutions that they had founded into something more conventional. While in Bologna this culture moved from a quasi-conventual model into something that was more distinctly lay, in Florence it seems to have gone the other way, with homes like the Pietà, the Carità, and eventually even S. Caterina all becoming convents in time.

On a certain level this was all abstraction. We have seen what it was like for administrators and politicians to open a home. What was it like for a child to enter one?

CHAPTER TWO

Entering a Home

Prescriptions and Procedures

Five children, five situations.

On 22 March 1560, 15-year-old Maddalena di Benedetto di Firenze went to a private home in Florence to be interviewed by five women. Her widower father was not able to care for her, and someone, likely a friend or neighbor, suggested that she might be enrolled in the Casa della Pietà, a conservatory supported by a network of women in the city. The five interviewers, lay women who were called mother prioresses and were led by a head prioress, Marietta Gondi, had interviewed over five hundred other girls since the Pietà had opened five years before. Sometimes they interviewed one girl at a time, and sometimes more. We don't know if the prioresses turned anyone down that day, but they accepted Maddalena into the Pietà as a novice. Arriving at the home, she was lodged in quarters apart from the other girls of the home, and put under the care of a mistress of novices who was herself an older *abbandonata*. For at least three months, the mistress trained her in Christian Doctrine, in the customs and rules of the house, and in proper deportment. Every day she sent Maddalena out with the other novices to beg for alms for the house, washing and clothing them in the morning and supervising them as they went through churches or to the houses of former Pietà girls who had married. After three months, she was able to give a good report to the five mother prioresses, and Maddalena was moved out of the novices' quarters and into the Pietà's main dormitory.[1]

On 22 June 1583, the procurators of the Poveri Vergognosi of S. Martino in Florence made a difficult request to their counterparts, the captains of the Bigallo. Andrea, the estranged wife of Piero Corone, called "the Swallow," had died four months earlier in the Hospital of S. Maria Nuova, leaving behind a boy and a girl. The Swallow had flown the nest, and now the children had nowhere to go. The procurators had managed to lodge the girl in the Conservatory of the Ceppo and then, hearing that the father was in Livorno, sent the boy to be with him. The father promptly sent him back, and now he was wandering the streets of Florence since there were no relatives or friends to take him in. The Bigallo captains checked into the details of the case, and in August formally accepted the boy into their Ospedale degli Abbandonati. A few years later, another boy, Bartolomeo, was simply left under the portico of the Abbandonati at night and, without any further investigation or vote, he too was brought into the home.[2]

On 27 August 1606, Domenica, wife of Luigi Pieracci, brought her 7-year-old stepdaughter Gracia to the doors of S. Niccolò in Florence. Luigi had just been sentenced to ten years on the galleys, and Domenica had no particular desire to raise his child on her own. She explained to the skeptical *madre priora* that Gracia's mother was dead, but the official sent her on her way, saying that unless she had proof of this there was no point knocking on the door. Two weeks later Domenica returned, waving the mother's death certificate (*fede della morte*) and Gracia's baptismal certificate (*fede di battesimo*), and threatening to turn Gracia out within a matter of days. The *priora* took Gracia in and began checking her head and throat for sores and diseases, all the while talking to the child in order to get a better sense of her personality. A week later, when S. Niccolò's governing council, the Five Deputies, met, she took the two *fede* with her and reported that the girl seemed to be both healthy and even-tempered: Gracia would fit in. The deputies discussed the case, and voted to accept the child into S. Niccolò.[3]

On 20 August 1609, the thirteen officials of the Casa di S. Croce in Bologna met to discuss the conservatory's business. Among the items were written applications for entry from six girls, among them Elena Fontana. The men discussed the applications, agreed to investigate the girls further, and appointed two of their number as visitors to examine each girl's background and situation: where she lived, who her parents had been or, if still alive, what they did, and particularly whether in her current circumstances she was vulnerable to rape or likely to be forced into prostitution. At the next meeting two weeks later, the visitors reported that Elena met most of the conditions set out in the statutes but one: at age 14 she was a year older than the age limit they had recently set for entrants. The men nonetheless voted to take their investigation to the next stage, and so S. Croce's mother prioress and nurse went to where Elena was staying temporarily and performed a physical examination in order to determine if she was a virgin. Elena passed this test too. Both male and female visitors prepared written reports on the case that were read aloud at the next meeting of the officials one month later. Elena won this vote with a comfortable margin. S. Croce's chief officers, the rector and chamberlain (*camerlengo*), signed a slip of paper that was sent to Elena, and that would secure a welcome for her. They also forwarded the list of summer and winter clothing, shoes, chests, devotional works, and other items that S. Croce required of entrants as a way of controlling its own costs.[4]

With hordes of orphaned children seeking shelter, and hordes of mostly single parents seeking someplace to take those children whom they couldn't feed or clothe, orphanages and conservatories had to be selective. Almost all adopted strict admissions procedures to allow them to choose worthy candidates from among the numbers seeking entrance. As the examples above demonstrate, procedures varied widely from home to home and weren't always practiced consistently even within the same home. Criteria common to a number of homes— usually having to do with age, health, and parentage—tell us who was deemed worthy of saving and who was thought to be either dispensable or a risk to the larger community of children sheltered inside the walls. That said, each home was distinct. We have already seen that different children—boys and girls, artisanal and poor, Bolognese and Florentine—could all expect different treatment. Bolognese homes for both genders quickly adopted a set of common bureaucratic procedures that used internal committees and civic documentation to weed out ineligible boys or girls. Florentine conservatories frequently left these decisions up to the will of the prioress and the ability of the girl herself to demonstrate her aptitude. Its orphanage of the Abbandonati framed restrictive entrance criteria that drew in the duchy's territorial administrators and local citizens, but these were continually undermined by the older practice of anonymous abandonment that had filled the older homes of the Bigallo, the Misericordia, and the Innocenti. And patronage played its part; in both cities, doors opened for the child who was promoted by wealthy or influential sponsors.

This chapter first reviews the regulations and procedures that homes adopted to control admissions, highlighting some of the common and distinct concerns that we can find between homes and between the two cities. But even as some homes layered safeguard upon safeguard, the prescriptions found in their statutes were frequently undermined by demographic pressures, by patronage politics, and by a host of quotidian factors that come down to the single reality that while Renaissance Italians were adept at framing rules, they were equally adept at avoiding or ignoring them. Statute prescriptions are necessary in order to understand what cities hoped to achieve, but the loopholes were numerous and wide, and the spirit of mercy and patronage could secure entry for children shut out by the letter of the law. As an Italian proverb put it, "Tra la dire e la fare c'e un mare" (Between the saying and the doing there's an ocean). Where records permit, data on actual entrants to the homes will be juxtaposed with these statute prescriptions in an effort to plumb the depths of that ocean.

One of the drawbacks in the data is immediately clear: guardians treated girls and boys differently. Conservatories in both Florence and Bologna carefully recorded their girls' origins, parentage, age, and assets at entry; updated these records until the girls left the conservatory or died; and in some cases periodically took censuses of the population that was in the home. By contrast, orphanages in both cities wrote down little on their boys, and kept no running records on the movements of their population up and down. The contrast highlights a critical difference in their obligations to girls and boys, respectively. The conservatory had to negotiate a girl's path back into society, and its work was immeasurably easier if she had the assets of dowry, honor, and virginity. Without careful vetting and recording of all of these she might become a permanent ward of the home because no home would turn a girl out on the street. Orphanages, by contrast, had no necessary obligations beyond feeding and sheltering a boy until the exit door opened in late adolescence. Some homes aimed to do more, and most tried to place boys in a workshop or some other work, but if necessary they could simply release their wards into the world with little more than their own resourcefulness. Beyond this, most girls remained enclosed in the home until they were formally passed over into the care of another guardian, while boys left in stages, gradually passing from the care of the home into that of a master before striking out on their own.

Prescriptions

Children had to meet a host of particular conditions before they could enter a home, but these came down to a few critical concerns in both cities: vulnerability, honor, and health. Beyond this, Bolognese homes wanted to accept only those children who had a good chance of leaving the surrogate nest by late adolescence, and added conditions aimed at securing this goal.[5]

The most vulnerable children were those without parents, and many homes stipulated that they would only take those who were *veri orfanelli*, lacking both mother and father. But not all. Other homes accommodated a range of children whose parents were incapable—or judged unworthy—of raising their children, and over time even this looser definition expanded as some homes began taking in fee-paying children.

Homes for boys in both cities were quite firm on taking in only "true orphans," though this was usually understood to mean fatherless children. In some instances, statutes specified that eligible children should have neither father nor mother, nor any brothers who were old enough to be responsible for them. That said, it was quite common for boys to have at least a widowed mother in the city; widowed fathers received less consideration. Of forty boys nominated for S. Bartolomeo di Reno in 1588, only six had lost both parents, while thirty still lived with their mothers. When it revised its statutes, Bologna's S. Onofrio began requiring that boys show their father's death certificate and be able to demonstrate that the widowed mother was unable to raise the child.[6]

Florentine state authorities sternly ordered that all children who had some family remaining be excluded from the Abbandonati orphanage, but their very insistence suggests that popular perceptions were a little more flexible on this point. In his 1542 decree establishing the magistracy that would run the Abbandonati, Cosimo I stipulated that it take in only those who were "derelict and totally abandoned by their fathers, mothers, blood relatives and any other human and spiritual protection." A public regulation circulated to all territorial administrators later that year to inform them of procedures reiterated the point and ordered them to personally countersign the *fede* or testimonials nominating a child for the home. The proclamation threatened public defamation both in Florence and in his hometown for any person, regardless of standing, who tried to enroll a child for whom he was responsible, be it his own son, a nephew, or some other boy.[7] Yet these threats do not appear in the first statutes for the Abbandonati that were drawn up only a month before the proclamation. The issue was one that the Medici dukes seem to have taken more seriously than the Abbandonati's administrators. When the latter appealed to Duke Francesco I for financial assistance in 1579, he responded that he knew that "among those called abandoned there are enough who have father and mother, and these shouldn't take the bread of the poor abandoned ones." His brother Ferdinando I responded in much the same way when administrators pleaded the case of families that were starving as a result of the famine of 1590.[8] The dukes need not have been quite so suspicious. Although no enrollment records for the Abbandonati remain, formal applications called *fede di bambini* survive from 1574. Of the 316 submitted from that year to 1590, almost all reported on the fate of the father, and in 88.6 percent of the cases, he had died. The mother's fate was reported in only two-thirds of the cases, and 66.5 percent of these had died.[9]

What the dukes were trying to avoid, and what the Abbandonati was forced to accommodate, was the procedure of anonymous abandonment by parents. It had filled Florence's foundling home of the Innocenti to overflowing. Yet the practice had predated the Innocenti's opening in 1445, and was even memorialized in the fresco painted on the exterior walls of the Bigallo's headquarters on Piazza S. Giovanni. Parents continued abandoning their children under that building's loggia, and later started abandoning children under the loggia of the dormitory on Via S. Gallo as well. The Bigallo magistrates were caught in a bind. Most of these boys were only 4 to 8 years old and clearly in need, yet most would not ordinarily be accepted in the *ospedale* because at least one parent was still living.[10] The dukes, if not unmoved, were certainly adamant. In a cold January of 1580, Francesco I ordered the governors to shelter such children only for the few days it would take to "restore" them from cold and hunger, and then turn them out again in the expectation that their parents would pick them up again. The prospect of pushing 4- and 5-year-old children onto the winter streets was less troubling to the duke than another prospect: "taking in all these *putti* [young boys] that are left," he complained, "would be making another Innocenti."[11] Abandonments continued, and a few years later the magistrates gained permission to post stern notices under the arcades at both Piazza S. Giovanni and the dormitory itself threatening that those who abandoned their own children would be subject to serious penalties that could include being sent to the galleys.[12]

The Medici dukes wanted to prevent the culture of parental abandonment from extending from foundling homes to orphanages, but with conservatories the situation was far more ambiguous. Certainly the Florentine conservatories with the closest ties to the state, S. Maria Vergine, S. Niccolò, and S. Caterina, all stipulated that eligible girls must have no living parents. S. Maria Vergine went beyond this to exclude any who had brothers or other relatives over age 28, or any who had been living with someone else for over four months—by this point guardians who attempted abandonment would be motivated more by boredom or inconvenience than need.[13] In practice, only one-quarter to one-half of the girls entering S. Niccolò and S. Caterina were clearly orphans under this strict definition. Two-thirds of those entering S. Caterina had brothers, sisters, uncles, or other family. For the remaining one-third, the death of the father had triggered the virtual death of the family. Of the first one hundred girls recorded in its registry, thirty-one had been abandoned by their mothers after the deaths of their fathers, while three had been abandoned by their widowed fathers. As we saw earlier, a man marrying a widow had no obligation to take her children from a previous marriage and, even when not confronted with this ruthless choice, some widows could not on their own scrape together the subsistence for all their children.[14]

Aware as they were of these realities, none of the other conservatories in either city was quite so explicit about their wards being "true orphans." Indeed, some saw that her parents' situation was the main reason for stepping in to help a girl. Bologna's S. Marta took in girls as an extension of its work in helping the "shamefaced poor," stating that being relieved of the care of the child would help reduce the strain on family budgets. On the other end of the social scale, S. Croce began as a shelter aimed at rescuing the daughters of prostitutes, recognizing that a nubile girl was a potential asset for a destitute family, and that parents or relatives could not be trusted to resist the temptation to capitalize on her. S. Maria del Baraccano echoed this when stipulating that in cases where parents survived, it must be clear that it would not be good for the girl to be with them.[15]

Poverty forced many young women into occasional or longer-term prostitution, and so this was a second, more gender-specific element in children's vulnerability. Most of the girls who came to the attention of the homes were poor,

Table 2.1. Ages of Boys Applying to Orphanages

Ospedale	Dates	Total	Age Given	> 4 years	5	6	7	8	9	10	10+
S. Bartolomeo di Reno	1588–94	75	30 (22.5%)				7	6	5	9	3
Abbandonati	1574–90	312	125 (40.06%)	32	20	20	22	16	2	6	7

Sources: ASB, PIE, S. Bartolomeo di Reno, ms. 7#2; ASF, Bigallo ms. 1459.

but not all were in danger of becoming prostitutes. The Bolognese conservatories all made danger to a girl's sexual honor a critical consideration for entry, and would even speed up their review and entrance procedures to remove adolescents from compromising situations as soon as possible.[16] S. Croce, of course, was very explicit, seeking "daughters of women of a not good life, and in the most obvious danger of losing their *honestà*, such that not accepting them, you know very well, is [for them] to lose honor and come to ill."[17] Others wrote more obliquely of "saving" the girls and putting them to more honest work. S. Maria del Baraccano exercised an additional caution from 1647. Thinking that beautiful girls were in greater danger than their more plain counterparts, its officers required that girls come in person to the final review of their application so that the men could get a good look at them and judge whether they had "a beautiful, or at least pleasing, Face, and thus [were] not secure from the threats to their honour."[18] Significantly, none of the Florentine conservatories mentioned the threat of prostitution in their statutes, or made the defense of a girl's sexual honor a criterion for bringing her into the home.

Age was a final factor determining boys' and girls' vulnerability. How young was young? Boys' vulnerability was clearly linked to their youth, though as Table 2.1 demonstrates, the two cities set this at slightly different ranges. Florence's Abbandonati initially took in those ages 3 to 10, though as conditions worsened in the city in the later 1570s, it found places for boys as young as 2 and as old as 16.[19] Bolognese institutions were more restrictive, preferring those ages 7 to 12, roughly corresponding to the years when boys were no longer considered infants, or *bambini*, but were old enough to take up apprenticeships or enter school.[20]

Girls' vulnerability was more evidently tied to their sexual maturity, and so most homes saved their spaces for those who were entering puberty, or what one described as a "dangerous age" (*pericolosa età*). None of Bologna's homes wanted to accept girls under age 10, and a number specified lower limits of 11 or 12

Table 2.2. Ages of Girls Admitted to Conservatories

Home and Source	Dates	Total	Age Given	2	3	4	5	6	7	8	9	10	11	12	13	14	15	16	17	18	19	20	20+
Bologna																							
S. Maria del Baraccano	>1570	161	129 (80.12%)			1		4	5	9	5	14	5	28	18	12	11	5	3	3	2	1	3
S. Maria del Baraccano	1570–84	121	40 (33.05%)											13	14	11	6	1	1	2			
S. Giuseppe	1616–41	112	45 (40.17%)				1				1		3	12	7	7	6	5	1	2	2	2	3
Florence																							
S. Maria Vergine	1552–55	93	80 (86.02%)							2	2		4	13	25	10	11	10	1	3			
Pietà	1555–59	361	361 (100%)		1		9	9	17	23	22	33	30	35	32	32	28	31	21	16	8	9	3
Pietà	1560–1623	708	511 (72.07%)	1	3	8	24	29	60	75	47	73	42	43	22	23	23	20	4	2	0	6	8
S. Niccolò	1571	54	53 (98.15%)		1	2	1	2	2	6	3	3	4	9	6	5	6	1	1	1	1	1	
S. Niccolò	1571–98	133	76 (57.14%)			4	4	1	7	8	9	13	3	9	5	5	2	3	3	3	1		
S. Caterina	1594–1635	276	165 (59.78%)		3	1	10	12	9	16	12	14	4	19	5	17	8	10	11	11	1	6	8

Sources: Bologna: ASB, PIE, S. Maria del Baraccano, mss. 6.2, 7; ASB, PIE, S. Maria del Baraccano, mss. 6.2, 7; ASB, PIE, S. Giuseppe, ms. 23; Florence: ASF, Ceppo mss. 59, 145; ASF, CRSF mss. 112/78, 79; ASF, S. Caterina, ms. 17.

years. Most also avoided older girls, judging that these had either already lost their virginity, or that they would have difficulty adapting to the discipline in the home and that it would be impossible to tell them what to do. Girls passed this point by about ages 14 to 16.[21] One home initially took in girls ages 12 to 18, but soon narrowed this, arguing that by age 15 girls became "difficult to put under obedience, to rule, or govern"; by age 17 they were so intractable that there had to be unanimous agreement of all the governors before accepting any-one of that troublesome age; and at age 18 it was better to simply try and arrange marriages for them.[22] This same set of homes also looked more closely at the girls' personalities, and shut the door on those who were bad tempered, were uncooperative, had poor work habits, or were slovenly; what they wanted was not so much passivity as adaptability and obedience. As can be seen from Table 2.2, homes by and large followed these guidelines in practice. Although a few children below and above the age limits always found their way into S. Maria del Baraccano and S. Giuseppe, almost 80 percent of the former's group were be-tween 8 and 15 when they entered, while 66 percent of the latter's group for whom ages are available were between 11 and 16.

Florence's conservatories adopted looser age restrictions that suggest they saw a somewhat different role for themselves, but Table 2.2 demonstrates that in practice they faced the same demographic and sociological realities as their Bolognese counterparts. Only S. Maria Vergine and S. Niccolò followed Bolo-gna's example and stated a minimum entrance age of 10 (neither specified an upper limit) or echoed its concerns about temperament. Both aimed to steer girls through adolescence and into marriage or domestic service by late adoles-cence. In practice, S. Niccolò took in girls as young as 3, and 80 percent of its girls entered when they were between 8 and 15 years old. S. Caterina at the end of the century specified ages 6 to 10, the youngest of any conservatory, and pos-sibly a reflection of its brief to offer temporary shelter to the neediest orphans in the dearth of the early 1590s. Yet in fact under 40 percent of its entrants fit this range and over half were older.[23] The picture becomes clearer in Table 2.3, which compares statistics on five homes in the two cities. The average ages of girls entering these conservatories are generally quite close, but the comparison of cohorts within particular homes demonstrates a couple of trends. Girls enter-ing a new home in either city averaged ages 11.5 to 14, with median ages from 12 to 14. Yet differences emerged as each home matured: in Florentine homes girls entered at younger and younger ages. In Bologna, they became older.

The picture is clearest at Florence's Pietà, where steadily dropping average

Table 2.3. Entrance Ages by Cohort of Girls Admitted to Conservatories:
Average, Median, Mode

Bologna, 1554–1641

	S. Maria del Baraccano		S. Giuseppe
	>1570	1570–84	1616–41
Total with Age	129 of 161	40 of 121	45 of 112
Average	12.38	13.62	14
Median	12	14	14
Mode	12	14	13
Maximum	26	18	5
Minimum	4	12	25

Florence, 1570–1635

	S. Niccolò		S. Caterina	
	Pre-1579	Post-1579	1594	1594–1635
Total with Age	71/94	59/116	87/100	78/176
Average	11.43	9.88	13.71	9.85
Median	12	10	14	8
Mode	12	10	12	9
Maximum	20	18	26	68
Minimum	3	2	5	3

Pietà (Florence), 1554–1624

	1554–59	1560–68	1569–1623 all	*Libro Nuovo*
Total with Age	361/361	142/165	355/372	96/106
Average	12.56	11.56	9.45	8.56
Median	13	11	9	8
Mode	12	11	10	8
Maximum	30	42	28	28
Minimum	3	2	3	3

Sources: Bologna: ASB, PIE, S. Maria del Baraccano, ms. 6/1; ASB, PIE, S. Giuseppe, cart. 23;
Florence: ASF, Ceppo ms. 59, cc. 105v–128v, 135v–193r; ASF, S. Caterina, ms. 17 (np); Pietà:
ASF, CRSF mss. 112/78 (1554–59), 112/79 (1559–1623).

and median ages mark the four stages in its development from conservatory to
convent. The girls entering the new conservatory in its first five years averaged
12.56 years (median = 13). This dropped to 11.56 (median = 11) in the decade that
followed while the Pietà was still in the Borgo Ognissanti neighborhood, and to
9.45 (median = 9) after the move to the new and more remote location in 1568.
If we separate out the final group of girls whose names were transferred over to
a new and no longer extant record (the *Libro Nuovo*), and most of whom became

nuns, the average drops to 8.56 and the median to 8. A simpler before-and after-picture is given in Graph 2.5 (see below). This is the most extreme and steady decline of any Florentine home, but the trend appears in all of them. It suggests that Florentine families early on saw these homes as affordable lay convents, and wanted to pass on their orphaned or abandoned wards as soon as possible so as to avoid the costs of raising them. Bolognese families may have had similar motivations, but entry to the homes was more tightly policed.

Many children were vulnerable, but fewer were honorable. Concerns about honor involved not just the *qualità* of children themselves and their families, but also the honor of the home and the city. Some of the prescriptions coming out of this concern had to do with the child's immediate situation and need: had he been begging, was she still a virgin, had they been servants in someone's house? Others had to do with the city's concern for maintaining a certain standard of citizen: was the child legitimately born of local parents who were moral and reputable? Would the city itself be dishonored if it did not care for this child? On these latter points, Bologna was generally far more restrictive than Florence, preferring to keep its homes for the use of local children of worthy families, and reviewing children more rigorously as a result. If charity was blind, politics had its eyes wide open.

Local origin was the critical point on which the homes of the two cities divided: all of the Bolognese homes—and none of the Florentine ones—mentioned it. Florence's Abbandonati orphanage had been opened to take children from the entire dominion, and local conservatories followed its example. The homes did not consistently identify their wards' origins, but most noted the neighborhood, town, or locality that the father had come from. This can give us an idea of the child's origin, but can also be misleading—after all, Leonardo da Vinci spent less than two years in the town that gave him his name. Yet even if a deceased father like Pietro da Mugello had raised his children in Florence, the name suggests that he was still considered a foreigner. His Florentine neighbors had no investment in keeping his children alive, and the brothers, sisters, and cousins who could have raised these children after he died were too far outside the city or too long out of touch to be of much help. This was even more the case with those children whose fathers were craftsmen up from Rome or soldiers over from Spain. Using patronymics, we can see that 60 to 70 percent of children entering into S. Niccolò, S. Caterina, the Pietà, and the Abbandonati came from families whose homes or roots were outside the city.[24] Some of these children definitely walked the distance from Pistoia, Pontassieve, and the Mugello—most "foreigners" were in fact from the *contado*, that administrative district of Tuscany that ranged from 20 to 60 kilometers beyond the city walls, though a few were from the *distretto* that pushed beyond this to the duchy's borders.

By contrast, the Bolognese intended their homes to be for the relief of their own local families. Sometimes it was the child herself or himself who was to be born locally, sometimes the child's father; the mother's origin is specified less consistently. Many homes toughened this regulation through the sixteenth century. If not actually a citizen, the father had to have lived honorably in the city for ten years (S. Croce) or even twenty (S. Marta). Sponsors had to produce a child's baptismal certificate in order to prove that he or she had been born locally, and S. Maria del Baraccano required officials to check this against the municipal baptismal records in order to prevent forgery and fraud; less than 10 percent of its girls seem to have come from families with roots outside the city.[25] Local origin was cited more frequently than legitimate birth in the case of boys' homes, suggesting that some of the Bolognese orphanages took in the illegitimate children of local worthy citizens. By contrast, conservatories required evidence of the family's good standing and reputation—the catch-all phrase "buona vita, fama, e costumi" (worthy life, reputation, and habits) echoes through the statutes— and this implicitly ruled out those girls born out of wedlock. With this combination of requirements, Bologna's homes were clearly aiming to preserve the honor of the city by demonstrating that it took the effort to care for the orphaned and abandoned children of those families, or at least those fathers, who were thoroughly Bolognese. One home went a step further and specified that if any men of its sponsoring confraternity died and left children destitute, these had the first chance at entry.[26]

The children's own honor was specified less often and revolved around two related points. A girl's sexual honor, as symbolized by virginity, was almost universally specified or at least implied, and few homes were prepared to take the word of either girl or guardian on the point. A woman, either the resident *guardiana*, a gentlewoman of the sponsoring confraternity, or a nurse, conducted a physical exam and submitted an oral or written report. Only Florence's quasi-conventual Pietà and the two homes for girls of the "shamefaced poor" (Bologna's S. Marta and Florence's Carità) omitted the concern, the former because it was a moot point, and the latter two because in the curious code surrounding the so-called *poveri vergognosi*, the family's honor was assumed and not tested.

The second point of honor had to do with the activities that the child had been engaged in since being orphaned or abandoned. Suspicions of sexual violation and other dishonorable activities lurked beneath the restrictions that banned those children who had been begging on the streets, who had been domestic servants, or who had tended livestock in the fields. When children were raped or assaulted, it was almost inevitably in these settings. These were also seen as the devious and disruptive children, thieving, fighting, throwing rocks and insults in the streets, and unlikely to be readily tamed through applications of hygiene, discipline, and Christian Doctrine.[27] Bologna's S. Giuseppe went further and excluded those who had spent time in other charitable hostels, and particularly in the city's large and overcrowded (but gender-segregated) Ospedale dei Mendicanti.[28]

The child's health animated a final set of concerns that comes through the statutes. With the possible exception of Florence's Pietà, no home wanted to become the repository of children abandoned due to infectious disease or some permanent physical or mental disability. Children with disabilities had few if any prospects of work or marriage, and so would become permanent wards. If that was a major reason for their abandonment by desperately poor parents, it was an equally strong reason for homes, dependent as they were on the economic contribution of children's work and counting as they did on eventually restoring most of these children to society as artisans, servants, wives, or nuns, to keep them out. Most linked health to a child's prospects of eventually leaving the home. The language of the statutes is brutally frank. S. Caterina excluded the blind, deaf, mute, hunchbacked, or lame so as not to "weigh down the place" ("per non gravare il luogo"); any girl found to have one of these impediments after she'd been formally accepted should be summarily thrown out. S. Giuseppe specified that its girls could not have itchy sores, be sick in the head or possessed of bad humors, be lame, or have bad eyes—anything that would keep them from their eventual destiny of working in the homes of gentlewomen should keep them from the conservatory as well. In a 1596 statute reform, S. Maria del Baraccano excluded those with any deformities, but used a term—*mostruosità*—that put these children beyond the natural and the moral realms, and so implied that they were beyond any help that the charitable home could provide.[29]

Beyond disability, homes worried about physical and moral contagion. Since many diseases were considered a form of divine punishment, it is not surprising to see them connected in the statutes.[30] The threat of contagious disease to all children and staff of the frequently cramped homes does not have to be spelled out. The Pietà, which alone among all the homes considered here had no regulations on health, had a staggeringly high death rate, losing almost half its first year's group of 156 girls to disease within five years. S. Maria Vergine wanted girls healthy in mind and body, saying that a blemish in one or the other would infect a home that had been brought, apparently with difficulty, to such a clean state ("oggi ridotto a tanta nettezza"). The *madre priora* and the nurse were personally to examine each girl before she was voted on, paying particular attention to the head and throat and the rest of the body to find signs of any physical infection or incurable disease. The men of the home's supervising confraternity were to give the girl's *qualità*, sponsors, and experiences an equally searching examination, looking in particular to see whether she had had the opportunity to see or hear dishonest words or actions that would have blemished her mind. "Keep your eyes open on this" ("con questo pero apra bene gli occhi"), the statutes warned, because we've been the victims of numerous frauds and deceits on this score.[31]

If physical and moral contagion were linked, so too, through the doctrine of the humors, were the concepts of health and temperament. As we saw earlier with regard to age, girls in particular were to be checked for their habits and disposition: the home didn't want to deal with bad tempers, laziness, gossiping, or what S. Croce described as a "nasty disposition" (*indispositione cattive*) since these too would have a contagious effect on the other girls and make the home an unhealthy place to live. By the same token, the good habits, vivacity, openness, virtue, and modesty of individual girls and boys could be reinforced if every entrant to a home shared these characteristics.[32]

Procedures

How could homes identify children who were genuinely vulnerable, appropriately honorable, and sufficiently healthy? The far-ranging and explicit conditions laid out in the statutes point to ambitious standards, but equally suggest that the children who passed through the doors were a decidedly mixed bunch. Typically for statutes of the period, the more often a prescription was repeated, the more likely that it was difficult to enforce or that it sought to repair recent negative experiences.

That notwithstanding, those writing the statutes did not shirk from giving themselves major roles in policing the standards they had set out. Men interviewed neighbors, priests, and kin, and checked through civic records to verify what they were told. Women examined the girls physically, and spoke with them in an effort to determine whether they had the right attitudes. Staff members watched to see how incoming children interacted with those already there, and noted whether the new ones fit in or not. In at least one instance, the children already in the home had the chance, after two months of living, working, and playing together, to vote on those who had applied to come in. All of these oral and written reports were brought forward to meetings of the governing confraternities, congregations, and officials, where the candidates were discussed and their case was put to a secret vote. There were few standardized procedures, but homes borrowed freely and adapted from the kind of rules their members had themselves experienced when seeking to enter a guild or confraternity, or what their spiritual advisors could tell them of procedures for entering a convent or monastery. A review of a few of these procedures will demonstrate the various degrees of oversight practiced in different homes, and so help show whether they could be as selective in practice as their rules suggested.

Homes opening or writing statutes in the mid-sixteenth century tended to have somewhat looser procedures that gave extensive latitude to the founder or to the small group of officials who were responsible for administration. While Florentine homes retained this somewhat looser system, Bolognese homes generally and those for girls in particular adopted progressively more restrictive procedures that relied on a series of votes and visitations, and employed baptismal and death certificates. At what must have been, bureaucratically, the furthest end of this development, S. Bartolomeo di Reno required by the late seventeenth century that its visitors have in hand baptismal certificates for father and son, the parents' marriage certificate, and the father's death certificate. When clerics and dioceses after the Council of Trent pushed for parish priests to register the major rites of passage, they likely didn't anticipate that the resulting certificates would become a means of making charity more restrictive.[33]

The loosest system of control left admission in the hands of a single individual—inevitably the founder—or a small group of officials. As we saw in the previous chapter, Bonifacio dalle Balle devoted his life and fortune to establishing Bologna's S. Croce as a shelter for the daughters of prostitutes, and it was only with great difficulty that he was encouraged to share the responsibility for determining who ought to get in. Vittorio dell'Ancisa played the same role when establishing Florence's Carità, though the girls he aimed to help were at the opposite end of the social scale. Each man judged individually who ought to enter and who not, and neither left a record of how he arrived at his decisions. As each home became more dependent on outside resources, and so had to draw more people into its work, these procedures were opened up and decisions were shared. The Carità briefly had two forty-member Congregations, one of women and one of men, but this system generated too many fights and was soon replaced with something closer to the procedures found in convents, a hint of the Carità's own future evolution. S. Croce moved closer to the common Bolognese model of governing councils and extensive reviews, for reasons and with results that we will see below.

A number of homes, chiefly Florence's Pietà and S. Caterina, entrusted admission decisions to a small group of volunteer officials who worked with some of the resident staff of the home and made their decision based in part on a trial period that the child spent in the home. As we saw with the case of Maddalena di Bernardino at the opening of this chapter, the Pietà gentlewomen who had ultimate authority for the home interviewed the child and, if they found her acceptable, allowed her a trial period of at least three months during which a mistress of novices would teach her and judge on her compatibility. Up to this point, she was to have no contact with the other girls in the house. S. Caterina experimented with a similar process forty years later, but encouraged more contact between new and resident girls, and initially allowed a committee drawn from the latter group a chance to vote on whether to accept the novice after her two-month trial period (though the final decision still rested with the Five Deputies who oversaw the home). This was clearly drawn from the practice of convents, where nuns had a say in the admission of novices, in part out of fears that obvious incompatibilities could tear the community apart through tensions and fights. This was also the model that the Carità adopted as it moved away from Vittorio dell'Ancisa's extremes of a one-man show and eighty-person anarchy. In its place the home adopted a three-stage process by which girls entered as novices, graduated to the status of *giovane* with their own teaching mistress, and, after four years, could graduate to the status of *stabilite*. Novices had no contact with the other girls outside of the chapel and dining hall, and the *stabilite* were entitled to vote on those *giovane* who wanted to join their number. Not surprisingly, all three of these Florentine homes developed into enclosed convents within a matter of decades.

Some homes tried more consciously to distinguish themselves from convents, and aimed more deliberately to reintegrate their charges into lay society. These drew in a larger number of lay participants to examine the children and to vote in what were often restrictive review processes. In Florence, the Abbandonati and S. Maria Vergine (and with it S. Niccolò) both relied on staff and, to some extent, on votes of the administrators. But in both cases, there were loopholes or even contradictions that could make these procedures a dead letter. As we saw with Gracia Pieracci at the opening of this chapter, girls coming into S. Niccolò or S. Maria Vergine had to pass initial inspection by the resident *guardiana* and the Five Deputies before their cases were turned over to two visitors who had a week and a day to check how well they met the conditions. Their report went to the forty-member Compagnia di S. Maria Vergine for discussion and a vote, though in urgent cases the Five Deputies could act alone.

The Ospedale degli Abbandonati's procedure took this a step further, relying on the resident guardian and on the formal written nomination called the *fede di bambino*. Written by a local priest, neighbor, family member, or friend, the *fede* laid out the child's circumstances and appealed to the *ospedale* to take him in. Nominees submitted 647 *fede* from August 1574 through November 1606. Some described a single child, but many emphasized the desperate circumstances of a set of siblings in the hope that the Abbandonati would take more than one.[34] Reading through them is a disheartening exercise. There seems to be no clear connection between the seriousness of the case and the child's admission.

The 315 *fede* submitted from 1574 through 1590 resulted in 133 boys entering the home. Entries did not increase in winter, and seem to have fallen rather than risen in time of famine when the need was clearly greater. The numbers admitted and excluded were extremely close regardless of locality, of whether the father and mother were dead, and of whether there were siblings.[35] Patronage and string-pulling no doubt played a large part in determining who came in, but all evidence suggests that the *fede* were certainly taken seriously. In 1583, Abbandonati officials began checking on the facts laid out in the *fede*, going so far as to track down the signatories and examine them under oath. The investigators wrote their findings on the back of the *fede* and sometimes had the guarantors sign a second time. Within a few years, as word spread of how serious the exercise was, the number of individuals signing each *fede* grew to three or four and, in a couple instances, to nine and even fifteen (though neither of these latter was successful). Nominators were no doubt as much concerned with spreading personal responsibility as with persuading the Abbandonati officials to accept a particular boy into the home.[36] Cosimo I's plan to have Florentine governmental representatives like the *podestà* or *capitano* control access to the Abbandonati by conducting a preliminary review and countersigning the nominations seems to have become a dead letter; the *fede* were almost entirely the petitions of private citizens directly to the Abbandonati. The few exceptions were appeals from other charitable institutions, notably the Ospedale di S. Maria Nuova, that the Abbandonati take in the children of adults who had died within their walls.

Notes on some of the *fede* show that the Bigallo captains read them closely and formally voted to take in certain boys and reject others. Significantly, the *fede* seldom if ever mention the training or skills that a boy might bring to the institution and that, like a girl's dowry, might speed up his exit from the shelter; they focus instead on his dire need. The boys and those nominating them had to wait from a few days to a week between submission of their request and the opening of the Abbandonati's door, though in some rare cases everything happened in a single day. During this time, the boys might be housed in a small local paupers' hostel, or lodged with the nominator. Yet the *fede* were always a gamble, and as the process was becoming progressively more bureaucratic, a loophole yawned large in the form of anonymous abandonment on the steps of the dormitory itself or under the portico on Piazza S. Giovanni. While the Medici dukes ordered that boys abandoned in this way had to be turned out again after a few days, the reservations and excuses frequently voiced by the Bigallo captains and gaps in the *fede* suggest that many were quietly accepted. In 1586 and 1588–90, years when the Abbandonati was complaining of overcrowding, only twenty-six *fede* were submitted and none was successful. When times were grim and families were desperate, boys were clearly entering the hospital by other means, most likely by abandonment at the door.

Florentine conservatories did not have *fede* as such, but from 1566 the Pietà came to rely on sponsors or promoters to bring girls forward. The first was Maria Margherita Bonsi, an early administrator and frequent benefactor who went on to nominate four more. Sponsors ranged from individuals of no particular status to leading families like the Soderini, Buonacorsi, and Salviati, and even the grand duchess. Priests referred local girls, administrators of other Florentine hospitals turned to the Pietà if a recently deceased patient had left a child, and even charitable institutions like the Buonomini di S. Martino and government agencies like the Magistracy of the Pupilli figured among sponsors of needy girls. The range of sponsors shows how quickly the Pietà had worked its way into established patronage relations and how much it had become part of Florence's network of charitable homes.[37]

Since Bologna's homes were far more determined to enroll only local orphans who met numerous conditions, they not surprisingly adopted far more complex and restrictive entrance procedures. And since, as we saw in the previous chapter, the Bolognese homes operated more clearly as an interlinked network with a strong albeit indirect political component, these procedures varied little from home to home and often gave a large role to the home's rector, the supreme head who was usually drawn from the city's senate and who served a six-month term.

Initially the rector had almost complete control. In a few of the homes he nominated those children whose cases would be considered by the governing confraternity. Children could be brought to his attention by means of a written *memoriale*, which was similar to the Florentine *fede di bambini*, or through his own network of clients. In March 1610, the executive committee of S. Croce filed into the palazzo of their rector, Girolamo Boncompagni, to discuss their business and receive, among other things, his nomination of Margherita, a girl then sheltered in the palazzo. Margherita was formally admitted at the next meeting, even though she did not fit all the statute requirements. A month later, Rector Boncompagni nominated 10-year-old orphan Cornelia Zagni, asking that she be taken in for five years, during which he would pay 5 lire monthly for her upkeep and after which he would supply a dowry. It is not clear how long the *confratelli* debated Cornelia's case while sitting in Boncompagni's chairs, admiring his well-decorated room, and possibly eating the food from his kitchen, but Cornelia was accepted that day.[38]

There was clearly a push and pull here. The Bolognese homes wanted senatorial rectors for the influence and funds that they could provide. Senators themselves appreciated the influence that the office provided, and worked collaboratively to ensure that the homes operated in a quasi-governmental sphere that was under their authority but out of the realm that they shared with the papal legate. At the same time, influence was meaningless if it did not mean that individual senators couldn't put individual girls and boys into particular homes at particular times. Certainly few senators would have been willing to put in the time and effort that the office required without some concrete quid pro quo. The paradox of the Bolognese system is that at the same time as it adopted this informal system of rectorial patronage, it laid out a far more elaborate formal system of visitations and checks on girls and, to a lesser extent, on boys. At S. Maria del Baraccano, over one-quarter of the girls were recommended by sponsors who ranged from maternal uncles to the wives of senators, and it is not clear what their impact was on the increasingly precise entrance procedures.[39]

Every entry began with a formal written nomination, establishing at the outset that the Bolognese did not want to deal with children dropped off at the door. A number of homes distributed printed forms that explained what information the administrators wanted to have and what certificates they wanted to see.[40]

Whether coming from the rector or from a *memoriale* that a parent or guardian had submitted, the nomination was first discussed by the home's four or five chief officials (the *confratelli* who managed its finances and day-to-day affairs, and who served rotating terms of six months or a year). If sympathetic, they proposed the child to the next meeting of the whole confraternity. *Confratelli* heard the *memoriale* read aloud, got a report on the discussion that the officials had had, and then voted secretly on whether to conduct a more complete investigation. This would be the work of two, or sometimes three, visitors, chosen either at the time from among the *confratelli* present, or serving fixed terms as other officials did. The visitors took the *memoriale* and went to the child's parent or guardian to check its details and ask why none of the relatives could care for the child. They talked to the local priest, to some of the neighbors, and possibly to the men who had worked alongside the father. If the home had a particular target group, these visitors had to make sure that the child matched it. So it was, for example, with S. Marta's focus on the "shamefaced poor." Early modern Bolognese seemed to have as much disagreement about who was truly "shamefaced" as modern historians do, and S. Marta frequently returned to the point in order to guide its visitors.

The first statutes of 1554 offered no definition of the term *poveri vergognosi*, but the confraternity clarified this in 1567 by setting out quite explicitly who fit in this group: gentlemen, merchants, and superior artisans who had lived civilly for at least twenty years. In 1580 the confraternity reiterated the point and clarified the definition, and in 1641 it cautioned that a family's fall into poverty could not be due to any fraud or deceit. But visitors also guarded loopholes. Lucia Ferrante, the only historian who has worked in the group's closed archive, has found in her investigation of entrance records that many of the girls' families did not meet the tightening definition of *poveri vergognosi*. Girls of lower status might be admitted if their families had a connection to the civic government or the confraternity, and girls of a far higher status might be admitted in *conserva*, a status closer to boarding under which the families retained more direct control.[41]

Statutes often required that visitors complete their investigation within five to eight days, but in reality governing confraternities seldom met more than once a month, and so it would normally be that long before the child could be discussed once again. The visitors read out their report, and after discussion of the case, the *confratelli* voted secretly with their black and white beans. The bar was quite high, at least in theory: children had to receive at least two-thirds and sometimes as much as three-fourths of the votes cast before they could be admitted.

Girls faced further and more intrusive investigation. In some cases, the vote taken after the visitors' report merely authorized a second visitation, this time by a team of female visitors drawn either from a parallel consorority or from the female staff of the home. These women examined the girl physically to ensure that she was still a virgin, something which, as noted above, all the Bolognese homes and none of the Florentine ones required. Initially performed at the girl's own home, by the mid-seventeenth century the *consorelle* and staff more often performed their physical examination in the home itself. Since girls were often proposed and examined in groups, we can imagine girls lined up and waiting, perhaps outside the home's infirmary, to be called in and be examined by a nurse in the presence of two or three gentlewomen of the consorority. These latter would ask some further questions of their own, and like their male counterparts could carry their investigation into the girl's neighborhood. If the *confratelli* checked the reputation and worth of the family, the *consorelle* had the harder task of establishing the honor and temperament of the girl herself. All of this went into a report that the women passed on to their male colleagues, either to be read out with the male visitors' report or at the later and final meeting called to consider the child's eligibility.

Under this process, orphaned and abandoned Bolognese children faced at least three and sometimes four votes on their application. It was closely reviewed by anywhere from two to six generally high-born citizens, and had to be approved by a senator before being put to a vote of anywhere from twenty to a hundred *confratelli*—memberships, quotas, and attendance varied widely—with a margin of not less than 66 and often over 75 percent. Though rigorous in theory, the system could fail in practice. Graph 2.1 tracks nominations and acceptances at the Bolognese orphanage of S. Onofrio over a three-decade period when *confratelli* investigated 138 boys, but accepted 157. Through the first five years, the home investigated roughly twice the number of boys that it accepted (53 to 28). At that point, administration began deteriorating and from 1587 through 1594 no effort was made to review applicants formally; they were accepted by the resident *guardiano*. Or so we must assume, since he was the one who took the blame when *confratelli* woke up in 1594 and claimed self-righteously in their minute book that their statutes had been grievously violated. Their next act was to formally admit the twenty-eight boys then resident in S. Onofrio. They proved only marginally more adept after this, and according to the records now accepted more boys than they had formally investigated (129 to 85). This could indicate lassitude, but more likely points to a deeply ingrained culture of patronage under

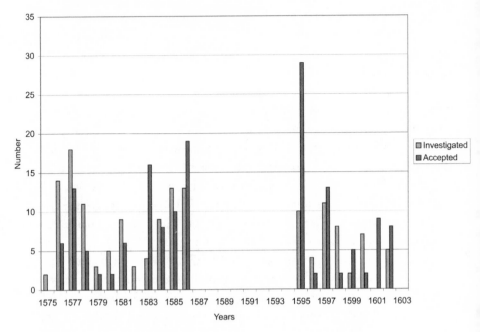

Graph 2.1. Nominations and Admissions at S. Onofrio, 1575–1603
Source: ASB, PIE, S. Maria Maddalena, mss. 4/VIII and 5/IX.

which *confratelli* and senior administrators assumed the right to place children directly in the home. Other homes certainly followed this practice—it may have been the only way to get volunteers to do the administrative work expected of them. At the same time, S. Onofrio seems to have been unusually generous in this regard. The case of S. Bartolomeo di Reno discussed below suggests a ratio of three acceptances to four investigations, while both S. Maria del Baraccano and S. Croce were closer to S. Onofrio's pre-1580 practice of accepting only about half of the children that they investigated. But this was just an average; Graph 2.2 shows that while investigations always outpaced acceptances, in some crisis years (e.g., 1582 and 1594) there were four times more girls looking for shelter than there were beds available.[42]

While loopholes and lassitude might open their doors unpredictably, Bolognese homes adopted ever more restrictive statutes in the hard times between the later sixteenth and early seventeenth centuries. Homes across Italy were struggling to cope with rising admissions caused by famines, plagues, and economic stagnation, and one common solution was to set an upper limit on the number of children that would be accepted. Florentine and Bolognese homes both took

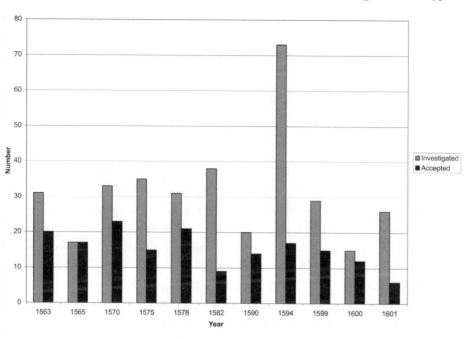

Graph 2.2. Nominations and Admissions at S. Maria del Baraccano, 1563–1601
Source: ASB, PIE, S. Maria del Braccano, busta 12, ms. 1.

this route, but only the latter adapted their procedures to ensure that the limits were enforced. This typically led to uneven recruitment by large cohorts rather than by individuals let in one at a time. The *confratelli* who ran S. Bartolomeo di Reno refused repeated applications through the first half of 1588 on the grounds that the home was too full. Meanwhile, three of their number looked through the dormitories to determine who could be released. In a meeting on 7 June, 13 boys were dismissed; the same meeting accepted 2 new boys and launched proceedings on 13 others. From June through December, *confratelli* considered a total of 40 applications, and allowed 29 boys into the home. The doors then rapidly closed again: only 12 boys entered in 1589, 3 in 1590, and no more than a handful each year to 1594, all of them years of extreme famine. Dire conditions in the city dried up opportunities for boys outside the home, and as residents stayed longer there was no room for new applicants. The rector was determined to keep the total number of boys around 100, which was all that the residence or the budget could accommodate.[43]

S. Bartolomeo's practice worked its way into the statutes of almost all of Bologna's homes, and most came to require that the home could not even consider a new application until they had located a vacant bed for that child to sleep in. S. Giuseppe ordered its members to sit down at the beginning of the year and determine what its rental and investment income would be, and how many children could be accommodated with those funds. The members were not to guess on what donations might come in or what the girls might raise through alms gathering; all of *that* was to be extra. S. Maria del Baraccano's *confratelli* had to meet periodically in order to determine what spaces were available within its self-imposed limit of seventy-five (reduced to fifty-five in the 1647 statutes) and formally declare an opening. Only then could it publicize that it would accept *memoriali per l'accettatione*, no doubt releasing a pent-up demand and leading eventually to the lines of girls awaiting their physical examinations for health and virginity in the Baraccano infirmary and the follow-up lines (no doubt shorter) of those waiting to be examined by the Baraccano *confratelli* to determine if they were pretty enough to be in danger of sexual assault.

And that was not all. Having identified a supply of vulnerable, honorable, healthy, and beautiful virgins, the Baraccano *confratelli* wanted to be sure that they would not have to shelter them for long. A final review went back to the family and guardians, and back to the bottom line. Bolognese conservatories wanted to ensure that if, all their visitations and examinations notwithstanding, the girl proved either sick, "experienced," disruptive, or incompatible, they could turn her out again and there would be some place to receive her. Hence, to a degree not found in Florence, a girl's admission was always conditional and always reversible. And indeed, the same S. Croce *confratelli* who had accepted Rector Boncompagni's nominations while enjoying the hospitality in his drawing room had a year earlier sent Maria Faccari out of the door and into the care of her sisters because she was ill.[44] Even more attention was paid to ensuring that there would be a dowry waiting in a few years when the girl became eligible for marriage. Since conservatories typically provided at least a basic dowry as part of their charitable care for girls, the temptation for parents and guardians of modest but adequate means to fake greater poverty in order to enroll their daughters or wards was considerable.

Visitors were supposed to question their motives closely on this score. Yet into the seventeenth century, Bolognese conservatories adopted additional strategies to deal with the potential problems of worthy, but not needy girls, coming in. Some, like S. Maria del Baraccano and S. Marta, asked that family and guardians pledge a particular amount that would be available at the appropriate time or, preferably, supply that pledge in advance. This money was either registered on the books as being to the individual girl's credit, or deposited into the *monte del matrimonio*, the civic dowry fund, and then drawn on when she left the home. While a girl wasn't to be rejected if her family could not provide a dowry, the amount of funds and their liquidity certainly figured in the discussions that preceded a vote.[45]

The opposite strategy, adopted by S. Giuseppe, was simply to refuse to get into the dowry business at all. The gentlewomen starting this conservatory wanted to give girls interim shelter for a few weeks or months rather than a surrogate home for a few years, and so made it known that they would neither accept dowry pledges nor offer dowry funds.[46] More to the point, they would not arrange marriages. That would be done, if done at all, by the Bolognese families who took the girls in as domestic servants. The gentlewomen's resolve was based more on practicality than principle. Like other Bolognese conservatories, they offered shelter for a fee.

This was another point on which the two cities differed: only one of the Florentine conservatories (the Casa della Carità) admitted fee-paying girls, but all of the Bolognese ones did. Each stipulated that a fee-paying girl had to meet all the same conditions as charity girls, and could only be accepted after the same strict process of visitations and votes. Yet it is hard to escape the suspicion that this was little more than a well-lubricated loophole opened up to accommodate more conveniently the offspring—possibly legitimate, probably not—of the city's more prosperous families. The same S. Giuseppe women who high-mindedly refused to offer dowries advertised that they had a separate and superior dormitory and a better diet available for fee-paying girls. In the later 1620s, 10 lire monthly—double what Rector Girolamo Boncompagni had offered the *confratelli* of S. Croce to take in Cornelia Zagni two decades before—could secure a girl a place at S. Giuseppe, and slightly less than half of the girls in the small home were fee-paying. By 1633 the ratio began tilting toward fee-paying girls until, by 1636, nine of the twelve girls admitted were paying fees. Or not paying in too many cases. Of the ten girls admitted before 1633, all but one left with debts outstanding. When they started taking in more paying girls, S. Giuseppe's administrators also started giving more attention to actually getting paid; of the seventeen fee-paying girls admitted from 1633 through 1636, only four left with debts. They may by then have adopted the rule that found its way into the 1641 statutes, requiring that all fees be fully paid up in advance every three months or the girl would be dismissed.[47]

What were the results of these procedures? The *confratelli* of S. Maria del

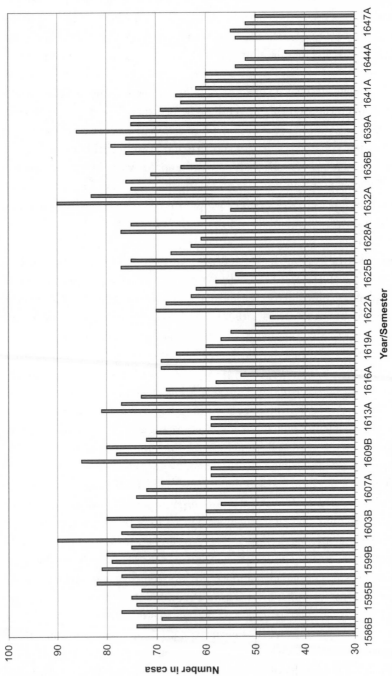

Graph 2.3. Biannual Censuses at S. Maria del Baraccano, 1586–1647

Source: ASB, PIE, S. Maria del Baraccano, ms. 7.

Baraccano kept excellent records on the girls coming into their home and, from 1586, took two censuses annually of the number of girls under their care. Graph 2.3 gives the results of these semestral censuses and shows that the efforts to keep within the seventy-five-person limit were reasonably successful from the 1580s through to about 1605. At that point, while keeping within the limit, the home developed a wave pattern something like that just seen in S. Bartolomeo di Reno, which expelled and admitted adolescents in groups. The number of girls in S. Maria del Baraccano would be allowed to fall to something under 60, at which point an opening would be declared and 20 to 25 girls would be allowed in at once. From 1605 through 1645 we can track 9 such waves, the last ending with a deliberate reduction to 40, and then a resumption of the wave pattern aimed at sustaining the new and lower limit of 55. Looking more closely at the records confirms that the confraternity organized the nomination, investigation, and approval process to culminate in a single meeting where brothers voted on the finalists of its long selection procedures.[48] Although the wave pattern is most clearly visible from 1605, Graph 2.3 shows that it was at work in lower numbers and smaller oscillations of one to two years through the 1590s.

Since the pattern was clearly the result of administrative procedures and, as we have already seen, since Bolognese homes tended to draw on each other's example in the gradual development of local administrative norms, can we find it in other homes? S. Bartolomeo di Reno appears to have followed the same pattern as its companion institution S. Maria del Baraccano, though the data are too rudimentary to say definitively. A similar pattern is evident in S. Onofrio (see Graph 2.1, above), though the gap from 1587 to 1594 skews the run of data. More tellingly, even S. Giuseppe, where short-term entrants and fee-paying arrangements might also be expected to distort the data, shows the same pattern, with four peaks at roughly three-year intervals through the 1630s (see Graph 2.4). By contrast, the oscillations in Florence's S. Niccolò (Graph 2.5) are more irregular and far more drawn out, with roughly twelve years separating peaks in the early 1570s, the mid-1580s, and the late 1590s.

Seventeenth-century statutes were inevitably more specific than those of the sixteenth century: what took a few lines for S. Maria del Baraccano in 1548 expanded through revisions of 1554, 1596, and 1608, until it ended up as twelve distinct steps over ten printed pages by 1647.[49] In some cases this reflected inflation in requirements, fed by rising standards (or pretensions), by a greater concern to limit aid to more select groups, or by a desire to take advantage of the bureaucratic tracking allowed by such innovations as baptismal, marriage, and

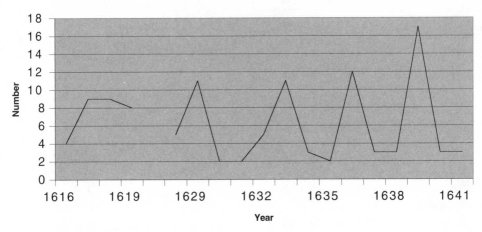

Graph 2.4. Admissions to S. Giuseppe, 1616–1641
Source: ASB, PIE, S. Giuseppe, ms. 23.

death records. In other cases, the succession of statutes reflects the sad experiences or power struggles found in particular homes. The situation of S. Croce is by turns sad and comic in its clear depiction of both these cases and the gradual bureaucratization of a home.

When Bonifacio dalle Balle finally got around to writing a set of statutes for S. Croce, he was financially vulnerable. Yet he still enjoyed the absolute control that had allowed him to choose, possibly in consultation with the four friends recruited into the work in 1592, the girls who would enter the shelter on Via S. Mamolo. The first statutes, undated but most likely written in 1605, describe the usual Bolognese conditions for girls—virginity, health, even temper, good-looking, younger than 12, imminent danger—without specifying any procedure for choosing them.[50] Even as the statutes were penned, rivals were joining the group of Franciscan tertiaries with whom dalle Balle formally shared governance. One of these, Alessandro Mazzarenti was particularly determined to push dalle Balle aside. He began levying accusations against dalle Balle's integrity, morality, and administration, which culminated in formal charges in the archiepiscopal court in 1607. Mazzarenti wanted to recruit more high-born Bolognese into administration as other homes did, and to this end began making promises to some that with the appropriate considerations—chiefly dowries or other donations—he would ensure that any girls they nominated would get in. Among those he approached were two high-born women, Isabella Vizzani and Cornelia di Ricci. Supplied with a dowry from the former and 200 lire from the latter, he secured admission for a 15-year-old girl who was so infirm that her mother and father, both in their 50s, could no longer care for her. Dalle Balle later charged that Massarenti faked the records of her acceptance and entry. The girl hadn't been visited, hadn't been voted on, and moreover, in four years' residence at S. Croce, hadn't worked a day. Massarenti, he claimed, was interested only in promoting his friends and family, and that if this way was to be followed, they may as well scrap any formal procedures for getting into S. Croce: "it can be said to those who ask that it's all done for the one who has the ready money in his hands."[51]

The accusation is a little disingenuous. Whatever dalle Balle's own practice on visits and votes, when that particular girl had come to S. Croce, there were no written procedures in place. Dalle Balle moved to remedy this with an absurdly convoluted set of provisions in statutes that he drafted and put to the confraternity for approval in January 1609. The rector and other officials would propose girls to the confraternity, which then voted for a review by two visitors. Each visitor prepared a written report on the girl's life, family, and qualities, and

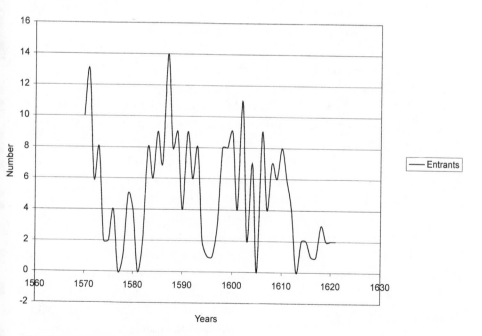

Graph 2.5. Admissions to S. Niccolò, 1570–1621
Source: ASF, Ceppo, ms. 59.

if the two reports did not agree, the girl was removed from consideration. If they did agree, another two visitors were sent out to do exactly the same review. If one of these demurred, a third set of two visitors repeated the process. All the written reports—up to six by this point—were discussed by *confratelli* before they voted for yet another review, in this instance, the test of the girl's virginity. The usual thunderous prohibitions against change to these rules were added at the end, and the archbishop had to be consulted before any deviation from them.

We are a long way from Rector Boncompagni's drawing room here, but to judge from subsequent events *confratelli* found that setting more agreeable than dalle Balle's report-writing nightmare. They refused to ratify his proposed statutes, and three months later adopted a simpler set whose two reviews—one by males of a girl's reputation and situation, and another by women of her virginity—matched the practices then current in Bolognese conservatories. Two large loopholes were added. Pressing cases could be handled by a simple majority of the officials and the visitors, and all rules and requirements could be suspended for particular girls if three-quarters of the *confratelli* approved. Alessandro Massarenti could continue with his recruiting, assisted by Isabella Vizzani, who joined S. Croce's consorority of gentlewomen and was elected prioress a few years later.

It is easy to portray dalle Balle as either a fanatic or a victim. Certainly the heated letters and memorials in his papers suggest a level of commitment far beyond noblesse oblige, and S. Croce did change significantly in the years that followed. High-born men and women took over administrative committees, power shifted decisively to rectorial drawing rooms, and dalle Balle's fears that doors would open for "the one who has the ready money in his hands" were fulfilled. More fee-paying girls entered S. Croce, and fewer of them were the endangered daughters of prostitutes. More families could make particular arrangements for short- or long-term care of their daughters or sisters, paying varying sums for different levels of help. Twenty-two girls applied for admission over the next three years, and of these eleven won admission, taking the places of eleven who left. Yet only three of these new girls came through the prescribed process of two visits and votes. Four were allowed in after the initial investigation, and four were admitted immediately. Each of these gained rapid entry because guardians promised to pay fees or provide other goods, and not because the *fratelli* feared for their immediate safety or honor. It appears to be a clear betrayal of dalle Balle's ideals, yet we only know these details because formal records of meetings, with nominations, visits, votes, and exceptions scrupulously recorded, only appear in the archives after the showdown with dalle Balle in 1609. And while these meetings shifted to rectors' drawing rooms, dalle Balle himself secured significant privileges, including a permanent seat on S. Croce's governing council, the right to place one girl annually in the home, and continued occupation of his private apartment in the S. Croce complex—a living arrangement that Massarenti had openly questioned before the 1609 showdown. We can guess that dalle Balle's is one of the two negative votes consistently recorded in votes on those girls proposed by the likes of Girolamo Boncompagni and Isabella Vizzani who did not meet the statute guidelines, but his disappointment was short-lived. Dalle Balle died in October 1612, and his brother Pietro took over his permanent seat on the council. Alessandro Massarenti took over his private apartment in the conservatory.[52]

In the decades that followed, S. Croce continued evolving closer to the Bolognese bureaucratic model and civic focus. By the 1660s, the confraternity determined annually whether it could shelter more girls, and issued announcements that it would accept nominations. Printed forms assisted the visitors in a two-month period of review that culminated in a single marathon meeting where the fates of as many as two hundred girls were decided, with just over 14 percent winning admission. The home recorded admission statistics according to the city's four quarters and, though no statute stipulates this, there appears to have been a rough quota system in place to ensure that each quarter received its share of spaces in the conservatory. Some of the sheets note the names of other convents, conservatories, and individuals that took in some of the individual girls who had been turned down by the S. Croce *confratelli*. This suggests that the Bolognese had further refined their interlocking network of homes by this point, and that shelters of various kinds communicated directly among each other about the fates of particular girls, though here too we have no clear documentary evidence of this.[53]

Reviewing entrance procedures and practices highlights the different aims that drove the Bolognese and Florentine homes and the dissimilar roles they played in their cities' social and political worlds. Bolognese homes had more prescriptive entrance requirements and in particular placed a priority on parents' citizenship and girls' virginity. They were very cautious, devising formal reviews of applications that could go through three or four stages, and requiring that guardians or parents stand ready to take back their disruptive charges or dower their more placid girls. Yet their close ties to the local political system opened avenues for personal patronage by high-born rectors who could sidestep all these elaborate entrance requirements. Determined to avoid bankruptcy, they became more open to fee-paying customers, and adopted financially driven entrance procedures that resulted in recruitment of girls and boys by cohorts. Florentine homes tended to be larger, somewhat less class-oriented, and attuned to the needs of the Medici dukes for territory-wide social assistance. Bolognese homes were smaller, organized quite decidedly according to social origin, and aimed more directly at the needs of the city, particularly its artisans, merchants, professionals, and elite. Florentine homes were shaped by the model of the Innocenti foundling home and the general *ospedale*, and so took in children with fewer questions asked and greater obligations incurred. Bolognese homes were shaped by the models of the confraternities that ran them and, eventually, the boarding schools that multiplied across sixteenth-century Italy. They demanded considerably more of their charges, and were prepared to give a great deal less. While Florentine shelters, particularly conservatories, accepted that they might be the permanent home of many of their charges, Bolognese homes clearly saw themselves as temporary shelters and worked as hard to get their children out as they had to get them in.

CHAPTER THREE

Making a Home with Girls

In late March 1575, a cart enters the large arched tunnel at one end of the façade of S. Maria del Baraccano that gives access to its inner courtyard from the busy Via S. Stefano—this is a only 100 meters or so from the major city gate of Porta S. Stefano used by traders and pilgrims heading out across the Futa Pass to Florence. The cart carries Valeria di Bartolomeo di Pavia and all her belongings. Her father is dead, her mother unable to keep her. Possibly her brother Cristofaro, who pledged 100 lire for her dowry, pushes the cart.[1] At the door, the keeper asks their business and quickly calls for the *guardiana*, or matron. At the moment, this older woman has her hands full preparing space in the dormitories for a new contingent of girls. It has been at least five years since she had to deal with the sudden entry of a large group of girls.[2] Sixteen new girls are to be entering S. Maria del Baraccano in the space of a few days, and in keeping with the home's customs, everyone moves around as the newest entrants are put into the least pleasant quarters while those who have been there for a few months or years can all move their beds to better parts of the dormitories vacated by girls who have just left to rejoin their families or to start new lives as wives.

Valeria and her fifteen novice companions are the lucky remainder of a group of thirty-five whose loss of a parent and resultant poverty had been described on application forms drawn up by family, friends, neighbors, and priests when the Conservatory of S. Maria del Baraccano had posted notice that it would open its long-closed doors to some needy but worthy girls.[3] These were girls whose family backgrounds had been investigated by some of Bologna's leading gentlemen and gentlewomen, whose strategies for staying alive over the past few months since the deaths of their fathers had been closely questioned, who had been brought into the home about a month ago and examined to see whether they were still virgins, and who had subsequently returned a few weeks later for a formal meeting in which more gentlemen had looked at them closely to see whether they were attractive. The number of girls had been whittled down at each stage of this process, until the *confratelli* finally voted on 23 March to take in sixteen of the abandoned and orphaned who had been proposed to them. These girls had spent the days since then assembling what goods they could muster to keep them through the years ahead: a bed, some linens, a few pieces of clothing for winter and summer.

At this point, the matron orders one of the conservatory's girls to prepare an inventory of all the goods on Valeria's cart. The only things worth noting specifically are a chest, a bed, and a mattress. The list goes to the *guardiana*, who later passes it on to one of the home's administrators, who in turn writes it on a fresh page of the ledger where he records the names, backgrounds, and fates of all the girls in the home. Cristofaro's dowry pledge is already there, and any further pledges that come in will be recorded as well. Cristofaro can't bring the bed farther than the door, since no men are allowed in the home regardless of their family connection to the girls there. Even visits outside of the home are not allowed; Valeria may not see her brother or mother again for a few years. As her brother leaves, a group of girls helps Valeria bring her things to a spare spot in the dormitory where, over the next few days, she meets the girls that she will live, work, and sleep beside for the next few years. Angelica di Benay, who in eight years will be expelled as a witch—possessed and "a servant of the devil." Ortensia, who at the same time will be returned to her family because she is "a good girl, but broken [*guasta*]" and because the home's authorities fear the effects of her broken state—physical or emotional—on the others. Ana di Caratini, who will die in a year and be buried in the local parish church. Laura di Filippo Maria, already ill with fever and dead in five months. Caterina Zanotta, described as "a quiet girl," and Isabella Prossero, "a good girl." Constancia, the only one of the group who will eventually become a nun.[4]

For better or worse, these sixteen girls move as a pack, bound together by their arrival together in a home where alliances and enemies have already been made, and where it has already been almost two years since any new girls—only two that time—entered.[5] Their beds, most of them brought along from their own homes, are clustered together in the dormitory. Their earliest lessons in the customs of the home are taken together with a senior girl who acts as mistress of novices. They all enter equally untrained into the workshop of the home and begin with the most basic forms of needlework and lacemaking. They will mature into adolescence within the walls of S. Maria del Baraccano, seldom even getting onto Via S. Stefano, much less into the rest of the city beyond. Most will eventually leave together: nine of the group will exit in eight or nine years, most of them to become the wives of Bolognese craftsmen. By this point, four of the others will have died and Constancia will have already spent four years in the Convent of S. Lorenzo. Is it the loss of her companions that "breaks" Ortensia and leaves her so distraught that the Baraccano expels her for fear of the effect she will have on younger girls? Though they have come from homes across the city, and from families that have been broken and broken up in different ways, these sixteen girls become something like sisters in the years that follow their entry into the quiet conservatory on busy Via S. Stefano. Having managed to get into the home, what kind of life do they lead there?

Valeria and her companions entered a home meant to protect their bodies, shape their character, and prepare them to return to the streets and neighborhoods of Bologna as wives and mothers. Locked doors and strict timetables could achieve some of this. Yet ultimately the girls' interaction with each other and with the older women who lived in the home and took on its day-to-day operation created the community that shaped them. Some of these older women were hired on the basis of their connections to *confratelli* or their experience in other homes. Others were members of a religious community who saw life in the home as a form of religious service. Yet others had come decades before as *abbandonate*, and had never found the opportunity or the will to leave. Since all homes employed girls in a range of administrative duties, the movement from *abbandonata* to administrator was a path of imperceptible degrees. The ones who remained might have some physical disability that made it difficult to find a husband, but might equally be those who chose to stay out of religious conviction, out of the emotional attachments they had made, or out of the fact that despite all its difficulties, this was a life that they preferred over any other option before them. For while statutes and confraternal overseers laid out a rigorous and often difficult life, the conservatory was in the end a space that women made. In some ways, they could do more here than they could elsewhere as wives, domestic servants, or nuns.

This chapter looks first at what a girl like Valeria di Bartolomeo di Pavia could expect to do in a day or a week at Bologna's S. Maria del Baraccano, and how these duties and opportunities changed as she matured in the conservatory. We will see the structures set in place—the timetables and the older women who supervised daily life—and, as much as possible, what the sources tell us about how life actually was lived. As we saw in the previous chapter, the prescriptions found in conservatory statutes suggest a rigorous and disciplined life, but minute books and other records tell a much more complicated story.

Daily Rhythms

Renaissance people were early risers. Valeria and her companions were wakened just before daybreak by the *guardiana*, or by one of the older girls that she had assigned to go from bed to bed down the length of the old pilgrims' dormitory shaking each girl awake. The bells sounding matins at the nearby convents of S. Pietro Martire and the Trinità provided the cue, and in these first hours of the day the convent's nuns and the conservatory's girls followed similar routines. The girls gathered around a common basin to splash water on their faces, and then drew some clothes out of the chests at the foot of their beds. Some girls had simple chests, while others may have had the more elaborate decorated *cassoni* in which over the years they had been gathering the linens and goods that they would need when getting married. Families began assembling this trousseau early, and after the death of a girl's father, the *cassone* remained a reminder of her parents' hopes and long preparations for her marriage. If the mother had also died, this chest might well be her own old *cassone*, containing a few of her clothes and some of the items that she had brought into her marriage. These wooden chests were typically longer and narrower than a modern steamer trunk or blanket box. Wealthy families commissioned painters to decorate them inside and outside with images suggesting both the wife's fertility and her submission to her husband, and sometimes had more erotic images painted on the underside of the lid. At a time when clerical ceremonies were less important than legal arrangements or property transfers in marking a marriage, the celebratory procession of the bride and her *cassone* through the streets from her father's to her husband's house was the common way of publicly demonstrating that she was passing from the authority of the former to that of the latter. Whether simple chest or decorated *cassone*, the box that held her clothes would eventually accompany Valeria in the same way when she left the conservatory in nine years to become the wife of Antilio de M. Erchole Agochiarolo.[6]

Valeria pulled a dress of modest cut and sky-blue color out of the chest. Whatever she had worn up this point, on gaining admission to the conservatory she had to adjust to its dress code, and this was something that caused frequent fights. Girls defended their right to wear their own clothes, particularly if they had come from more comfortable homes. That shifted the financial burden of dressing the girls away from the conservatory, but there were drawbacks. S. Marta wanted its girls to dress as equally as possible because, its statutes claimed, clothing was one of the main triggers of jealousy and fights between the girls. For the peace of the home "there should be no recognizing superiority among them" ("tra loro non si conoschi maggioranza")—as clear a sign as any that girls had been fighting repeatedly over clothes.[7] Clothes were a key marker of status, particularly for young women of marrying age, and families of modest and middling means often had more invested in their dresses, capes, hats, vests, and shoes than they had in furniture or real estate. When parents died, attire became the legacy left to their children. Flaunting a silk dress, a fine woolen cape, or an expensive linen blouse in the conservatory could stir up envy and fighting. Some poor girls came into the conservatory with very few clothes, particularly in the case of homes like Florence's Pietà and S. Caterina. On the other hand, many of the girls accompanying Valeria into S. Maria del Baraccano were from reasonably comfortable homes, where they had accumulated clothing in colors and styles that their parents' ambitions and budget would allow. In spite of the strict sexual morality of the time, prepubescent girls faced fewer sumptuary prohibitions, and their parents used less restrictive clothing as a means of advertising their charms and attracting the interest of a future husband. As they matured into adolescence, their parents put them into more modest styles to protect them from what could become the more threatening attention of older boys and men. Yet on the breakup of her home, all of Valeria's clothing—fine and plain, revealing and modest—had been packed into the chest. When the *confratelli* of S. Maria del Baraccano finally admitted her into the home, they informed Valeria and her guardian what kinds of clothing she would be allowed to wear and what she would have to give up or keep stored away.[8]

Valeria, like S. Marta's girls, could bring in modest clothes: no frill or decoration and no excess cloth in ruffled sleeves or heavily pleated skirts and bodices.

In lieu of a particular uniform, the *confratelli* and *consorelle* of S. Maria del Baraccano had decided that as much as possible, these clothes should be sky-blue so
that the girls could be identified as being part of a single community.[9] Picking
up on the idea that the clothes of a Renaissance girl were in part about attracting a spouse, the S. Marta statutes told the girls that their dresses should have
the modesty expected of a bride of Christ. Friends, family, and guardians could
send gifts of clothing to S. Marta's girls, but these too were to be modest. Poorer
girls or those not lucky enough to have patrons outside the home were told to
be patient and to be happy for the good fortune of their sisters. More practically,
they could also share the clothes that others had outgrown and no longer wanted,
or that had been donated to the home. S. Maria del Baraccano had two ways of
handling this. If there were a lot of needy girls without sufficient clothing, from
time to time their names were written on slips of paper, put into a bag, and then
drawn out one by one. In this lottery, the first one chosen had the first choice of
clothing in the communal store, the second drawn had second choice, and so on.
In cases of extreme need, the gentlewomen who acted as visitors could intervene
and assign a blouse or skirt or underclothing to a particularly needy girl. These
same gentlewomen were also encouraged to donate clothing to the home, though
it all had to be in the signature sky-blue color. The home preserved the girls'
right to keep their own clothing. Yet the ever more insistent orders that these be
modest and unadorned—by 1648, S. Maria del Baraccano wanted them "cut
soberly by the tailor" ("tirata con gravità dal Sartore") to avoid giving the impression that these were vain and giddy girls—suggests that at least some girls
entered the home with very individual and sometimes questionable outfits.[10] The
outfits—and perhaps the girls—would not have lasted long. By 1648, this conservatory tolerated no exceptions to its regulations on cut, color, or cloth. The
resident *guardiana*, or warden, was to enforce this, and the gentlewoman visitors
made sure she did.

Clothes were clearly a preoccupation. They affected the girls' emotional state
and behavior and for some homes they became a tense focal point for arguments
and discipline. But others saw them more creatively as an avenue for getting
through to the girls. Pietà girls who mistreated their uniforms were sentenced
to wear the most patched-up ones in the storeroom. A bit more creatively, when
Vittorio Dell'Ancisa wanted to get through to the girls of Florence's Carità home,
he wrote a pair of pamphlets that compared their spiritual choices in life to two
sets of clothing they could wear: *It's hard to strip yourself of the clothes of the unre-
generate soul* (*Il vestito dell'anima vecchio e brutto da spogliarsi*) and *It's nice to dress*

yourself in the new clothes (Il vestito nuovo e bello da vestirsi). Vittorio went through almost every bit of clothing an adolescent girl could hope to wear—with the exception of underwear—and then added the cuffs, garlands, and crown that she may have dreamt of or dressed a doll in a few years before. Each item could be bad or good, depending on the girl's spiritual disposition: the dress represented either charity or cold-heartedness; the veil, humility or complacence; the belt, modesty or hostility. Vittorio's double-sided Pygmalion could top herself off with the crown of prayer—or of pride, and carry with her the little book of devotion— or of idle curiosity. Fashioning the theme of the Old and New life around cloth- ing made more immediate sense to a 16-year-old girl than a traditional sermon about suppressing the Old Adam (or Eve) or putting on the armor of God. Vit- torio aimed to convince the doubters by promising that modest clothes on earth would win a girl the most lavish clothes she could dream of in heaven. Vittorio left all undergarments apart from a petticoat (*sottana*) out of his imaginary trousseau, but did include a ring, necklace, earrings, and gloves, items that could point either to the somewhat better class of girls living in the Carità or to the dreams that girls regardless of class might share. But whether new clothes or old, they could only hold Vittorio's outfits in their imagination. Like their counter- parts in S. Marta, the girls of the Carità wore modest colors, with no silk, no ornaments, and no superfluous decorations or excess of cloth.[11]

If in their early years conservatories could ill afford uniforms, and so preferred to stipulate what the girls should bring with them, many eventually came to the point of recognizing that a uniform was the only way of keeping peace between the girls. Homes with poorer girls adopted this practice almost immediately out of necessity, since the pauper girls they accepted would have little beyond the clothes they wore on entry to the home. Uniforms were also more practical for girls as they cleaned the rooms, worked in the kitchen or laundry, and entered the home's workshop. A modest cut and color could be guaranteed, and in the larger homes the problem of cost was overcome to some extent by having the uniforms made internally by a group of the girls who had been trained as seam- stresses. The sheer uniformity of these standardized outfits also helped the homes when they sent the girls out into the streets, markets, and churches to collect alms, or on those occasions when they marched in ritual processions marking the feast day of their home's patron saint, a parish feast day, or even a city-wide procession like that held on Corpus Domini. The girls became known by the color of their uniform: the *fanciulle* of Bologna's S. Croce and Florence's S. Caterina were the blue girls, while those of Florence's Pietà were the white girls, and, from 1709, those of the Ceppo were the black girls.[12] When Valeria di Bartolomeo di Pavia was told to stock up on sky-blue clothing, this was one step toward a uniform; a girl entering a century later would not have the choice. There was more than practicality going on here. These ever-tightening restrictions on what they wore were part of a broader effort to have the girls fit a single model of what they should be.

Having donned her sky-blue dress, where does Valeria go? S. Maria del Baraccano's statutes do not lay out a specific routine, but other conservatories like S. Croce and S. Giuseppe do. Of these two, S. Giuseppe's strict schedule is timed down to the quarter hour and focuses on getting the girls through their work and associated duties, while S. Croce rounds out physical labor with an extensive set of spiritual exercises.[13] The girls of S. Maria del Baraccano, and those of Florence's various conservatories, followed routines that embraced these two emphases to greater or lesser degrees.

Girls in S. Giuseppe had an hour after waking to dress, make their beds, and generally tidy up before heading off to the conservatory's workshop. S. Croce's girls were to make the sign of the cross with the Holy Water that each had in a container at the head of her bed and recite a litany of prayers, including one to their guardian angel. Having made their beds, the girls headed first to the conservatory's chapel, where all of S. Croce's two dozen girls, together with the six or seven Franciscan tertiaries of S. Antonio who looked after their daily needs, gathered to recite the Divine Office. New girls sat together to listen, possibly for the first time in their lives, to this liturgy of prayers and psalms. An older girl, the mistress of novices, sat with them. Teaching them these religious exercises was among the first of the mistress's duties, with the Morning Office being simply one of a set of prayers that they must memorize. She taught them the responses that they were to make in the Mass, the Ten Commandments and the Apostles' Creed, and prayers like the Our Father and Hail Mary that they were say through the day. She also trained them how to use the Rosary to structure these prayers. Some girls knew these basics of the Christian catechism, but others had barely heard of them.

In homes with a resident community of tertiaries like Bologna's S. Croce and S. Marta or Florence's Pietà, the daily regimen was much like that of a convent. Frequent trips to the chapel for communal prayers marked the day, and the sisters used religious exercises to shape the girls' habits. Waking, work, meals, and bedtime were all marked by the girls' filing together into the chapel. S. Croce's six or seven tertiaries cared for twenty to twenty-four girls, while S. Marta had three for twenty to twenty-six.[14] In each case, the tertiaries had already been living in community when they were approached by the conservatory's founders and were asked to help out. As we saw earlier, Italy had a long tradition of women living communally in looser religious communities bound by religious vows but not as strictly regulated or enclosed as the convents of the major religious orders. There was a spectrum of communal styles. Some came about when a charismatic individual or small group of women gathered others together in a single house to share their goods and life, adopt a rule of prayers and religious services, and carry out charitable services in the streets of their local communities.[15] Many were widows, but the communities eventually came to include women who desired an active communal religious life but did not want to live as nuns or lay sisters in a cloister. Some could not afford the dowry, some did not fit into the often upper-class environment of the convent, some wanted more freedom in their practice of public charity than enclosed nuns could exercise. In the end, they were still lay women who could move about the streets more freely than a nun. Some stayed in these communities for a few years, others for the rest of their lives. Some of these communities fashioned individual rules based loosely on conventual and confraternal models, but others associated themselves more closely with the mendicant orders as tertiaries.

Through the later fifteenth and into the sixteenth centuries, these tertiary communities were coming under increasing pressure from local bishops and their host religious orders to adopt a more restrictive and cloistered life. While many did eventually turn themselves into enclosed convents, others resisted and some seem to have taken on the management of a conservatory as a kind of halfway step. It allowed them to live in an enclosed community under the somewhat looser supervision of a local house of friars and in conjunction with a confraternity. Regulations laid on them suggest that some of these women aimed to continue their other charitable work as well; the confraternity that controlled S. Marta insisted that its tertiaries not leave the home without permission, not go out to help the sick, and not stay out overnight. It could not stop them from regularly going to help their clerical overseers at the Franciscan Observant house of the Annunziata, a magnet for Bologna's sick and poor, but it did require that at least two tertiaries always remain behind to supervise the girls.[16] Tertiaries took the name of "sister" and wore a habit (different from the girls' uniforms) but they were frequently older widows who had raised their own children and looked after the day-to-day needs of a family home. They transmitted the joys, challenges, and skills of this experience to the *fanciulle* with a conviction that nuns could not echo, and they passed on practical tips about everything from shopping to sex based on experience that nuns weren't supposed to have. At the same time, while they may have avoided the restrictions of conventual life themselves, they brought into the conservatory community a more disciplined life of religious exercises than was found in communities run by hired lay women.

S. Maria del Baraccano did not have a community of tertiaries, and so we do not know whether Valeria's first stop in the day was the conservatory's chapel or its workshop. Regardless, she was in the workshop at an early hour working on her quota of spinning, lacemaking, or needlework for four hours before eating. After the morning meal, Valeria and her fifteen new companions were taken in hand by their older mentor and initiated into the procedures and schedules of the conservatory. As noted above, some conservatories appointed an individual, either a tertiary sister or more often a *fanciulla* who had already lived in the home for few years, as the official mistress of novices. One of S. Caterina's mistresses took on the job in 1623, when she was 43 and had already been in the home for twenty-nine years; she served a further eighteen years.[17] In other homes, the *guardiana* made more informal arrangements. In these first days at S. Maria del Baraccano, Valeria's mentor showed the sixteen girls around the workrooms, the kitchen, the laundry, and the chapel of their new home. Along the way, they learned of the various duties that they would take on and where they would help out as cooks, laundresses, and sacristans. The mistress also introduced the novices to the staff and other girls of the home.

Valeria had to keep her eye out for two of these staff in particular. On entering the day before, the first person she had met was the *portinara*, or gatekeeper, an older woman named Lena de Fiore. Lena sat at the entrance to the home and made sure that no one went out or came in without the proper authorization and supervision. She had checked her own records and called the *guardiana* to make sure that Valeria was allowed entry.[18] Most residential institutions, from convents, to hospitals, to brothels, had a gatekeeper of some sort for security purposes. Here at the conservatory, the *portinara* Lena guarded the boundary between Valeria's old and new lives. Neighborhood friends could not visit, and even family members needed special permission to come to a room that conservatories, like convents, called the *parlatorio*, where they might exchange some words with the *fanciulla* under the eyes of the *guardiana*. Valeria herself could not leave the conservatory unless she had a particular mission that had been authorized by the *guardiana*. Even then, a chaperone would have to go with her.

The *portinara* may have arrived years before as a *fanciulla*, and exercised her office as much out of experience and personality as according to any rules written down for her.

Individual gatekeepers might pass messages or discretely allow some contact, but doing so was strictly forbidden; breaking these rules may have been one reason why S. Giuseppe went through four *portinaras* (each hired from outside the home) in the space of ten months in 1629–30 before finally finding one who lasted the next five years.[19] Tight enclosure worked two ways, keeping the girls off the threatening streets and preventing curious tradesmen or packs of boys from bringing their own kind of trouble within its walls. Even the men of the confraternity that governed and funded the home had to pass the *portinara's* scrutiny and, apart from a few officials who came regularly for business, had to show her the permission slips that proved that their visit had been discussed and approved in a confraternity meeting. S. Giuseppe alone of all the conservatories had a male employee, though this gardener could conceivably work around the home without ever getting past the *portinara* or meeting the *fanciulle*.[20]

Valeria would only see the *portinara* on those rare occasions when she passed through the doors—the gatekeeper could not leave the doors until they were locked tight at night and the key was handed over to the conservatory's resident head. This person, whom Valeria would see far more often, was variously called the *guardiana* (warden), the *priora* (prioress), or the *madre generale* (head mother).[21] These three possible titles suggest the different models of hostel, convent, and home that one or another conservatory emphasized. Groups of tertiaries might nominate one of their number to this post, but supervising confraternities had the final say here even as they did in homes without tertiaries. The *guardiana* who greeted Valeria was a widow named Lutia, recruited by the gentlewomen who effectively ran the Baraccano conservatory and subsequently appointed by the administrative confraternity.[22] In her mid-40s or older, possibly a former *fanciulla* or a woman who had experience in other charitable institutions, she walked its halls from morning to night overseeing the girls' education, work, worship, and recreation, and visiting the sick *fanciulle* daily; she had so much work that larger homes gave her an assistant. A good *guardiana* or *priora* was priceless, and homes recruited and held on to them carefully. Former *abbandonata* Antonia di Simone reentered S. Maria Vergine in 1599 after having been out in the home of *confratello* Altobianco Buondelmonte's, under the supervision of his wife Margherita. When Margherita died, Altobianco urged that they take Antonia back into the home since she had "a judicious spirit, apt for

governance" ("e di spirito giuditioso, et di governo"), qualities then in short supply in the home. Though Antonia was too young at that point for serious responsibilities, the governors agreed to take her back in and give her some minor
duties as part of an apprenticeship for greater duties later on. It is not clear if
Antonia ever rose to become S. Maria Vergine's *madre priora*, but in 1611,
S. Caterina appointed as *priora* Domenica di Lanberto dalle Rete, who had arrived seventeen years before at age 20 and had presumably held various positions in the home in that time; she served as *priora* for the next forty-five years.[23]

S. Maria del Baraccano's *guardiana* Lutia had first come to know Valeria when
the girl was going through the lengthy nomination process. While the gentlewomen involved were preoccupied with Valeria's virginity and family background, and the gentlemen wanted to be convinced that she was pretty and vulnerable, Lutia wanted to make sure that she would fit in and pull her weight—a
temperamental, lazy, vain, or sick girl would only make her own work that much
harder. For all intents and purposes, she would be Valeria's mother for the next
nine years.

In most conservatories the *guardiana*'s word was law inside the gates, though
some like the Baraccano and S. Giuseppe hedged this with frequent visits by the
gentlewomen who outranked her and had no reservations about intervening.[24]
When S. Giuseppe's governatrice quit suddenly in 1639, possibly after a dispute
with the visitors, one of these, Margherita Angiosoli Fantuzzi, took the dramatic
step of temporarily moving into the home with her children to govern the *fanciulle* directly.[25] Nonetheless, if the *portinara* was the home's face on the street,
the *guardiana* or *priora* was its face with society. She accompanied every person
from outside, whether it was a gentlewoman visiting, a priest coming to hear
confessions, or a family member. She kept mental and written records on all the
girls, and reported regularly to her confraternal employers when one was ready
to leave, when another had the skills to take on administrative or supervisory
responsibilities, or when another needed special discipline. She kept all the accounts and inventories, and checked these with the confraternity's financial officers. She tailored the menu to whatever food was bought or donated, and negotiated piecework with merchants and craftsmen who might want to bring their
goods into the home for processing by the girls.

The *guardiana* had to be careful in her relations with the confraternity; one
Baraccano *guardiana* so exasperated the *confratelli* with demands that it expel difficult girls—for bad behavior, insubordination, and even bed-wetting—that they
turned around and threw her out instead.[26] S. Croce didn't allow her to enter-

tain visitors or keep pets, in part out of concern that what food there was go to the girls, but also because brothel madams used exotic pets, food, and drink to set an open and sophisticated tone for their establishments, and S. Croce wanted to keep its home for prostitutes' daughters as far as possible from those associations. S. Caterina housed the daughters of the poor generally, and could afford to be slightly more generous with its reputation, if not quite its food. It allowed family or visitors from far away (or poor Florentines) to eat a bit if they came to visit their daughters or nieces, but these girls could not sit with them while they were eating—they ate alone behind the locked doors of the refectory, with the *guardiana* or *priora* keeping watch. In the end, watching was what the *guardiana* did most: she had to, in the words of S. Maria Vergine, be solicitous and vigilant and trust no one but herself, "remembering that all the others sleep under her eyes."[27]

Having met the people who would structure her life in the days and years ahead, Valeria had to learn the rules that they operated by. Her mentor started by instructing the girls in the fundamentals of the Christian faith, using some of the catechetical books that were being produced at the time by confraternal Schools of Christian Doctrine in their free and very popular Sunday School lessons—in order to do this, the mentor herself had to be literate.[28] Beyond prayers, the Rosary, and confession, she taught them how to sing *laude*, the vernacular praise songs popularized by confraternities three hundred years before and still commonly used in worship. And beyond religious exercise, she also began instructing them in the rules of the house: what they couldn't do, where they couldn't go, when they had to be in one place or another, and whom they had to obey. These lessons expanded into a general education in manners and proper deportment. S. Caterina thought this work so important that it had two older girls, a mistress of novices and a mistress of children (*maestra delle giovane*), who worked together to root out insolence, aggression, and foul language, and to mold their charges into girls who were discrete, grave, respectful, clean, capable of standing in line, and, above all, silent. In some cases, she might even instruct the more capable ones how to read and to sing more complicated works than the *laude*.[29]

The mistress-mentor had to be sensitive enough to understand how best to bring a girl through the potentially wrenching transition from her old life with her own family in a home, with access to friends and the street, to a new life with a set of girls in an institution, with no access to family, friends, or street. We cannot portray her as a college dorm counselor, and should not overestimate any conservatory's investment in the psychological well-being of its new charges. But nor should we underestimate the realization in many homes that a girl's rough entry could make problems for everyone who lived there. This is a point at which we have to read between the lines of statute regulations in order to extract from the strict prohibitions some sense of what some mistresses of novices might have been up to. What are we to think when we find the author of Florence's Pietà statutes so vexed about romantic *novelle* and the dreams that they might put into a young girl's head that he prohibits its mistress of novices from giving them to the girls, and even threatens to dismiss a mistress who carries them around? Clearly this was the kind of thing that the girls circulated among themselves to pass the time and help lift them imaginatively outside the conservatory walls. Some mistresses must have passed these romances on to the few girls who could read, or read them aloud to those who they thought were having a particularly hard time making the break from their old lives. So too the restrictions against chatting together, playing games, or singing popular songs; the exasperation of the statutes hints at how often the girls passed their time in this way.

Those writing the statutes had an abstract model of what they wanted their wards to become, but women like the mistress of novices had to live with these girls day to day. And, for all their firm prescriptions, the statute writers too seem to have had some inkling of what human qualities this required. Together with its frequently firm and disciplinary line, the Pietà wanted the mistress of novices to have "a loving and charitable spirit," to sleep in that part of the dormitory where the novices slept, to wake them in the morning and make sure that they washed and dressed and ate, and to pray with them before they went out to their work.[30] She was the older sister who helped girls like Valeria step by step through the many rapid adjustments in their new lives.

Even if her formal novitiate lasted three or six months, Valeria did not spend much of it in lessons. She moved quickly into the world of work, picking up in a more regulated way the domestic chores and paid work that all Italian children had been doing since they were 6 or 7. Valeria's work had two purposes. On one hand, it contributed to the income that helped the conservatory put food on the table, wood in the fireplace, and clothing on the backs of the girls. On the other, it provided the discipline, skills, resources, opportunities, and mentors that should help Valeria and her companions find a way out of the home as a servant or wife once they reached late adolescence. All of these institutions embraced work as much from conviction as from necessity. Orphanage and conservatory statutes sounded a consistent refrain: although work would not get you to heaven, it fore-stalled the idleness that would certainly send you to hell.[31] It also prepared chil-dren for the realities of adult life: S. Giuseppe's statutes warned the *priora*, "Mind that you don't keep them too softly, so that (domestic) service won't be strange to them later."[32] As we try to assess the work, we can distinguish between work routines—and homes—which emphasized sending children out into the city at the earliest opportunity, and those which employed children internally.

Many homes initiated their newest girls like Valeria with alms gathering in churches, streets, markets, and homes. Some conservatories thought alms col-lecting was undignified and unsafe, but practiced it nonetheless out of economic necessity. A few had *confratelli* do the rounds, and others employed profes-sional collectors, though this cut into receipts and didn't take advantage of the sympathy—and alms—that a 10- or 11-year-old girl could generate.[33] Youngest girls were favored for this, both because they did not yet have the skills to work in the conservatory workshop, and because an older girl on the street would at-tract suspicion, no matter how worthy her cause. Alms gathering was labor-intensive and systematic, since each home targeted particular markets, neigh-borhoods, and churches on particular days, and tacit agreements between the homes kept each out of the other's "territory." The girls' distinctly colored uniforms helped donors keep the conservatories apart, and distinguished girls like Valeria from the collectors for convents, friaries, hospitals, and foundling homes who worked the same churches, streets, and piazzas. Strict guidelines safeguarded the girls' safety and honor, and the reputation of the conservatories themselves. The Pietà allowed only its novices to go around the streets collect-ing food and money because once a girl had become fully inducted, the restric-tions of enclosure prevented her from going out on the streets. Two women called *servigale* who ran messages, picked up food supplies, and generally did all the "outside" work for the Pietà accompanied and kept an eye on them.

Pietà novices went out in pairs every second day first thing in the morning, and began by visiting churches.[34] They arrived early so as to say confession before Mass began, and then during the Mass they moved discretely among the wor-shipers with their alms boxes. Other *abbandonate* and beggars would be there, and the Pietà girls were under strict orders not to leave their companion's side, not to talk to the girls of S. Niccolò, not to gossip with relatives, and not to stand around chatting with the poor or with any others who were canvassing for alms; they were to stand silently. This would have been a hard rule that was easily vio-lated, since the Pietà novices no doubt ran into friends and neighbors that they had known for years and talked to frequently before moving, only days or weeks before, into the conservatory. These people would be full of questions about what conditions were like in the conservatory, and the girls for their part would want to know about how things were with other friends and family. It is hard to imagine them standing silently, though they had to talk discretely so as to avoid the eye of the *servigale*.[35]

However hungry, the girls were forbidden to eat while they were collecting. This was a practical matter, since many people supported the conservatory with gifts of food, and it would be tempting for the girls to take a bit of what they had received in their baskets and big canvas bags. Girls generally collected alms in the morning as people attended Mass before starting work, while they more often gathered food in the evening as marketers were clearing out older and half-rotten items that no one wanted to buy. The girls—and the home's reputation—were most vulnerable when they were out on the street, so traveling in groups with a chaperone was a given. S. Marta paired *fanciulle* with one of the resident tertiaries, while S. Maria del Baraccano had an older girl go along, and ordered that this chaperone should never let the girls out of her sight, and certainly not let one go into a shop on her own. Similarly, Florence's S. Caterina noted that girls shouldn't fall for the old trick of a man inviting them to accompany him home and get the alms there.[36]

Among the few private homes that the girls could visit were those of former *abbandonate* who had since married and set up their own households. These women sympathized with the young girls and might have a strong enough sense of obligation to give some alms. They might also want to hear news of what had happened to some of their former companions, or to some of the longer-serving tertiaries or staff. Visits like this also allowed the home itself to keep up with its former *abbandonate*, over whose life and property it sometimes tried to keep some claim, and who might be encouraged to, like Caterina Trigari Providoni of S. Croce, remember the home in their will.[37] Yet even here the novices were to be cautious and discrete. The Pietà ordered that when they went in to a former *abbandonate*'s home, they must never speak with any men who might be there, and shouldn't gossip with the women. Prohibitions like this might seem impractical and moralistic, but conservatories aimed to help their wards preserve their honor, and one way was to remove them from the suspicions, speculations, and knowing nods that animated gossip. S. Bernardino of Siena had preached against gossip's corrosive effects over a century before, and keeping a girl behind enclosure was a means of preventing her name from circulating in conversations outside the home.[38]

Having spent a few hours gathering food and alms, the girls returned immediately to the conservatory. They shouldn't play along the way; they shouldn't stop to watch the performances of street players or charlatans or listen to street musicians. At the same time, they shouldn't pass up the opportunity to thrust the alms box in front of passersby and gain a few more pennies. Arriving back at the house, they gave the alms boxes and baskets to the *portinara* or reported directly to the mistress of novices or the *guardiana*. The girls told her where they had been, what had happened to them, and what they may have learned from visiting the homes of former *abbandonate*, and she in turn gave whatever cautions or warnings were necessary. In most instances, the alms box itself could only be opened when the supervising confraternity's bookkeeper had arrived—having two or three locks with separate keys held by various officials ensured observance of this rule—to carefully record receipts in the conservatory's ledgers.

Alms gathering was an important means of what we might now call "marketing" the home, and it was vital to meeting costs. In 1553, Florence's S. Maria Vergine gained 85.8 percent of income from alms, with the girls' efforts accounting for 7 percent of this. In 1556, the second year of operation for Florence's Pietà, alms accounted for 72 percent of total income and the girls themselves collected 39 percent of this sum. At the end of the century, S. Caterina sent out about one-quarter of its girls, most between ages 8 and 12, and these gathered over 40 percent of its income with their alms boxes.[39] Table 3.1 shows what percentage of conservatory income came from alms, and how those donations were in turn broken down. As homes matured they relied less heavily on girls collecting funds in regular trips around the city and drew more on alms boxes placed in churches, pledges ("ordinary"), and special appeals ("extraordinary"). Taken together, alms continued to generate between one-half and two-thirds of total income for most conservatories. Florentine homes relied more heavily on pledges from regular donors, while Bolognese homes collected alms in the public churches that were part of their complex and then made appeals to guilds, confraternities, citizens, and the senate when crisis hit.

Florence's S. Maria Vergine soon took its wards off the street, but its poorer homes of S. Caterina and S. Niccolo could not have functioned without the girls' efforts. And while the balance sheets on which Table 3.1 are based leave out the Pietà's alms gathering in the 1570s, we know from other sources that by

Table 3.1. *Alms Gathering in Conservatories*

Institution	Years	Percentage of Income	Alms Box	Church	Ordinary	Extraordinary
Bologna						
S. Croce	1620–25	47.7	2.3	2.8	10.8	31.8
S. Maria del Baraccano	1575–85	77.1	6	16.2	12.6	42.3
S. Maria del Baraccano	1592–99	38.2	n/a	10.2	4.6	23.4
Florence						
S. Caterina	1591–1625	71	41		30	0.2
S. Niccolò	1560–74	74.5	51		22	1
S. Maria Vergine	1565–83	69.9			30.3	39.9
Pietà	1557–58	67.2			34.9	32.3
Pietà	1566–71	59.18			30.18	29
Pietà	1572–78	31.1	n/a		21	10.1

Sources: Bologna: ASB, PIE, S. Croce, ms. 149; ASB, PIE, S. Maria del Baraccano, mss. 264, 265; Florence: ASF, S. Caterina, ms. 25; ASF, Ceppo mss. 147, 149; ASF, Pietà, mss. 55, 57.

the end of that decade, the Pietà girls regularly collected almost 8 to 12 lire in their circuits every second day through the city, and up to 17 lire around Christmas or Easter. Ten lire bought over 40 pounds of meat, while 15 paid for a month's worth of firewood, so these were not insignificant amounts; in fact, as we will see below, the girls collected enough each month to cover about half of the Pietà's food costs.[40] As local economies rose and fell, and girls and collectors were more or less effective, alms receipts varied widely. S. Giuseppe, which from 1629 to 1639 got anywhere from 15 to 75 percent of its income from alms, tried not to base its operations on this unstable income, but few other homes had the luxury of doing without it.[41]

Valeria di Bartolomeo di Pavia may or may not have carried the S. Maria del Baraccano alms box through the churches of Bologna. What is more certain is that she carried brooms and laundry through the home's corridors. In the most common form of work, the girls themselves washed the floors, cooked the meals, did the laundry, and in many instances made the uniforms. The mentor or mistress of novices introduced the new girls to these tasks as well, and the kind of domestic work each girl performed depended in part on the size and organization of the home, and whether there was a community of tertiaries to handle some of these chores. Homes with a few dozen residents like S. Giuseppe and S. Croce worked it into the daily schedule, with each girl sweeping, washing, drawing water, bringing in wood, and doing other chores for an hour in the late afternoon between their shifts in the conservatory workshop.[42] Larger homes, and bigger tasks like laundry and cooking, required more concentrated labor for more than an hour a day. The youngest girls started off with the most basic duties, much as they would have had they been working in private homes as domestic servants: cleaning vegetables, hanging wet sheets and clothes out to dry, scrubbing floors.

Homes with a hundred residents or more, like Florence's Pietà and S. Caterina, appointed more experienced and able girls as mistresses of distinct operations. They fulfilled immediate domestic needs, trained all the young girls in basic household skills (*funzione domestiche*), and apprenticed a few of the more promising girls in more responsible roles. S. Caterina organized this domestic work most precisely, appointing up to twelve girls to keep the home clean and the girls fed. At least two girls handled the kitchen, one cooking the evening meal (the midday meal was simply bread and wine) and the other cleaning the pots and dishes and putting things back in order after meals. The Pietà appointed one girl as cook, and brought others into the kitchen in two-week shifts so that over time more of them could learn how to cook. Along with staples like oil, vinegar, and salt that the home bought, these cooks worked with whatever seasonal fruits and vegetables or other perishables like fish and meat that the alms collectors might gather in their visits to the city's homes and markets. The more prosperous Bolognese homes got fresh fruits and vegetables thanks to the sharecropping system employed in their farmlands. In 1613, S. Giuseppe calculated that its farms ought to bring in 88 capons, 58 hens, 21 geese, and 2,225 eggs, and it used these figures to set limits on how many girls it would shelter that year.[43]

The food homes purchased seldom went beyond staples like cheese, legumes, grain, and small amounts of pork or other meat, but they occasionally added seasonal treats, so as the girls sat to table they might find cherries in June and melons in August. Table 3.2 compares the Pietà's monthly costs for three staples: meat, flour, and the catch-all term *camangiare*, which incorporated fresh fruits, salad, vegetables, legumes, and bread. While roughly half the food budget went to purchase meat, each of the 100 to 125 girls ate the equivalent of only a little more than a pound of meat per month, except for Lent, when the only meat purchased went to the sick. While Italians generally did not eat as much meat as northern Europeans, most ate four to eight times more meat in a year than these Pietà girls.[44] The bits of beef, mutton, and pork flavored the stews and soups that a Pietà girl ate alongside the chief staple, bread. The Pietà bought grain in

Table 3.2. Basic Food Purchases at the Pietà, 1578–1579

Month	Meat Quantity (pounds)	Meat Price (lire/soldi/denari)	Flour Quantity (staia)	Flour Cost @ 3 lire/staio*	Gabelle	Camangiare Items	Camangiare Price L.s.d.	Total L.s.d.
1578								
April	151	35.12.08	96	[300]	22.01.04	Legumes, vegetables	12.11.00	379.05.00
May	184	45.03.11	192	[576]	35.13.04	Legumes, vegetables	5.07.04	662.03.09
June	174	41.06.08	96	[300]	17.07.00	Squash, cherries	10.07.08	369.01.04
July	145	32.18.02	39	[117]	07.09.00	Beans, citrioli, zucche, finocchio	25.09.00	182.16.06
August	156	32.14.00	1192 lbs + 2 staia	14.03.04		Squash, melons, figs, cavolo, onions, beans	21.13.04	68.10.08
September	121	32.10.08	48 + 3 sacks	[144+]	14.00.00	Squash, onions, lupini	15.04.00	205.14.08
October	136	30.05.08	192 + 1 staio	[579]	36.18.00	Onions, vegetables, eggs, chestnuts	28.02.08	678.06.04
November	224	51.10.00	192	[576]	32.12.04	Onions, chestnuts	26.14.08	686.17.00
December	59	9.12.08	96	[300]	19.00.00	Beans	4.08.00	333.00.08
1579								
January	163	30.06.04	60 lbs	4.06.08		Beans	34.03.00	68.16.10
February	204	41.03.08	96	[300]	19.01.04	Onions	13.02.00	373.07.00
March	[for the sick]	8.06.04	48 + 10 sacks	[144+] 8.02.00	9.14.04	Rice, chickpeas	43.04.08	214.07.04
April	45 + 2 sheep	13.13.00	1 staio	4.00.00		Vegetables	10.03.04	27.16.04
May	134	31.14.00	96	[300]	18.10.00	Beans, cherries	8.05.08	358.09.08

Source: ASF, CRSF ms. 112/81, cc. 69r–102r.
*When making bulk purchases, the Pietà paid just over 3 lire per staio. The figures in square brackets represent the pro-rating of these bulk costs, while other figures represent real costs for occasional purchases on the market. For calculation of bulk costs, see ASF, CRSF ms. 112/81, c. 81rv (bulk purchase on September 6) and ASF, CRSF ms. 112/2, c. 102r (gift of 48 staia in 1565).

bulk at harvest time in order to cut costs, and stored it with farmers or millers, who then carted sacks of flour into the city every couple of weeks so as to stretch out the costs of the gate tax (*gabelle*). Bulk grain cost a little over 3 lire per staio (at 24 liters, roughly two-thirds of a modern bushel), and the Pietà brought in the equivalent of between a half and a full staio per girl per month, buying extra bread as needed when donations of the staple failed to meet needs. Through the summer, the Pietà girls found squashes, beans, and cabbage on the table, and in the fall the home bought up items like chickpeas, onions, and chestnuts that would appear in their soup bowls through the year. Unlike meat and flour, these *spese di camangiare* were seldom recorded by weight or volume, so we cannot determine how much salad the girls ate through the year, or how much zucchini squash they faced through the summer.[45]

Food was precious and in demand. The cooks had to keep the kitchen door locked and couldn't allow anyone in but the *guardiana's* assistant (who helped with inventory) or the home's nurse (who oversaw preparation of medicinal broths and special dishes for sick girls). Bread was what the girls ate most often. It was so important that S. Caterina entrusted it to two pairs of girls who rotated weekly, rather than to the two mistresses of cooking. Every weekend these two mistresses of bread ground as much flour as they would need for the week, and twice weekly they baked the bread that would supplement whatever the collectors brought in, always making sure that they had at least a two-day supply on hand. The mistresses of bread could bring in some other girls to help them, waking them at the first bell of the nearby Annunziata convent to boil the water used in the bread. Bakers had careful instructions on preparing the dough, making sure that the wheat was well sifted to remove the chaff, measuring out all the flour and water for consistent results, kneading the dough well, and letting it rest twice for best results.[46] When meals were ready, another girl looked to getting the tables ready and food out on them. The *refettoraia* closely rationed the bread and wine, putting them on the table just before the meal began, making sure no girl ate too much, and then returning them to a locked closet after meals. When supplies were running low, she told the bakers to get busy. Girls in other conservatories could have some bread for breakfast, but the S. Caterina girls normally ate only at midday and in the evening. A bit of bread was allowed to them if they needed a breakfast on summer mornings, when waking at sunrise meant a long wait before lunch, but this was generally frowned on as an indulgence, "because eating so close to lunch is very unhealthy" ("perche il man-

giare cosi vicino al pasto e tutto veleno"). S. Caterina eventually allowed breakfast only for those girls whom the prioress judged to have a weak stomach.[47]

Outside the kitchen and refectory, S. Caterina was most concerned with making sure the dormitories and clothes were clean. Apart from keeping the girls
close to godliness, clean clothes and sleeping quarters helped keep them far from
plague, at least according to the medicine of the day. Every day two girls washed
the dormitory floors and threw open the windows in order to air out the nox-
ious vapors that collected overnight in the crowded space. Bad air in the sleeping quarters led directly to plague according to contemporary doctors, so the
Pietà ordered its nurse (*infermiera*) to take care of making the beds and ensuring that the sheets, floors, and walls were clean. S. Caterina's dormitory crew
also cleaned out the lamp and filled it with oil so that it would be ready to burn
though the next night, "for any accidents that might happen." Yet these cleaners weren't the personal servants of their companions. Any girl who failed to
make the bed—her own or what she shared—and generally tidy up her small area
before heading off to work in the morning risked being reported to the prioress
and being disciplined for her sloppiness.

Clean clothes and linens were the job of the *bucatiera*. Most homes did this
weekly or biweekly, but the impoverished S. Caterina conserved its soap, to the
point where we can wonder how seriously its administrators really took the
health threat of dormitory vapors. Once a month in summer and every two
months in winter, the *bucatiera* set a cauldron boiling and gathered a large work
crew to strip the linens from all the beds, gather up all the towels and tablecloths,
and assemble the clothes. Washday was a Monday and the *bucatiera* began getting busy the night before, filling the washing cauldrons on Sunday after vespers
so as not to lose any time the next morning. And as in any town or village of the
time, laundering was a celebratory communal event with singing, laughing, and
joking as the girls sorted the clothes, stirred them in the boiling water, wrung
them out, and hung them up in S. Caterina's small courtyard. They had done
this kind of work since they were children. Things could get so out of hand that
the *bucatiera* was told to try and at least keep the laundry crew talking quietly so
as not to disturb any girls who might be resting in the conservatory's infirmary
nearby. Some conservatories washed more frequently, but outside of its monthly
or bimonthly wash times, S. Caterina's dirty laundry just piled up. Only the linens
for the chapel could be washed in the weeks between.[48]

Having washed, dried, and folded the home's linens, the *bucatiera* distributed
some to the girls and brought others to a colleague who made, repaired, and

stored a good deal of the conservatory's cloth goods. The *sarta* had extensive responsibilities and special training, and may have been hired from outside. She had to know how to prepare and cut linen and woolen cloth, she worked closely with the *bucatiera* to make sure that they weren't damaged in the washing, she repaired and refashioned items when necessary, and she stored a great deal of the girls' clean and dirty clothing so it didn't add to the crowding in the dormitory. Girls received their fresh linens from the *sarta* on a regular schedule: clean white shirts every two weeks in winter and weekly in summer; smocks, neckerchiefs, ribbons, and caps weekly through the year; napkins every two weeks; sheets monthly or bimonthly. In winter the *sarta* distributed leather shoes, heavier shirts, and gowns. These schedules kept most of S. Caterina's girls in cleaner clothes than they had ever worn. But different expectations could surface as often as spills and accidents. When girls came to the *sarta* in between these scheduled times, pleading perhaps for a clean shirt or new smock, she could only tell them to wait and, if it seemed that a change was justified, to get the prioress's permission.[49]

Valeria di Bartolomeo di Pavia swept the halls, joined in the laundry drill, and possibly worked in S. Maria del Baraccano's kitchen. Yet only a few girls could fill these full-time domestic positions, and then only after a long time spent proving their abilities. After she had passed her novitiate, with its alms gathering and minor domestic duties, Valeria's most likely destination in the morning would be S. Maria del Baraccano's workshop.

The largest single sectors in both cities' economies were the labor-intensive and still largely profitable textile industries (wool and silk for Florence, silk and hemp for Bologna).[50] Across both cities, thousands of workers in hundreds of small and large shops spun linen and silken thread, wove cloths of all kinds, and finished silk cloth. Paying by the piece for particular forms of processing, cloth brokers and merchants moved raw materials, thread, and bolts of cloth back and forth across the cities from one workshop to another before exporting them to markets across Europe. Conservatories could easily become a stop along the way in this process, particularly for those steps that were labor-intensive but that required little in the way of training, machinery, or even specially outfitted quarters. These steps included unwinding the silk cocoons in basins of hot water (reeling), winding the skeins of raw silk, and spinning the raw silk into thread.[51]

A single superintendent, the mistress of workers, organized tasks in the smaller and medium-sized homes like Bologna's S. Croce, S. Giuseppe, and S. Maria del Baraccano, or Florence's S. Maria Vergine and S. Niccolò.[52] Other homes like S. Marta clearly engaged in spinning and weaving, but say nothing in the statutes about how this was organized, leaving it up to the *guardiana* or to the resident tertiaries. In many cases, the conservatories initially recruited these supervisors from outside, because they needed to have enough familiarity with a variety of processes to be able to lead the girls through the steps of whatever work came in. There was no question of a trained male master coming in to oversee the work, but the widow of a cloth master would have precisely the training, experience, and gender required. The arrangement worked to her benefit as well, since the mistress, like all the conservatories' workers, moved into the home, taking with her any female children she might still have. So in August 1555, Mona Betta came to the recently opened Pietà to teach the girls weaving, bringing her 7-year-old daughter with her. Chiara di Antonio came at the same time to teach the *fanciulle* how to prepare wool and woolen cloth, receiving room and board as her pay.[53] Like guild masters in their workshop, women like Mona Betta and Chiara supervised the girls' piecework as they taught, apportioning more work as the girls gained a more confident grasp of the techniques. And, like guild masters, they trained their own replacements. Most homes aimed eventually to pass these supervisory jobs on to older girls—Valeria could, in time, become a mistress of work.

If the smaller and medium-sized conservatories had flexible workshops (what S. Croce called the "scuola de loro lavorieri") that might handle linen at one time and wool at another, the larger conservatories were more like factories, with dedicated workrooms and specialized superintendents who trained and supervised piecework of various types. Florence's Pietà had separate mistresses for silk, spinning, and weaving, while its S. Caterina had officials designated the mistress of weaving, mistress of silk, and mistress of gold—the gold in this instance being gold thread that the girls used for embroidery or cloth of gold.[54] With captive populations averaging from sixty to eighty and sometimes reaching over 150, these larger homes could engage in more specialized training and production, and could even designate specific rooms for the different operations. As the girls entered the workroom, the mistress assigned them their work and watched closely to see where they needed correction. This is where tension could arise, particularly as more of the girls were promoted as mistresses; as the Pietà warned, "be vigilant that the demon doesn't come between us." Anger could flare up quickly if the mistress assigned more work to one girl, or held back too much of another's because it wasn't done well enough and had to be fixed, or accused a girl of stealing some of the materials. A girl who spun as her mother had taught her, or wove cloth as she had seen her father do, would not take well to correction from someone who might be only a few years older and who most likely hadn't been professionally trained. The Pietà aimed to defuse some of these tensions by rotating these offices regularly, and by trying to invest them with spiritual authority.[55]

Smaller homes also specialized over time, and some gained a wide reputation for their work. Valeria di Bartolomeo di Pavia may have spun thread or woven silk cloth, but she may also have made lace, another of the low-paid and labor-intensive tasks that came naturally to conservatories. Lace required a higher degree of training and artistry, and the clear eyes and nimble fingers of young girls. Because it was lighter and more decorous work, S. Maria del Baraccano assigned it to respectable girls while keeping those of a lower station tied to physically strenuous silk production. S. Maria del Baraccano became a significant center of lace production by the seventeenth century and even developed some of its own signature patterns and a reputation for quality that its girls carried right into the twentieth century.[56] Similarly, the Pietà girls quickly developed a reputation as the finest weavers of brocades in Florence, and even supplied fabrics to the ducal court. Professional training—always female—was most often recruited for silk work, since there was a potentially bewildering variety of processing methods employed and a mix-up could be costly for the home. Over a period of just a couple of weeks in 1601 and 1602, S. Niccolò recorded at least twelve different types of raw silk brought in from all across Italy for various forms of processing.[57]

Beyond training and supervising the girls, the mistresses kept account of raw materials coming in and finished goods going out, and ensured that the girls maintained their quota. Individual girls worked on different pieces for various workshops, and the mistress had to keep all of this separate, so that each girl received her due, and also so that each workshop received back the same pieces that it had sent in. S. Caterina attached a tag to each piece of silk, recording the shop, the work needed, and the weight, and the mistress had to weigh the items after each step to make sure that they matched the tags. At the end of the day, the girls returned the bolts of cloth, unfinished pieces of lace, and lengths of gold thread to the mistress, who locked them away in special chests.

Mistresses were also expected to maintain records of the amount that each girl earned with her textile piecework, ostensibly so that this could be applied toward her dowry or her keep.[58] According to various statutes, the figures were passed on to the *guardiana* or *priora*, who in turn submitted them to the conservatory's bookkeeper or administrator so that he could record them in the girls' accounts. But it is difficult to determine how or even whether these injunctions were followed. The first statutes for Bologna's S. Croce required that the *priora* and *camerlengo* record each girl's production, but added that "all the works are to the benefit of the casa."[59] The rare extant account books titled *Libri di Lavori* record goods consigned and not wages earned by individual girls and, more to the point, all conservatory accounts record piecework as part of the institution's general income. Large ledgers like the one in which S. Maria del Baraccano recorded Valeria di Bartolomeo di Pavia's admission, goods, dowry, and fate have their equivalents in the archival deposits for Florence's S. Maria Vergine, S. Niccolò, Pietà, and S. Caterina, and also for Bologna's S. Giuseppe, but there are no extant volumes for any of these institutions that record the amounts that particular girls earned through their piecework.

The mistresses were not the only ones looking over Valeria's shoulder to see how she did their piecework. Confraternities elected, appointed, or chose by lot visitors who, in the course of terms ranging from a couple of months to a year, came regularly to check all the girls' work.[60] Bolognese homes adopted more formal procedures for this than Florentine ones. The smaller and medium-sized homes that had fewer and less specialized mistresses made up for this with more visitors, and required that they come by the home a few times a week and sometimes even daily. This had to be handled delicately, particularly in the case of confraternities that were made up primarily of men. As with entrance procedures noted in the previous chapter, each of these appointed a parallel congregation of women to have closer contact with the girls. These women visited the homes most often, arriving in their carriages to mount thorough inspections accompanied by the *guardiana* or *priora*. They walked through the dormitories to check for cleanliness and tidiness, peeked into the kitchen, and talked to the different mistresses in charge of domestic and piecework to see how individual girls were working out. Indeed, one of the qualities that S. Caterina sought in its mistress of weaving was knowing how to talk with a gentlewoman on one hand, and a common artisan on the other.[61] Apart from the advice or discipline that they could offer, the gentlewomen kept an eye out for girls who would work out well as servants in the city's homes and workshops, since moving such a girl out would open up space to take in another *abbandonata*.

On occasion they were accompanied by one of the male visitors—in spite of their ultimate authority, none of these latter could so much as enter the conservatory unless it was in the company of one of the gentlewoman visitors and the *guardiana*. Male visitors came through less regularly—about once a month—to see about conditions and necessary repairs, to see which girls might soon be of marriageable age, and to update a notebook recording how much each girl was earning toward her dowry. At the next monthly meeting of the confraternity, they would report on all of this. But they also talked to the workshop mistresses, showing them how to carry out particular operations, checking on the quality of the cloth that was being produced, asking about the skill levels of particular girls, and correcting problems where necessary. These visitors aimed to find out just what the girls were capable of producing, since on leaving the home they had to work their network of contacts in order to find more piecework contracts.

Some piecework came in at the door, particularly as a home's reputation spread, but much of it still had to be sought out by the home's officials or by members of the supporting confraternity, many of them merchants and some of them guild masters. Some of these used the homes as an extension of their own workshops, and this could lead to charges of abuse. Four of the six merchants who contracted silk work from S. Croce's girls in 1606 were members of its governing confraternity. This was in the early stages of the fight between founder Bonifacio dalle Balle and the patricians like Alessandro Massarenti who aimed to make S. Croce more like Bologna's other conservatories. Among dalle Balle's frustrations was the fear that his colleagues were forcing the girls to work too much and too often. Those in the workshops now had to continue spinning through the time designated earlier for prayer and lessons in Christian Doctrine, while others were forced out at the earliest opportunity into domestic service. Dalle Balle's vision of an alms-supported quasi-convent was fading, but worse than that, the girls were losing hope of their prospects and the tertiary sisters were unsure of what their role ought to be; they had come to the home to be charitable helpers, not textile overseers. In the administrative duel of statutes described in the previous chapter, dalle Balle's rejected rules of January 1609 were long on spiritual exercises but vague on work. The set actually adopted in April 1609 kept many of the spiritual exercises but gave far more explicit guidelines for supervising work, and emphasized that girls needed to be trained and put into productive work as soon as possible upon entering S. Croce, since the greater number of girls spinning, the greater the benefit for the home. Within a couple of years, the confraternity appointed a team to negotiate better terms from the merchants who were providing silk piecework. Two silk merchants, Hieronimo and Alfonso Salani, responded a year later with a proposal for a monopoly on silk weaving that would, they argued, benefit the home far more than its existing haphazard piecework arrangements did. The S. Croce *confratelli* refused the Salani brothers' proposal, perhaps because the merchants among them didn't want to surrender their own access to this low-priced workshop, but they did tighten up discipline, expelling Antonia di Santi for her *mali portamenti* (bad behavior) and for her refusal to work.[62]

The dispute highlights the difficulty of running these workshops efficiently. S. Niccolò's first *Libro di Lavoro*, covering 1589–1627, initially records a substantial number of small commissions by a host of small spinners, wool workers, silk merchants, and the like, for a multitude of distinct and, in the case of silk, specialized operations. After the larger and better-organized S. Maria Vergine took over its administration in 1620, this was simplified radically: only three merchants appear in the records after this, one for gold thread and two for silk spinning. It is not clear whether these are contracting jobbers or whether the three merchants had succeeded in gaining a monopoly over the girls' work, as the Salani brothers had attempted to do at S. Croce.[63] Even if jobbers were in place most piecework was highly seasonal, and conservatory workshops had to deal with wide fluctuations in demand for their labor. A rare set of financial records that tracks how many girls worked for how many weeks each month at S. Maria del Baraccano in the 1590s shows just how elastic that demand was. Table 3.3 tracks the number of girls who performed a full week's worth each month, and calculates averages over the months for which statistics are available. Between seventy-five and eighty girls lived in the conservatory through this period, and removing at least twenty of these for cooking, cleaning, and laundering leaves fifty-five to sixty girls available for textile piecework.[64] If sixty girls each worked a full four weeks in a month, the figure for that month's labor would be 240. In fact, work available averaged only one-quarter of that, and a girl might work only one full week per month in this economically depressed decade. But this average obscures the fact that there could be as little as nine weeks of work available in a particular month (January 1594), and that even the busiest month (August 1596) fell significantly short of "full employment." Given seasonal demand, Valeria di Bartolomeo di Pavia would be most likely to be performing paid piecework between March and June, and least likely from December to February.

Volatile labor demand meant volatile earnings, and this became a problem when work became critical to the bottom line of many conservatories. It usually brought in more than the girls' alms-collecting efforts did, but Table 3.3 underscores how receipts ranged widely, both because of the number of girls working in a particular month varied and because a low-skill job like spinning paid only a fraction of what a more skilled job like weaving earned. In the Pietà's first year

Table 3.3. Seasonal Work Patterns at S. Maria del Baraccano, 1593–1599

	1593	1594	1595	1596	1597	1598	1599
January	56	9	?	19	16		
February	38	24	?	80	?		61
March	60	147+	23+		77	79	157
April	?	?	92	86	103	45	21+
May		?	68	144	36	61+	64
June	?	?	78	66	74		74
July	?	?	94	72	16	?	59
August		?	49	164	29		85
September		?	?	71	7+	?	39
October		?	14	30	?	?	26
November	108	?	19	133	35		65
December	128	?	46	31	31		50
Monthly average	78	60	54	81	42	62	64
Annual earnings (in lire)	2,678	2,713	2,645	2,850	2,538	3,156	2,564

Source: ASB, PIE, S. Maria del Baraccano 265 (*Libro Mastro*, 1587–1600), cc. 129r–v, 193r–v, 223r–v, 273r–v.
Note: Figures represent number of girls paid for a week of work in a month (e.g., January 1593, fifty-six girls each worked one week).

(1555) work comprised just under 10 percent of income, rising to 22.43 percent the following year. As Table 5.3 shows, piecework rose to 40 percent of the Pietà's income through the years when it remained at Borgo Ogni Santi, and then climbed as high as 64 percent after the move in 1568. Table A.2 demonstrates that by their piecework the girls usually generated from 20 to 44 percent of a conservatory's income, with figures somewhat higher in Florence than in Bologna.[65]

Work also served as one means to instill discipline in the girls, though it could be as much the problem as the solution. Girls who had grown up helping their fathers at the bench or their mothers at the spinning wheel were already familiar with a workshop culture that the conservatories didn't want to bring within their walls. The singing, story spinning, and gossip that passed the time in many workshops created a camaraderie and atmosphere that were far from the silence, modesty, and self-control that conservatories aimed to build in their girls' characters and project to the city. A good part of work discipline went beyond production quotas into the more delicate questions of deportment and reputation. The Pietà and S. Caterina ordered their mistresses to avoid talking about worldly matters while working, because they were afraid that people passing by on the street would get the wrong idea if they heard wild fables, laughter, and popular songs wafting from the workshop's windows. Likewise, the girls of S. Croce were taught spiritual songs and prayers in part so that they could use these in the workshop in place of the popular tunes—possibly lascivious and certainly worldly—that workers outside used to pace their production. S. Caterina thought that the Rosary was equally good as a means of pacing work, and so the silk and weaving mistress who went around gauging production had to measure the girls' progress through it as well. Rules weren't just about work discipline: "the work brings affliction and melancholy sadness," said the S. Caterina statutes, using a word often applied to madness or depression (*maninconia*), and they seem to have assumed that using *laude* and prayers to pace the work could give the girls some hope and comfort too. Bonifacio dalle Balle spoke of the girls' "despair" when he complained that his opponents at the S. Croce conservatory were pushing too much work on them.[66]

With this understanding of how hard and depressing the conservatory workshop environment could be for adolescent girls, it is impossible to determine how much the mistresses could or would enforce these rules. Yet the girls were drilled in obedience to them, and beyond them they would have to face the censorious actions of the visitors, the prioress, and any other officials passing through. A few tried using mutual surveillance to keep everyone on edge. S. Croce visitors came weekly, and once they had interviewed the *guardiana* and gatekeeper, they talked to some of the girls to ask how the paid staff were doing their jobs. Pietà staff who failed to punish girls for swearing, sloppy work, singing popular songs—or indeed any fault in an extensive list further described below—would themselves incur the corresponding punishment. Girls who were particularly disruptive could find their behavior recorded in the register alongside the inventories of their property and accounts of dowry pledges; Maddalena di Domenico Marino, one of Valeria's companions at S. Maria del Baraccano, was described tersely in 1584 as one who "doesn't want to work, is a liar, and steals from others." Later visitors might look for improvements in Maddalena's behavior, but it is doubtful they passed their assessments on to the artisan Ghalandro, whom she married in November of that year.[67]

Work filled most of the day for girls like Valeria di Bartolomeo di Pavia, but it was broken up with meals and periods of recreation on a schedule that may have resembled that for the girls of S. Giuseppe or S. Croce.[68] Arriving in the workshop first thing in the morning, she worked there for about four hours before breaking for a midday meal. The girls filed into the refectory, washed their hands at a basin there, took their assigned places at the long tables, and waited for the mistresses and *priora* to enter before they began eating. They were expected to spend this time in silent prayer, and once she entered the *priora* led them in a blessing on the food. Pieces of bread and watered wine had already been set out on the table by the *refectorara*, and as they ate another girl or a staff member read to them from some spiritual work, as much to keep them from laughing and chatting together as to instruct them. Table manners were becoming a marker of class and breeding by this point, and Valeria had to learn how to eat properly for her own good and for the reputation of the home. When a Bolognese wag wanted to mock Bonifacio dalle Balle and his S. Croce conservatory, he spread the rumor that dalle Balle let the girls dry their just-washed hands on their smocks and shirts, and that he had them eating their soup with their fingers rather than spoons.[69]

After half an hour the mistress gave the sign and the girls all rose for a closing prayer. They then cleaned their places and had an hour for recreation. This was a diversion from work, but not free time. Younger and newer girls like Valeria were taken in hand by their mentor and given some of their lessons in house rules, basic reading, or Christian Doctrine. Older girls could spend the time a little more freely, and likely talked together as they tidied up part of the dormitory or looked busy while they enjoyed the sun in the conservatory courtyard. The rules forbade them from standing together in pairs chatting, but a bit of routine or meaningless work no doubt helped many girls find a way around this. Then it was back to the workshop for a further six hours of work through the afternoon, broken into two three-hour shifts by another hour of recreation, which they spent in the same way. The girls then returned their various pieces to the mistress, who weighed them and recorded each one's progress before locking the pieces away and freeing the girls to walk in pairs to the refectory. Any girl who hadn't finished her daily quota had to work through her recreation time, and couldn't eat until the assigned piecework was done. The evening meal also featured bread and watered wine, but would include at least a soup of some kind based on dried beans and whatever the alms collectors had been lucky enough to find in their rounds that day—rarely some meat or fish but almost certainly some seasonal vegetables. The mistresses' sign and prayer closed this meal and freed the girls for another hour of recreation before they did their bedtime prayers and went to bed. In the winter, S. Croce allowed the girls to gather around the fire in the kitchen for a few minutes after meals and in the evenings before bedtime, since neither the workroom nor the dormitory was heated.

The rules that Valeria learned in recreation time were like those that she learned in the workshop: kneel to priests and to the gentlewoman visitors who come to the house, don't stand in pairs gossiping, eat and drink modestly and politely, pray frequently through the day, keep yourself neat and clean, particularly your head and clothing. On the other hand, don't engage in horseplay, don't talk too loudly, don't sing worldly songs, don't insult others, don't be impudent, don't swear, don't act immodestly, don't keep secrets, don't go where you're not supposed to. If Valeria broke these rules, she typically lost food, the most immediate currency in the home and traditionally a focus for women's self-discipline; here it became the tool of a discipline used to bring her into line. If a S. Giuseppe girl failed to get up on time in the morning, didn't wash, dirtied the house, or went into the garden or other locked places without permission, she ate only bread and wine for a day. If she talked out of turn, or when she was supposed to be silent, like mealtimes or during prayer or chapel, she was cut off of wine. If she failed to show proper reverence to the mistress, it was bread and water. If caught lying, she couldn't eat the evening meal. If she put wood on the fire without permission, lit too many candles, or stole something small, she went without food altogether (a bigger theft earned expulsion).[70]

Other punishments aimed to humiliate. A Pietà girl lost food if she didn't work but other rule-breaking brought on penalties that were levied in front of all the other girls in the refectory. Torn clothing or badly performed work was slung around her shoulders through mealtime. A girl who swore by calling on the devil had to spend a mealtime standing with a piece of metal in her mouth. Girls who gossiped or talked about things in the home that didn't concern them had to stand through the meal with a sign on their back saying "For Prattling," and those who went into the novices' dormitories without permission did the same with a sign reading "For Presumption." Singing worldly songs earned fifteen lashes in front of the others, or the shame of kissing the feet of all the Pietà's *fanciulle*—easily over a hundred at any one time. Vices that might bring the wrath of God on the home or lift the protective care of guardian angels had to be punished in a different place: taking God's or a saint's name in vain brought a girl to her knees through the Mass, after which she circulated to ask the pardon of each of the *fanciulle* individually. Irreverence or insubordination to the resident prioress also kept a rebel on her knees through Mass. With such a strict regimen, it is not surprising that the first Pietà rule had to do with girls who talked about escaping: these had their hair cut. If they managed to get over the walls but were caught and returned, the barbering was followed by a spell in *prigione*.[71]

The rules aimed to cut off actions that might breed broader rebellion or discontent, or to punish other actions that couldn't be spoken about directly, even in the statutes. These girls were all maturing sexually, and their dreams and emotions could prove disruptive. The statutes don't say much specifically about how to work positively with them—though all officials are encouraged to be loving and charitable and gentle—and even the prohibitions are phrased obliquely. We already saw that the mistress of novices wasn't to allow the girls access to *novelle*. The stories of chivalric knights and ladies or, if it was Boccaccio, of priests, wives, and cuckolded husbands, could inspire dreams and corrode morals. Pietà girls who joked about sex or marriage had to spend a mealtime on their knees holding two distaffs loaded with raw hemp out in front of them, a punishment more ironic than painful.[72] The girls in Florence's Carità were strictly forbidden from having paper, pen, and ink, unless it was required for their duties in the home. Were their guardians afraid that they would attempt to write letters to people outside the enclosure, or perhaps pen plays or *novelle* for their own amusement? Into the sixteenth century, many people had slept two and even three to a bed. By the seventeenth century, conservatories seemed to have feared that this would lead to sexual experimentation: any S. Giuseppe girl caught going into another girl's bed was sent immediately into the house's prison and expelled as soon as possible.[73]

Of course, these rules should be taken with a grain of salt. Many were written by men—sometimes clerics—who took their strict regulations from books of manners or sets of spiritual exercises and not from much direct experience raising adolescent girls. Yet many girls chafed under these rules, and we have enough signs that the atmosphere in some homes could be quite turbulent. A few *fanciulle* managed to escape their enclosures, but they had to be either athletic or clever. Twelve-year-old Amelica de Galusano Sagorij fled the Baraccano after throwing herself out of the window. Some ran away from the homes where they had been hired as servants, or from the hospitals where they had been sent due to serious illness. Others simply resisted all the rules and created so much havoc that they were finally expelled. Apart from a pair of "ungrateful and disruptive" ("ingratitudine e malportamento") girls who broke out and fled together in 1598, S. Caterina noted of another that she left "by her will and to our satisfaction; she was never much use, and was ungovernable." Yet another girl was sent back to her mother because "she was always a scandal here, and not very useful," and a couple of others were let go by the authorities after they had tried and failed numerous times to flee. Antonia di Santi was expelled from S. Croce and returned to her mother in 1611 because of her bad behavior (*mali portamenti*) and the fact that she refused to work. On a slightly more sinister note, Orsolina di Benedicto Savorina was one of a few Baraccano girls described in the records as "possessed" (*spiritata* or *indemoniata*).

Possessed or self-possessed? One of Valeria's companions, Laura di Francesco "il Bologna," was expelled in 1584 for being "possessed," but her case shows that there could be more to bad behavior than met the eye. Marginal notes in Baraccano records suggest that father "Francesco il Bologna" was a fiction and that Laura was almost certainly the illegitimate daughter of Senator Francesco Maria Casale, who sometimes served on the Baraccano's governing councils. Entering the Baraccano dormitory at age 12 was an unpleasant shock for a girl of some standing, and Laura did not take it well. "She is wicked with lies, with swearing, with not wanting to work, with talking back to superiors, and in sum she is incorrigible." Or so the authorities wrote when they declared Laura to be possessed and shipped her out four years later to board with a widow. Yet this was still Casale's daughter, so the Baraccano paid the widow's fee and at age 18 welcomed Laura back long enough to marry her off in its church with a large dowry that Casale had provided.[74]

We can only imagine the kind of determined resistance, violent protests, fighting, depression, or even insanity that may have led officials to describe a girl as "possessed." It puts the strict rules on deportment into a sad and almost surreal light, and should remind us that the prescriptions for order, silence, and downcast eyes did not match the daily reality of conservatory life. Many girls were deeply unhappy, but only a few were expelled. Was there any alternative for the girl who took the conservatory enclosure as a prison? The individual cases of escape and expulsion noted above are spelled out in the records, but many similar stories of anger and rebellion may lie behind the numerous records of girls who were returned for unspecified reasons to their families.[75]

Weekly Rhythms

Work, prayer, eating, and recreation marked the rhythms of Valeria's daily schedule through the years that followed her entry into S. Maria del Baraccano. Spells on bread and water or even some days in the Baraccano *prigione* made sure that she kept to the discipline. There were weekly and more irregular rhythms as well. Chief of these were her religious duties. Led by confraternities or assisted by communities of tertiaries, the homes assumed considerable responsibility for their own worship life. At the same time, their spiritual exercises were modeled on those of the convents. Apart from morning and evening offices every day, the girls periodically headed to the chapel to perform the Office of the Dead for deceased *fanciulle, confratelli*, or benefactors—donors regularly required this when giving alms or property, and *confratelli* expected it as part of the normal reciprocation between givers and receivers. S. Caterina appointed one girl as the *cantora* to make sure the *fanciulle* knew the right words and notes, and could sing the solemn *canto fermo*. The girls also confessed and took communion regularly, observed the feast days of their patron saints, and fasted frequently. Every Friday was a fast day, but in Advent and Lent the girls might be fasting three days or more per week.[76]

Many of their spiritual duties took place within the conservatory's own chapel, though in their early years the Pietà girls lined up weekly to go across the Arno to the convent of S. Maria Angeli for lessons in Christian Doctrine and singing. One of the girls, or possibly a tertiary, acted as sacristan and kept the chapel clean and appropriately furnished, and made sure that the lamps had oil and were lit. She also kept the inventory of all that was in the chapel, much of it no doubt donated by various benefactors. Beyond this housekeeping, her duties could verge into those of a chaplain. S. Giuseppe's and S. Croce's female sacristan made sure that each of the other *fanciulle* prayed, did confession, and took communion as much as they were supposed to, reporting any lapses to the *guardiana* or *priora* so that the girl could be disciplined. The sacristan also kept records of when and for whom the girls were to say Offices of the Dead. Benefactors demanded requiem prayers in different numbers on various anniversaries, and the sacristan ensured that there were girls ready in the chapel to read through the various offices.[77]

There was a sacramental limit to what the girls could do on their own, and so another official whom Valeria would see often was the priest, whom S. Maria del Baraccano called the *padre spirituale* and others the *padre confessore*. These titles summed up the spectrum of the priest's main duties and the home's broad or narrow expectations. He was not a resident spiritual guide, but a periodic—certainly frequent—visitor who came to hear the girls' confessions, conduct the Mass, and possibly give a brief sermon from time to time that addressed problems that had arisen in the home. Some, like S. Maria del Baraccano, were indifferent to whether he was a regular or secular priest while others, like S. Marta, stipulated the mendicant house from which he was to come. Valeria's confessor was to be over 50 years old, though other homes would take a priest as young as 35 when, according to Aristotle, the passions had cooled. Strict regulations kept him within the walls of chapel, and like any other visitor or male official, he had to be accompanied by the *guardiana* or *priora* if he ventured into the house itself. S. Caterina warned against any familiarity or friendship between the priest and the girls, yet his sacramental duties helped him understand the tensions within and between individual girls and their supervisors, and S. Marta among others wanted him to work deliberately to keep the peace in the home.

The priest could easily become a powerful figure in the home. As we saw earlier, in less than a decade's service the friar Alessandro Capocchi moved Florence's Pietà to new quarters, rewrote its statutes, and intervened for it frequently with the Medici. His statutes ordered the girls to call their priest "father" and to treat him as such (matching the resident female head, the "mother," or *madre di casa*), though they equally required that he distance himself from the details of daily administration. Some homes certainly tried to limit the priests' authority. S. Caterina's first statute writers gave the priest power to make new rules governing the girls' spiritual or corporal life, but a later hand stroked these lines out. Bologna's Bonifacio dalle Balle wanted only a *confessore* for the girls, reserving for himself and the tertiaries care for the girls' broader spiritual life, which he conducted through sermons and lessons.[78]

Homes believed that a healthy soul needed a healthy body, and so Valeria's schedule included regular baths and shampoos. This may have upset some girls who shared the fears of the day that frequent bathing caused illness through the dangerous opening of the pores. Yet with lice abounding, sixteenth-century homes still preferred a clean head above all, and a clean body if possible, as a matter of health. Every two months, girls at the Pietà lined up to get their hair and feet washed by the *medica* (though girls who went out alms gathering could get their feet washed every two weeks). Working over a large brass bowl, she applied a shampoo made of herbal extracts and, after rinsing, went through the girl's hair with a special set of combs that would catch any lice there. This work was not about appearance or even, for that matter, about hair. If the *medica* came across a girl with long hair who was preoccupied with keeping it clean and well-dressed, she simply reached for the shears and cut it to a length that made it easier to manage. The combs were the real tools of her trade, and the *medica* worked through all the girls in shifts to keep head lice at bay. With over 150 girls within its walls, the Pietà gave her a particular challenge, and beyond organizing the girls into shampoo shifts, she took her combs to the infirmary and even to parts of the home where girls were on duty and worked on them there. This was professional work requiring a keen eye and hand, and as if to further emphasize that it was about health and not vanity, the girls were not allowed to comb each other's hair.[79]

However much she was scrubbed and combed, Valeria would certainly fall ill from time to time. Minor illnesses resulted in her transfer to the infirmary that all the larger homes maintained out of fears of contagion. Here the *medica* or *infermiera* (nurse), likely an older *fanciulla*, examined Valeria within the bounds of her training and competence, and prescribed a regimen based on rest and a diet heavy in broths and infusions. It might be the most rest a girl would ever get, and fearing perhaps that some girls would use the infirmary to get out of work, Florence's S. Caterina limited stays there to eight to ten days. The Pietà bought meats and some vegetables specifically for its ailing girls, and also had a *ricettario*, or set of medical recipes that the *medica* could use to nurse them through seasonal ailments, work injuries, and contagious infections. She could prepare most of these recipes with herbal materials at hand or readily purchased, but a few could only be bought through the apothecary. The *ricettario* was written in a few different hands, most likely in the 1560s.[80] It raises more questions than it answers about the girls' health and sickness, since most of the fifteen recipes say nothing about how they are to be used. The remedies are not for pills, which could only be prescribed by licensed doctors, but are for ointments, plasters, suppositories, and elixirs, the kind of external remedies and light medication that someone without professional training or guild certification could prepare and apply.[81] They were still very serious—if a girl contracted the contagious skin disease ringworm (*tigna*), the nurse shaved her head and bathed it with mallow, ash, and plantain before smearing on an ointment made of pig fat, pine resin, and powdered wild celery or smallage (*altea*). Other remedies addressed work injuries or the health problems specific to young girls. There were remedies for sore eyes and for burns, both injuries that girls could expect to suffer as they bent over boiling pots to reel the silk cocoons. Chickpeas, barley flour, and dried lupins were slowly roasted together before being mixed with honey and vinegar to create poultices for skin sores and inflammations. Mixing linseed oil together with fenugreek and iris, or turpentine with resins, pitch, and wax, the *medica* created ointments which, according to contemporary and classical gynecological guides, helped girls who had painful menstruation or no menstruation at all.

These latter recipes raise questions of their own because remedies that stimulated menstruation sometimes could do double duty as contraceptives or abortifacients. The most complicated recipe in the Pietà nurse's recipe book was for an "unguento appostolorum da Vicenna." Did the phonetic rendering of the

great Arab scientist's name indicate that the recipe was dictated orally to someone who knew its purpose but not the reputation of its author? The Roman physician Soranus had listed most of this recipe's active ingredients—birthwort, resin,
panax, lead dross, frankincense, myrrh, and galbano—as abortifacients and/or
contraceptives in his *Gynecology*. A series of scholastic authors had passed down
this Greco-Roman-Arabic knowledge in their encyclopedias, and it had been further diffused through midwives' manuals and Renaissance herbals.[82] But this was
not just knowledge for those who could read books. Birth control remedies were
known and exchanged by the prostitutes who walked the streets surrounding the
Pietà, which in these years still made its home in the heart of Florence's red-light
district of the Borgo Ognissanti. Some of the girls coming into the home could
have been prostitutes, and some of the mothers abandoning them may have been
too. Abandonment to charitable shelters was one of the ways that prostitutes
aimed to give their daughters a better life, though these homes frequently complained that their wards found it hard to leave the profitable work behind.[83]

Some of the girls going out to domestic service may have been raped, a not
uncommon fate for female servants generally and always a bigger danger for
those who had no fathers or brothers to protect or avenge them. Getting the girls
out of this dangerous location was one of the main reasons that Alessandro
Capocchi put forward when he successfully brokered the conservatory's move
from the seedy Borgo Ognissanti to the northern edge of the city in 1568, and
helps us understand why he was so determined to tighten up entrance procedures and enclosure at the Pietà. The Pietà's situation and the *ricettario's* terse-
ness lend plausibility to these scenarios, and may even help explain why the
recipes are quite literally hidden away in the inner pages of a volume that, judging by its title, ostensibly recorded textile accounts. Did the Pietà's *medica* ever
prepare these remedies or administer them to the girls as abortifacients or contraceptives? The clues are tantalizing, but in the absence of any other corrobo-
rating evidence we cannot say for sure.[84]

If a girl's medical problems worsened, the *guardiana* could summon the doctor that conservatories commonly kept on retainer. Bolognese conservatories
seem to have done this more frequently than Florentine ones, perhaps because
of the city's pride in the university medical school and its graduates. Valeria would
get a visit from the *medico* Domenico da M. Santo, who received 20 lire annually for being on call. He could use a broader set of diagnostic tools and move
the treatment beyond Galenic rest and broths into more complicated medicines
and procedures like bleeding.[85] If her condition failed to improve, the girl was

moved out of the house altogether. Here again, the Bolognese homes were more proactive in returning seriously ill girls to their family or guardians, while holding open the possibility that they could return once they regained their health. In one year alone (1609), S. Croce returned four of its roughly two dozen girls to their families for this reason.[86] Valeria could also end up convalescing in the greater quiet and better care of an upper-class home; S. Marta and S. Maria del Baraccano allowed its gentlewoman visitors to take girls into their own homes to nurse them, provided again that they were returned when healthy. Florentine homes more often passed girls on to the city's main hospital, S. Maria Nuova, which usually had excellent success in restoring patients to health. But a doctor's medications were expensive, and in the public hospital a *fanciulla* ran the danger of being morally infected with bad examples. For these reasons, S. Caterina initially called for only light and cheap remedies (*medicine leggieri* as opposed to *medicamenti grandi*) and forbade transferring girls to hospitals. It is a small surprise that these lines too were soon struck from the statutes of a home that civic officials had opened to deal with the plague and famine of the early 1590s. Of the first hundred girls in S. Caterina's register, thirteen died in the hospitals of S. Maria Nuova or S. Matteo. The Pietà had never ruled against public hospitals, perhaps because it needed them almost from the time it opened. Of its first 361 entrants, 210 died in S. Maria Nuova, S. Bonifacio, or S. Matteo. Going to the hospital was, for most Pietà girls, a one-way trip; only one of them returned from S. Maria Nuova.[87]

Outwork—Domestic Service

Escaping over the walls or out the windows was not the only way out of a conservatory. Firm enclosure relaxed slightly for a few girls who got work outside the home. Apprenticeships were not usually an option for conservatory girls like Valeria di Bartolomeo di Pavia, but she might be allowed to become a servant in a private home.[88] This could come after she had lived in the home for a period, had proven her moral stability and domestic skills, and was ready to be gradually reintegrated into society. It could also be the best way of handling a girl who chafed under the home's restrictions. Whatever the circumstances, domestic service was not the kind of work from which the *fanciulla* would return to the conservatory at night. It brought a girl back into the kind of noninstitutional fostering arrangement that we saw earlier, and that was the fate of the majority of orphaned and abandoned children. Servant girls left for contractually defined periods of time, but this was really supposed to mark their permanent departure from the home. Employers undertook to arrange the girl's marriage at the end of the contract period, and offered a dowry as her pay, together with the usual room, board, and clothing. Anyone wanting to take Valeria di Bartolomeo di Pavia out of S. Maria del Baraccano in order to be a servant would have to set out all of these arrangements in a notarized agreement that specified the size of the dowry and date of the marriage before the confraternity would even vote on it.

As we saw above, service clearly had the potential to demean or dishonor a girl and left her open to sexual exploitation in particular; the majority of infants abandoned at foundling homes were illegitimate children born to servant girls who lived in a master's home. It is not surprising that conservatories for girls of better families forbade it or made no provision for it, or that girls from homes like this frequently lasted only a few weeks before returning to the conservatory. Only a handful of girls took this route from Bologna's S. Marta or S. Maria del Baraccano. At Valeria's Baraccano, none of the 161 girls in the first register from 1554 to 1570 are listed as servants, and only 5 of the 182 in the register that picked up the record from 1570. Yet Valeria knew all these 5; one entered the day she did in 1575, and the other 4 arrived in April 1578. Jacoma, age 20, "a good girl, quiet and works," would do well in the home of Mona Lucia di Frascatti. It is less clear what success Mona Castelani had with 18-year-old Laura, "full of lies and blasphemies and does not want to work or respond to her superiors." When Baraccano authorities decided that she was possessed, she was freed (*liberata*)[89] to live and work with Castelani.

At first glance, the situation looked much different in Florence's S. Maria Vergine. Its first matriculation book registered 85 girls entering in the first 4 years. The bulk of these (46) were still in the home at that point, when their records were transferred to a second no-longer-extant volume and out of our sight. Of the remaining 39, 28 (32.94% of the whole group of 85) were sent out on domestic service contracts, while the rest died, fled, or were expelled. The contracts for the 28 serving girls set terms of anywhere from 3 to 8 to 10 years. Yet 19 (67.85%) of these girls returned to S. Maria Vergine, most within weeks or months, because of disagreements with employers or inability to do the work. A further 7 simply fled soon after getting to their new employers. Only 2 were still with their employers when the new book started in 1556.[90] With so many girls returning or fleeing in such short order, it seems that domestic service was beneath their dignity and far from their experience. They considered the

Vergine's quasi-conventual arrangements more congenial and more appropriate to their station; the fact that the conservatory doors opened to them so quickly suggests that their overseers shared this view.

Since dishonor and exploitation always threatened, strict rules aimed to make service safer for girls. Almost all homes strictly forbade domestic service with members of the sponsoring confraternities or congregations, to avoid the suspicion (or reality) of confraternity members exploiting their wards. But even this could be reversed for the right reason. The gentlewomen of Bologna's S. Giuseppe organized themselves as a kind of employment agency and temporarily took girls into their own homes to polish their manners and skills before passing them on as servants to other gentlewomen or citizens. In the decade 1628–38, for which records are relatively complete, slightly less than one-third of S. Giuseppe's fifty-seven entrants went from the conservatory into domestic service arrangements, often passing first through the private homes of the gentlewomen who acted as their sponsors and mentors. The girls ended up in the homes of some of the leading families of the patriciate, including the Bentivoglio, Leoni, Grassi, and Guastavillani (only two employers were artisans), and since most of the employers were women, the *fanciulle* clearly got their positions thanks to the strong network that linked upper-class women together.[91]

The Bolognese conservatories only placed their girls with gentlewomen and citizens, and consistently required that any arrangements had to be approved by the whole confraternity before the girl could pack up and go. Florentines tended to be a little more relaxed about destination and process. The men who ran S. Maria Vergine and S. Niccolò kept their ears open for any respectable people who needed servants, or for weavers or artisans who might need semiskilled helpers, and the five executive administrators could approve a contract without consulting the other members of the confraternity.[92] But whether strict or relaxed, all homes closely scrutinized the morals and domestic life of the person who would take the girl in. In the case of S. Croce or S. Maria Vergine, they paid a follow-up visit after one or two months to see whether the girls or the employers were unhappy with the arrangement. This helps explain why so many Vergine girls returned to the shelter. But beyond this visit, officials spent little time over the following months or years policing the arrangements. None of the homes required their male or female visitors to keep tabs on the conditions of those girls who had become servants, even though their counterparts at male orphanages usually did exactly this for the boys who served as apprentices in workshops in the city. This underscores the fact that conservatories saw domestic service contracts as a form of fostering that effectively relieved them of ongoing responsibility for the girls.

Conservatories that took in girls from respectable families, like Florence's S. Maria Vergine and Bologna's S. Marta, might avoid domestic service, but those serving a more common clientele had little choice. Not surprisingly, the Florentine conservatory that served the artisinal ranks of society used domestic service most frequently and with the greatest success. Initially, S. Niccolò's record of its girls listed *only* those who had been "settled [*acconciate*] with others" before expanding to become a general census of girls both in and outside of the home. The first group, covering 1558–66, numbered forty-two girls.[93] Most (thirty-three) came from outside the city or had shallow roots there at best. Almost one-quarter (nine) went into service with women, four of these being widows and only one noted by occupation; she was a painter (*depintore*). When noted, the male employers (twenty-three) tended to be in the cloth trade. Beyond room, board, and clothing, girls earned about 10 lire per year; some contracts specified that this would be given as a lump sum dowry at the end of the period. Only a few contracts specified a complete term, and this could be anywhere from four to ten years. Since the girls' ages aren't recorded, we cannot tell whether the term was set to finish at the time when the girl might normally be expected to marry.[94] Not all girls made it to the end of their terms: Caterina di Domenicho da Fiesole left Girolamo di Nicholo da Ferrara six weeks into a five-year contract, and went instead to Maria, wife of Felice della Chanpana. Lamenacha di Meo da Pistoia lasted for almost three months in the home of a tailor, and three months in another home before disappearing from the record.[95] Apart from these girls, six eventually returned to S. Niccolò. Because the records are sketchy, it is hard to tell what proportion of the whole this represents.

From 1571, S. Niccolò expanded its record to include all its girls, and we can tell that over the long term just under one-quarter of its *fanciulle* left to become servants in a private home. It began in 1571 with a census recording 57 girls in the home. Some had entered in the 1550s and were now in their late 20s or early 30s; 35 more girls joined this group through November 1579. Of this total of 92, almost half (39, or 42.39%) left the home through the decade for domestic service or fostering arrangements. Most of them were quite young. Of those for whom ages were given, over half were less than 12 years old. Almost two-thirds of the girls who left to become servants were from outside of Florence or from non-native families.[96] A second census in 1579 recorded 54 girls (including 13 from the earlier cohort). Of these, 12 (22.2%) went to domestic service. From this point through 1598, 113 more girls entered S. Niccolò. Though records through this period become even more sketchy, 26 girls (23%) left the home to become servants in private homes in the city.[97]

We might assume that domestic service was even more commonly the fate for those girls sheltering in the two homes at the bottom of the Florentine social scale, S. Caterina and the Pietà. It was not. S. Caterina originally prohibited its girls from going out as servants with gentlewomen, "so that they won't happen to fall into evil" ("accio non habbino da capitar male"). Like so many of the high-minded intentions in its statutes, this line too was scratched out. Yet the prohibition did not make it far out of the mentality of the home's administrators. The first hundred girls in S. Caterina's *Libro di Ricordi* entered from 1591 through the time the famine eased in November 1594. Only nine went out as servants, and one of these returned. All but one came from families rooted outside of Florence. Four left within two years of arriving at S. Caterina, one after approximately six years, and the remaining four after approximately fifteen to twenty-five years. Over the next thirty years, only five more girls went out as servants. S. Caterina's administrators may have cooled to domestic service after some early experiments, or perhaps the girls themselves were difficult to place, or perhaps attitudes in Florence had changed by the end of the sixteenth century. This was certainly far from the determined effort that had regularly sent almost one-third of the Vergine's girls, and between one-fifth and one-quarter of S. Niccolò's girls, out as servants earlier in the century.[98]

What was up? Florence's Pietà home may provide an answer, because we can track cohorts and see a deliberate shift in practice over the decades. Three hundred and sixty-one girls passed through the doors of Florence's Pietà home in the five years after it opened in January 1555. Of these, at least 61 (16.89%) went out into domestic service. A handful (three) left the institution within a month, perhaps because they were either very unhappy and disruptive, or they had simply lodged at the Pietà temporarily until they could move into some prearranged position. Most stayed from two to five years before going out as servants, and at this point most were in their mid to late teens.[99] We do not know the contract terms for very many of these girls, or how much their previous experience played a part in determining where they went. How many girls were like the baker's daughter who was sent out to work for a baker on a two-year contract? Did she eventually return to the Pietà, like almost one-quarter of the other servant girls? One 13-year-old left on a seven-year contract but was back in eight months; she was barely in the door before the Pietà returned her to her mother. This was very likely a girl who didn't take readily to the discipline of either a home or a master. Most of the others who returned were seriously ill and died soon after.[100]

In its early years, the Pietà initially sent fewer of its girls into domestic service than either S. Maria Vergine or S. Niccolò, the only other conservatories open in Florence at the time. We might assume that this was because of its location in the red-light district of Borgo Ognissanti, but in fact the number plummeted after it moved north to a safer district. Table 3.4 divides the 819 girls recorded in the Pietà's registers into 3 cohorts. The first group of 361 includes those girls enrolled from 1554 to 1559. The second group of 165 includes those registered from 1560 until the home relocated out of Borgo Ognissanti in October–November 1568. The third group of 293 includes those registered from January 1569 through the end of 1601.[101]

Just under one-fifth of girls (17 to 20%) left to become servants as long as the home was in Borgo Ognissanti, but after the move the number dropped to a handful. The decrease is even more dramatic than the table implies, because domestic service actually declined almost immediately following the move, and the last girl to exit the Pietà on a domestic service contract left in 1584. Thinking back to the Pietà's collection of medical recipes, and particularly its puzzling birth control remedies, this precipitous drop may confirm that this conservatory's guardians had decided that domestic service was simply too dangerous and should be abandoned. It is certainly clear that the move itself was part of a larger refashioning of the home away from its founders' intentions of offering emergency temporary aid in a lay shelter that would return girls as quickly as possible to secular society as wives and mothers like the homes in Bologna did.

The Pietà was turning into a factory. As we saw above, it had a reputation for producing the best brocades in Florence, thanks to an enclosed workforce of orphaned and abandoned girls whose options for leaving were swiftly evaporating. Moreover, it still had the highest mortality rate of all Florentine conservatories, and few financial resources beyond what the remaining girls could earn. It could ill afford to let its most skilled workers leave the home. S. Caterina had a similar problem with high death rates, and with a higher percentage of its girls leaving through either marriage or a return to their families, there was yet more pressure on the remaining girls to maintain the home economically. Bolognese homes, all sustained by the accumulated legacies of their founding confraternities, had no equivalent financial pressures and so could work more deliberately at passing the girls back into society. But while economic necessity might re-

Table 3.4. Girls in and out of Domestic Service at the Pietà, 1555–1601

Cohort	Total	Number in Service	%	Number Returned	%
> 1559	361	61	16.89	9	14.75
1560–68	165	30	19.63	9	28.12
1569–1601	293	14	4.77	5	35.71

Source: ASF, CRSF ms. 112/78 and 112/79.

quire Florentine conservatories to hang on to skilled workers for the good of the home, the city had no model for a forced-labor factory in which orphaned and abandoned girls would be compelled to remain enclosed and working until their deaths. The closest model it had was the tertiary convent, an enclosure of lower-class women who, lacking the resources and family connections of higher-class convents, also worked hand to mouth and were prevented by their vows from returning to secular society. Not surprisingly, both the Pietà and S. Caterina, Florence's poorest conservatories, metamorphosed into convents through these decades. Economic necessity and restricted cultural horizons were perhaps the main factors leading to this result, but politics and administration also played a part, as we will see in chapter 5.

Valeria di Bartolomeo di Pavia spent eight years in S. Maria del Baraccano. Her life there was far more regimented than it would have been in a private home. At the same time, in the work she did and in the obedience she owed to adults who controlled her movements and chose her husband, her experience was not much different from that of other girls of her age and class. One of the greatest differences is the one that is hardest to measure. Valeria lived in a world made by women, and had very little contact with men until she left in 1584 as the bride of Antilio di Erchole Agochiarolo. Almost everything she had learned, from domestic and employable skills to religious doctrine, had come from other women in an environment closed to men. Unlike a convent, all the women in this community were lay, and most were adolescent. However much the statutes may have tried to shut their mouths and regulate their thoughts, Valeria and her companions were girls wrenched out of a previous life and thrown together in a new and strange world. Together they faced the drudgery of institutional cleaning, the meagerness and blandness of institutional cooking, the chill of under-heated dormitories, the endless hours of lacemaking and the harsh tongue of a work mistress, or the overcurious gaze of a male visitor who might want to check whether their beauty was intact. Could they avoid talking about this? Together they saw some girls break under this discipline—fleeing, imprisoned, or declared to be possessed. Wouldn't they share sympathy, scorn, or fear? Together they saw new girls come in from time to time. Could they avoid asking them what had happened to the city and people outside the walls? Together they saw companions leave from time to time, and themselves looked ahead to the almost certain prospect of leaving the home to marry a stranger and raise a family. Could they avoid dreaming or dreading who would it be, what he was like, what he did, where he lived, how they would be received in his family, or whether they would see their own relatives again? In the end, Valeria lived in a world constructed more by her adolescent companions than by adults' regulations. If anything, enclosure heightened this reality by putting such large numbers of girls together with such small numbers of supervisors. Living in the enclosure of the home freed her from the threats and dangers of the streets and gave her a life which, despite all its difficulties, was almost certainly better than what she would have faced if she hadn't been allowed in. Was this true for boys as well?

CHAPTER FOUR

Making a Home with Boys

As Valeria di Bartolomeo di Pavia was settling in to the routines at S. Maria del Baraccano, Ruggiero di Lorenzo da Castelfocognano was mounting the steps of Florence's Ospedale degli Poveri Abbandonati. Barely more than 7 years old, he had been down busy Via S. Gallo many times before in the company of his mother Rosa. Shortly after he was born, his father Lorenzo had abandoned the family for the life of a soldier. No one had heard a word from him since then, and Rosa had no idea where he was, who he was fighting for, or even if he was still alive. For seven years Rosa had struggled to find enough for the two of them to eat, but she was evasive on the details of how she had managed. In her efforts to find a better home for Ruggiero, she had gone up and down the streets of Florence from one monastery to the next trying to have the boy accepted as an oblate or even a servant, but the doors were always shut. Ruggiero was a bright boy, but too young, or at least so she was told. Finally, at the end of 1575, Rosa managed to find work as the servant of a Florentine citizen, Girolamo Honesti. The pair moved into Honesti's house, where Ruggiero and Rosa swept, hauled water, and kept the fire fed through the winter months in return for a bed under the eaves and a place at the kitchen table. This was a common enough fostering arrangement, but within months Honesti was penning a *fede* to the magistrates of the Bigallo, asking that they take Ruggiero in.

Had Girolamo Honesti found that Ruggiero was just too much trouble? Had he agreed with Rosa to shelter the boy only through the winter months? It is impossible to say. Girolamo praised the boy as smart and quick-witted (*bello ingegnino*), but claimed that he simply didn't have the means to sustain both mother and son. He wrote that he had no idea how Rosa had managed to feed Ruggiero through those years—clearly there had been little if any help coming from Lorenzo's father Bernardo or his kin, and there was no mention of any of Rosa's own relatives. He also described her unsuccessful efforts to make a friar out of him. Girolamo felt that this was still the best option, and speculated that with a bit of formal education, sharp little Ruggiero would easily pass through the monastery doors. He was even willing to put money on it, in the form of alms for the Abbandonati if the magistrates would take the boy in.

They did. Ruggiero was hardly the most needy child around, but if the records are to be believed, he was one of only three children admitted into the Abbandonati on the basis of *fede* during 1576–77. Honesti may have had better connections than most, or perhaps he was just lucky that his timing fit the home's cyclical recruitment. The Abbandonati was still absorbing twenty-six children it had enrolled through the previous year. It had been a difficult winter and the door remained shut to many more desperate cases, like the widow with four children under 9 years old, or the boy whose father had died seven years before and who had just been rejected by his new stepfather. Even well-connected sponsors were having trouble: Pandolfo de Medici had requested entry for a 2-year-old abandoned boy so that the woman caring for him could nurse his newborn son instead. The magistrates discussed his request, but didn't record their decision.[1]

When we try to sketch Ruggiero's circumstances and determine who his companions might have been, we come up against a problem common to all the orphanages studied here: they kept few records. Conservatories in both cities filled large registers with careful entries on each of their girls, recording their backgrounds and sometimes even the vote tallies when they had been accepted, listing their resources, sometimes describing their personality, and explaining the circumstances of their departure. Orphanages were extraordinarily lax in recording anything about the boys in their care. None of the homes kept the kinds of registers found in conservatories, even though their statutes ordered the officials to do so. From time to time a more conscientious *segretario* would enter the names of boys into the minute books of the confraternities that ran these homes, but at the end of his term he would inevitably be replaced by someone who took a more lax view of things and the record would peter out.

S. Onofrio recorded the names of the boys it investigated and accepted, but nothing further. S. Bartolomeo sometimes noted which master artisans its wards apprenticed with, and occasionally even noted their salaries, but this too was uneven. It required officials to inventory the chests, clothes, and other items that boys brought in and to credit a boy's account if these were sold, but nothing this individual has survived. Some record was kept at the time. A few S. Bartolomeo boys who had brought in the tools of a craft received them back when leaving, and a few *confratelli* were appointed to oversee the house another boy inherited until he too was ready to leave.[2] Florence's Abbandonati was worst of all: the bundles of *fede* petitioning for boys' admission tell the backgrounds of some, and occasionally record whether one or another made it into the home. Yet as we saw in an earlier chapter, other boys found the door opening after a parent had left them under the portico, and were never recorded anywhere. As for boys finding their way out, the Abbandonati records are silent.

Compounding the problem, neither the Abbandonati nor S. Bartolomeo ever got beyond writing drafts of statutes, and any that S. Giacomo may have adopted on opening in 1591 are no longer extant. Only Bologna's S. Onofrio published and later revised the procedures governing its home.[3] Compared to the tightly regulated conservatories, the orphanages seem to have been run on ambition tempered by large doses of ad hoc improvisation. *Confratelli* could turn to the advice books that clerical authors like Erasmus, Andrea Ghetti, and Silvio Antoniano were writing around this time. It is tempting to use a book like Antoniano's *Dell'educazione cristiana e politica de'figliuoli* (1584) to fill in the gaps in these sometimes fragmentary statute drafts and administrative records, particularly since there was no part of childrearing that the childless Antoniano considered outside his ken or competence. Running to 281 topical chapters, Antoniano's tome was frequently reprinted into the twentieth century. While we can turn to it to find early modern concepts of child psychology, the limits of corporal punishment, and the ways of keeping boys chaste, it is a far greater jump to assuming that early modern fathers and orphanage guardians did the same. Or whether, when these men read their Antoniano, they found practical ideas to help with the day-to-day challenges of running an orphanage. They may have had copies of such texts around, and may even have made them required reading for the teachers, chaplains, and guardians that they hired to look after the boys. Yet the argument from silence—unwritten registers, incomplete inventories, and unfin-

Figure 4.1. Orphan boy, drawn on the back of an admission application (Archivio di Stato di Firenze, Magistrato del Bigallo, ms. 1459 #242)

ished draft statutes—suggests that in the end they relied more on their instincts, experience, and connections than on the advice of a celibate clergyman.[4]

Given these gaps in the records, we cannot tell with certainty who may have joined Ruggiero di Lorenzo di Castelfocognano at the junior end of the Abbandonati's dining table or the back of its chapel. We know, from those periods when records were more precise, that Florence's main orphanage more often enrolled individuals or small groups of two, three, or five children. And in spite of their fragmentary state, the surviving records allow us to see something of the life that boys led, and to see how different it was from that of girls like Valeria di Bartolomeo di Pavia. Differences began with the children's ages, and were amplified by social mores. Most conservatory girls were over 12; most orphanage boys were under 10 like the solemn boy in an Abbandonati uniform whose portrait an anonymous artist sketched on the back of a *fede* in 1582—a boy whom Ruggiero, then only 14, likely knew (Figure 4.1). Younger at their entry into the home, the boys were more sheltered in their first years, but quickly gained some of the freedoms that their peers outside the walls enjoyed. Though their domestic chores were minimal, they worked in order to keep the home afloat. Since it was not necessary to protect the boys' honor with strict enclosure, none of the homes operated workshops like those found in conservatories. Many boys worked outside of the home during the day and returned only for meals and sleep. Bolognese orphanages went further and developed a profitable business in attending at funerals, which put their boys on the street many times a week.

In short, girls lived their lives almost entirely within the conservatory walls and were subject to its strict discipline until they could be returned to their families or passed on to the authority of a husband, employer, or convent. Boys never lost their contact with the culture of the streets, but through the years gained more and more tools for making a life there. Girls created a community, while boys shared a residence. While it is possible to work out daily and periodic rhythms for a girl like Valeria, a boy like Ruggiero had his life structured more by his age and by the progressive steps by which the Abbandonati reintegrated him into Florentine life. In the end, all these diverging practices underscore a more basic difference: while conservatories aimed to protect girls for a later life whose details would be arranged by family or institutional guardians, orphanages aimed to shape boys with education, self-discipline, and self-reliance to the point where they could step out on the street as independent agents by late adolescence.

Daily Rhythms

On entering the Ospedale degli Abbandonati, Ruggiero had gone through a formal ceremony of becoming part of the family. He put on the rough brown woolen smock uniform and stood while an official prayed over him and blessed him in a rough parallel to the vesting ceremony that awaited him if he fulfilled his mother's dreams and entered a monastery. Orphanages had none of the problems that conservatories wrestled with when it came to clothing, though this was due more to the boys' younger age and poverty than to any lack of vanity; the adolescent Renaissance male was certainly as fashion-conscious as his female counterpart.[5] Most homes kept a generous supply of clothes on hand in the event that a boy entering had nothing decent to wear. In 1562, when S. Onofrio had no more than about two dozen boys resident, its *guardiano* recorded 112 new and old shirts in stock. Boys entering the newly opened Abbandonati twenty years before had received shoes, shirts, vests, and russet-colored smocks.[6] Orphanages did not build spiritual lessons around physical dress, but Bolognese homes did insist that boys wear clothes appropriate to their class. S. Onofrio outfitted its boys with the handkerchiefs, caps, and shirts in wool and silk worn by the well-mannered sons of middling guildsmen, and it paid for the clothes of those of its boys who lived with guild masters, no doubt in part to ensure that they were up to standard.[7]

Orphanages built identity around their uniforms just as conservatories did, since their boys also walked up and down the streets gathering alms or in procession. Some provided robes for their administrators, priests, teachers, and older boys, though of a finer cloth and cut than what the boys wore. Ruggiero might eventually wear one of the processional robes of Lombard cloth that the Abbandonati purchased when it opened, though he likely began with only the rougher russet-colored smock. In procession the two uniforms set up a before-and-after moralizing lesson. The bulk of younger boys tumbled along without much order or pace, their woolen smocks advertising the mendicant humility and simplicity of their current state. The smaller cadre of older and better-disciplined boys processed with more dignity, their better-quality robes announcing their future status to be something closer to the guildsmen and *confratelli* who marched ahead and behind them. Dress robes could be quite extravagant. S. Bartolomeo di Reno clothed its boys in red gowns and white shoes, "so that they will be recognized," on feast days, for alms collection, and when they walked in procession with the patrician *confratelli* who ran the home.[8] Had the boys worn these robes when going out as apprentices to the shops of tailors or shoemakers, they would have been targets for the stones and mud that Bologna's young toughs liked to throw at those they hated, envied, or just were annoyed at.

No one had entered the Abbandonati on the same day as Ruggiero, but most of the two dozen who had come in the previous twelve months were under age 7 as he was. Many of his experiences through the first few years would be shared with this larger group of young boys. The boys were too young to benefit from a master of novices guiding them through the hallways and customs of their new home, as happened in conservatories. Older boys seldom stepped in as the mentors of younger ones, or as staff running the kitchens, the infirmary, the laundry, or any other part of the home. Ruggiero would not rise through the ranks, as Valeria might, because there really were no ranks to rise through. Orphanages in both cities hired cooks, teachers, laundresses, and sacristans, who ate and slept in the home and became a supportive community that in smaller homes was modeled more closely on the nuclear family. Larger homes certainly had a more institutional feel. The men who drafted the Abbandonati's first statutes planned on a major institution much like Florence's main hospital of S. Maria Nuova, with a specialized staff of at least fifteen, including cooks, medics, cleaners, teachers, and *ministri* who were jacks of all trades. They hoped for a *cerimoniero* who, like a master of novices, would teach the boys the customs of the house and the manners they were expected to adopt, and who would take particular care of the little ones, waking them in the morning, putting them to bed at night, and helping them with their shoes. Yet high costs curbed many of the founders' ambitions by the time Ruggiero came in the Abbandonati's door. An undated list of the sixteenth century notes only twelve resident staff for 187 boys, so it's most likely that the resident teachers or chaplain took on the *ceremoniero*'s duties, if they were taken on at all. By contrast, a century later S. Onofrio's sixteen boys were under the care of a married couple (the *guardiano* and *guardiana*) and a priest who were themselves assisted by a male and a female servant.[9]

Though he may not have had a master of novices or *cerimoniero* to take him by the hand, Ruggiero would have to find his way around the halls and rooms of his new home. At the time, the Abbandonati still occupied the old Broccardi *ospedale* on Via S. Gallo. We do not know what it looked like inside, though Ruggiero probably slept in one of the large open dormitories that was typical of old hostels. Descriptions available for two Bolognese homes give us some idea of the sharp contrasts between larger institutional complexes like the Abbandonati and smaller homes. S. Bartolomeo di Reno began as a compact pilgrims' hostel in 1530, but the confraternity quickly embarked on an ambitious building program that extended it on all sides and upward, and by the time the work finished in the 1580s, it could shelter about a hundred boys. Local architect Alessandro Fontana began the renovation not with dormitories but with a church.

Oriented to but also set back from Via Imperiale, the church gave S. Bartolomeo new architectural prominence and the appearance of a spacious front courtyard on a street where real estate was at a premium. More to the point, it also gave the orphanage a place to offer public religious services and collect alms. Boys entered around the side and to the rear of this church, coming through the doorway that was situated under the portico that ran adjacent to the Reno canal immediately south of the building. Through the door boys and visitors entered an inner courtyard ringed with a loggia from which one could reach the public church and sacristy to the right, or the refectory, kitchen, and pantry. A second courtyard connected to this first one, and here there was a stable and rooms for staff, servants, and officials. Taking a stairway down, one entered an underground laundry room outfitted with reservoirs to store the water that was piped in directly from the Reno canal. Taking another stairway up brought the boys to the second-floor loggia that ringed the courtyard. The boys slept here in two dormitories, one facing south over the Reno canal and the other north over an adjoining street. Putting their dormitories on the second floor meant windows could be opened during the day to catch the breezes and air the buildings out. The teachers gathered the boys in a couple of classrooms on this level, and any tools or valuables that they had brought in to S. Bartolomeo could be stored in a locked room where the records were also kept. From this second-floor loggia, the priest or music teacher could also shepherd the boys into two small choir rooms that looked down into the public church. The boys practiced music here, and by the eighteenth century could even provide music for Masses without ever leaving the orphanage; convents had similar grated rooms once enclosure became more tight, but in the case of S. Bartolomeo boys these rooms were more likely for convenience than for security. Back on the second-floor loggia, one could find another stairway that led up to a third and top floor, where there was a granary, a sun porch (*solana*) that looked over the city, and the private rooms and oratory of the confraternity of S. Bartolomeo di Reno.[10]

Following the path of the Reno canal eastward for five or six blocks brought one to the corner of Via Mascarella, where Senator Ercole Bentivoglio was building an imposing palace within sight of the ruins of an even more massive palace that Giovanni II Bentivoglio had built a century before. Bolognese mobs had torn that would-be *signore*'s palace down in 1508, and the debris-ridden site would remain barren for another two hundred years until, appropriately, an opera theater rose on the site. The ruins sheltered many of Bologna's homeless, including some of the boys who later made their way over to Via Mascarella and into the orphanage of S. Onofrio, which was in view of Ercole Bentivoglio's palace and certainly under the protective care of his family. S. Onofrio was far smaller than S. Bartolomeo, housing a *famiglia* of less than two dozen. In 1568, the *confratelli* who had started it bought a house and began renovations to accommodate its staff and boys. Entering from under the portico on Via Mascarella, a boy came not into a loggia-ringed courtyard, but directly into a large room that served as a public space and kitchen outfitted with pots and pans. From here he could enter a small chapel or the refectory, where he ate at one of three tables. He likely could not enter the so-called *massaro's* (overseer's) room where the confraternity stored various goods and where there was a bed for the *guardiano* and his wife. Beyond these rooms and out a back door there was a yard of sorts with a small pergola, a stable, and a room in which to store firewood and kindling. Underneath the kitchen was a cantina for the flasks of oil and wine and many other kinds of tubs, barrels, and bushel measures used to collect and store food. The boys all slept on the second floor. In keeping with Bologna's architectural vernacular, there was a small dormitory over the portico; the city's characteristic porticos had first developed in the twelfth century when a flood of university students hit the city and were lodged in second-floor rooms built out over the street. A larger dormitory beside this held most of the home's sixteen beds. Both of these rooms had locks fitted into the doors. Leading off of that and directly above the kitchen was a smaller room with a bed: more private and certainly warmer in winter, this was most likely where the chaplain slept.[11]

Whether large or small, most homes aimed to blunt the abstractions of institutional staff with the fictions of family life. The *confratelli* who ran the homes as rectors, visitors, and accountants often wanted the "father" title for themselves. So, for instance, S. Bartolomeo di Reno initially drafted statutes that described the *confratelli* as the boys' parents and obligated them to visit frequently. But in practical terms, the father and mother of Ruggiero's very extended surrogate family were the *guardiano* and *guardiana*, usually a married couple who lived in the Abbandonati home. Since most boys had grown up in situations where one parent (perhaps both) was dead, in prison, at war, or absent, this was an unfamiliar domestic arrangement. Orphanages struggled between ideal and reality on this point, believing that a resident couple could provide a model for the boys, but equally concerned that they might defraud the place by inviting their own family and friends to the orphanage table, and perhaps suspecting that the kind of couples who would take on such demanding work might not make the best fathers and mothers. Some couples confirmed this low estimate by remaining only a few months before leaving or being sacked, and in any event, few remained for more than a few years.[12]

We can read the suspicions of S. Bartolomeo's *confratelli* in the many scratched-out deletions and emendations to their draft statutes. They initially thought that the ideal *guardiano* should be over 40 and so well-cooled (in Aristotelian terms) in his passions that the flesh could not tempt him—the first draft even prohibited him from having a female companion. But some *confratelli* realized that a single male might raise suspicions in a home full of boys regardless of his age, so they scratched this out and allowed him a wife. But *only* a wife—the *guardiana* had to be beyond her childbearing years so that all her energies could be directed to the boys and so that S. Bartolomeo's food wouldn't end up going to her own children. The couple were to live in a separate apartment that had no access to the boys' dormitory beyond a small internal window through which they passed food to the boys and staff on the other side. If the wife were ever caught alone in the dormitories—or indeed in any room on the orphanage side—both she and her husband were to be thrown out immediately.

These statutes were written before S. Bartolomeo built the new quarters described above, and in the event the *confratelli* seem to have thought better of these restrictions. They may have had a more realistic view of their own limitations as well. Taking on the father role for themselves required them to come to the home more frequently than was practicable for most merchants, professionals, and patricians. The confraternity wanted them there every day, but the repeated reminders of this obligation in minute books suggest that most visitors took a somewhat looser view of things. They remained careful in their choice of *guardiano*, however, and when the job came available they reviewed a number of applicants, requiring references, and subjected candidates to the same level of scrutiny that the boys themselves received. At one point when forty-seven of S. Bartolomeo's *confratelli* gathered for a meeting couldn't decide on the basis of reports which candidate of three they ought to hire, they called both the men and their wives in for interviews on the spot.[13] And they were even flexible when it came to the relationship between the *guardiano* and *guardiana*. When the Abbandonati's *guardiano* proved to be a little *pazzo* (mad) in 1550, the home's administrators fired him and recruited a priest and his 60-year-old mother as replacements.[14]

The couple divided their duties according to convention, with the *guardiana* and one or two assistants cooking, cleaning, laundering, and making the beds in the home's dormitory. The couple nurtured the youngest boys who, for all they had seen and experienced, were no doubt still somewhat anxious and unsure of themselves in their new home. The Abbandonati wanted them to raise the boys with "that affection and love as though they were their dearest sons."[15] The women should seldom be out of the home during the day (and certainly never for more than a day at a time) and had to be available all night, when the boys would no doubt be the most lonely and upset. Each morning one or the other went through the dormitories waking the boys where they slept, most often two to a bed. They made sure that Ruggiero and his companions washed their faces and put on their smocks and shoes, and then allowed the boys into the refectory, where they could eat a little bread for breakfast. There at table Ruggiero would meet some of the other staff. In homes with two to three dozen boys, like S. Onofrio and S. Giacomo, the couple did much of the work themselves. The seventy-five to one hundred boys at S. Bartomomeo di Reno and the 150 to 180 at the Abbandonati required more helpers and this blunted the couple's role as surrogate parents. Regardless of size, all homes had at least a priest and one or more teachers. These adult males also moderated the parental authority of the *guardiano* and *guardiana*, particularly since they were certainly more educated than that couple and possibly of a higher social standing as well.[16]

Despite these limitations on his authority, the *guardiano* had ultimate responsibility for affairs in the home. At breakfast he told Ruggiero where he would be spending the day. There weren't a great many options: the youngest boys went to classes in the orphanage, and the older ones went to work, either in workshops in the city or sometimes in the home itself.

After eating, Ruggiero and most of the two dozen boys who had entered in the past year followed the teacher to the room appointed for classes. For the rest of the day until dinner, Ruggiero and his companions would be in the teacher's care, learning from books and engaging in some recreation.[17] Both Florence and Bologna had well-established traditions of public education and in both cities many children also learned through proprietorial schools or the charitable Schools of Christian Doctrine. At the beginning of our period only about one-third of Florentine or Venetian boys normally received a basic education, so on this score entering the orphanage had improved Ruggiero's chance to learn reading, writing, and the commercial math skills of *abbaco*. If he was adept, he could go even further.[18] The Abbandonati and S. Bartolomeo di Reno actually had a number of teachers for the scores of boys in their care. The Abbandonati statutes projected at least three, teaching progressively more advanced materials to ever-smaller classes.

Ruggiero would begin with the first teacher, *lettore primo*, who taught the basics of Christian Doctrine and ensured that the boys knew their prayers, the Apostles' Creed, and the Ten Commandments. *Lettore primo* also arranged the readings during morning and evening meals, doing this himself or appointing one of the older boys if necessary. Like the mistress of novices in the nearby conservatory of the Pietà, he likely used one of the small manuals of Christian Doc-

trine produced by confraternities for their Sunday School classes. A manual published in Bologna around this time catechized children by having them memorize questions and answers on basic doctrine. They learned the creed and prayers
that would serve in personal, family, and corporate devotions through the rest
of their lives, but the text rounded this out with social and sexual lessons to govern their lives as mature Christians in the world. They memorized the works of
corporal and spiritual charity, but also "The Four Sins that God will Avenge":
voluntary homicide, sodomy, oppression of the poor, and failing to pay a worker
his wages. They encountered the Three Enemies (the Devil, the World, and the
Flesh) who would assault them as they matured into men and the Three Powers of the Soul (Intellect, Memory, and Will) that would help them fight back.
If the boys' attention flagged or memory failed, *confratelli* could buy inexpensive
broadsheets of moral codes that itemized this same message of chaste social dis-
cipleship in a few dozen rules and post them on the school room walls. The
broadsheets reminded the boys to observe feasts and fasts, to offer prayers, and
to respect relics and clerics, but also to keep from gambling and blasphemy, to
never spend more than they earned, and to avoid prostitutes, theaters, and
lawyers.[19]

More ambitious or well-funded teachers could also draw on popular works
like an edition of *Epistole e Evangeli*, a large traditional text that gave the Gospel
and Epistle readings for the Mass (often with an explanatory homily) or perhaps
the early-fourteenth-century *Fior di Virtù*, whose forty chapters catalogued virtues and vices through a combination of legends, maxims, and cautionary tales.
Selections from these texts, from lives of the saints, or from other spiritual works
were read out during the morning and evening meals by *lettore primo* or a boy he
appointed.[20]

If Ruggiero proved as quick-witted as his mother Rosa and Girolamo Honesti claimed, he could move rapidly into the classroom of *lettore secondo* and begin learning basic reading and writing. Promotion and advancement through
schools generally was based on skills acquisition and a willingness to pay fees.
With fees not an issue in the orphanage, Ruggiero could rise as quickly as his
abilities merited. Reading was considered the easier skill and the one more necessary for survival as an artisan, yet many boys were never able to do more than
sign their names. *Lettore secondo* may have used what contemporary Venetian
teachers described as *libri de batagia*, chivalric romances of battling knights, in
order to get their boys more interested in reading. These were the very *novelle*
that conservatories fought to keep out of the hands of their girls, but parents

liked them for their boys, and they were widely used in many civic and proprietorial schools. These stories spilled out of the books to become the imaginative currency of street ballads, traveling theater, and popular poetry. Their easier morality of stolen kisses and adulterous courtly love contrasted to the moralizing *Fior di Virtù*, but a middle ground could be found in the equally popular and more recent *Vita di Marco Aurelio*, a vernacular text that its courtier author Antonio de Guevera (ca. 1480–1545) claimed to have translated from a classical Latin biography of the emperor that he had found among texts collected by Cosimo de Medici. This was the *studia humanitatis* in translation, history teaching philosophy by example in a historical narrative heavily larded with maxims that demonstrated the key modes of rhetoric. The pseudo-classical text was wildly popular in schools across Italy and through Europe, and may have found its way into the classrooms at the Abbandonati and S. Bartolomeo di Reno.[21]

If Ruggiero picked up reading quickly and easily, he might be allowed to stay in school to learn writing. He would likely begin with *mercantesca*, the script used by merchants and bookkeepers in their records, and often favored by Italians as they wrote their personal letters or diary-like *libri di riccordi*. Depending on his skills and prospects, he might then be introduced to the humanist chancery cursive scripts that had emerged in the fifteenth century but had started to spread rapidly after the development of printing. Through the sixteenth century, Italians came to favor this far more readable and beautiful script for correspondence and public documents. Yet it was hard to learn, and orphanages may have decided that they could not afford to invest the time it took to master. One sixteenth-century author estimated that most conventional techniques took two or three years to learn, though this was in the context of advertising his own far easier method that a bright student could master in three months and that even an average student could learn in about half a year.[22]

Oddly, the duties assigned the Abbandonati's teachers do not include *abbaco*, the merchant arithmetic that taught future craftsmen, masters, and accountants how to balance their books. Florence was a center of *abbaco* teaching, and from the fourteenth century Italian communes had been hiring Florentine masters to teach in communally supported schools and so ensure that they would not lack for well-trained merchants and bookkeepers. *Abbaco* training did not center on an abacus, but aimed to build an ability to use pen and paper, arithmetic, algebra, geometry, and algorism to keep accounts and solve business problems ranging from currency exchange and interest calculations to weights and measures. Math books typically posed problems in very concrete terms: if a braccio of lombard cloth costs 5 Florentine lire, what will it be worth in Provencal soldi? If the sickly husband of a pregnant woman writes a will giving his spouse and anticipated heir different percentages of his estate, what happens to his 1,000 lire legacy after he dies? How are the proportions recalculated if she bears twins after he dies? If one twin is female? As tortured as these examples sound, they were precisely the practical problems that young men would face in the future. Depending on the status of the legacies that their own parents may have left them, the boys may already have faced these problems. Florentine students typically began studying *abbaco* after they had mastered reading and writing, and before moving on to grammar. Gaining a working knowledge of *abbaco* took about two years if one went to one of the city's many specialized *abbaco* schools. Given the more specialized skills involved, it is entirely possible that the Abbandonati sent its boys out to such schools rather than try to bring an *abbaco* master onto its own staff.[23]

If Ruggiero was among the bright students, *lettore secondo* would begin teaching him *grammatica*. This was almost certainly in Latin, and learning it carried Ruggiero over a major cultural divide and opened to him a far broader range of occupational possibilities. The most common textbook was called the "Donatus," though it was not the medieval *Ars minor* of Donatus, but a more elementary systematization of it that bypassed metaphysical speculations and prepared students more quickly for the challenge of reading classical sources.[24]

It might take Ruggiero four years to get as far as the grammar text, and by this time only a handful of the two dozen boys who had begun classes with him would still be taking lessons. Studying for much of the day as they did, they likely passed through their schooling more quickly than their peers outside the home who typically took classes for a few hours before returning home or to a workshop to begin working. Ruggiero had by this time received the kind of education that less than one-third of young males in Italy received at schools run by towns, by private schoolmasters, or by religious orders. As religiously motivated volunteer *confratelli* and *consorelle* began teaching afternoon Sunday School classes from the mid-sixteenth century, basic vernacular literacy shot up to almost half the population, including many young women. In Bologna through the 1560s to 1580s, when the number of children in the city ages 5 through 14 ranged from seven to ten thousand, anywhere from three to four thousand young children learned reading, writing, and religion at these Schools of Christian Doctrine. Piarist and Barnabite friars expanded this educational revolution through the next century with more formal charitable schools for the children of artisans, craftsmen, and merchants. Both the Jesuits and the Somaschans had started out teaching the children of these more modest social ranks, but moved by the seventeenth century into becoming "schoolmasters to the upper classes."[25] As the bar rose for the whole population, a relatively advanced education was one means by which an orphanage could improve the chances of one of its wards finding an apprenticeship in a workshop.

Or more. Ruggiero was sharp and had an ambitious mother. With Girolamo Honesti's help, he might well enter a monastery, but his chances would improve dramatically if he could join the small number of boys who were allowed to go on and work with *lettore tertio*. Here Ruggiero would apply his budding Latin skills to the *studia humanitatis*: history, poetry, rhetoric, moral philosophy, mathematics, and advanced grammar. As he mastered these, he would also be introduced to theology, and would start to engage in public exercises like debate, where his learning was put to the test. Ruggiero would be meeting the standards that reformers set—and less often could enforce—for the new model of clergy, and could hope to find the monastery doors now opening for him.

Of course, that new model was seldom encountered on the streets, and in the 1570s remained largely a dream. It is not even clear whether Ruggiero would have encountered the three teachers that the ambitious magistrates projected in 1542, let alone whether his talents or Honesti's alms could take him beyond primary lessons. Yet orphanages definitely placed a high premium on education and took it beyond the basics. Around the time that Ruggiero might have been beginning his studies in the liberal arts, S. Bartolomeo was firing the friar who had come in to teach music to its boys. This did not mean that music was no longer part of the curriculum, however, since seven years later in 1585 S. Bartolomeo hired a full-time *maestro di musica*. The *confratelli* clearly felt there was work enough for its teachers, since around the same time it ordered them to stop teaching privately outside the home, and appointed some of the more capable older boys to help teach the younger ones, likely filling the role of *ripetitori*, the lesser-skilled assistants who drilled boys in grammatical rules and *abbaco* arithmetic.[26] As these *confratelli* were firming up their educational resources, a Bolognese silk merchant was writing a will that would allow smart boys like Ruggiero to take their education to the very highest level. Francesco Pannolini framed his legacy to allow twenty orphans at a time to study toward doctorates at the University of Bologna. The boys were chosen from the foundling home of the Esposti and the orphanages of S. Bartolomeo di Reno and S. Onofrio. Of 146 boys who were Fellows of the Collegio Pannolini from the time it started in 1617 until Benedict XIV suppressed it in 1745, thirty-six came from S. Bartolomeo di Reno and thirty-five from S. Onofrio. Only one-third actually completed their doctorates, most choosing law, but a few taking medicine or philosophy; the rest entered religious orders. Their humble origins did not prevent these boys from taking positions as university professors, secretaries, and medical practioners.[27] This was far more than Valeria di Bartolomeo di Pavia—or, for that matter, Ruggiero di Lorenzo di Castelfocognano—could ever dream of.

While larger homes like S. Bartolomeo di Reno and the Abbandonati could build school rooms and hire specialized teachers, S. Onofrio had more modest resources for its two or three dozen boys. Its single teacher, a priest called the *precetore*, taught reading, writing, grammar, and use of the abacus to all levels of students, and had to be ready to teach everything from the moral lessons of Antoniano and the *Fior di Virtù* to the techniques of public disputation. If there happened to be a lot of students due to a wave of entrants, he could draft some of the older boys as assistants. Since many boys would be out during the day working in workshops or searching for alms, the *precetore* had to teach in the evening or on feast days. While firm, he wasn't to be so severe that the boys began to hate him. He also took the boys' lessons quite literally into the street. On feast days he led the uniformed boys through the streets, singing the psalms and hymns they had been taught in the classroom and keeping an eye on their manners as the group entered one church after another. Every Saturday afternoon he led the boys into the orphanage's adjoining public church, where they recited litanies and penitential psalms for the souls of benefactors and *confratelli*. From time to time he took a few of the better-mannered ones on special trips to the homes of some of S. Onofrio's larger donors and better prospects. The *precetore* was teacher, chaplain, and fundraiser, and, as we will see shortly, this merging came directly out of the kind of work that many of S. Onofrio's boys performed for the orphanage.[28]

Merging duties was common in cash-strapped orphanages. Though many orphanage teachers were actually priests or friars by vocation, all the homes also hired a separate chaplain to confess and communicate the boys at least once every two months, to lead them in daily matins and vespers services, and to give sermons and hold Sunday Masses for the boys and any *confratelli* who might come. Apart from the moral example that he taught and was expected to demonstrate, a resident priest guaranteed prospective donors that the requiem obligations that they loaded onto their legacies would be observed. These obligations inevitably drew the children in as well. Ruggiero had to pray at set times of the day for Duke Francesco and his family, for the late Duke Cosimo, and for all other founders and benefactors of the Abbandonati. He and his companions were also expected to get down on their knees during the times when their governors, the magistrates of the Bigallo, were meeting. His counterparts at S. Onofrio had to start their day with a "De profundis" and end it with a "Misere mei" for one donor, while the boys at S. Giacomo had to follow dinner with a "De profundis" for another.[29] And so it multiplied.

Guardiano, teacher, and priest were all resident in the larger homes, and each had a distinct kind of authority. The *guardiano*'s supreme local authority could easily conflict with the priest's broader social authority, and it could be difficult to balance the latter's insistence on time-consuming religious exercises with the former's efforts to get the work of the home done. *Confratelli* had to adjudicate the frequent disputes, and one reason for having visitors drop by regularly was to make sure that everyone was doing his or her own work, that disputes among the staff were resolved, that the boys were learning what they had to. We might expect the resulting reports to be a mine of detail on daily life, but on most occasions when S. Bartolomeo's visitors were asked how things were going with the children, they replied laconically, "things are going well enough" ("le cose passano assai bene").[30]

But there were exceptions. In 1588, S. Bartolomeo's priest stormed over to the confraternity rector to complain of his treatment by the *guardiano*. The charges that flew back and forth over the next few days were so confusing that the confraternity called nine of the boys in one by one to relate what had happened. At some point the priest had been having a hard time getting the boys to settle down and be quiet for some religious exercise, and in frustration he had accused the *guardiano* of egging them on rather than helping to set the proper example. Thrusting his face at the cleric, the *guardiano* responded, "I don't take orders from a priest!" He then began a slow, deliberate, and loud clapping, like the kind he used in the mornings as he walked through the dormitories waking up the boys. All the boys present immediately began clapping in time as well, shouting insults and mocking the priest until he retreated angrily into the classroom, "accompanied by that noise." This left no question of who the more popular official was, but the *confratelli* could not countenance this kind of deliberate disruption and so fired the *guardiano*. At the same time, however, they laid out a more precise schedule of times for confession, communion, and sermons as a means of keeping priest and *guardiano* out of each other's way.[31]

As Ruggiero grew older, he could look forward to getting out of the home in order to work. None of the orphanages in Bologna and Florence followed the example of conservatories and set up internal workshops, because none placed as great an emphasis on the protective enclosure of their wards.[32] Each had grates over the windows and locks in the door, but none lay out the kind of complicated restrictions that conservatories commonly adopted to keep their wards from walking the streets or readily receiving visitors. S. Bartolomeo likely had a gate-keeper of some sort guarding the entrance to its complex, but of all the orphanages only the Abbandonati seems to have thought strongly enough about its *portinaro* to outline his duties in the statutes. Most of these were conventional: he couldn't leave the door between dawn and midnight, couldn't let boys like Ruggiero go out without a written license from the *guardiano*, and had to lock the boys and staff in over night. More unusually, the authors who drafted the first statutes added some oddly liturgical aspects to his duties, ordering the *portinaro* to make the sign of the cross on all those entering and leaving, to say an Our Father and a Hail Mary together with them, and to sprinkle them with holy water while saying the "Asperges me." The authors may have felt that if their magistracy was going to extend control over all lay and clerical *ospedali* in Florence it might need some way of lending religious legitimacy to its flagship institution. This ersatz ritual was hardly suitable to the home's staff and clientele, and whatever the intentions of these authors, it is unlikely that the *portinaro* kept his holy water for long.

When Ruggiero first passed by the *portinaro* to work, he would likely be collecting alms in Florence's churches, streets, markets, and homes just as conservatory girls did. The Abbandonati statutes had projected a cadre of professional alms collectors, but also offered instructions on how the boys were to behave as they circulated in pairs through Florence's churches collecting alms. Ruggiero and his companion would have to take their hats off on entering, go to the main altar and kneel to offer prayers, stay for the whole Mass if it was in progress, kiss the ground in front of the priest, give a blessing to all who gave alms, and then leave with reverence. Did the authors of these statutes really think their boys could manage this? Apparently not, for they followed these fine rules with stern warnings that the boys weren't to start swearing, gossiping, or mocking others once they hit the street.[33] Regardless, the Abbandonati never did hire alms collectors, and Ruggiero most likely joined with his counterparts at S. Bartolomeo di Reno, S. Onofrio, and S. Giacomo in taking to the streets with his alms box and food bag.

A carpenter had made four small and two larger locking alms boxes for the

Table 4.1. Alms Gathering in S. Bartolomeo di Reno, 1582–1598

	Alms Boxes		Church		Ordinary		Extraordinary	
	Lire	%	Lire	%	Lire	%	Lire	%
1582	1,424	16			685	8	3,813	42
1583–84	2,537	13			326	2	5,270	27
1585	2,534	25			1,634	16	3,549	35
1586	2,929	18			849	5	5,113	32
1588	1,688	15.7			1,380	12.8	3,655	33.9
1589	1,710	13			1,846	14	3,008	23
1590	1,337	20			1,900	9.6	3,684	31.6
1595	1,273	17	113	2	133	2	1,458	20
1596	960	12.5	151	2	1,775	23.2	812	10.6
1597	714	9	99	1	2,224	27	687	8
1598	453	6	131	2	2,003	25	775	6

Source: ASB, PIE, S. Bartolomeo di Reno, ms. 138, cc. 40r–v, 190r–v, 242r–v, 295r–v, 314r–v; ms. 139, cc. 172r–v, 235r–v, 254r–v.
Note: % = percentage of total income.

Abbandonati soon after it opened, and S. Onofrio went even further and commissioned an alms box for each of its two dozen boys to carry, plus a larger one to put in its church. Its boys seem to have been so effective that other confraternities hired them to collect alms on their feast days, giving a portion of the proceeds to the orphanage at the end of the day. As with conservatories, this labor-intensive and systematic activity targeted particular markets, neighborhoods, and churches on certain days. Saturday mornings were an especially good time to go around to the workshops of craftsmen and collect money. The boys were old enough to go out without chaperones, but at the end of the day the *guardiano* checked the boxes closely for any signs of tampering, and recorded what had been gathered. The money each child could take in was as significant for orphanages as it was for conservatories. As Table 4.1 demonstrates, the boys' alms gathering earned from 6 to 25 percent of S. Bartolomeo di Reno's total income through the 1580s and 1590s, and until 1595 it regularly brought in two or three times as much as pledges. For S. Onofrio two decades earlier the amount was even greater; in 1576 the boys' alms gathering brought in 39.5 percent (lire 1,035.16.0), and general alms a further 36.5 percent (lire 955.4.10).[34]

Even more than income, this activity brought in significant amounts of food and other necessities. Like the *fanciulle*, groups of boys took special bags with them to go door to door through every quarter and neighborhood collecting bread or vegetables from shops, private homes, monasteries, and convents. One stronger boy might take a yoke along to string on flasks of wine like traveling vendors did, and a few others might push a cart, particularly when they moved out beyond the city walls into rural areas in order to get firewood from farmers. All of this was coordinated by the *guardiano*, who sent out the teams in the morning and greeted them again at the end of the day. He made sure that boys visited regular donors on schedule to collect on their pledges of oil, bread, or wine. He had to know where the merchants' stalls were, and which squares and streets held markets on which days so that boys could go and get vegetables and fruit. S. Onofrio's *guardiano* sent them to the meat markets on Thursday and Saturday, knowing that there would always be some cuts available at the end of the day that the butcher couldn't save over the following day's closing and then offer for sale again after that. He also got and gave the refrain that was familiar among local institutions looking for charity: "On fish days, fish among the fish-mongers."[35] S. Bartolomeo for its part recommended that the food gatherers fish among the politicians. In the early stages of the famine that crippled many homes in the later 1580s and early 1590s, it told them to go around the palaces of Bologna's senators, many of them located up and down the street from its own quarters on Via Imperiale, in order to shame them into providing for their juvenile neighbors.[36]

Some boys reveled in the chance to get back on the streets and move through the familiar and unfamiliar parts of the city. To control their behavior, the Abbandonati statutes echo conservatory rules against visiting, chatting, or playing. The Florentine home seemed to take a pretty dim view of its boys, because it went on to forbid them from drinking, clowning around or horseplay, sweet-talking fraud, and entrepreneurial free-lance working for their own profit.[37] That notwithstanding, none of the homes provided chaperones to keep the boys in line while on their food patrols. But if some boys found the work liberating, others found the trek for food and alms overly onerous, possibly degrading, and occasionally dangerous. Ruggiero and the Abbandonati boys would have to be cautious and discrete as they went around with their alms boxes. Florentines walking the streets could sometimes turn a corner and find a gauntlet of boys blocking their way with long sticks and demanding payment of a toll. Ruggiero and his companions had to collect in such a way, and in such places, that they wouldn't be identified with these street gang extortionists—hence the strict regulations on their behavior. And while the gangs most often singled out young women, orphanage boys in brightly colored uniforms loaded down with food and rattling alms boxes made a choice target for everything from thieves to apprentices out for a mischievous good time.[38] It all became worse in times of famine. This is likely why S. Bartolomeo's boys refused to go out in 1590, when famine was particularly bad in Bologna. They had a history of resisting this job, and the orphanage had supplemented their efforts with professional alms collectors for decades, sending them into the streets of the city, and also into outlying towns like Faenza, Forli, and Imola, where they sometimes encountered stiff resistance. Priests in some of these towns had sometimes confiscated the alms and refused to hand them over until ordered to by their own bishops. In good times, it was easier and cheaper to send the boys out to work the streets of Bologna, but the boys' early modern strike forced their sponsoring confraternity to send its own members out into the streets and to hire more professional alms gatherers. The boys were soon back on the streets, but attempted a second strike two years later.[39]

But there was more to alms gathering than carrying *cassette* and food bags. At a fairly early stage, Bolognese orphanages realized that even more alms could be generated by using their wards as the lay celebrants of liturgical rituals. All Italian cities dressed their children as angels and put them at the head of celebratory or propitiatory processions that beat the parish bounds or wove from shrine to shrine on feast days. Bologna's *bastardini*—the children from the foundling home of the Esposti—annually marched in white cloaks and angel wings to help celebrate the feast day of their sponsoring confraternity of S. Maria degli Angeli. Florence had a broader tradition of recruiting youths and adolescents into activist youth confraternities and allied religious reform movements, and under Savonarola teams of boys had staged pious processions and patrolled the streets hunting down the card-players and blasphemers who were undermining the holy republic.[40] Under the duchy, that city's merchants did not aim to generate anything more than moral capital out of their poor youths. Perhaps the uncomfortable Savonarolan legacy kept the Medici loyalists who ran the Abbandonati from using their boys in this way. By contrast, Bolognese orphanages made their fresh-scrubbed, well-mannered, and uniformed boys into a cornerstone of institutional finance. S. Onofrio developed a particularly profitable business of funeral attendance and performance of requiem observances.

The idea of using boys as paid mourners may have come to the orphanage's confraternal founders when they first lodged their juvenile charges in the brotherhood's quarters, an old *ospedale* dedicated to the fourth-century saint Onuphrius, whose legend had been frescoed on an exterior wall by Cristoforo da Bologna in the fourteenth century. The Egyptian desert hermit was commonly identified with burials, though less for anything he had done than because two attendant lions had dug his grave.[41] The S. Onofrio boys were not, so far as we can tell, gravediggers. They sang and marched in the procession that brought the body from the home to the gravesite, and then sang again at the service that was later held in a church. The confraternity aimed to support this work by buying uniforms for the boys, by building up the spiritual treasury of its adjoining church of S. Maria Maddalena through indulgences and aggregations to religious orders and to Rome's famous hospital, S. Spirito in Sassia, and by outfitting the church with the liturgical trappings and other equipment needed for funerals and requiems, and even an organ to allow for more impressive sung Masses. The orphanage priest was, of course, available to perform whatever monthly or yearly anniversary Masses a legator might wish, and the boys in their turn would sing at these Masses and also recite the offices. Teachers like S. Onofrio's preceptor and S. Bartolomeo's music master helped prepare the boys for this work by teaching them the appropriate hymns and responses, and by drilling them in the reserved deportment that was proper in processions and requiems. Ultimately, it was the business of funerals that made sense out of the merging of the preceptor's duties as teacher, procession organizer, Mass celebrant, and alms gatherer.[42]

Funerals and requiems were a potentially profitable business that had pitted parish priests against the regular clergy across Europe for centuries, and that had made the former in particular somewhat suspicious of confraternities for at least as long. Confraternities had gotten into the business from at least the twelfth century, and many continued to attract members in part because they acted as burial societies. From the later fifteenth century, as Sharon Strocchia has noted, civic governments across Italy judged women's extravagant funeral mourning disruptive and distasteful, and passed regulations to limit their participation in the processions.[43] Humanist notions of stoic reserve and propriety had already brought educated public opinion to this point. The funeral of a worthy individual was still thought to need large numbers of mourners, but sumptuary regulations typically limited their costs. The timing could not have been better for the wards of the newly opened orphanages. Well-regulated and somber children in uniform were impressive as public mourners, and could be recruited for less than the cost of professional mourners or clergy. The fact that they had themselves lost their fathers or mothers or both made all the more poignantly dramatic their taking the role of the *puer senex* (aged child).

Their choreographed mourning also targeted directly a very different association of youths and funerals. Young boys had more often been found hauling bodies out of graves than helping them in. The public enemies ranging from traitors hanged on a beam to moneylenders who had died in their beds could rightly fear that shortly after the last shovel full of dirt had been put on their grave, a gang of youths would dig it all out again and lift out the body for a ritualized game of humiliation. Dragged down the streets, hung up in public, hacked to pieces, thrown to the dogs, and finally tossed in the river or on unconsecrated ground: this was the fate awaiting a few unpopular individuals after interment of their corpses. While it was all strictly speaking illegal, the youth gangs who performed these rituals frequently enjoyed the enthusiastic support of their neighbors and the tacit approval of their civic governments.[44] Yet the tide was slowly turning on this carnivalesque mob violence through the sixteenth century, and some governments and social reformers were growing anxious about its unpredictability and the ease with which such violence could be manipulated and turned against legitimate authorities. Enlisting adolescent boys as funeral mourners set them up as models of order and restraint rather than disorder and abandon, and so underscored the experiment in social engineering that the orphanages, on one level, represented. At the same time, highlighting these opposite dynamics of interment and disinterment allowed confraternities to send a subtle message to civic authorities: redeemed from the streets and educated in manners and social responsibility, abandoned boys could become supports of the governing regime. Left to their own devices, these same boys could end up as the unruly apprentices of a criminal and potentially rebellious underclass.

All three of Bologna's orphanages catered to the potentially profitable trade. In January 1574, the month in which S. Onofrio opened new quarters for the boys, 27.3 percent of income was derived from funerals, as compared to 0.75 percent of income from its share of what boys earned in craftsmen's workshops; through 1576, funerals generated 17.7 percent of S. Onofrio's income (lire 465.15.2) and salaries only 2 percent (lire 52.15.00). These figures understate the economic impact of funeral attendance, since many families paid with a few dozen loaves of bread or some white or yellow wax.[45] Similarly, S. Bartolomeo di Reno derived 15.8 percent of its income from this activity in the later 1580s, twice what it took from boys' salaries in workshops.[46] Competition for this business may have been one of the reasons why S. Bartolomeo adopted the new and more dramatic red uniform that would make its boys more impressive in processions. Presenting a *bella figura* in one funeral would certainly lead to more inquiries and commissions. This alone justified sending the boys out regularly in small processions with a cleric-teacher to discretely solicit business. Funerals normally brought the boys of S. Onofrio into the streets a few times a week, though in times of plague this could rise to every one or two days.

When famine hit the city in 1590, Archbishop Gabriele Paleotti dangled the promise of a license to attend at funerals in front of the *confratelli* of S. Giacomo in order to convince them to turn their pilgrims' hostel into an orphanage. Paleotti was hitting two birds with one stone, addressing both the need to bury the dead and the need to care for the children the dead had left behind. S. Giacomo's orphanage opened within months, and one of the first acts undertaken by its boys was attendance at the funeral of the patrician Orazio Bombelli. Like early modern ambulance chasers, S. Giacomo's *confratelli* pursued the sick and dying with a vengeance; signing the boys up for funerals or anniversary requiems was one of the few things that members of the confraternity had to do. In their efforts to attract legacies, *confratelli* built a new church in 1606–7, and offered a range of funerary and requiem services. Three accounts of the first half of the seventeenth century show how quickly this business expanded. Work that the boys performed in artisans' shops represented just under 13 percent of total income in 1612, falling to 7.7 percent in 1646 and 3.7 percent by 1652. In the same period, income generated through legacies that required some requiem observances rose from 12 to 51 to 60 percent. Moreover, through this period, gross annual income almost doubled, from lire 2,996.17.8 to 5,375.2.4.[47]

The boys did more than walk in funerary processions. S. Bartolomeo's musically trained boys sang motets and *laudi* at the open air shrine of the Madonna delle Asse behind the Palazzo Communale every Saturday and on every Marian feast day on commission of the chaplain of one of the city's traditional governing bodies, the Anziani; this wasn't a requiem request, and the donor didn't want attention brought to himself.[48] S. Onofrio's aggressive solicitation of business across the city and locally extended to such traditional parochial duties as bringing the Eucharist to the sick and dying, an activity that further connected them to the S. Onufrius legend and also generated alms. They also brought in painters and colored paper to stage an especially lavish festival on the feast day of S. Mary Magdalene, after whom their church and governing confraternity were named. When people of the neighborhood began bypassing the parish church a few doors away in order to go the orphanage's chapel, things got nasty. Both parish and orphanage tried disrupting the other's services by staging competing sermon cycles and by ringing their bells vigorously at strategic times to drown out the sound of the competitor's priest or preacher. Mediation efforts by some of the company's patrician members began in 1590, and by 1609 the warring parties required mediation from Rome, where the Sacra Rota set out eight rules governing their mutual relations. The rules showed how far the confraternity had elbowed its way into traditional parochial *cura animarum*. The boys would now have to take at least their Easter communion in the parish church, they couldn't bring the Eucharist to the sick and dying, and the priest had to be invited to attend at the burials of any of the parish dead. Tensions and competition continued nonetheless, to the point that the Camera Apostolica had to re-issue the rules in 1692.[49]

Ruggiero di Lorenzo di Castelfocognano may not have marched in Florentine funeral processions for more practical reasons than these. Most immediately, the confraternity of the Misericordia acted as the city's ambulance and burial service, and the Misericordia brothers were unlikely to share their virtual monopoly.[50] Beyond that, however profitable for the institution, funerals and requiems were not work that prepared the boys for much beyond the priesthood. By late adolescence, it would be all the more difficult to resolve the question of a boy's future if he hadn't put in his time as an apprentice. This was where the *confratelli* earned the right to call themselves the orphans' fathers, since they took on the parental duty of finding apprenticeships for the boys. And where a father might have to do this only a few times with his own boys, some of whom might end up in his own shop or farmed out to relatives, the *confratelli* had to be looking out continually for new apprenticeship opportunities as new boys arrived periodically in the homes.

How did one do this? In his effort to frame a perfect republic, contemporary Venetian author Giovanni Maria Memmo emphasized that boys needed to learn a trade at an early age, before inactivity turned to laziness. They should start working by about age 7, when most normally left the domestic sphere overseen by mothers and began their first step into the public sphere controlled by fathers. This broader transfer of authority no doubt encouraged some orphanages to prefer boys of this age over those who were either older or younger. Memmo added that since a man is more likely to perfect the art that he had a natural inclination for, fathers should expose their boys to a number of different *arti* and *essercitij*, so that the child could determine his inclinations and abilities and choose wisely. Fathers should not selfishly force their children to follow them in their own occupation, since as often as not, these boys ended up discontented and died ignorant.[51]

The larger number of boys in their care narrowed the options for *confratelli*, but statutes echoed Memmo in enjoining them to consider the boys' skills and abilities before placing them with craftsmen. Florentine and Bolognese guilds do not appear to have resisted putting *abbandonati* into apprenticeships as their Venetian counterparts did. While the Abbandonati orphanage was in the care of patrician magistrates, guild masters were the backbone of the confraternities that operated Bologna's orphanages, and they could expect to be called on frequently to test the boys and possibly find places for them. They came regularly to the orphanage to discuss individual boys with the teachers, priest, and *guardiano*, and to set their own eye on the children, bearing in mind the needs of masters they knew who could take on an apprentice. If Ruggiero di Lorenzo di Castelfocognano were a boy of moderate abilities or prospects, he might even be put into domestic service.[52]

Memmo argued that fathers should not be ashamed to put their boys in a house with another master, suggesting that at certain social levels the boarding out of apprentices was not widely practiced. In Memmo's view, the boys would more likely become better masters as a result of living in someone else's care than if they stayed in the parental shadow. Nervous parents ought to be more concerned with ensuring that the master was a moral man who wouldn't teach bad habits or involve the boy in illegal activities. They should also ensure that he was humane and not cruel like the many masters who beat their charges severely, sometimes to the point of injury, illness, or death.[53]

Orphanage staff and confraternal or magisterial supervisors were not in such a hurry to unload their charges that they ignored questions of shame or security when it came to apprenticeships. They looked for "worthy" ones. S. Bartolomeo di Reno, for example, insisted that supervisors avoid the unstable weaving trade, unprofitable occupations like spinning, and any dishonorable crafts. Beyond that, it echoed Memmo in cautioning against work that the boy didn't find enjoyable. A similar concern with the institution's reputation and with the orphans' long-term prospects led Amsterdam's Burgerweeshuis orphanage to forbid its charges from shipping out with the East India Company.[54] In both instances, these institutions turned their backs on some local employers who were often short of workers because the *confratelli* felt the work was not honorable. There was at least as much concern that the supervisors not make themselves vulnerable to embarrassing charges of exploitation. All the homes firmly prohibited the *confratelli* or magistrates from employing the boys in their own homes or workshops. Rather, as guardians they were to place the boys carefully and then visit them regularly in their new workplaces to ensure that the boys were behaving themselves and that they were not being mistreated. In the early stages of his apprenticeship, an orphanage boy might expect to see an orphanage visitor as much as once a week, but after a few months these visits would drop off sharply. In order to preserve the dignity of his office, the visitor's role was limited to investigating the boy's performance, deportment, and treatment. Collecting the boy's salary was left to an employee—S. Onofrio's *guardiano* spent part of his days going from shop to shop for this purpose—or to one of the confraternity's financial officials.[55]

If Ruggiero was unproductive, uncooperative, unhealthy, or desperately unhappy he might come back to the orphanage. Yet if his own misbehavior triggered that return, it would not be a happy homecoming. The boy's new home with a master was encircled with an invisible enclosure, and he could no more leave without formal permission than if he were in the institution itself. The ambitious idealists who penned the Abbandonati's statutes freely consigned to the galleys all those boys who for laziness, insubordination, or other *difetti* (defects) were dismissed by their new masters. If they had the temerity to flee, they would be permanently exiled from city and state—though this was just putting the seal of law on something the boy had achieved with his own two feet, and it was largely unenforceable anyway.[56] Statutes seldom spelled out either crimes or penalties, and seemed to assume that most masters and boys would simply follow the commonly accepted standards of the day. These could be quite rough, for apprentices were not known for their restraint or polite manners. Orphanages dealt with this discretely, particularly if the boys did not live with their masters.

Religious holidays were often wild times when apprentices from different shops and even different trades would get together for games, conversation, and various sorts of trouble. Memmo complained that the young boys' carousing overshadowed the spiritual purposes of these feast days and recommended that at the very least they go to church first thing in the morning. Orphanages went even further, by keeping the boys in for the day and using the opportunity to give them their lessons.[57] Even those who had spent the minimum time with *lettore primo* or the preceptor could learn more of reading, writing, and keeping the books of the shop or store. In this, orphanages implicitly followed Memmo, who argued that someone who didn't know how to read, to write in his mother tongue, and to handle numbers lacked what it was to be a human being ("mancare del proprio esser dell'huomo"). Virtues, *arte*, and letters are, he wrote, what make us different from "gli altri animali" (all the other animals) and orphanages aimed to ensure that as many of their boys as possible achieved this balance.[58]

Where, then, did boys like Ruggiero end up? Most of his companions at the Abbandonati worked with weavers, though some turned to other cloth trades or construction.[59] Bolognese boys ended up in a range of crafts, merchandising, services, and painting. Boys in other institutions like Florence's Innocenti apprenticed in a similar variety of shops and workshops, and at least some seem to have moved from one shop to another in a protracted search for the work or master best suited to their own abilities. Bartolomeo, called "Abbracci" by his friends, worked with at least four different silk spinners from his first assignment in 1655 at age 9, while around the same time Domenico "Beco" began with a tailor but eventually worked with seven different masters in at least three trades, and Lorenzo "Grillo" began with spinner and ended up as a servant in the home of the cleric Carlo Altoviti.[60]

Many apprentices continued to live in the orphanage itself, as much to save money as to save their morals. The fee owed to a master was lower if room and board were excluded, and as with *fanciulle* whose piecework earnings went to their conservatories, the boys could pass on at least some of their earnings to the orphanage to cover their maintenance. That said, the amounts earned from boys' wages in Bolognese orphanages were nowhere near as great as what they could earn from either alms gathering or liturgical services. Through the 1580s and 1590s, earnings from boys' wages comprised 6 to 10 percent of S. Bartolomeo's income. The picture in Florence is less clear. In the same sample years just noted, boys' paid work generated between 2.6 and 5.3 percent of the Abbandonati's income. Yet an undated account that seems to come from earlier in the sixteenth century paints a very different picture. Of 187 boys then at the home, 80 were out in *botteghe* (shops) learning crafts and doing other work, and their work brought in 52.9 percent of the home's income.[61] Part of the difference here lies in accounting. The earlier list omits both the proceeds of the alms boxes and also the funds remitted to the Abbandonati from other Florentine *ospedali* under the terms laid down when Duke Cosimo established it in 1542. Yet beyond that, the Abbandonati was boarding more of its boys outside the home by 1590. The old Ospedale Broccardi on Via S. Gallo was so overcrowded that many boys were getting sick and some were dying in the close, airless rooms. Famine brought in more boys and made the old shelter only worse. While they waited for Duke Ferdinand to agree to let them move over to the S. Caterina convent by the city

wall, the Abbandonati administrators boarded some of the healthier boys outside of the institution in private homes. They may also have let some of the
healthy working boys take room and board with their masters, sacrificing part
of their earnings as a result.[62]

Those working boys who continued living at the Abbandonati home returned
by early evening in time for a meal. They may have taken their larger meal of
the day around noon at their master's table, but even the lighter meal offered to
them in the evening was more substantial than what girls ate in their conservatories, with regular helpings of cheese, meat, and fish adding protein to a diet
otherwise heavy in bread and legumes. When he reached the age of 10 or 12,
Ruggiero went to the doctor for a physical examination and, if he was deemed
ready for it, he would be encouraged to begin fasting on Fridays and through
Lent. This meant skipping breakfast and lunch and having only a simple salad
or some apples at dinner. If he wanted to try fasting at a younger age, he would
be allowed some watered wine and a bit of bread to see him through, but if he
was still in the home by age 18 or 20 there would be no such indulgence and also
no excuse for avoiding the Lenten fast.

Homes generally worked hard to ensure that the boys received the diet that
their gender and station required, and they were helped in this by their sharecroppers and donors. S. Bartolomeo di Reno followed contemporary patricians
and institutions in buying up land in the rural community of S. Giovanni in Persiceto northwest of the city, and by 1588 had at least four sharecroppers there
turning over half of their yields. An anonymous donor to S. Giacomo gave 1,000
lire in 1627 with the stipulation that it be invested and that the income be spent
buying fish or meat for the boys to eat on Tuesdays. Up to that point, they ate
that well only on Thursday or Sunday, thanks largely to what butchers and fish-
mongers gave when the boys came with their bags and baskets at the end of the
market day. Fearing perhaps that the donation would be folded into general revenues, the donor warned that if S. Giacomo failed to give the meat to its boys,
the legacy would revert to the boys of S. Onofrio.[63]

Those boys already enjoyed food that thoughtful donors put on their table.
Festive customs and seasonal availability determined what arrived in the S. Onofrio kitchen. Through 1574, for example, donors sent cheeses, meat, eggs, and
pies, together with the more common gifts of bread, flour, wine, and oil. At the
end of February, the boys went door to door and collected eggs, cheeses, and
various pies or *torte* for a carnival feast ("per fare carnevale"). At Easter they collected even more eggs—291, according to the account book—and some *torte;*

Alessandro Gandolfo provided them with a live lamb, and Francesco Calice sent over a quantity of beef. Gandolfo came through at Christmas as well, this time with some pork, and Laura Bentivoglio and Piero Rastelo provided more pork and some beef for that feast. Private individuals like Gandolfo and Bentivoglio were dependable donors of meat and bread who wanted to make sure that the boys would enjoy a decent *festa*. While Gandolfo's gifts were modest, Laura Bentivoglio sent baskets of legumes, containers of flour, and loads of firewood every few weeks from the imposing palace just up the street. With relatives sitting on the confraternal governing board and serving periodically as S. Onofrio's rector, she considered this group of orphaned and abandoned boys to be her own particular charge, and periodically nominated one for entry. Officials were expected to be generous with food, and those serving S. Onofrio did not disappoint. Groups based in the neighborhood might feel the same way; the *confratelli* of S. Sebastian sent quantities of cheeses over from their *casa* a few blocks away as a way of celebrating the feast day of their patron saint, while the guild of Salaroli gave sacks of flour a few days before Easter. In times of need, S. Onofrio sent individual *confratelli* to visit the guilds directly and appeal for food, targeting those whose members more often drew apprentices and laborers from the orphanage, and possibly those whose own liability had been eased when the orphanage took in the orphaned child of a dead guild member.[64]

Donors of treats wanted the boys to have a party, but there was also more to their generosity. Food was one of the most common markers of class, and these Bolognese and Florentines still worked with medieval codes that stipulated that different classes ate different foods as much for natural as for cultural reasons. When nobles and patricians ate white bread, artisans a brown loaf, and laborers a coarse dark bread, it was not just cost that determined their selection. Mothers and doctors knew that a laborer's tough constitution required a rougher bread to keep it going; white bread would not have enough substance or nutrition. By the same token, a laborer's loaf would be indigestible for a person of better breeding. This code carried on to legumes, vegetables, fruits, and even garlic which, growing underground, was considered the very badge of the lower classes who lived close to the earth.[65] The social politics of diet helped set the orphanage table. The regents of contemporary Amsterdam's Burgerweeshuis orphanage were obligated by their own statutes to spend more per person on food than their counterparts at the same city's Aalemoezeniersweeshuis. The former institution sheltered the orphans of craftsmen and citizens, while the latter sheltered the orphans of the poor and indigents. The regents were true to

their statutes, spending over 50 percent more per child on their charges to ensure that these enjoyed meats, vegetables, and sweets—particularly sugar, for
which the Dutch were developing an insatiable sweet tooth—that the indigent
children, facing bowls of gruel meal after meal, could only dream of.[66]

That said, Italian orphanage diets and food budgets are extremely difficult to
describe and calculate since so much was built on donations and the rents in kind
offered by sharecroppers, and both of these were often recorded imprecisely if
at all. More to the point, in the absence of a continuous registry of boys, it is
impossible to determine how many mouths were consuming the quantities of
grain, wine, and meat that are listed.[67]

Culinary treats evaporated in times of famine. Even staples were hard to come
by as doors shut in the boys' faces, pledges of flour and bread went unfulfilled,
and prices rose. As conditions began worsening through 1588 and into 1589,
S. Bartolomeo di Reno took stock: through the first half of 1589, its boys had
collected 855 kilograms of bread, but eaten 12,105. They had collected almost
5,000 liters of wine, but drunk almost 16,000. The situation had become desperate almost overnight. In 1588, the home spent lire 3,718.3 on bread and wine
alone, but took in lire 6,100.05 in alms and boys' salaries. A year later bread and
wine had soared to lire 4,936.04, and alms had collapsed to lire 4,810.12.[68] The
crisis was compounded by an ambitious purchase of real estate in S. Giovanni in
Persiceto that S. Bartolomeo had made on the very eve of the famine. The farm
had cost more than double all the *ospedale*'s property purchases over the previous twenty-five years, and S. Bartolomeo counted on its rental revenues to carry
the remaining loan, but the famine threw over all its careful calculations. Further liquidations made no significant impact, and with the succession of *anni ster-
ili* the urgent need to feed and clothe the orphanage *famiglia* finally forced it to
sell the property again. Marc Antonio Fibbie, a member of the board of Twelve
Conservators who guarded S. Bartolomeo's finances and someone who had also
been involved in S. Onofrio for many years, bought it for the original purchase
price less than a year later, paying part of the price directly to the creditors in
cash and part to S. Bartolomeo in food. By the end of October 1591, with the
disappointment of yet another meager harvest, the *confratelli* authorized 500 lire
to buy food for the boys "who don't have bread, so they can live," another 35 lire
to gild the cross of the flagellant *fratelli* who would process through the city seeking more alms, and a sum to make an "honorable" funeral shroud to cover the
boys who died of hunger.[69]

The hunger years of the late 1580s and early 1590s had a profound impact on charitable institutions that housed large numbers around Europe, and some of them adopted strategies or rules meant to prevent a recurrence of the crisis that had almost resulted in their collapse. S. Bartolomeo's *confratelli* threatened in the depth of the famine to simply open the doors and let the boys free. When that raised no public response, they approved a plan to approach noble and patrician families and ask each to shelter a single boy until the famine had passed. Both of these ideas had been raised at different times by promoters of Bologna's central poorhouse, the Ospedale dei Mendicanti, and in neither case did the threats or ingenious alternatives gain a positive response. Members of the senate ignored an invitation to attend a special meeting in September 1593, and even after more liquidations, emergency strategy meetings, and appeals to the archbishop, the visitor was still reporting that things would only get better when the children had enough to eat.[70] Smaller S. Onofrio required that any grain removed from its internal storehouse be immediately replaced, and this strategy together with its far smaller size seems to have allowed it to weather the period of 1588–93 with less distress than S. Bartolomeo.

Far to the north, Amsterdam's Burgerweeshuis took a more businesslike approach by entering into futures trading on the Baltic grain trade and requiring its regents to have a minimum of a year's requirements in storage at all times. According to Anne McCants, the experiment in buying grain futures ultimately increased the orphanage's food costs, but even had they known this in advance, the regents would likely have been willing to pay for the peace of mind that it gave.[71] In late-sixteenth-century Bologna, as Matt Sneider has shown, *ospedali* like S. Francesco and S. Biagio (for pilgrims) and S. Maria della Morte and S. Maria della Vita (both for the sick) traded farms and plots in order to get rid of low-producing lands, consolidate far-flung holdings into larger farms, and so improve their ability to supply their own needs. More followed S. Onofrio's practice of stockpiling grain, and S. Maria della Vita and della Morte became major players in the city's grain market. Though not liquid capital, land proved to be a remarkably fluid resource. Heavy mortgaging of their properties helped *ospedali* weather the subsistence crisis of the early 1590s, and many began redeeming these mortgages by the beginning of the next decade.[72]

Bodily Disciplines

In the Abbandonati home, Ruggiero followed some of the same domestic rhythms that conservatory girls did, though he was not expected to do any domestic duties. The deputy nurse ensured that he had a bath at least once a week and had his head washed when required; she also aired out the dormitories so that miasmic vapors could not collect and make him sick. If he did fall ill, Ruggiero took rest and medication in the Abbandonati infirmary. In a smaller home like S. Onofrio, the battle against head lice was waged by the *guardiana*, who washed the boys' heads in a great brass basin every two weeks. A professional doctor on retainer handled serious illnesses, visiting the home when necessary and likely examining the health of boys nominated for entry. Were Ruggiero to become more desperately ill, he might be sent on to Florence's S. Maria Nuova hospital; his Bolognese counterpart might go to the hospital of S. Maria della Vita or, more likely, be returned to family or guardians until he regained health.[73] For all that, plague could throw the home into chaos. Adding to its *annus horribilis* of 1588–89, when the *guardiano* was sacked for challenging the priest and property was sold to buy food, S. Bartolomeo had to contend with plague. Its first victim may have been the new *guardiano*, Horatio Mangardini, dead in March 1589, only three months after taking the job. In view of the immediate crisis in the home, he was quickly replaced by Giovanni di Bianchi, one of the three candidates who had lost out to Mangardini. Thinking perhaps that the orphanage doctor Alfonso Riccobone hadn't sufficiently scrutinized the ten boys accepted the previous December, officials replaced him with another, Hieronimo Bellintani.

A year later, company historian Alessandro Stiatici wrote of the plague in his chronicle of S. Bartolomeo. Stiatici claimed that some of the new boys had been infected with "tigna & altri diversi mali." Also known as *tegna* or *tarma*, *tigna*'s symptoms included head rashes and open sores with worms that any but the most negligent doctor, visitors, and *guardiano* should have seen immediately. Still, some contagious boys came into the beds of S. Bartolomeo's dormitory, where almost a hundred slept. In Stiatici's graphic account, like "a sick sheep who infects the whole sheep pen," their worms wriggled across the bedcovers and into the brains of the healthy boys sleeping in the shut-up dormitory and infected them. Stiatici's diagnosis may be imprecise and dramatic, but he had watched the plague march through the home claiming one after another. The priest and teacher both fell deathly ill, as did the new *guardiano* Giovanni di Bianchi. While they recovered, Bianchi's wife and 20-year-old son did not. The contagion then hit the professional alms collector and the *invitatore*, a man who ran errands through the city including delivering door to door the written notices calling confraternity members to their meetings. This brought the plague uncomfortably close to the homes of individual *confratelli*, and the *massaro* and Doctor Bellintani acted quickly to contain the rapidly spreading contagion by isolating the worst cases in the home's infirmary. Remarkably, none of the boys died. The last victim, alms collector Thomaso Belfante, died in late October, leaving three daughters. S. Bartolomeo di Reno dowered these girls, but there is no record of them entering its companion institution, S. Maria del Baraccano, when that conservatory next accepted girls the following April.[74]

Cleaning the soul was more important than cleaning the body, since hell would burn more intensely than any fever. Beyond daily matins and vespers services Ruggiero went to Mass weekly and took communion at least every second month. The home prepared him for some of the devotional rhythms practiced in confraternities, though this did not extend to flagellant discipline. This didn't mean, though, that Ruggiero might not feel the whip. Blasphemy, disobedience, and complaining about the officials were all considered spiritual faults that needed quick correction. By the same token, going out without a permit, fighting, or damaging furniture also pointed to a boy who had to be wrenched off a downward slope. From time to time, boys fled in order to escape the life and discipline, and the Abbandonati held that they could never return. S. Bartolomeo lost boys through its open windows, but kept the door ajar for their return, so long as they passed a second time through the formal review process. At the same time, the home secured its main entrance with a metal gate in 1587, and heard from a visitor in 1593 that the most important problem in the home at the time was ensuring that the bars over the dormitory windows were locked at night to prevent the boys from escaping and, presumably, to keep thieves and sodomites from entering.[75]

We can assume that sexual propriety was an issue very much on the minds of all adults who were trying to shape the lives of adolescents. They read their Antoniano, even if they didn't aim to apply all its lessons. There is an implicit ambivalence in efforts to shape the boys' sexual morality, probably because many of these men were themselves fathers and assumed a degree of license. We can see a bit of this from the griping of a Bolognese teacher, Giovanni Antonio Flaminio, whose *Dialogus de educatione liberorum ac institutione* (1523) gives an unvarnished if perhaps exaggerated view of the merchants and professional men of his day. Flaminio complained of corrupt and depraved pupils who echoed the contempt their fathers demonstrated toward teachers, treating them like cooks or stablehands. They snorted at religion and mocked clerics. In front of their sons, these men boasted of the women they had seduced and the men they had murdered. They armed them with knives, recruited them into their feuds, and applauded when the boys were audacious or impudent. Flaminio's solution was to hustle the boys into boarding schools away from the subversive example and active encouragement of their fathers.[76] The men who poured their time, energy, and money into running orphanages probably had a less laissez-faire or libidinous view of childrearing. Yet in contrast to the stern warnings and overt enclosure that preserved girls' virginity, orphanages used circumlocution in their statutes and never guarded the gates quite as closely.

Though not quite a "boys will be boys" indulgence, the general impression we get from statutes and other records seems to be that their supervisors, like many parents, were more concerned that the boys' activities would throw the institutional family into disrepute than that they might pervert or ruin the boys themselves. Ruggiero's *lettore primo* and his counterparts in other homes had drilled their boys in catechisms that counseled chastity, and we can imagine the *precetore*, chaplain, and *guardiano* trying to discuss the lessons of someone like Antoniano at the dinner table. We don't find boys being thrown out of homes or forced into marriage as a result of getting girls in trouble, though given what we know of adolescent culture then, the argument from silence is hardly compelling in this case. Did the adults, armed with popular superstition, try to dissuade boys from masturbation by warning them that it would use up their limited lifetime supply of semen?

Sodomy seems to have been the sexual activity that worried Ruggiero's guardians more. Renaissance sources used the term to describe both fellatio and anal intercourse, and may have extended it to fondling and kissing between boys as well. But while it seems to have concerned the guardians more than heterosexual activity, the evidence in orphanage records is so scanty and indirect that it is difficult to either confirm or qualify Michael Rocke's assertion that "sodomy was an integral facet of male homosocial culture" in Renaissance Florence, much less that it was a common, if limited, experience for many Florentine adolescent males that their parents and guardians tacitly accepted. Children as young as 6 were involved, but only rarely; passives were more often ages 15 to 18, at which point most ceased participating in it while a few became involved as active partners. Prosecutions had waxed and waned under the Office of the Night from 1432 to 1502, but its judicial activity seemed to bear out the view common in Italy and beyond that this was a particularly Florentine vice: in their periods of activity through the fifteenth century, a similar magistracy in Venice convicted 268 people and one in Geneva only 5. Florence's Office of the Night investigated 15,000 to 16,000 men over seven decades, and convicted almost 3,000 of them.[77]

Despite the stiffening of prosecutions under Savonarola and the republican government of 1527–30, the Office had been so slack during periods of Medici rule that some believed that the Medici saw sodomites as a constituency worth courting. Cosimo I initially followed this pattern, if pattern it was, until 1542, when earthquakes in his home territory of the Mugello and lightning bolts that hit both church (the cathedral dome) and state (some government buildings) in the city of Florence brought a sudden change of heart and the promulgation in short order of new laws against sodomy and blasphemy. The senate passed these laws on the same day (7 July), and contemporary chronicler Bernardo Segni certainly saw them as Cosimo's moral prophylactics against divine wrath. Opening the Abbandonati orphanage fit in with both laws. One-third of the fines from the new blasphemy laws went into the Abbandonati's coffers, continuing a long local tradition of using vice to support virtue. From 1440, half of the fines collected by the Office of the Night from convicted sodomites went to support various convents on Via S. Gallo, and in later years proportions went to the Convertite convent for reformed prostitutes and to the foundling home of the Innocenti. The connection to the sodomy laws was more preventative. The Abbandonati took the city's most vulnerable boys off the streets and away from those who might prey on them sexually. In the 1550s, Cosimo I ordered the S. Niccolò conservatory opened to shelter orphan girls who were vulnerable to sexual assault, and the Abbandonati served a similar purpose for preadolescent boys. The 1542 sodomy law was passed only four months after the Abbandonati began operation. Unlike some earlier codes, this law levied penalties against young passives who usually had been almost overlooked, and it raised penalties for those passives who were repeat offenders. Both provisions would have hit those young abandoned boys who made—or at least were suspected of making— a living as male prostitutes. The Abbandonati could provide such boys with an alternative way of surviving after the death of one or both of their parents. In the end, after roughly a decade of more intensified prosecution, convictions (if not punishments) declined considerably from the 1550s.[78]

Of course, if one of its purposes was to keep boys like Ruggiero from prostitution, the Abbandonati also had to work to make sure that its dormitories didn't turn into schools for sodomites. Orphanage statutes never named sodomy directly, but it was the perceived threat looming behind a number of precautions and prohibitions. Since apprentices often slept more than one to a bed, and were thought to be particularly vulnerable to the suggestions, inducements, and assaults of journeymen and masters, there may be more than just cost behind the common practice of having boys work in shops during the day but return to the oversight of the orphanage by night. But the threats and gossip weren't just outside. Youth confraternities and flagellant companies that raised their whips at night had always been subject to raised eyebrows and suggestive gossip. How much more so a dormitory of boys who were looked after by some adult males that slept under the same roof? Rocke has noted the "strong collective character" of sodomy, but the orphanages do not seem to have been identified as brothels in the public imagination.[79] Clearing boys out of the homes by age 18 may have helped control some of the gossip, though it would not prevent younger boys from servicing each other. S. Bartolomeo di Reno thought it worth recording in 1583 that its newly opened dormitory had a single bed for each boy—it did not spell out the reasons for its pride or relief, but individual beds certainly reduced the opportunities for consenting encounters or assaults. What *had* been stated in its 1550 statutes was that the *guardiano* had to prowl the halls and dormitories of both the boys and the staff day and night at all hours on the look out for anything dishonorable or dishonest, and had to report these activities immediately to the confraternity's rector and *massaro*. The officials, for their part, were to expel any boys or staff whose vices, scandals, or fighting dishonored the home. The passage was repeated twice in two pages, with added emphasis on reporting *any thing* (*cosa alcuna*), and the final note that if the *guardiano* failed to report any dishonorable activities, he would be considered guilty of them himself and would be thrown out immediately. S. Onofrio had similar regulations.

Given the prevailing culture of sodomy, adult males like the preceptor, the priest, and the *guardiano* were likely to be seen as a greater threat to the boys than older *putti* (boys) were. Popular plays, songs, and gossipy legend stereotyped teachers as irrepressible sodomites. Ruggiero's teachers and supervisors at the Abbandonati were warned that the best way to keep the "wolf of human nature at bay" was to keep themselves in the "collective eye" (*occhio corporale*) of the guardian and rector. None of them should sneak off to the storerooms, or bedrooms, or remote corners of the house, and when they met with the boys, there should always be at least eight in the group. The rules condemned silence as much as the act itself, judging that anyone who failed to report was complicit.[80] These concerns help us understand why homes routinely wanted their male staff to be over 30 or even, in the case of S. Bartolomeo di Reno, over 40;

in late-fifteenth-century Florence, the overwhelming number of active partners arrested by the Office of the Night were between ages 18 and 30.[81] Ruggiero's overseers at the Abbandonati were to make sure that the boys received training in moral virtues, and that day and night they were kept occupied so that they wouldn't fall into the dangerous leisure that would give opportunity to commit "an infinity of sins."[82]

Prayers and a diet of bread and water were the first tools used to correct a wayward boy, but if he continued his slide into immorality then by the third or fourth time he could face a whipping. The *guardiano* and rector could certainly impose this, but homes wanted to both build self-discipline and get their wards ready for the kind of discipline that they might face once they entered a craft and became subject to the justice of the guild. To this end, if Ruggiero broke the rules, the Abbandonati's *guardiano* and rector could empanel a tribunal of seven of his most God-fearing and upright peers ("piu timoratj e piu recti di tutta la casa") to hear the case against him and give a punishment that did not exceed the regulations. The experience was considered as valuable for the juvenile judges as it was for the juvenile delinquent, though it no doubt left lingering resentments in the home and may have opened the judges to some kinds of unpleasant retribution. If a boy simply would not submit to discipline, then he could be expelled. Only the Abbandonati, whose early supervisors were eager to send malefactors to pull the oars on Florence's galleys, set out the procedures for expulsion.[83]

As Ruggiero grew into adolescence, he spent more and more of his time outside the home working with craftsmen, collecting alms, or participating in public liturgical life. It was an experience opposite that of the girls in the conservatories, whose movements were ever more restricted as they matured into their late teens. But all of this was not far from what adolescent girls and boys who still lived with their parents experienced. Orphanage children were being prepared to enter their new lives with the best possible advantages: virginity and a dowry for girls, and education and an occupation for boys. Ruggiero would have to be able to handle the culture of the streets confidently if he was to survive, and for that he needed to be allowed to experience it in manageable doses while he was still under the protective care of those he could consider his surrogate parents, the Abbandonati staff and the Bigallo magistrates. Having seen something of the life of girls like Valeria di Bartolomeo di Pavia and boys like Ruggiero di Lorenzo da Castelfocognano, we can turn our attention now to the adults who stood to them *in loco parentis*. Who were these people, and what motivated them to take on the challenge of caring for orphaned and abandoned children?

CHAPTER FIVE

Running a Home

Early on a Sunday morning, 5 July 1562, the members of the Compagnia di S. Maria Maddalena gather in their church to contract the business of the orphanage of S. Onofrio. Recently adopted statutes require that they keep every Sunday morning free for such a gathering, though whether in fact they will meet as a *corporale* after the Mass and sermon on any particular Sunday is up to the rector. A patrician who may or may not be a member of the confraternity, the Maddalena *confratelli* chose him to be head of the orphanage for a six-month term. Early in the week, the rector will signal the *guardiano*, who will in turn go through the city to the home of every member of the confraternity telling them that the rector wants them to show up. With a few dozen homes to visit, the *guardiano* may enlist some of the older boys to help. He is not to hang around for a tip, but he may reserve for himself those members known for their discrete generosity. If the member is not at home, he may have to leave a message or return. In a few years, he will be able to simply fill the date in on some printed forms and leave them at the members' houses like mail.

In the later summer of 1562, the rector is Cavaliere Gian Galeazzo Bottrigari, a patrician who had served as rector only a few years before, and under whose watch the new statutes had been drafted and approved. His return so quickly could be a sign of deep interest in the home, or of a desire to keep his finger on the pulse of this institution at a critical time of dearth in the city, or even of some frustration that the new statutes don't seem to have taken hold yet. Boys are still being let in without formal approval, the previous *guardiano* has been sacked, and no one seems to understand the rotation of offices or their duties. The home is at a turning point. The generation of men whose charitable zeal had launched S. Onofrio is dying off. Some of them had joined the company decades before when it began as a youth confraternity, and simply hadn't quit or retired. Now they were dying, and Bottrigari was among those civic leaders who were trying to ensure that S. Onofrio would make the transition from a group's labor of love to a city's stable institution.[1] The statutes had been a step in this direction. Drawing on the example of Bologna's longer-running orphanage of S. Bartolomeo di Reno, they aimed to bring order, accountability, and broader involvement of confraternity members into the home by establishing a trio of officers with particular duties assisted by eight "conservators," all elected from the membership and all rotating every six months.

Thirty members of S. Maria Maddalena show up that day, a good number but just barely a quorum according to the demanding statutes. After Mass in the confraternal oratory, they convene as the *corporale* to hear reports from the rector; the *massaro* (overseer), who supervises the home, staff, and boys; and the *priore*, who looks after the confraternity's devotional life and also oversees the public church next to the S. Onofrio home, where funerals are held and alms collected. The thirty *confratelli* vote on motions by dropping black and white beans in a container. They readmit Bastiano di Agostino, an orphan who had fled but now wanted to return to be with the other boys. They commission an inventory of goods in the home, and set in motion the process that will allow them to appoint Giovanno da Giovanno Liardi as *guardiano* at their next meeting at the end of August. And that will be it until December. By statute, the *corporale* is where everything happens: members review and appoint officials and staff, they decide which of their number will take a turn as visitor, they hear the visitor's reports on boys and the home, they examine accounts, review the dealings of officers who have reached the end of their terms, debate the lack of alms, strategize when times get difficult, vote on boys coming in and interview boys going out. In theory, the *corporale* is deeply involved in every stage of S. Onofrio's life, but in practice some rectors call it together infrequently because meeting weekly with just the *priore* and *massaro* is far more convenient and efficient than calling the entire fractious *corporale* together; Bottrigari only calls it three times in his half-year term. Moreover, even when called, some members decide not to appear—the same manuscript statutes that set a quorum of thirty members over age 25 have an undated note penned in the margin reducing it to twenty members over age 18.[2]

Meanwhile in Florence, Francesco Rosati meets weekly with four companions at the S. Niccolò conservatory. All are bureaucrats appointed by Duke Cosimo I when he ordered S. Niccolò be opened to shelter homeless girls in the dearth of the mid-1550s. The duke's charge went to Florence's prison magistracy (the Otto di Guardia e Balia) and landed with Rosati both because of his experience running the Stinche prison, and because he was a member of the Company of S. Maria Vergine, the confraternity that ran Florence's other conservatory. But the two conservatories are quite different. S. Maria Vergine, like Bologna's S. Maria Maddalena, delegates duties to a core of officers who serve limited terms and periodically report back to the confraternity. At S. Niccolò there is no reporting, no rotation, no relief, and, for that matter, no religion as such: Rosati and his four companions discuss business together without breaking for religious services, and they have no community of confraternal brothers to advise, audit, or otherwise share the load. They set policies within the ducal mandate, appoint staff to implement these policies, visit periodically to check on both staff and girls, and worry incessantly over expenses that frequently threaten to outstrip a meager income generated from alms and the girls' work. Their other collective action is complaint: a steady stream of interventions to Cosimo I claiming that they are exhausted and that the current situation simply can't continue.[3]

Previous chapters have focused on life inside the homes. While the boys, girls, and their resident guardians created much of their lives together, many of the decisions that they worked with or around were taken outside their homes' walls. Individuals, or more often groups of men and women, met regularly to plan, budget, or fundraise; to let children in or usher them out; to hire staff, expand the premises, or even consider whether it was time to close the doors altogether. In the most direct way, these people acted *in loco parentis* to the orphaned and abandoned children in their care. What motivated them? Some, like the early *confratelli* of S. Maria Maddalena were driven by an intense sense of religious mission and poured their lives and resources into the homes. Others, like Bologna's Gian Galeazzo Bottrigari or Florence's Francesco Rosati, took on the administrative work as yet another charge in long careers of government or political service. Almost all found the work overwhelming.

A related question is, how did they organize this care? And more to the point, why did they organize it as they did? Whether driven by divine mission or ducal decree, administrators worked within a political and religious environment that defined the shape of their work as much as any famine or plague. Bologna and Florence had distinct traditions of charitable relief that governed how the homes were run in each city. Moreover, these two cities took two very different political paths in the course of the sixteenth century. Bologna lost the de facto independence that it had enjoyed through much of the fifteenth century and reverted decisively to subordinate status within the papal state. Florence moved in the opposite direction as the Medici dukes turned it into the capital of a new territorial state which they hoped could act on the European, and not just the Italian, stage.

These political realities were in turn shaped by changes in the Catholic Church and in religious life generally. The Church's spiritual and organizational life was intensifying under movements of reform that combined competing and sometimes contradictory elements. Laypeople and clerics alike agreed that Christians of all stations needed to develop their spiritual lives and express this more fervent interior state through charitable works that would support and redeem the poor and needy. Charity would have to be better organized if it was to be focused and effective. But who should organize it? The fiery Florentine friar Savonarola (1452–98) thought that regular clergy had the motivation, time, and experience required, and Ignatius Loyola (1491–56) established the Society of Jesus to exercise the same conviction. Neither wished to cut the laity out of the picture; far from it, both had a healthy respect for lay activity and managed to attract many animated and dedicated followers. Yet both also saw the laity as distinctly subordinate disciples who implemented and paid for the plans that a cleric had devised. Not all of their lay followers agreed with this assessment. Other reformers like Bologna's archbishop Gabrielle Paleotti (1522–97) thought that the secular clergy should be the animators, led by a resident bishop whose palace drawing rooms would be active centers of command—or at least persuasion. Civic magistrates like Gian Galeazzo Bottrigari and Cosimo I, on the other hand, thought they had the requisite combination of spiritual awareness, administrative skill, and legal power to organize charity, particularly since clergy had allowed many hospitals to fall into ruins. Many looked to the experiments being tried in cities and towns like Catholic Ypres, Lutheran Wittenburg, and divided

Lyon for general inspiration and specific policies. Individual lay men and women outside the political class, and various groups of laypeople gathered in guilds or confraternities, practiced direct action in establishing new charities and consolidating existing ones.

Networks of charitable homes for orphaned and abandoned children developed in both cities—and indeed in cities across Italy and Europe—through the interworking of these often competing agendas. Magistrates fought with bishops, bishops fought with religious orders, Savonarola's disciples fought among themselves, and laypeople fought with all of the above. But they also worked together, and in the end it was that cooperation as much as the periodic tensions that governed how homes opened and sheltered children. The demands of church, state, and charity frequently dovetailed in the orphanages and conservatories, and in each case local traditions helped shape the dialogue among the competing and cooperating figures involved. And here again, nothing was fixed: administration was a constantly evolving experiment in which statutes were written one year and improvised on the next as homes lurched to meet financial crises and political necessities. The mix of factors generated paradoxes: in Florence many people advocated centralizing charity under lay and civic control, yet their hopes ran counter to Medici efforts to negotiate authority between pressures from patricians, Savonarolans, and local communities, and so were consistently stymied. Bologna had no similar pressure group, yet gained a high degree of de facto centralization of poor relief under lay and civic control because this fit the needs of a governing class that was still negotiating the city's subordination to the papal state.

This chapter first sketches how those local charitable traditions and political realities shaped the running of the homes in Bologna and Florence. It then turns to gender, and asks whether women administered homes any differently than men did, and whether these differences could survive the efforts in both cities to develop more unified networks.

Confraternities and Local Charitable Traditions

All the conservatories and orphanages of Florence and Bologna were started or eventually taken over by confraternities, voluntary brotherhoods of men (and sometimes women) who aimed to imitate some of the disciplined worship, collective life, and charity of the mendicant friars while remaining lay. Did this fact have any particular significance? On a purely practical level, confraternities provided a traditional institutional format for lay charitable administration. They had organized and distributed charity in both cities for centuries, whether this meant giving bread to the starving, opening infirmaries for the sick and dying, comforting prisoners and those condemned to die, or gathering and burying the dead. When spiritual and charitable revivals moved across Europe from the high middle ages, they typically left in their wake confraternities whose members pledged to treat each other as brothers and sisters in Christ. Their theology built on the notion of kinship as expressed in Matthew 25, where Christ teaches that an act of charity offered or refused a poor person is an act of charity offered or refused to him. If you aimed to count Christ a brother, you inherited obligations to the sick and destitute whom he considered to be his family.

A happy band of charitable equals is easy to romanticize. In practice, most confraternity members were as class-conscious, self-serving, factious, bored, calculating, or indifferent as any other collection of Renaissance Italians, particularly once the brotherhood was a generation or two removed from the devotional movement, charismatic preacher, or plague that had first stirred its founders into action. After a few decades, when the founders had died, the second and third generations of *confratelli* looked desperately for ways of convincing—or forcing—existing members to serve in office, and finding new members to pay dues. Some increased terms of office from six months to a year, and others did precisely the opposite; all toughened up their statutes with dire threats of what would happen to members who refused their turn. Yet who could actually dare expel a member who might occasionally give alms, or relent and actually serve a term as a visitor or *depositario?* S. Bartolomeo di Reno charged one of its officials with keeping the members *caldi*—we could almost say "stoked up"—but in fact most groups resorted to dreary and desperate nagging.

This could pose some challenges to running the infirmaries or hostels that many confraternal founders had opened to succor Christ's poor kin. Hardening of the spiritual arteries might be countered briefly by devotional reform movements, but cities quickly grew too dependent on the new charitable institutions to entrust their survival to sporadic religious revivals. In most places the politically dominant or the merely ambitious moved into the confraternities in sufficient numbers to ensure that their work carried on. With such a close identification of civic and lay religious elements, confraternities in many cities became quasi-governmental welfare agencies through the fifteenth and sixteenth centuries. Tax revenues turned into bread or medicine when funneled through confraternities, and with volunteers performing the time-consuming work of assessing need and distributing charity, civic governments were spared considerable administrative costs. In the early fifteenth century, many governments consolidated numbers of small *ospedali* into larger unified *ospedali maggiori* by encouraging mergers among their governing confraternities. A similar process took hold in the mid-sixteenth century as new shelters emerged for orphans, syphilitics, battered women, and Jews converting to Christianity. In short, confraternities dominated the early modern stage on the continuum from the ecclesiastical charities of the middle ages to the state welfare bureaucracies of the industrial period, with all the paradoxes that this entailed: they were both lay and religious, both private and civic, both autonomous and regulated.

But however "useful" they were, practical considerations alone cannot explain the broad reliance on confraternities, particularly for a time not ruled by bottom lines, quality management strategies, or the nostrums of modern business administration. Caring for needy children was a religious duty. The active participation of confraternal overseers in screening orphaned and abandoned boys and girls underscores the fact that the confraternities who sponsored these homes saw themselves as far more than simply fundraisers or managerial advisors. Lay brothers and sisters took an active, direct, and time-consuming interest in the day-to-day management of conservatories and orphanages. Overseers recruited, supervised, and disciplined the staff of teachers, cleaners, porters, guardians, and priests. Financial officers balanced the income from alms, rents, and children's work with expenses. Two or more visitors circulated regularly around the halls and workrooms within the homes, and around shops in the city where children might be serving apprenticeships or fulfilling domestic service contracts. Entering children had to be scrutinized. Exiting children needed someplace or somebody to receive them, whether it be a shop, a home, a convent, or a husband. All of this work was in the hands of the executive members who had their own families, properties, shops, or occupations to care for. They no doubt breathed a sigh of relief at the end of their terms.

The many *confratelli* and *consorelle* who ran the homes for orphaned and abandoned children drew on different confraternal models. Gender brought some of the greatest differences in approach, as we will see later. Beyond that, there were at least two models of confraternal administration, which we can distinguish as the collegiate and the congregational. Briefly, collegiate administration was favored by large confraternities that undertook many different activities, and that found it easier to allot these to different subgroups or companies that might be designated a *collegio*, or *compagnia*, or *scuola*.. This was the model that Gian

Galeazzo Bottrigari worked with at Bologna's S. Onofrio orphanage. Congregational administration was leaner and more focused, with all (or almost all) members of a much smaller confraternity or congregation taking a hand at running the group's charitable home. This was how Florence's Francesco Rosati and his colleagues ran S. Niccolò.

In the collegiate model, the confraternity might number hundreds of members. Besides regularly gathering to sing songs, hear sermons, march in procession, or bury their dead, they might establish a hospital for the sick, a shelter for pilgrims, or a service to bring food to prisoners. Bolognese laypeople had formed four such groups in the early fourteenth century, roughly corresponding to the city's four quarters. Hundreds of members gathered at least monthly to sing the vernacular praise songs called *laudi*—hence the groups' colloquial name, *laudesi*—and to support the charitable work of the large pilgrims' hostels that each ran for the benefit of travelers passing through Bologna on their way to and from Rome. Joining one of these *laudesi* confraternities gave members access to charitable and spiritual resources ranging from disability insurance and dowry funds to burial and requiem services. All members could expect to be drawn into the public charitable work at some point as overseers or in-house volunteers, but this began to change by the fifteenth century. Each of its organized charitable activities—and over time a large confraternity came to sponsor several—came to be entrusted to a separate, subordinate group. Each of these separate groups had its own limited autonomy: it selected members from among the broader confraternity; it elected its own officers; it had its own statutes, accounts, financial officials, and possibly its own priest; and it reported periodically to the larger brotherhood on its activities. Members of the broader confraternity could join one, some, or none of the smaller groups, depending on their interest or suitability for the work. This is the model we find in Bologna's S. Marta (under the sponsorship of the Compagnia dei Poveri Vergnognosi), S. Maria del Baraccano, S. Bartolomeo di Reno, S. Maria Maddalena (sponsor of S. Onofrio), and S. Giacomo.

Confraternities organized on the congregational model were far smaller, often numbering only a few dozen members or less in contrast to the scores or hundreds of members typical of collegiate-organized groups. Members fixed an upper limit on their size, and only added a new member when one of their brothers had died. They tended to be stricter about who could be nominated, and far more careful about reviewing and voting on those proposed. The congregational group was usually far more restricted its charitable work, most often focusing its energies on one activity only. It frequently had far less in the way of a collective devotional life or much in the way of charitable obligations between members. It looked more like a board of directors than a devotional group. This is the model we find in Florence's Bigallo, S. Maria Vergine, S. Niccolò, S. Caterina, and Pietà, and in Bologna's S. Croce and S. Giuseppe. The congregational model was a far cry from the traditional, medieval confraternity, and some might argue that it should not be considered with the other lay brotherhoods discussed here. Yet that would be drawing the analysis too narrowly. Across early modern Italy, the conjuncture of ennobling and Catholic reform introduced new forms under the confraternal rubric, and in the eyes of many reformers the congregations represented a reformed model of the traditional confraternity. It certainly fit the needs of evolving bureaucratic governments, and toward the end of the sixteenth century this was the model that newer groups adopted and that older groups reformed themselves by.

Before looking at why the two cities divided so neatly on this point, it may be helpful to describe how the two forms worked. The differences, while real, had less to do with immediate care for the boys and girls, and more to do with local traditions and political realities.

All confraternities appointed a small group of executive officers to take on the day-to-day work of administration in conjunction with the paid staff.[4] Florentine congregational administrations were almost all very "flat," and their statutes spent little effort distinguishing one office from another. As we will see below, Florence's flagship Ospedale degli Abbandonati was directed by a hybrid of historical confraternity and modern bureaucracy—a hybrid so deliberately crafted that it stands out as one of the best examples of this early modern merging of the two. Its twelve captains operated on the level of policy, like a board of directors, while paid officials took on the real work of balancing books and arranging new homes for the boys. This was initially how Francesco Rosati and his four colleagues looked after S. Niccolò. A similar model held with S. Caterina at the end of the century, where a small group of six self-perpetuating *signori* met every Thursday (later monthly) to hear the reports of one of their brothers serving his one-year term as *proposto*, and also from a couple of hired administrators. The *provveditore* handled expenses—making sure that there was food in the home and that the various staff members did their jobs—while the *camarlingo* handled income—making sure that the alms box receipts were tallied, that legacies were tracked and their rents paid, and that girls' wages were collected annually in July.

It is possible that these two officials were members, but the statutes do not stipulate this, and the first ones were not.[5]

The Abbandonati, S. Caterina, and S. Niccolò in its early years were fundamentally state homes, even if the pretext of confraternal organization put this relation at arm's-length. Their captains and *signori* had little direct involvement in the lives of their wards, though statutes required them to visit periodically. At their regular meetings they focused on reviewing the actions of paid staff. They were also expected to review and approve admissions, though this happened inconsistently. Things were somewhat different at Florence's S. Maria Vergine and Pietà homes, and also at S. Niccolò after Rosati and his colleagues finally convinced Cosimo I to change the administration. We will look more closely at the Pietà when considering how women ran homes. Cosimo solved S. Niccolò's problems in 1564 by merging it with a confraternity, as he had done with the Ospedale degli Abbandonati and the Compagnia del Bigallo. In this instance, however, the confraternity did not have a 300-year pedigree and deep pockets. S. Niccolò's new "parent" was the company of S. Maria Vergine, established by the Medici a decade and half earlier to run the eponymous conservatory. And there was a circularity here, because one of its founding members was Rosati himself. Sixty years later the two would merge their books, and eventually their quarters, but at this point they remained two separate institutions under one confraternity.

The thirty members of S. Maria Vergine shared seven offices that involved real work—it is not at all surprising that they had to meet weekly in order to get it all done. The offices were much like those of S. Caterina noted above: under the chairmanship of the *padre proposto*, a *provveditore* looked after expenses and a *camerlingo* recorded income from alms and the girls' work. S. Maria Vergine added a *scrivano* to keep the records and then, like all confraternities, added four *consiglieri* (counselors) to keep the others honest. All officers served for a year, so in the normal course of things, a member of the confraternity could count on being part of the administrative team at least one out of every four or five years. While there was a rough effort to match recruitment with deaths and resignations, the group enrolled cautiously and was consistently a few members shy of its limit of thirty.[6] When taking over S. Niccolò in 1564, it initially resisted expanding the responsibilities of the existing officers, and instead added a group called the Five of S. Niccolò. This quintet supervised staff much as Rosati and his colleagues had. Finding twelve officers annually from thirty volunteers meant everyone was now on the hook every two or three years, and this proved unsustainable. S. Maria Vergine first addressed the situation by raising its size to forty members (1584), and then decided to redefine the Five of S. Niccolò as meaning the four *consiglieri*, together with the *proposto* (1598); this meant that members were once again serving every four or five years, a level that everyone found easier to sustain. It also made S. Niccolò's eventual absorption into S. Maria Vergine that much easier to achieve.

Cutting expectations to meet diminishing volunteer energy available—this was the administrative calculus applied in Bologna as well. Yet here the adjustments were more dramatic because the original administrations had been far larger, reflecting equal measures of charitable optimism, bureaucratic zeal, and mutual suspicion. With four distinct administrative layers, the two orphanages of S. Bartolomeo and S. Onofrio were roughly similar, largely because the latter borrowed the former's statutes. A rector held supreme authority, but in a somewhat ceremonial fashion. The statutes spoke of him as guarding the peace and adjudicating disputes, sign enough that some of these homes tottered on a deeply divided confraternal foundation. He might not even be a member of the confraternity, but should come from among the "più nobili et gentiluomini et antichi cittadini di boni famigli" (high nobles, gentlemen, and established citizens of worthy families)—in short, a referee and figurehead representing the urban elite who, in practice, was frequently drawn from the city's most influential families, like S. Onofrio's Gian Galeazzo Bottrigari. Below him in dignity were the two officials in charge of charitable and cultic activities. The *massaro* made sure there was food in the kitchen, a roof overhead, and staff in place; his work brought him into the home every day as the official most immediately responsible for every aspect of day-to-day operations, and he could have a couple of assistants to help him carry it out. The *priore* ensured that the confraternal church was furnished, that flagellant *confratelli* had their capes and marched in processions, that the priest was hired and the sacraments honored. He was the spiritual cheerleader who, as S. Bartolomeo wished, kept the *confratelli* "hot" (*caldi*).

On the third layer below these two were a larger group of *conservatori* and *sindici*, eight or twelve members on life or limited terms. They were the institutional memory of the place, whose oversight and audits made sure that rectors, *massari*, and *priori* didn't scheme together to defraud the home. No property could be bought or sold without their approval. A complicated electoral process rooted in medieval guild and communal traditions brought the top three officials into office. The oldest *confratelli* prepared a long list of suitable candidates from within the company who were age 30 and over and who had been members for over three years, and then brought this list to the membership, which represented the fourth and broadest layer of administration when it gathered periodically as the *corporale*. Each name was voted on, but only half—those with the most votes—got into the bags from which officers were drawn every six or twelve months. Their heavier responsibilities meant that these officials met every one or two weeks to conduct orphanage business. It also meant that some of those extracted turned down the job.

Bologna's conservatories had similar administrative tiers and oversight. All employed a small core group of nine or twelve men, called *deputati* (S. Maria del Baracano) or *procuratori* (S. Marta). These were drawn from the sponsoring confraternity, served life terms, cycled repeatedly through a set of administrative offices, and were subjected to the oversight of conservators and sindics. The two key offices, lasting six or twelve months, were those of *priore* (daily administration) and *depositario* (finance); beyond that, each member of the core group would serve a two- or three-month term annually as a visitor. Most included a distinct Congregation of Gentlewomen, whose operation and relation to the male administrators will be considered more closely below. And all included various groups of overseers: S. Maria del Baraccano's twelve deputies had four superintendents scrutinizing them from above, and six supernumaries awaiting below; these latter filled in if one or more deputies couldn't make it to a meeting, but could only participate in discussions and not in votes.

Only the conservatory of S. Croce had a rector serving the kind of ceremonial and political functions seen in Bologna's orphanages, but then it started with the most elaborate administration and ended up with one of the leanest. It wanted so badly to fit into the city's charitable, political, and religious networks that in 1609 it allotted executive seats for members of every major social group: a rector representing the senators; a *sopraintendente* representing the cathedral canons; a prior representing the Franciscan tertiaries who held titular authority over the *ospedale* quarters; a *camerlengo* representing the city's merchants who footed the bill and employed the girls; twelve life conservators and eight annual conservators drawn from the ranks of gentlemen, citizens, merchants, and tertiaries; and a parallel congregation of twelve gentlewomen to deal directly with the girls. They were following a model common across Italy that had emerged locally four or five decades earlier as the city was defining its citizenship categories more closely, and was using these to shape the administrations of large financial-charitable institutions like the Monte di Pietà and the Monte del Matrimonio.[7] Yet finding two to three dozen people willing to serve a home that sometimes gathered barely that many girls was more than a little quixotic; while many were called, few wanted to be chosen. In its first statute revision four decades later, S. Croce reverted to a lean, congregational administration of five: rector, prior, *camerlengo*, and two visitors.

Florence's lean administrations seemed focused on getting the job done efficiently, while Bologna's many-tiered "thick" ones seemed oriented to making sure that everyone got a shot at holding office and a chance to look over everyone else's shoulder. This contrast of neat and narrow congregational bureaucracies with broad and sometimes fractious collegiate cooperatives reflected both the evolution of the two cities' confraternal and charitable traditions through the fifteenth century and the shifting political culture of the sixteenth century. Florence's charitable traditions were shaped by the fact that most of its hospitals were in some way proprietary. The families or guilds that had established and maintained them jealously guarded their rights and property by concentrating power in small, appointed boards that operated with a high degree of secrecy and little or no public accountability. The governors and rector of S. Maria Nuova, Florence's largest *ospedale*, were descendants of Folco Portinari through the male line, while a small *ospedale* like S. Caterina dei Talani on Via S. Gallo was firmly in the grip of the Talani family, in spite of their demonstrable corruption.[8] Bologna's hospitals, by contrast, had almost all grown out of the large *laudesi* confraternities of the thirteenth and fourteenth centuries, and even when patricians began infiltrating and co-opting them in the later fifteenth and early sixteenth centuries, the tradition of a broad membership electing an executive board remained strong. The only Bolognese institutions to adopt the congregational model were founded by individuals late in the sixteenth century. Moreover, a closer examination shows that both traditions evolved in close connection to the new political realities of the two cities.

Bologna and Collegiate Governance

The collegiate model had first emerged in Bologna in the fifteenth century. Paradoxically, it was not aimed first at practicing institutional charity, but at avoiding it. When some members of the large confraternities that ran the city's pilgrims' hostels and infirmaries were caught up in the observant devotional movements promoted by traveling preachers like Bernardino da Siena, and wanted to practice the rigorous devotional exercises that these movements entailed, they found that the time and effort of running their charities simply wouldn't allow it. Moreover, some of their brothers and sisters were nonplussed by the notion of shifting from a somewhat relaxed set of spiritual exercises toward one that demanded weekly gatherings for the Divine Office, monthly confession to the priest, and regular periods of fasting. Most challenging of all, these strict new exercises included gathering a few times a year to strip to a special robe and whip one's self until the blood flowed. In the 1430s, these worship wars brought some Bolognese confraternities to the brink of splitting up until one, the Compagnia di S. Maria della Morte, came up with the idea of separating into two linked groups that would share quarters, resources, and name but divide responsibilities: thus was born the collegiate model. Those who wanted to wash their hands of the chores of running the *ospedale* and instead follow a strict life of prayer, sacraments, and flagellation took the name *compagnia dell'oratorio* or *compagnia Stretta*. Those who preferred washing sheets, greeting pilgrims, fixing beds, and occasional worship services took the name *compagnia dell'ospedale* or *compagnia Larga*. Both were equally members of the Compagnia di S. Maria della Morte. The terms *oratorio* and *ospedale* designated function, but *Stretta* and *Larga* were the terms that made it into the city's confraternal vernacular, perhaps because they referred as much to the size and exclusivity of the group as to the relative amplitude of their spiritual exercises. Larga membership could be in the hundreds, while the Stretta seldom numbered more than a dozen or two. All members of the Stretta were automatically members of the Larga, and could gather with these spiritual kin to vote in the confraternity's overall governing board of officers, to worship in its church, and to march in the confraternity's processions. Members of the Larga, however, could not join their Stretta brothers unless invited, and all they knew of the Stretta's activities was what the latter group's representative on the confraternity-wide governing board of officers chose to tell them.[9]

Despite—or perhaps because of—the disequilibrium between the two parties, the collegiate model became a widely practiced and characteristic element of Bolognese confraternal life. Its flexibility made it adaptable to most any circumstance. Within a couple of decades, the four major charitable confraternities of S. Maria del Baraccano, S. Maria della Vita, S. Francesco, and S. Maria dei Guarini divided in this way, and in the sixteenth century many more followed their example. Allowing distinct subgroups to function with a degree of autonomy within a larger corporate body matched the status that Bologna aimed to create for itself as a city within the papal state or that colleges possessed within a university.[10] Under this system, different styles of worship and charity could be accommodated within a single confraternity. Members whose devotional preferences ran in new directions need not quit, and confraternities could avoid schisms that would divide the properties that had been built up over decades or centuries, and that funded the dowries, sickness benefits, or funerary provisions that all members drew on. Moreover, through this device, a single confraternity could take on a variety of only loosely related charitable activities that would have strained the resources and attention of a more traditional group.

Here again, S. Maria della Morte led the way through the later fifteenth and sixteenth centuries by establishing separate groups for those members who aided prisoners (*compagnia dei poveri prigionieri*) and for those who spiritually assisted criminals condemned to execution (*scuola dei confortatori*). Its patrician members used the model quite deliberately in order to turn the brotherhood into Bologna's most powerful confraternity, with representatives heading out from its rebuilt quarters on Piazza Maggiore to their responsibilities in the prisons, on the scaffolds, by the hospital bedsides, at the shrine of the city's most important religious icon, and collecting rents from houses and farms throughout Bolognese territory.[11] Because so many people had direct experience of this administrative convention, it was easily adapted in the 1520s to create Congregations of Gentlewomen that would directly supervise girls in the conservatories, and then again in the 1540s and 1550s to form distinct devotional consororities within existing confraternities.

For all its flexibility, the collegiate system could cause as many problems as it answered. Larga-Stretta relations were seldom placid, and hostile disputes frequently broke out over confraternal identity and control of property. These troubled Bologna's shelters for children because in almost every case, their governing confraternities were driven to create a subgroup out of financial necessity rather than devotional fervor. In a reversal of the usual historical pattern, S. Bartolomeo di Reno, S. Maria Maddalena, and S. Giacomo deliberately created Larga cells after opening their orphanages precisely in order to accommodate those higher-born Bolognese who had the capacities and connections for administration but who were less interested in flagellating with artisans. The administrative fiction of *massaro* and *priore* acting as equals under the overall authority of the rector fit in here because, apart from their formal offices, the *massaro* represented the Larga and the *priore* the Stretta. Neither could be seen to dominate, and the rector had to have peacemaking as one of his chief goals because of the frequent tension between the two groups. Yet even this was a convenient fiction because rectors and *massari* might rub shoulders in civic councils, patrician palaces, and social events where the *priore* and his Stretta brothers could never appear. In each case the high-born charitable administrators of the newly created Larga companies soon made moves to control the whole confraternity and appropriate its revenues, inevitably straining the connections between the confraternity and its officers. The S. Maria Maddalena brothers accepted this as a necessity in 1560, and the S. Giacomo brothers embraced it as an opportunity in 1604; S. Bartolomeo's Stretta was considerably less accommodating.

Many S. Bartolomeo di Reno *confratelli* had resisted having anything to do with orphans when they were first approached by civic officials in the 1530s. They fought it in confraternal councils and local law courts for decades before submitting to what was really nothing less than an internal coup. Meetings held to discuss the situation turned into angry debates between older members who wanted to kick the orphans out as soon as possible and younger members who favored cooperating with communal authorities and turning the home into an orphanage. The latter group won the argument but, for all intents and purposes, lost the confraternity. Cooperation with communal officials entailed an expensive building program for a new dormitory that so stretched their resources that they were obligated to sell some of their endowment properties. In 1534 they negotiated the sale of a small house close to the *ospedale* with Cavaliere Lodovico Fellicini, who promised half the 800 lire price in building stone and half in cash; twenty years later, the confraternity brought Fellicini to court for having failed to pay either the price or the interest.[12] New and wealthier *confratelli* were required, but no Bolognese matching this description wanted to join this small group of flagellant artisans meeting in an industrial district. The brothers obliged by establishing a separate nonflagellant group within their confraternity, designated the Larga according to the local custom.

A 1590 history by one of the winners, Alessandro Stiatici, described the change in terms of social class: the lay brothers, realizing that they were of low condition and little ability, sought the administrative expertise and financial resources of citizens who had greater *qualità*.[13] In view of the long-running dispute simmering under the surface, this was a convenient justification of events. With brothers skilled in the arts of politics and patronage, the Larga soon dominated the confraternity and the orphanage, while the artisans segregated in the Stretta were on the verge of extinction by the early 1550s. They had sold their rental properties to provide space and funds for the dormitory, thereby losing a major source of income. By 1554 they would have been bankrupt had not a legacy claimed by the Larga been settled in the Stretta's favor.[14] These deep disputes were the context for the statutes drafted in 1550 with their convoluted electoral process that aimed to balance the old and new orders. The three oldest members (those initially opposed to the home) prepared nominations for executive positions that the whole *corporale* voted on, and the rector—a short-term officer drawn from a patrician family outside the brotherhood—was cast as the confraternity peacemaker with the power to throw out troublemakers.

But whom would he throw out? The rector was hardly disengaged from the civic politics of charity that animated the *confratelli*'s internecine disputes. In the 1550s, the senate was aiming to firm up its grip on local governance. It established eight subcommittees of *assunti* charged with overseeing distinct areas of civic administration, justice, infrastructure, economy, and social life. This gave senators a much more effective means of controlling and extending the local government bureaucracy, particularly since the mandates of particular *assunterie* expanded to what might at first sight seem to be unrelated parts of the city's social life. This was the critical decade in the emergence of Bologna's network of civic welfare, culminating in the opening of its beggars' hostel, the Ospedale dei Mendicanti, in 1563, and the senate assigned the Assunteria del Pavaglione to oversee the new institution. The Pavaglione was the major annual fair where merchants traded the cocoons that provided the raw material for Bologna's rapidly expanding silk industry.[15] While it may seem an odd choice of bureaucratic committee to oversee a charitable shelter for the poor, the senators clearly realized that cheap semiskilled workers would be needed to help the silk industry expand, and saw the labor potential in an enclosure for poor women and children. So as it took shape from the 1520s to the 1560s, Bologna's charitable network deliberately wove together political influence, economic needs, and forced labor.

Other European cities expropriated charitable institutions and put them under the control of a magistracy. Bologna's approach was more indirect and deliberately rooted in its republican polity. Patricians gradually moved into the Larga companies of charitable institutions, spearheading or securing shifts in their charitable activity, and frequently stimulating disputes in the process. This is when we see the first examples of the practice that S. Croce adopted in 1609, when it designated seats on its executive to distinct social groups like doctors, merchants, artisans, and clerics. Within these broadly representative executives, the rector was to be both a figurehead and a referee standing above the fray.[16]

Senators fit this role and soon predominated as the rectors overseeing the major homes. In return for the work expected of them, they often received the power to place girls or boys in the homes during their term. Balances were built into the system: to prevent consolidation of power and to preserve the relative openness of the homes, senatorial rectors served only a six- or twelve-month term. At the same time, some senators moved from one home to another or even served in two at once. When the brothers asked Francesco Sampieri to take on the duty in 1591 (a year after taking up a seat in the senate), he declined on the grounds that he was already serving as rector of both the Ospedale dei Mendicanti and the Opera dei Poveri Vergognosi, which ran a number of charities, including the S. Marta conservatory. Sampieri was a busy man, having earlier (1578) been a member of the congregation that ran Bologna's Monte di Pietà, agreeing a year later to take on the S. Bartolomeo rectorship (1592), and then eventually moving over to serve twice as rector of S. Maria Maddalena (1597, 1602), where some of his relatives were also active.[17] Similarly, Gian Galeazzo Bottrigari moved from the rectorship of S. Maria Maddalena to serve two terms as the chief officer (*principe*) of S. Maria della Morte (1564, 1568) before joining the senate (1570–1600), the Monte di Pietà (1584), and the Morte's prison charity, the Poveri Prigionieri (1597).[18]

We can see two related phenomena here. On one hand, a few senators like Sampieri appear and reappear in one home after another, taking on more of these time-absorbing duties than political expediency alone could justify. On the other hand, a few families took leading roles in particular institutions, becoming virtual patrons of them. We saw earlier that the Bentivoglio family frequently sent gifts of food, wood, and oil 100 meters down the street to S. Onofrio, and that the *pater familias* Ercole Bentivoglio sat frequently on S. Onofrio's governing councils or served as its rector.

The shuffling of senatorial rectors from one home to another brought some consistency and semiofficial policy to the network of homes that was emerging in Bologna. But it ensured that when push came to shove between a devout artisanal Stretta and charitable patrician Larga, most rectors would side with the latter. Stretta were *caldi* for all the wrong reasons. This reality puts recurring complaints about members declining to attend meetings or serve as officers into a different context. Artisanal members who were disenfranchised had little motivation to attend. Reducing the numbers and duties of officials could be read as a necessity imposed by the numbers of *confratelli* who had gone *freddi* (cold), but could also reflect the status quo that was developing as rectors like Gian Galeazzo Bottrigari declined to call the *corporale* and simply met regularly with his *massaro, priore*, and staff. Turning the blame back on the membership was a convenient, self-justifying rhetorical stance, but as scholars of voluntary organizations have argued in other contexts, apathy is often the result rather than the cause of disengagement and disenfranchisement.[19]

S. Maria Maddalena had left open the possibility of weekly meetings of its *corporale*, but from 1562 through 1603, the mean was slightly more than six annually. Two rectors managed to get through their six-month terms without ever calling a meeting of the *corporale*, only one ever managed monthly meetings, and over the forty years there had only been sixteen times when two meetings were held in a single month. While S. Bartolomeo's draft 1550 statutes called for regular meetings of the *corporale* and the executive congregation, there are no records extant for either of these groups until 1588. Both started new minute books that year and prefaced the blank pages with a commitment to reform and renewal. The Bartolomeo Stretta wrote new statutes the same year, suggesting a deliberate and broad effort to turn a new leaf from the informal management of the previous decades (for which the financial records remain) to something more organized. Yet reforming zeal inevitably flags. The new minute books are initially rich with detail on the boys passing through the homes, but within a year or two revert to a more telegraphic mode.[20]

A bureaucratic congregational model was gradually replacing the participatory collegiate one in Bologna. It became the new convention for groups established or reformed from the early seventeenth century, like S. Croce and S. Giuseppe. Maintaining and controlling a broad membership was not easy. The disputes raging in S. Bartolomeo were not just about charity or property, but about class or, as company historian Alessandro Stiatici had put it in the code of the day, *qualità*. S. Bartolomeo and S. Maria Maddalena were caught in between the two models. While moving to a less participatory congregational administration, they required a large base of dues-paying members to handle expenses. Only six new members went through S. Bartolomeo's process of nomination and review from 1588 to 1593, the period when conditions in the city steadily worsened and the *corporale* debated sending most boys out onto the street. But membership was always very fluid. At the end of August 1593, 46 of 47 members present at the *corporale* voted to accept 98 new members, a dramatic act that both confirmed the idea of a broad membership undergirding the collegiate system, and yet indicated that this system could only be maintained by desperate expedients.[21] The move was no doubt made in desperation, but it accelerated the process of ennobling that had long been underway. Yet we should not make too much out of comparisons between two lists that are at best snapshots of a moment. A meeting in September of the same year attracted 26 members, of whom 11 were on the June matriculation of 48 members, 3 were of the August influx of 98, and 12 were on neither.[22] Members fluctuated so much in their attendance and commitment that the matriculation taken at any particular meeting is no index of total membership.

S. Maria Maddalena had an even harder time. Its 1560 statutes had intoned, "better the number of the few and the good than the confusion of the many," but within decades it was seeking as much of that confusion as it could get.[23] About forty to fifty confratelli supported it through the 1560s and 1570s, perhaps two dozen of these being Stretta, although of course fewer than that number would come regularly to meetings. On 25 March 1580, fifty-four of these members voted to accept a group of forty-four recruits. It was the feast of the Annunciation, and joining the Maddalena and bringing the new members' gifts of alms and cake was the kind of charitable act toward children that was popular on that feast day. Two months later, the *confratelli* took in a second group of eighteen. This offered some immediate relief both in terms of new candidates for office—and both groups included some men who moved almost immediately into positions of influence—and new sources of revenue. Did it erode the sense of confraternal community? In October 1595, eighty recruits joined in a single meeting, and five years later, a further forty-eight; yet the number of members who came to vote in this latter group was only twenty-eight, or scarcely more than 20 percent of the many who had recently joined.[24] Indeed, here as at S. Bartolomeo, mass influxes usually resulted in little more than a dozen more members attending meetings regularly, if that. What, then, were the advantages of membership?

There were certainly immediate benefits for the institution beyond gaining people who could pay dues or take a turn in office. With broad-based memberships, orphanages like S. Onofrio, S. Bartolomeo, and S. Maria del Baraccano gained access to their members' broader networks of support, and used them to fight the battles of the moment. While the senate seldom granted much in the way of direct alms, a savvy member could negotiate exemptions from taxes, usually those levied on building supplies. In February 1567, eleven members of S. Maria Maddalena circulated to eleven guilds to lobby for alms, and a year later eight more did the same. At the same time, an appeal for help to newly appointed Cardinal Bishop Gabrielle Paleotti backfired badly; he responded that if the orphanage was in such bad straits, it ought to merge with S. Bartolomeo di Reno. The brothers immediately sent eight members to intervene with Paleotti and wean him from his inconvenient notion. The delegation included recent rectors like Senator Ercole Bentivoglio together with Marc Antonio Malvezzi and Antonio di Grassi, both of senatorial families. Their lobbying succeeded in killing the suggestion. Soon after, another member was sent as an ambassador to Rome to see if there might be help forthcoming from that quarter. Cultivating connections to Rome could prove profitable in other ways. When a conventual Franciscan friar, Arcangelo Scargi, was convicted of apostasy in 1581, all his property was forfeited to the papacy. Gregory XIII turned around and, on the Day of the Annunciation, donated one of Scargi's houses to "the putti di S. Maria Madalena."[25]

In Bologna's more decentralized government, power was shared and derivative, and everyone from junior politicians to the archbishop looked over their shoulders toward Rome. The senate shared power collectively with the papal legate, but all senators were in real or potential competition with each other, a competition that extended down into the ranks of families where the question of who would take on the senatorial dignity was a real one. This uneasy balance of interests characterized many Renaissance and early modern republics, and one way to counter uncertainty was to buy, negotiate, or usurp powers and privileges, and then seek legal means of cementing gains. One of the most notorious examples locally happened in 1434 and 1440, when a group of investors banded together to purchase the public treasury. They comprised the core of the oligarchy that ruled the city in the later fifteenth century, and fought tenaciously when Pope Paul II accused them of bleeding Bologna dry. By the sixteenth century the group had expanded somewhat, but the city's finances were still controlled largely by a small core of investors. And Bologna was not unusual—this was simply how power operated in small republics, particularly those like Bologna that were republics "by contract" or treaty with a sovereign power that had agreed to guarantee some local customs and rights. It led individuals, families, and groups to focus on preserving local authority in any way they could, and tended to make them insular and obsessed with consolidating local alliances against local enemies.[26] Ambitious politicians married locally, and families perpetuated fixed alliances down the generations. This gave women significant bargaining power, and made them critical to alliance building.[27] In this decentralized and competitive environment, a network of homes—each based in a distinct albeit informal alliance, and each with a membership structure that could draw in more patronage networks—simply made more political sense than a single home.

Did membership have its benefits? The ambitious professionals, merchants, and politicians who joined the confraternities running these homes had more than the prospect of onerous office or repeated financial appeals ahead of them. On an immediate level, *confratelli* knew that if they died in good standing, their needy children would have priority in entering the home. And even in spite of ennobling and the carefully guarded distinctions of *qualità*, membership brought aggregation of sorts to the upper ranges of society. An ambitious, careful, and willing guild master who made it onto a governing body could reasonably expect that at some point he too would have the chance to enter a patrician's palace in order to discuss the fate of an orphan or the problems in a *guardiano*'s accounts. The charitable confraternity was one of the few forums for members of different social classes to come together in common cause and with some degree of shared purpose. More directly, it also gave guild members and textile brokers immediate and privileged access to a young and cheap labor supply.

More intangibly, joining a group like S. Maria Maddalena or S. Maria del Baraccano brought significant spiritual benefits. Coming to Christmas Mass in the oratory brought a plenary indulgence, with more plenary and temporal indulgences on other feast days and on days when there were meetings or processions. From the late 1570s, the Maddalena confraternity devoted considerable energy to obtaining the kind of spiritual benefits that could attract members. Beyond the abstract benefits of public charitable service, members joined in a rich festive life that ensured them an honorable place in processions on major civic and religious feast days. If they chose, they could apply to join the Stretta and take part in its weekly Mass at the confraternal chapel and in more rigorous penitential exercises. Aggregations to the Franciscan and Augustinian orders and to Rome's S. Spirito in Sassia raised the spiritual calculus exponentially.[28]

This continued pursuit of indulgences and spiritual goods, together with other signs of an expanding devotional and cultic life, should keep us from interpreting the gradual shift to bureaucratic congregational modes of governance as an example of secularization, or from separating governors' motives into tidy categories marked "spiritual" and "temporal." The religious context was indispensable—indeed, it is unlikely that Renaissance and early modern people could even think of institutional care for children outside of it. Continual expansions in cultic life suggest that it was far more than just an afterthought or "mere ritual." It was at the core of the homes' identity and of their governors' ability to legitimate their claim to authority over society. This was all the more so as we move by the end of the sixteenth century into the period of baroque piety when spirituality found ever more extravagant expression in processions, shrines, and public acts of charity and devotion. Bologna's homes provided a cast of children who could be recruited into these public acts, their confraternities provided the lay religious framework, and their patrician members provided the contacts in archiepiscopal and papal circles that could inflate their churches' spiritual treasuries and elevate their images to a far higher status.[29]

So, for instance, at S. Bartolomeo di Reno, the first stage in the home's reconstruction from a pilgrims' hostel to a much larger orphanage came not in the dormitories but in the adjacent public church, which became the focal point of the expanded complex. Around 1534, architect Alessandro Fontana shifted the building's orientation away from the Reno canal, which bordered it on the south, toward Via Imperiale on the east. This simple action effectively turned an open space there into the church's forecourt, and accentuated its prominence on a street that was then emerging as one of the most fashionable in the city, thanks to palaces of the dal Monte, Fellicini, Fava, and Tanari families. The church's cultic locus was a Marian image which with some deft promotion during a drought of the 1550s became known as the miracle-working Madonna della Pioggia. The brothers kept the Madonna under wraps in the confraternal oratory for most of the year so as to preserve its spiritual charisma and the importance of their own patronage. On certain feast days *confratelli* brought it shrouded into the public church, and then dramatically pulled back the curtain. At other times, it accompanied the *confratelli* in procession.[30]

The body directing S. Bartolomeo's cultic life was its Stretta company, and this too underwent a metamorphosis in the central decades of the sixteenth century. As the artisanal flagellants who had opposed the orphanage died off, this branch of the confraternity, like the Larga, moved up the social scale and into a different set of devotions. The 1588 Stretta statutes include a matriculation list with a number of prominent families among the names. If many are still guildsmen, all these are now masters, and there are none of the patronymics found on earlier lists. The statutes themselves point to subtle changes by what they include and omit. Piety, too, has moved upscale. The usual emphasis on frequent reception of the sacraments, regular attendance at worship, frequent reciting of private prayer, a restricted and disciplined membership, and a personal life marked by reserve, morality, and self-control is certainly there. But no one carries a whip. Flagellant devotions, or indeed penitential exercises of any sort, are nowhere to be seen. And while Quattrocento Stretta had shunned the public streets, these statutes include a chapter on the public processions that will take S. Bartolomeo's *fratelli* around the city, carrying their image of the Madonna della Pioggia before them and trailing their costumed juvenile wards in their wake.[31]

These processions were a vital part of the confraternity's public promotion before various audiences, with none quite so significant as the Compagnia di S. Maria del Baraccano, the elite confraternity that directed the Baraccano conservatory. While the Baraccano and S. Bartolomeo homes were parallel institutions, their confraternities operated in different social spheres, and the latter deferentially referred to the former as "nostri Padri del Baraccano." Promoting the Madonna del Pioggia was quite clearly meant to provide the Baraccano with a miracle-working image similar to the Baraccano's own venerable Marian one. It was a special honor for the S. Bartolomeo brothers to be asked by the Baraccano to visit on a day like the Feast of the Annunciation, and for these occasions a few *fratelli* would be chosen in advance and drilled carefully in deportment. They were told to stand with

> reverence, fear, devotion, and modesty, forcing yourself in that place to be a mirror for all the people of goodness and devotion, as is appropriate to men of a spiritual profession; and if any of these elected ones should do or say anything that would be scandalous, or would dishonour the Company, he will be thrown out.

At the head of the 1588 Stretta matriculation list was the name of its oldest member, 89-year-old Alessandro Stiatici. Stiatici was a prominent scholar who taught law at the university and wrote five volumes in Latin on legal and notarial questions. He was also the chief human link between S. Bartolomeo and S. Maria del Baraccano for over sixty years, filling various executive offices at both homes and ending his distinguished writing career with a vernacular history of S. Bartolomeo that pleaded with the Bolognese to remember why these homes were so vital.[32] Writing in the early stages of one famine, Stiatici recalled the chaos of another—orphaned children wandering homeless and starving through the streets in the 1520s. As Stiatici's text circulated around the city, the governors of S. Bartolomeo, the Ospedale dei Mendicanti, and other charitable homes darkly hinted that the current famine might force them to open the doors and release their wards to forage in the streets again. The Bolognese rallied, the homes survived, and the doors remained safely shut with the poor inside. Stiatici is an example of the kind of person who found in Bologna's confraternities and orphanages a vehicle for expressing both his faith and his political and social ambition. The words of the passage quoted above may or may not be his, but the sentiment—bringing together charity, piety, and deportment for the honor of the group and the edification of the population—surely is. Charity and order were two sides of a single coin. In the convictions and the six decades of service of a Stiatici we find the argument against separating the spiritual from the bureaucratic, or for reducing all charitable service to political opportunism or economic advantage.

Florence and Congregational Governance

Congregational governance in mid-sixteenth-century Florence came out of the dovetailing of three elements: local charitable and confraternal traditions, the Savonarolan movement, and Medici state building. Each of these elements had a history with each of the others, and each had been fractured, compromised, and adapted in the revolutionary swings that marked Florentine politics after Lorenzo de'Medici died in 1492. Their interaction together shaped how the city's conservatories and orphanages would be set up and run. Moreover, the Medici dukes used newly formed or re-formed confraternities to achieve a degree of direct or indirect coordination of Florence's orphanages and conservatories.

Florentines had a curious love-hate relationship with their confraternities. On one hand, they were proud of them as demonstrations of Florence's piety and charity. Confraternities were, as elsewhere in Italy, woven into the warp and weft of social life at the overlap of neighborhood and parish, quarter and city. They delivered charity, socialized children, organized neighborhoods, conducted processions, and enacted a worship that was vernacular, participatory, and Catholic.[33] On the other hand, no other state in Italy interfered as much in its confraternities' operations. Florentine governments of all political stripes refashioned confraternal administrations, instituted mergers, appropriated or redirected legacies, and appointed or dismissed officials. From the early fifteenth century, no political turning in Florence was complete without the obligatory closing of the confraternities, all or some, in whole or part, for weeks, months, or years, and always on suspicion of being nests of conspiratorial intrigue. Whole or partial suppressions had closed confraternal doors in 1419, 1444, 1455, 1458, 1471, 1484, 1498, each year from 1502 through 1505, and from 1512 through 1517, 1522, and 1527.

Closures aimed specifically to keep politically active Florentines out of secretive confraternal oratories while they were serving in political office, or when scrutinies were underway to fill the bags from which those officers' names were drawn, but there was also a more general fear of "unlawful association." Closures became such a reflex motion that it is difficult to say whether it was simple paranoia, familiar tradition, or a realistic assessment of threat. Certainly the Medici and the Savonarolans (popularly called *piagnoni,* which could mean "wailers," "weepers," or "snivellers," depending on one's attitude) had each, in their turn, used the confraternities to advance their programs and undermine their enemies, and so the serial suppressions were motivated in part by the desire to withhold from the enemy the tools that had proven so helpful to one's own cause. The Medici were particularly fearful of the confraternities as fifth-column *piagnone* cells, and so draconian closures were among their last acts before losing power to the last republican regime in March 1527 and among their first upon recovering power from that regime in 1530. This latter closure lasted until 1533. True to familial form, one of Cosimo I's first measures upon riding into the city in February 1537 to claim the ducal crown from his assassinated cousin was a closing of the confraternities.[34]

Did he have reason? Savonarola's message of a disciplined, charitable, spiritually vibrant, and politically attuned Christianity had resonated well with those who chose to gather in confraternal oratories, as did his growing critique of lax and corrupt clerics. He and his followers believed that the clergy ought to stick to their sacramental and pastoral functions, and leave charitable work to the laity, who in turn ought to organize it as broadly and systematically as possible— through confraternities and with civic help if necessary—in order to ensure that the "poor of Christ" were sheltered, fed, clothed, and healed. As a result, many *confratelli* had rallied around Savonarola's standard in the 1490s, while many Savonarolans flocked to the confraternities in turn, seeing in them the lay religious arm of the Christian republic that he was building. Institutional charity was a cornerstone of that republic, and the *piagnoni* moved particularly to some of the key charitable confraternities that had started to flag in recent years, most notably (and ironically) the Buonomini di S. Martino, the group for the "shamefaced poor" that Cosimo de Medici had helped found in 1442 and which the Medici had heavily patronized. Among others they revivified were S. Michele Archangelo, which came to be known as the Compagnia di Carità because of its new focus on helping the poor, and SS. Filippo e Iacopo, which ran the Ospedale del Ceppo. Members cut out elaborate ritual activities in favor of simplified worship, and taxed themselves heavily in order to increase their confraternities' impact.[35]

They also taxed their neighbors heavily, though in different ways. Savonarola's *fanciulli*, those bands of holy teenagers who patrolled for sodomites, card-players, blasphemers, and prostitutes, and who processed for Christ and his Florentine republic, also took confraternal form. The coordination of their activities pointed to another Savonarolan inheritance that reflected both his Dominican background and the impulses of almost all Catholic Reformers who saw the lay brotherhoods as incubators of reform. If they were to be the coordinated vehicles of deliberate reform, confraternities themselves needed to be reformed out of their local, self-directed, and sometimes superstitious customs and habits, and made into groups whose thoughts and actions were more centrally directed and uniformly organized—in short, something more congregational. When clerics preached lay reform, the first casualty was lay autonomy. Savonarola reshaped Florentine confraternities so as to make them more effective vehicles for his movement, though he did not lack for willing—even eager—confraternal partners.[36]

The depth of Savonarola's legacy became clear only after his death. Persecution forced his followers underground, but the confraternities and charities were a refuge where they could continue their pursuit of the Holy Republic through lay preaching, spiritual exercises, help to the poor and sick, and even prophecy. Most of all, this network allowed them to connect with, patronize, and encourage each other such that when the political winds shifted, as they did in 1527, the *piagnone* movement was ready to take power. Lorenzo Polizzotto argues that the suddenness of the *piagnone* revival in 1527, with well-articulated plans for political and charitable action, can only be explained by a healthy *piagnone* underground existing in the confraternities and *ospedali* through the apparently placid 1520s, when it seemed that the movement had been all but killed by Medici kindness. The underground network operated at all social levels. When the sack of Rome made Clement VII a prisoner in his own fortress, Medici authority in Florence collapsed and the *piagnoni* were ready to assume power. Their sudden emergence from a long internal exile was, to their own minds, a fulfillment of Savonarolan prophecy. This conviction moved them beyond contradiction or compromise and into disaster. Millenarian apocalypticism prepared the *piagnoni* for everything but success, and the steady refusal of its clerics and leaders to fight the papal-imperial siege that settled around Florence by

1529 with anything other than prayer, charity, and hope steadily bled all but a hard core of true believers out of the movement. As a result, the republic of 1527–30 was at once the *piagnone* movement's greatest triumph and its greatest setback.

In demonstrating both the quixotic and self-destructive nature of devotional absolutism, and the extent of clerical resistance to lay efforts at compromise, the republic effected a change in *piagnone* moderates. These gradually abandoned revolution and moved to build their Holy Republic on a smaller scale, by immediate action, with a lay focus, and without directly challenging the Medici dukes—the dukes could, in fact, be allies in the cause. The Medici would exact a high price though. Popes Leo and Clement had pursued a moderate policy of winning over enemies through compromise, but the vigor of the *piagnone* underground had discredited this approach. After the family's restoration, Duke Alessandro executed twenty-five prominent republican leaders and imprisoned or exiled another two hundred. When a prophetic cell of *piagnoni* became recklessly public in their prophecies, the duke imprisoned and executed its leaders and closed the confraternities for one of the longest periods yet.[37]

Cosimo I's closing of the confraternities in 1537 fit this repressive policy, but even by then was perhaps an overreaction, since only a disorganized, and widely scattered remnant was ready to pick up the political fight they had left off at the beginning of the decade. If this closure continued one Florentine tradition of gagging the brotherhoods in times of political flux, Cosimo's suppression of the Compagnia di S. Maria del Bigallo five years later, and the transfer of its assets, name, and responsibility over to the magistracy meant to oversee hospitals and relieve the poor, was an act in an allied local tradition of shaping confraternal charity through political dictate. Communal, republican, and despotic governments had done this continually from the thirteenth century, notably with major public confraternities that distributed charity like Orsanmichele, the Compagnia di S. Maria della Misericordia, and the Compagnia di S. Maria del Bigallo itself. They consistently argued that corrupt confraternal officers were siphoning off the alms meant to succor widows and orphans. Orsanmichele had counted almost three thousand members in 1325, but had become for all intents and purposes a branch of government by the end of that century. The Misericordia and the Bigallo had histories of worship and charitable service extending back to 1244, but had been forcibly merged by communal decree in 1425 and then separated again in 1489 and 1525. Expropriating the much-battered Bigallo was, if anything, a family tradition, since both Cosimo the Elder and Lorenzo the Magnificent had been key players in its Quattrocento transformations.

Recurring closures had prevented many Florentine confraternities from retaining active members, and made it inevitable that a small congregational core of officials would look after legacies.[38] The suppression or expropriation of large confraternal charities had much the same effect. While the Misericordia seems to have emerged from its forced marriage with the Bigallo with an active membership that was ready to pick up the sick and bury the poor, the Bigallo itself seems to have atrophied at the grassroots level. In short, by the mid-sixteenth century Florentines had been prepared by the traditions of their existing guild and family *ospedali*, by the history of political suppressions and expropriations of confraternities, and by the Savonarolan movement for the kind of top-down congregational governance that characterized the groups that opened shelters for orphaned and abandoned children in the 1540s, 1550s, and 1590s. They were also prepared by both the Savonarolan and Medicean visions for Tuscany to welcome further bureaucratization as the best means of expanding charity beyond what confraternities themselves could offer.

Cosimo I moved gradually toward this goal. As famine gripped the duchy in 1540, he appointed Francesco Cavalcanti and Francesco Inghirami as commissioners and provisioners of the begging poor ("commissari et provveditori de . . . poveri mendicanti"), with a broad mandate "to order, provide, and manage in benefit, accommodation, and subvention of these poor."[39] Both Cavalcanti and Inghirami were members of the Misericordia confraternity, and had served terms as the Misericordia's *capo di guardia* during the critical period of 1527–28 when that confraternity was Florence's chief agency battling the plague.[40] Their immediate mandate was directed to finding and rationing food supplies in the 1540 famine, but as that crisis faded, Cosimo I apparently aimed for a less ad hoc approach to poor relief. It may have been around this time that an undated and anonymous *Regolamento* in the Pratica Segreta was written. The document is filed with others dated 1531–43, and proposes a "spedale de Mendicanti di Firenze" for four types of deserving poor: the crippled, the blind, abandoned orphans, and—more controversially—the unemployed. Florentines would receive shelter, food, and spiritual assistance aimed at helping them reform. Non-Florentines would receive alms before being sent away from the city.[41] With their confraternal background and provveditorial office, Cavalcanti and Inghirami are likely authors of this *Regolamento*. It indicates that by the early 1540s,

Florentines were joining in Europe-wide discussions about radical overhauls to poor relief. And they weren't simply talking. In March 1542, Cosimo I took the bold step of putting two hundred lay and clerical *ospedali* under the supervision of a magistracy of five gentlemen. Both Cavalcanti and Inghirami were among the first five appointments to the magistracy (although Cavalcanti died before he could take up his duties), and the magistracy itself was unusual in that one of its first tasks would be to determine its specific activities within the rather broad mandate that Cosimo I had given.[42]

These discussions took place under the direction of the new magistracy's *presidente*, Angelo Marzi de'Medici, bishop of Assisi and secretary to both Duke Alessandro and Cosimo after him. His colleagues were largely Medici loyalists, and they had great ambitions. Cosimo I had directed them to survey the income and expenses of the two hundred *ospedali*, and requisition their excess resources to provide for *derelitti e mendicanti*, that is, abandoned children and beggars. The magistrates drafted a plan that would have left them running a wide-ranging welfare plan whose charitable and disciplinary parts would extend out to all parts of the duchy. They would license and discipline beggars, distribute food aid, open a workhouse, care for poor prisoners, and run shelters in Florence for orphaned and abandoned girls and boys drawn from across Tuscany. Moreover, working together with local ducal police and administrative officials, they would keep a tight rein on local *ospedali*, which they took to be nests of fraud. Some of the worst, in their minds, were clerical *ospedali*. Cosimo I seems to have anticipated some conflict, because he secured approval for the plan from Archbishop Andrea Buondelmonti in October 1542 and from Pope Paul III the following year.[43] It was in between these approvals that he stabilized the magistracy's funding by suppressing the Compagnia di S. Maria del Bigallo and transferring its considerable assets over to the new magistracy. The quid pro quo here was that in taking on the Bigallo confraternity's assets, the magistracy also took on the Bigallo's name and testamentary obligations and even adopted the title of "captain" that Bigallo officials had used. Moreover, their numbers were increased from five to the twelve that the Bigallo had had, though none of these existing confraternity captains kept their posts.[44] The Bigallo's absorption by the poor relief commission in November 1542 was highly rational. It brought together a magistracy that had power but no income, and a confraternity that had a tradition of serving poor pilgrims and orphans, an effective institutional base in the territory, and significant rental properties. The merged body was a natural vehicle for spearheading Cosimo's restructuring of poor relief.

Table 5.1. Bigallo Captains' Terms of Office
(years)

Duke	1–10	11–20	21+	Uncertain	Total
Cosimo I	11	13	5	2	31
Francesco I	7	6	1	0	14
Ferdinando I	9	9	6	2	26

Source: ASF, Bigallo ms. 1669/IV, 199r–203v.

The merger confirmed the Bigallo confraternity's evolution into a purely congregational body without a broad membership of lay brothers who could be the eyes, ears, and hands of the operation. It is a critical example of how state welfare bureaucracies emerged out of earlier voluntary and religious charity, and paradigmatic as well since spiritual elements did not entirely disappear. The Bigallo magistracy retained all the cultic and testamentary obligations that the Bigallo confraternity had accumulated over the preceding two hundred years. It retained the limitations on the alienation of property. It retained the network of orphanages and *ospedali* in city and *contado (country)*. It retained the prominent public building on Piazza S. Giovanni with the loggia where Florentine children had been abandoned by desperate parents for years. Whatever ambitions its twelve members and their president Bishop Angelo Marzi de'Medici may have harbored for licensing male and female beggars, sheltering male and female orphans, caring for the poor in prisons, and supervising hospitals across the duchy, the scope open to them gradually narrowed until by the end of the next decade it fit the narrower channels developed by the Bigallo over the previous century. In law, the magistracy absorbed the Bigallo; in the public mind—and perhaps in the Medici dukes' minds—it was the other way around.

Who were the Bigallo captains? The first three dukes appointed 71 captains: Cosimo I, 31, Francesco I, 14; and Ferdinando I, 26. Captains normally served life terms, though the fact that both Francesco and Ferdinando made a rash of appointments upon coming to office suggests that vacancies were determined by more than captains' mortality alone. When one died, the others each nominated a replacement and then from this long list prepared a slate of three nominees from which the duke made his choice. The president was always a bishop drawn from a diocese in the Florentine dominion (from 1565 this was consistently the bishop of Fiesole), nominated by the archbishop and appointed by the duke in a procedure intended to mitigate the problem of a lay magistracy exercising control over ecclesiastical *ospedali*.[45] Table 5.1 compares in years the actual length of

Table 5.2. Bigallo Captains' Political Standing

Duke	Appointed	Priorial Families	Council of 200	Senate	Order of S. Stefano
Cosimo I	31	21 (67.74%)	25 (80.64%)	16 (51.61%)	24 (80.64%)
Francesco I	14	10 (71.42%)	11 (78.57%)	8 (57.14%)	12 (85.71%)
Ferdinando I	26	23 (88.46%)	24 (92.3%)	22 (84.61%)	25 (96.15%)

Sources: ASF, Bigallo ms. 1669/IV, cc. 191r–203v; ASF, Tratte 725; Gamurrini, *Istoria delle famiglie nobili*; Mecatti, *Della nobiltà*; Burr Litchfield, *Emergence of a Bureaucracy*, 339–82.

the life terms served by the captains appointed by the three dukes. These ranged in practice from one to thirty-three years; the mean among Cosimo and Ferdinando's captains was twelve years, while that for Francesco's was eight.

The captains were not political lightweights. As Table 5.2 shows, the bulk of them were members of the active and established political class of Florence.[46] A steadily rising percentage came from families that had held priorships four times or more through the fifteenth century. Beyond lineage, the prerequisite for political participation in ducal Tuscany was personal membership in the Council of 200, the assembly drawn from those who had passed scrutiny for magistracies. Most captains were members of the 200 before joining the Bigallo. A somewhat smaller, but steadily rising percentage of captains were also members of the forty-eight-member executive senate.[47] Finally, moving from the organs of power to the organs of ritual and prestige, most Bigallo captains were also knights of Santo Stefano, the chivalric-crusading order created by Cosimo I in 1562 to capitalize on the booming market for marks of honor and possibly sweep the Mediterranean of Corsair pirates in the process.[48]

If we move beyond the relative anonymity of political memberships and global percentages, we find some Bigallo captains had done exceedingly well by ducal patronage. Among the longest-serving of Cosimo I's appointments was Giulio di Alessandro del Caccia (served 1559–90), a doctor of law, frequent ambassador (to Ferrara, Milan, Parma, Savoy, the Holy Roman Emperor, Philip II of Spain), and governor of Siena.[49] Among Francesco I's appointments, Benedetto di Buonaccorto Ugaccioni (served 1582–90) was a favorite who supervised numerous public works projects in the dominion (in Livorno, Pratolino, Lampeggio) and in the city (working on the Palazzo Pitti, S. Maria del Fiore, and Ponte S. Trinità); he was also the first of his family appointed to the senate.[50] Finally, among Ferdinando I's captains we find Giovanni di Domenici Bonsi (served 1590–1601), a cleric and doctor of law who negotiated the marriage of Marie de Medici to

France's Henri IV, accompanied her to France as her almoner, and became bishop of Biziers and subsequently cardinal of S. Clemento.[51]

In short, the Bigallo captains were the personally powerful scions of traditionally powerful families. They had experience in Florentine and ducal government, were adept at gaining honors and position, and normally enjoyed long terms of service with the Bigallo. On paper, their influence increased over our period: while Cosimo I and Francesco I appointed new men and old, insiders and outsiders to the Bigallo, Ferdinando I overwhelmingly favored well-established senators and knights of Santo Stefano. As they never tired of pointing out in numerous letters to successive dukes, Cosimo had endowed them with great authority. How, then, to explain their mixed success in realizing the Bigallo's ambitious mandate?

Cosimo and his sons seem to have developed reservations about the power that the Bigallo captains could garner to themselves if they fulfilled their plan. They also seem to have developed reservations about the plan itself. Significantly, neither Cosimo I nor his sons ever ratified the magistracy's draft statutes, which became a virtual dead letter. Ambitious captains and an ambitious centralizing plan—even one dedicated to consolidating Medici authority—could undermine ducal relations with territorial communities. The vision of coordinated poor relief may have warmed the hearts of charitable reformers across the spectrum from *piagnone* radicals to Christian humanists, but it was anything but popular with local hospital administrators, who saw their livelihoods threatened. Towns and villages also resisted, because they rightly feared that their local charitable resources, built up over generations and a vital part of local self-sufficiency, would be drained away into the capital. From the time of the first, incomplete census of *ospedale* resources, local communities resented and resisted the efforts of the Bigallo to review accounts, approve nominations for office, or tax resources.[52] For both these reasons, a centralizing poor relief system in the hands of powerful magistrates could undermine the Medici dukes' own efforts to secure their personal authority.

Certainly Cosimo's most delicate relations were with the Florentine patricians, and particularly with those gathered in the Council of 200 and its executive forty-eight-member senate. They had written the new constitution in 1532, and after the assassination of his distant cousin Alessandro de'Medici in 1537, they appointed him in some desperation. While generally Medici supporters, they assumed that this inexperienced boy would act as a figurehead like the

Venetian doge. The collapse of the last republic in 1530 had brought many *piagnone* moderates over to the view that having a Medici on the ducal throne could provide some ballast to the regime so long as this duke left governance to a series of powerful magistracies of the Council. The Bigallo captains saw themselves as one such magistracy, and as their ambitions became clear through their draft statutes and their early actions of 1542 and 1543, it seems to have dawned on Cosimo that they could develop into the kind of body that could challenge his agenda rather than fulfill it. In the narrow area of poor relief, they could establish under their own authority the kind of network that Cosimo himself wished to control, and in the process they could certainly alienate locally influential *ospedale* patrons whose cooperation was vital to Cosimo's strategy of dealing directly with territorial leaders. While they were anything but Cosimo's political enemies, they were to some extent his rivals in a race for political supremacy whose outcome was, in 1542–43, by no means assured.[53] In the decades that followed, both Cosimo I and his sons consistently ignored the Bigallo captains' appeals for ratification of their broad authority or for the funds to fulfill their mandate. Their neglect was more deliberate than benign, and ensured that the captains could do little but supervise the Ospedale degli Abbandonati. If their centralizing ambitions did not extend beyond care for orphaned and abandoned boys, what then of the girls who were in a similar state?

The dukes refused the captains' persistent appeals to be put in charge of orphaned and abandoned girls until 1615. While they did not centralize that care in a single orphanage like the Abbandonati, or set up a parallel magistracy like the Bigallo, they did establish a congregational confraternity to oversee and coordinate care at arm's length. This was the Compagnia di S. Maria Vergine, whose members, as Rosalia Manno Tolu has shown, took an active role in establishing most of Florence's conservatories. The name at the head of the confraternity's first matriculation list is that of Francesco d'Astudiglio, a Spanish priest and doctor from Burgos who had come to the Medici court together with Eleonora of Toledo, who had funneled her alms giving to S. Maria Vergine and who was a witness to the will in which she pledged 200 scudi annually for dowries for the conservatory's girls. We have already seen that Francesco Rosati of S. Niccolò was also a founding member of S. Maria Vergine. Another charter member was Antonio di Francesco Cattanio, also known as Antonio da Milano, who was the first priest for the girls of S. Maria Vergine and who was instrumental as one of the founders of the Pietà conservatory that opened in 1554. When that conservatory needed an administrator who could oversee expenses and collect the income generated by the girls' work, they turned to Andrea di Benedetto Biliotti, who had joined S. Maria Vergine a year before. Among later members of the group, we find both Vittorio dell'Ancisa, the founder of the Carità conservatory, and Girolamo Michelozzi (a senator and cavalier of the Order of Santo Stefano), Friar Giulio Zanchini, and Giovanni Battista de Botti, the three founders of S. Caterina; certainly dell'Ancisa consulted the S. Niccolò statutes when he was framing the rules for the Carità. S. Maria Vergine steadily expanded its coordinating role with Florentine conservatories. Having taken over S. Niccolò's administration in 1564, it merged the two separate quarters into one building in 1620. Its early control over S. Caterina expanded to the point where five of the first six governors were members, including those who renovated the building and wrote the first statutes. By 1632, an anonymous S. Maria Vergine account noted the fact that it still controlled half of S. Caterina's six-man governing council. These connections went beyond the administrative level; some of the girls living in the Ceppo had sisters in S. Caterina, and the governors of the two homes allowed for visits on some feast days.[54]

For all its importance, S. Maria Vergine remains a somewhat shadowy confraternity that operated more as a behind-the-scenes charitable congregation than as a conventional lay religious brotherhood. In its early years it had a relatively high turnover; in its first four years, it had lost eleven members, or over one-third of its original strength, seven through death and four through resignation. The members addressed at least part of this problem by ensuring that more of their new recruits were in their 30s or 40s (with three in their 20s). Eight of the original thirty had some historic family links among the *piagnoni*, and at least one, the physician Giovanni de Rossi, was himself a member of the *piagnone* group in 1497. While most members came from prominent families like the Portinari, Frescobaldi, Pandolfini, and Alberghi, there were a few more humble ones identified by patronymics, like the cloth-shearer (*cimatore*) Lorenzo di Tommaso, or by their occupation, like Lionardo il Sarto (tailor). One charter member, Alessandro di Gherardo Corsini, was a Florentine senator, and in its early years the confraternity usually counted at least one senator in its ranks. By the turn of the next century there were two or three senators, another sign of its expanding importance in the informal network of state charitable aid. Like most brotherhoods, the confraternity chose its own members. Though technically at forty members from 1584, meetings at the turn of the century attracted only twelve to twenty participants.[55] Any continuing Medici influence was more indirect than at the Bigallo. Yet the choice to appoint its members to establish the new S. Caterina home four decades later speaks to the dukes' continuing regard for and investment in the confraternity. It suggests that however informally the links to the Medici were maintained, they were sufficiently strong that S. Maria Vergine could be considered a voluntary body parallel to the Bigallo, and that it acted primarily as an administrative body overseeing Florence's conservatories as the Bigallo acted for the orphanage of the Abbandonati. The relative paucity of its religious observances reinforces this impression.

So far as we know, S. Maria Vergine had no oratory or regular religious services. Almost all of its members pledged to give annual sums of money, grain, wine, or oil, and received for their generosity the grateful prayers of the girls in their care, yet S. Maria Vergine did not collect legacies on the promise of requiem Masses said by a confraternal priest in a confraternal oratory. The pastoral visitors sent around the Florentine archdiocese by Archbishop Antonio Altoviti in 1568 and Alessandro de Medici in 1589 made no mention of it, and it does not appear in M. Piccianti's 1589 census of 143 confraternities found in the city of Florence. While the 1632 anonymous history suggests that its members were proud of their achievements, the Vergine left few records and seems to have simply dissolved at some point in the seventeenth century. By contrast, the Bigallo is mentioned in archdiocesan records as a functioning confraternity performing Masses, even though its captains would have preferred to jettison the liabilities and obligations of confraternal identity and function simply as magistrates.[56] This brings a final interesting comparison: while members of S. Maria Vergine served in the congregations governing other conservatories, no Bigallo captains served in S. Maria Vergine. There was no overlap between these two groups, and each had its own particular patronal links to the Medici dukes.

Women's Governance

The orphanages and conservatories considered to this point were run by confraternities and/or congregations made up of men. Yet a few homes had parallel congregations of men and women working together, while others were run by groups of women alone, particularly the Casa della Pietà in Florence (est. 1554) and the Conservatorio di S. Giuseppe in Bologna (est. 1606). Did they do anything differently? Definitely—from the way they organized themselves, to the ways they raised funds, to the way they related with the children in their charge. Yet their difference was short-lived. In all instances, the women's mode of governance was within a few decades (or less) criticized and reformed to bring them closer to local (male) conventions. When opening shelters for needy girls, women did not use the model of institutional hospitals, but that of the informal communities of widows who fostered children as a way of realizing spiritual goals and achieving financial self-sufficiency. This was strongest in Florence, where the model of the widows' community dovetailed with Savonarolan politics. Some of Savonarola's strongest supporters had been among widows who seized on his message about building a charitable republic by devoting their own lives and resources to serving the needy. Three Florentine conservatories rose out of this ethic—the only three that were run by women, as it turns out. Yet all three were undone by Savonarolan politics: one by a suspicious Cosimo I and two by conflicts with Savonarolan male clergy who found the women's religious vision threatening.

As we saw in chapter 2, the earliest identifiable conservatory in Florence was the shelter that Lionarda Barducci Ginori opened in 1541. Though colloquially known as the Ospedale delle Povere Fanciulle Abbandonate, it in fact had no formal name or legal identity, and was little more than a community of widows who took in numbers of young girls. Florentines likely began using the name after Cosimo I opened the Ospedale degli Poveri Abbandonati a year later, and it suggests that they saw the two as companion institutions much like Bologna's S. Maria del Baraccano and S. Bartolomeo di Reno. Ginori rented the Ospedale di S. Niccolò dei Fantoni in Piazza S. Felice from the Compagnia di S. Maria del Bigallo where a possible kinsman, Giovanni Leonardo Barducci, was then a captain. To help in the work she recruited three other widows, Nanina, Antonia, and Piera, and then her own daughters Caterina Tedaldi and Maria. She was certainly not the only widow fostering orphans for a fee, because another of the Bigallo's tenants in the mid-1540s was Maddalena, widow of Sebastrella, who together with her daughter ran a similar home for boys, possibly on commission from the Bigallo itself, which had been merged into the magistracy that operated the Abbandonati orphanage.[57]

The Bigallo captain-magistrates offered Ginori alms from time to time, but Ginori also counted on informal alms giving by other women to cover costs. These women constituted a network of help that may also have sponsored girls and that certainly intervened on their behalf. After Ginori's death in 1549, three of them appealed to Cosimo I for a dowry to help a girl marry. The girl's three elder sisters had all passed through Ginori's shelter and gone on to marriage or a convent thanks in part to Cosimo's aid. Their petition, and others issued after Ginori's death, suggest that this conservatory was organized loosely, if at all. It had no clear entry procedures, no formal officers, and in fact no statutes; Ginori herself had decided which girls stayed and which girls left. This was a common enough procedure for a widow's community, but it left Ginori's daughters puzzled about how they ought to proceed. They believed that they were running a type of lay convent or community that offered shelter on some informal ducal commission, and so sought to draw the duke in more closely. Soon after their mother's death, they wrote to Cosimo I asking that they be allowed to take a girl into "*servanza*" in the "*monasterio*" of their late mother. Cosimo's secretary Lelio Torelli compounded the confusion by forwarding their letter to the captains of the Bigallo, possibly because of the common belief that the so-called Abbandonate and the Bigallo's Abbandonati home for boys were somehow connected.

The Bigallo magistrates, already the landlords of and frequent donors to the Abbandonate, and very eager to expand their mandate, welcomed the strengthening tie. Torelli forwarded at least seventeen petitions of this sort on to the Bigallo before writing in February 1551, "they can accept this one and no more."[58] Torelli and Cosimo presumably saw that this could mushroom out of control, and leave the state subsidizing dowries for any poor girl in its borders, and they now made moves to shut down Ginori's home altogether. More than that, they sought to expunge it. The three widows Nanina, Antonia, and Piera who had lived in the home appealed to Cosimo I for a small farm where they could continue living together, "because Your Excellency is resolved to no longer help care for abandoned girls." They claimed that they had given their youth and their possessions to care of the girls, and that Ginori had promised them the farm after her death so that they could continue living communally. Their request was refused.[59]

Cosimo did in fact carry on facilitating care for abandoned girls by establishing the Compagnia di S. Maria Vergine within the year. On one level his move marked the extension to conservatory governance of the kind of formal institutionalization and accountability that he had initiated with the centralized Ospedale degli Abbandonati and the magistracy that became known as the Bigallo. Yet why was he determined to close down the Abbandonate and eliminate its traces? The most likely answer is that he wanted to sever its connection to the movement of Savonarolan *piagnoni*. Lionarda Barducci Ginori was of *piagnone* stock, and had married into a *piagnone* family. Her daughter Caterina had done the same. The three women who had appealed to Cosimo for a dowry for one of Ginori's wards had also married into *piagnone* families, as was the girl on whose behalf they were writing. The Abbandonate seemed to be another instance of the *piagnone* charitable underground, and though Cosimo's suppressions since 1537 had taken the sting out of the *piagnone* tail, there was no point in allowing this institution to grow into something bigger, or to allow the *piagnoni* to take credit for charity that Cosimo was bankrolling. By contrast, S. Maria Vergine was loyal, organized on familiar institutional lines, and largely self-financing.

Closing the Abbandonate did not eliminate the group of *piagnone* women determined to find shelter for needy girls, any more than opening S. Maria Vergine took up all the demand for such shelter. If anything, ambitions grew as needs exploded. In three years, the *piagnone* women emerged stronger than ever as the force behind the Casa della Pietà. As we saw in chapter 2, the Pietà opened its doors in December 1554, but the women organizing it had already been working for months to raise pledges. Giving a pledge secured membership in the confraternal Compagnia della Pietà and with it the right to participate in the group's activities.[60] In five months, the chief instigators of the group, Margherita Borromei and Marietta Gondi, got 149 pledges, most of them for very small amounts from artisans, servants, and patricians, and all but one from women. Among those giving pledges were Lionarda Ginori's daughters Caterina and Maria Ginori. No doubt more of Ginori's former supporters were among those now joining the rapidly growing Compagnia della Pietà and pledging to support its home. The pledges were the early foundation of the home's finance, and most women renewed their support annually over the first few years of its operation— after a year, the Compagnia della Pietà had 270 members, and by 1558 it had 320.[61]

Most of these women pledged up to a florin annually, and while many donations fell below this level, only eighteen of the first year's cohort exceeded it. Practical and ideological motivations drove this kind of hand-to-mouth financing. In the absence of the large private legacies that had founded most Florentine hospitals, or of the guild or state support that underwrote others, only private pledges could open a new conservatory's doors. Moreover, Savonarola had taught that dependence on an invested, alms-giving community rather than an invested legacy kept religious charitable institutions honest, engaged, and less vulnerable to corruption, fraud, and theft. That said, funding by annually renewed pledges could work only if a few larger donors stood ready to make up the difference when larger bills came due, as indeed happened within months of the Pietà's opening. The shelter also needed another form of funding that Savonarola, and indeed all sixteenth-century poor-relief reformers advocated for financial and moral reasons: low-skilled piecework, usually in textile trades, that the enclosed poor carried out on commission from outside merchants.[62]

There are no statutes extant for the Compagnia at this stage (and likely none written), but there was a *madre priora* and a *consiglio delle maggiori* who helped her make decisions, such as which girls would get into the home. Girls had one interview with Marietta Gondi and four or five other members of the Compagnia (Borromei had died only days before the home opened its doors), who then decided immediately on their admission. This was far simpler than any other conservatory then operating in either Florence or Bologna, and certainly more reminiscent of widows' communities and Ginori's Abbandonate.

What we know of the early organization of the home comes in part through a chronicle of the home started decades later by one of its Dominican *padri spirituali* and carried on by a series of friars and nuns after its transformation into a Dominican convent. The chronicle must be read critically because it deliberately aims to obscure some difficult debates over the Pietà's administration and purpose, and to project the impression that its later evolution into a convent was not a result of these disputes, but an outworking of God's original plan for the home.[63] Reading it in conjunction with contemporary administrative records gives the acute impression that one is reading about two entirely different homes. In the account books, the work of Borromei, Gondi, and the two or three hundred women is amply evident. In the Dominican chronicle, the Pietà conservatory emerges as the work of pious clerics who recruited the women and directed or corrected their efforts. Between the lines we find latent *piagnone* connections and the intense struggles that erupted within the *piagnone* movement between lay women and Dominican friars for control of the Pietà home.

In a prosopographical study of the Pietà matriculation list, Rosalia Manno Tolu has found both a strong presence of traditionally *piagnone* families, and also signs that some of these were beginning to marry into traditionally Medicean families, bringing about a convergence of the two camps. The Pietà's *piagnone* links went to the very top and in many cases had generated considerable personal hardship. Many of the women who had joined the Pietà consorority were the widows, daughters, or sisters of prominent *piagnoni*. Priora Marietta Gondi had married Federico Gondi, an anti-Medicean who had been exiled for his service to the republic and had died in 1536. They had no children, and Marietta gave all her property to the conservatory when she died in 1580. Ginevra Bartolini's husband Lionardo barely escaped the city before being condemned to death in absentia in 1530 for his role in protecting Pieruccio de'Poveri, one of the charismatic leaders who had helped organize *piagnone* poor relief. Maria Strozzi's husband Lorenzo Ridolfi had opposed the arrival of Duke Alessandro in 1530, and had fought against Cosimo I at the battle of Montemurlo in 1537. Her brother Piero was fighting for the French against Cosimo in the war for Siena that was raging even as the Pietà was being established.

Other women had more mixed political connections. Ginevra Sacchetti Capponi was the daughter of Niccolò Sacchetti, a signatory of the petition defending Savonarola that was sent to the pope in 1497; she was a sister-in-law of Niccolò Capponi, first *gonfaoloniere* (standard-bearer) of the last republic. On the other hand, her sister Isabella had married Luigi Guicciardini, a fervent Medicean who gained important offices under the restored duchy. Maddalena Gondi was the widow of Pagnozzo Ridolfi, a once ardent Savonarolan who switched sides in 1530 and went on to take political office under the Medici. Monaldesca Monaldeschi Baglioni, widow of the mercenary Malatesta who had led the last republic's forces through the siege and had subsequently defied the republican government and negotiated with the imperial forces, was a member. So too were Lucrezia Girolami and Cosa Antinori, the widow and daughter respectively of that republic's last *gonfaloniere*, Raffaello Girolami. Yet other family links suggest that the informal networks among patrician families allowed for a degree of coordination in charitable institutions. Maria da Diacetto was the wife of Piero di Bartolomeo Capponi, who had joined Malatesta Baglioni in the surrender, but also the sister of Dionigio da Diacetto, one of the captains of the Bigallo from 1561 to 1574. Another sister was the stepmother of Caterina de'Ricci.[64] At this point, the Pietà was still a Bigallo tenant, occupying the Ospedale di S. Maria dell'Umiltà in Borgo Ognissanti.

These were clearly influential women with first- and secondhand experience of governance. They were deeply pious, but confident and canny enough in ecclesiastical matters that they aimed to draw spiritual directors from a variety of sources: lay and clerical, regular and secular, first and third order. Over the first two decades, the Pietà consorority found teachers for its girls from an unnamed confraternity, the Carmelite sisters of S. Maria degli Angeli, and possibly from the Franciscan friars of the S. Salvatore friary that was adjacent to their home in Borgo Ognissanti. They recruited spiritual directors from the Capuchin, Camaldolese, Dominican, and even Jesuit orders. Savonarolan sentiments among Florentine clergy extended far beyond the Dominicans, and by frequently shuffling their religious guides, the women of the Pietà could avoid falling under the control of a particular religious order. Confraternities commonly followed this practice, and while most orders accommodated it, Dominicans were less open to it and Florentine Dominicans were particularly resistant.[65] The women also gave the girls their own old breviaries and psalters for use in worship, and may have passed on other spiritual literature.

Savonarola's female disciples were self-assured activists who frequently clashed with the Dominican friars over the organization and direction of their charitable and devotional activities.[66] The Pietà women's nemesis was a fervent Savonarolan friar, Alessandro Capocchi. Capocchi was a seasoned combatant in church wars, having fought against his brothers at S. Maria Novella in order to see the friary moved under the jurisdiction of the Roman Province of the Dominican Order, where it joined S. Marco. He had been spiritual director of one of the key *piagnone* confraternities, S. Benedetto Bianco, and at the Carmelite convent of S. Maria degli Angeli, where he first had contact with the Pietà women and girls. Capocchi's public association with Savonarola could have generated more trouble politically had he not also been one of those who was subtly redefining the friar as a kinder, gentler, miracle-working proponent of Catholic spiritual reform—a Savonarola without the millenarian prophecies or the aggressively anti-Medicean republicanism.[67] In order to secure the position as the Pietà's spiritual director, Capocchi levied a charge of heresy against the Jesuit cleric who was then serving the women and girls. The charge stuck, the Jesuit was removed to Rome, and the gratified women of the Pietà appointed Capocchi in his place.[68]

Capocchi was a charismatic and determined director, and in the course of a decade (1558–68) he convinced the women of the Pietà to make some fundamental changes to their shelter and confraternity. The girls' eclectic worship forms were reformed to match current conventions, and all were enrolled in the Company of the Rosary, a confraternity founded and heavily promoted by the Dominicans. The Pietà's informal and open administration was described as "resulting more often in confusion than order," so Capocchi wrote statutes that regularized practices and vested authority in an executive council of seventeen, and later, nine members.[69] Yet the biggest change was a move to a new location.

The shelter's home in the old pilgrims' hostel of S. Maria dell'Umiltà in Borgo Ognissanti was cramped, surrounded by prostitutes and textile workshops, and next to a Franciscan friary—all threats to its integrity in Capocchi's estimation. In spite of the fact that they had just been given an adjacent property that would allow them to expand, Capocchi convinced the women to move, and then used all his influence and that of a courtier for whom he served as private confessor to intercede with the reluctant Medici. He was nothing if not persuasive. Both the Bigallo captains and Cosimo I's secretary Lellio Torelli also opposed moving the Pietà, and the shift involved some complicated property transactions. Capocchi aimed to get the Pietà closer to the neighborhood of San Marco, where the Dominicans had been slowly building up a community of women's enclosures, including the *piagnone* convents of S. Lucia and S. Caterina di Siena.[70] In December 1563 the Pietà bought three houses behind the Annunziata friary and over the next five years had them restructured into a more thoroughly enclosed conservatory with workspaces. The girls moved before reconstruction was even finished, with rituals that were a celebration of Florentine Dominican traditions. The date chosen was 10 May, the feast of S. Antoninus, the Dominican who had been Florence's archbishop from 1446 to 1459. One hundred and sixty girls donned white clothes and made the processional trek to their new quarters, likely accompanied by Gondi and some of the over three hundred Florentine women who had pledged to support them to that date. En route, they stopped at S. Maria Novella to hear Capocchi give a sermon and then, one by one, the girls kissed the relic of S. Vincent Ferrer kept there. They then issued from the church and moved north to the convent of San Marco, the center of Florentine celebrations of S. Antoninus's feast. A couple of priests met them at the door to sprinkle them with holy water before they proceeded to the saint's tomb. Each girl kissed the relic before the group headed out again and processed the short distance north to their new home. The new complex was on the edge of the city and in sight of the walls, a great distance and a far cry from the pimps, bawds, apprentices, and shops of Borgo Ognissanti.[71]

Capocchi had overreached himself. According to the Dominican chronicle, some women of *mali voli* (bad will) in the Compagnia della Pietà opposed the friar, adding mysteriously that "he left the Governing Council of those Abbandonate because he was not able to realize one of his ambitions for them."[72] A day after the new church at the new quarters was dedicated, arguably his crowning triumph, Capocchi was replaced as *padre confessore*. Administrative records show that the women of the executive council that he had put in place had discussed Capocchi's tenure three days earlier and voted 8 to 1 to replace their energetic Dominican; it is the only time in the Pietà records that the appointment of the priest is noted, and the only time that a vote tally is recorded.[73] In his place, they appointed a Camaldolese friar, Fra Franceschini.

It is not clear what constituted the last straw for the Pietà women like Marietta Gondi and Lucrezia Ricasoli. Capocchi's statutes, relocation, and changes to the girls' worship gradually made the Pietà more like a convent, but each move had been approved by the women. With these pieces in place, it could be that his unstated "ambition" was to now formally turn the Pietà into a tertiary convent, and that this galvanized whatever opposition there had been to individual changes in the past. Certainly the women's decision to appoint a Camaldolese in place of a friar from nearby San Marco suggests that they were now determined to put some distance between themselves and the Dominican friars' influence and expectations. Some difficult years followed. Now distant from the contacts, donors, and volunteers built up over fifteen years in Borgo Ognissanti, they were weakened financially.[74] More critically, local church politics entered the dispute as Cosimo I finally made peace with Florence's archbishop Antonio Altoviti and allowed him to enter the city.

Altoviti had been appointed twenty years before but had not since set foot in Florence. His father Biondo had supported the assassination of Duke Alessandro I in 1537, and had consistently opposed Medici rule. Antonio Altoviti himself was associated with the Savonarolan *piagnone* movement. Not surprisingly, Cosimo I took Altoviti's appointment by Paul III in 1548 as an affront. He refused to allow the archbishop to enter Tuscany, and confiscated his revenues. For two decades, Florence's ecclesiastical government was fluid at best, and this may have allowed the women of the Pietà to be as free as they were in supervising their young wards' spiritual lives. Their liberties were about to end. Altoviti finally entered the diocese in May 1567 and began an aggressive program of Tridentine reform. He conducted an extensive visitation from April 1568 to October 1569, convoked a diocesan synod in 1569 to formally adopt the decrees of Trent (which Cosimo I had already published in 1564), and planned a provincial synod for 1573 with the same purpose. Among the Tridentine reformers' goals was a determination to put more order, discipline, and regularity into the disparate variety of women's religious communities. In June 1570, Altoviti ordered the women of the Pietà to draw their next *padre confessore* from the Dominican Order, and from San Marco in particular. Fra Franceschini's fate is not clear.[75]

San Marco had been dealt a strong hand and used it to wring concessions that would permanently change the nature of the Pietà community. It agreed to provide a confessor on condition that the Pietà take only friars of S. Marco in perpetuity, and that the San Marco prior supervise future Pietà elections. He also took one of the three keys to the church. The new *padre confessore*, Fr. Battista Salvetti, immediately reenrolled the girls in the Company of the Rosary and

Table 5.3. Income Generation at the Pietà, 1566–1578

	Ordinary Alms		Extraordinary Alms		Work	
	Lire	%	Lire	%	Lire	%
1566–71	20,506	30	19,417	29	27,305	40
1572–73	4,998	21	3,580	15	15,623	64
1574–75	2,775	11	1,790	7	4,807	18
1576	7,294	34	3,571	17	10,289	48
1577	2,626	20	970	7.5	6,173	48
1578	2,799	17	371	2	5,398	33

Source: ASF, CRSF ms. 112/57, cc. 142r–v, 182r, 208r, 264r, 307r.
Note: % = percentage of total income.

secured spiritual benefits for the girls from the Dominican Order. As we saw in the previous chapter, before this time the Pietà had routinely sent out about one-fifth of its girls into private homes as domestic servants, but now the practice ended and the girls remained locked up inside their new enclosure. There they were set to work. As Table 5.3 shows, from 1566 to 1571, their work had generated 40 percent of the home's income and through the balance of the decade it averaged 42 percent and rose as high as 64 percent. The generosity of shopkeepers, textile workers, church goers, and prostitutes around Borgo Ognissanti had generated almost 60 percent of income before the move, but in the empty streets around the new quarters in Via Mandorlo, alms gathering of all kinds dropped to 36 percent of income and fell to under 20 percent by the end of the decade. Receipts from the girls' trips around town with their alms boxes disappear from the ledger, though this may simply reflect a change in accounting procedures. In one short decade, the Pietà moved from being an alms-supported open shelter to being a closed workhouse. This set the stage for a further radical shift: in 1586 a Flemish friar, Gherardo Fiammingo, arrived as *padre spirituale* and began moving the home definitely toward its eventual status as a third order Dominican convent. He vested the first eighteen girls as tertiaries on 25 March 1595, the Feast of the Annunciation and the beginning of Florence's new year.

Sensitive to the controversy stirred up by Capocchi a few years earlier, the Dominicans had bided their time until the last of the group of women who had founded and run the Pietà had died. Marietta Gondi died in 1580, after spending twenty-six years as *madre priora*. Her successor Lucrezia Ricasoli was the last of the founding group, and died in 1586. The first resident prioress, Alessandra di Girolamo Lignuaiolo, had died in 1583 after twenty-nine years of continuous service. With their long terms of service and close personal involvement in the Pietà's day-to-day operation, these women had given and guarded a particular communal identity. While they had been forced to take the friars of S. Marco as their confessors, most friars remained for only two or four years, and none attempted the ambitious changes launched by Fra Gherardo.[76] With his arrival the pattern of officeholding reversed, with the *madre priora* and the resident prioress serving shorter terms, while the confessors remained longer—Fra Gherardo was in office for eighteen years. As the founding group came to the end of its term and influence, the Pietà's hitherto clear and through record keeping deteriorated. While the Compagnia della Pietà had begun its work with a systematic and well-maintained set of records, none of the volumes bearing financial accounts are extant from the time of Madre Priora Marietta Gondi's death in 1580 until after Fra Gherardo's death in 1604.[77]

Changes also crept into the language used internally and the way it framed relationships. Early records specifically and consistently referred to the women collectively. Account books and *ricordi* are all headed with some variation of "this book is of the women and girls of the *Pietà*" ("questo libro e delle donne e fanciulle della pieta"), while letters sent to Duke Cosimo I regarding property transactions are signed not by Marietta Gondi or an executive, but by "The women who govern the abandoned girls of Borgo Ogni Santi" ("Le donne che governano l'abandonate di B. Ogni Santi").[78] The members present when girls were interviewed and admitted to the home were known as the *madre priore*, or mother prioresses, a term never restricted to Marietta Gondi. It emphasized their close personal and maternal connection to the home, a connection that they substantiated with frequent alms and periodic visits. Yet when one of the newly arrived tertiaries Caterina began contributing sections to the chronicle in 1593, she recorded a subtle shift. *Madre priora* now referred only to the resident prioress, an overseer whom the longest resident girls and women elected from among their own number on the model of conventual elections. By contrast, the gentlewoman who headed the Compagnia della Pietà was now called the *priora generale*, or more tellingly the *priora di Fuori*.[79] Sister Caterina's redefinition was consistent with the tone of the Dominican chronicle generally, which consistently asserted that the closest emotional relations in the home were not those between the women and their metaphorical daughters, but those between the clerical confessors and girls. It is subdivided into chapters organized according to the length of time that particular priests spent with the home, and seldom describes anything the women *do*. In the chronicle, the girls shed tears of gladness and grief for their confessors, but only hot tears of rage at the meddling women of the Compagnia della Pietà. Oddly, it says nothing at all about the tears that both girls and women must have shed over the many deaths that gave the Pietà the dubious distinction of having the highest mortality rate of all Florentine conservatories.

Any hot tears of rage dried up through the early and middle decades of the seventeenth century. The Compagnia della Pietà dropped from the records; the chronicles mention instead a panel of five *signore governatrice*, headed by a *priora generale* and willing to institute the restrictions characteristic of a self-sufficient convent: no more alms gathering in the streets by any girls other than novices (1623), no more instruction in reading and writing (1624), conversion of the *scrittorio* into a *granaio* for food storage (1624), and construction of an oven on site so that the girls would no longer have to go out on the street to buy or beg bread (mid-1620s). In 1624, the Pietà started a new matriculation list, the *Libro Nuovo*, and registered 106 women: the youngest was 8, the oldest 79. One-third had been there thirty years before when Fra Gherardo began vesting tertiaries. By 1634 the administrative records referred to the institution as the Monastero delle Fanciulle or the Venerabil Collegio delle Fanciulle della Pietà, and it had completed its metamorphosis into a third order convent.[80]

The same metamorphosis from conservatory to convent came over another Florentine home that was for a brief time run by women. The records are less numerous and the history more contested, but here again Savonarolan politics added heat to an administrative dispute. As we saw in chapter 2, the Florentine cleric Vittorio dell'Ancisa received his early spiritual formation in Savonarolan and Dominican confraternities, was *padre confessore* for the conservatory of S. Maria Vergine, worked with Philip Neri (another follower of Savonarola) at the beggars' shelter of S. Trinità dei Pellegrini in Rome for a decade, and then opened the Carità home as a paupers' hostel in 1583 using the proceeds of an inheritance. Orphaned and abandoned girls first entered the home six years later. Dell'Ancisa never got around to writing formal statutes but sketched out an administration based around two companies of forty, one of women and one of men. These were modeled on the *piagnone* charitable confraternities that he had known and joined as a young man, and also on the Compagnia di S. Maria Vergine, which he had rejoined after returning to Florence from Rome. The women and men of these two companies undertook the day-to-day work of the shelter, with men in charge of feeding beggars and women in charge of educating and governing the girls. Each met separately and elected from their number a *proposto* and some *deputati* to handle administration. Together they formed the Congregation of Charity (the name of a *piagnone* confraternity that dell'Ancisa had joined in 1568 but that had since disbanded), and while both sides had a voice, the men exercised ultimate authority. Dell'Ancisa was the *governatore* who brought the two together, much as Bologna's rectors brought together the Larga and Stretta groups of their charitable confraternities.[81]

Having a Company of Men and one of Women made sense as long as the Casa della Carità served both genders, but in 1595 dell'Ancisa bowed to pressure from the Buonomini di S. Martino and the duke, and made the Carità a shelter exclusively for young girls from the ranks of *poveri vergognosi*, or "shamefaced poor." The Carità's congregation sheltered them and groomed them for marriage or the convent, hiring the extended family of a widow Margherita Camerini to be the core of the residential community. A critical distinction from the daily lives of girls in other conservatories was that Carità wards were not expected to work for a living; relatives, sponsors, the Buonomini di S. Martino, and the Magistrato dei Pupilli paid fees to cover the costs. The superfluous Company of Men now disbanded, and the remaining women constituted the whole of the Congregation of Charity. Dell'Ancisa also sketched out notes for a set of statutes. He entrusted the now all-female Congregation of Charity with supervising widow Camerini and the girls, but set four male *protettori* over them to handle temporal affairs. Two of these men would be well-born administrators, while the other two would be experienced bookkeepers. The four men together with dell'Ancisa would also choose the gentlewoman who headed up the Congregation of Charity for a three-year term, and who joined the men to discuss and vote on business. The Congregation of Charity could not make a decision without the approval of the men.

The women reacted strongly against these new rules. They met and wrote a letter to dell'Ancisa claiming that they recognized his authority in spiritual matters only, that the home was *their* main charge, and that they would take the lead in administration.[82] Though no record of their names survives, theirs was described as a company of gentlewomen. Given the status of the girls in their care, they most likely had the kind of rank, experience, and skills found among the founders of Pietà. They may also have shared the *piagnone* orientation that dell'Ancisa had deliberately highlighted when naming his shelter and its governing Congregation of Charity. Their letter suggests that they wished to turn the Casa della Carità into a lay conservatory on those lines. Were they reacting against the fact that only a few months before the Pietà had begun its transition into a convent? They felt strongly, and seem to have enlisted others into their cause. The controversy became so violent that dell'Ancisa had to take shelter in a convent for a few days to avoid being beaten up, and Archbishop Alessandro de'Medici was forced to intervene.[83]

The women's rebellion, if we can call it that, was short-lived. Dell'Ancisa died three years later, while in the process of writing new statutes. The Company of Women, the Congregation of Charity, and indeed most laypeople were effectively written out of the conservatory. In the decade after his death, the move began to transform the home into a convent under the authority of the archbishop. New rules adopted in 1607 removed laypeople from all but financial administration and gave the archbishop final say in everything, including which girls entered through its doors.[84] Girls entered as *novizzi* (novices) and passed to an intermediate stage as *giovani* (youths) before applying to become *stabilite* (fixed, established). A *fanciulla stabilite* at the Carità was neither a nun nor a tertiary, but neither was she going to leave the home. As at the Pietà, the first women to take this step were older women who had lived many years in the home and who had no dowry to ease their way into a conventional convent: 36-year-old Christina Giorgi was a twenty-year veteran, having entered when dell'Ancisa opened the Carità. She was prioress when she was *stabilite*. Seven other women ages 24 to 39, who had lived at the Carità for between eight and nineteen years, joined her. This was almost half the residents of the small home.[85]

The next step in the Carità's evolution into a religious house came in 1627, when the archbishop assumed full authority and imposed full enclosure. New statutes of 1644 cleared up the remaining ambiguities.[86] The Carità sisters wore the habit and were under the authority of the diocese of Florence. Neither widows nor married women could enter the enclosure for lessons, devotions, retreats, or retirement. The nuns' chief work was precisely that of sheltering and educating needy girls, both fee-paying and pieceworking, age 16 and older. It was *serbanza* in all but name. Some of these girls would eventually leave as wives, others might be *stabilite* and join the nuns, and yet others of greater *infermità* or lesser *qualità* might stay on as servants.[87]

Women in Bologna generally had more rights, greater influence, and a broader social sphere in which to operate compared to women in other cities in Renaissance Italy. Historians and art historians have uncovered a vibrant cultural life embracing both female artists and patrons. More secure dotal rights, the patriciate's preference for marrying within the city, and the frequent absence of patrician men on diplomatic or bureaucratic missions made upper-class women significant and active players in the political game.[88] Moreover, the city was completely untouched by the politics of Savonarolism, and had a tradition of using lay institutions like confraternities and hospitals as a vehicle for resisting— or at least circumventing—ecclesiastical authority. Did this make a difference in who ran conservatories and how? In the long run it did not. The local politics of charity worked against shelters built on the model of the widows' community and pushed instead toward institutional forms in which men dominated. Women were necessary participants in these homes, and at least one was established and run for a period by women alone, but by the mid-seventeenth century all followed the local administrative template in which men dominated. That said, none became convents. They were too valuable as lay institutions to be allowed to slip under clerical control.

Women took a leading role in Bolognese conservatories from the start, though not as founders. As we saw in chapter 3, Bolognese conservatories set strict entrance requirements and actually followed them in order to ensure that girls were local and respectable. Determining reputation, health, virginity, and resources could require three or four separate steps, complete with written nominations, interviews with neighbors, checks of civic baptismal records, and votes of the executive and confraternal membership, and could take six months or more. These time-consuming and physically invasive procedures were too important to be left to female staff, and could not be conducted by male administrators, so women were drafted into conservatory administrations from the very beginning, and usually formed a separate group within the collegiate model.

Two of the confraternities overseeing Bolognese conservatories, S. Maria del Baraccano and S. Croce, recruited parallel companies of laywomen, who in turn elected a trio of officers to conduct some of the more delicate exchanges with girls. These women checked the virginity of applicants to the homes, visited periodically to see that living conditions were acceptable, and even kept tabs on women who had married out the home and now lived in the city. The Baraccano gentlewomen were active from the time the former pilgrims' hostel began sheltering orphaned and abandoned girls in 1527. Women like Pantasilea, Camilla, and Alexandra Bentivoglio, Julia and Gentiles Paleotti, Helena Guastavillani, and Ginevra Lambertini came from the highest social class. They reported to the twelve-member male executive, which reported in turn to the confraternity as a whole. These women were an integral part of the collegiate system, sharing authority with the men much like their brothers, husbands, and fathers in Bologna's senate shared authority with the papal legate. While they kept no separate records, the gentlewomen of S. Maria del Baraccano did have a set of statutes directing their activities. Approved in 1548, they were extremely rudimentary, but this in itself is not surprising since they predated the general statutes for the conservatory, and indeed would appear to be the first statutes of any kind for a conservatory in Italy.[89] Names of all the confraternity's women (one list accompanying these statutes notes fifteen names, and another twenty-six) went into a bag, from which three were drawn monthly to oversee the group's activities and visit the home regularly. On this rotation, each woman would serve at least one month's term in the year, and some might serve two. Girls had to pass a secret vote in the women's company, with two-thirds of the beans cast before the men would even consider their application, and the men could not allow into the home a girl who hadn't been approved by the women. The women also appointed the conservatory's resident female warden and the chaplain who heard confession and administered sacraments to the girls.

The Compagnia di S. Maria del Baraccano expanded its statutes for the conservatory five years later in order to describe more fully the procedures for administration, accountability, and the *governo* of the girls. While the provisions on girls' age, citizenship, virginity, and honor remained unchanged, the power to determine entrants into the home shifted decisively to the sixteen male officers. Under these 1553 statutes, the women didn't vote at all, although they still interviewed and inspected applicants and passed on recommendations orally to the twelve male deputies and their four superintendents, all of them serving life terms. The women had been demoted from their original status as co-governors of the conservatory to a level not far above the staff, whom they no longer had the authority to appoint.

This subordination in 1553 seems to have come out of a few intersecting forces. It may have been a price for the resolution a few months later of a long-standing fight between the Baraccano's Larga and Stretta companies. These had warred from 1439, when the confraternity was one of the first in Bologna to experiment with this internal division. Stretta devotional values were aggressively male, stereotyping women as the source of sin and temptation, and requiring men to atone for their own sins and the sins of their communities by whipping themselves. This was a devotional exercise that few thought appropriate for lay women and the flagellants' whips effectively drove women out of most confraternities. Though Bolognese women had traditionally made up half the membership or more of some of the large community-based *laudesi* confraternities, they inevitably lost any public or administrative role—and sometimes even membership—in companies undergoing the Larga-Stretta division. This had not happened in S. Maria del Baraccano, perhaps because of the extreme animosity between the groups, but also because of the women's wealth, power, and determination.[90]

Yet something changed in the early 1550s, that period of conjunction when Bologna's senators began consolidating their administrative grip on the city, when individual charitable homes were drawn into a network, and when all of Bologna's conservatories and orphanages received new statutes that enshrined a roughly standard collegiate model headed by an executive and a patrician rector. It was also a time when confraternities across the city were starting to devise, within the collegiate model, separate companies for well-born women that had a collective devotional life, but little real authority or even independence within the larger confraternity. These consororities would presumably blunt the appeal for women of heterodox groups like the Protestant conventicles that were known to gather in Bologna.[91] Catholic reformers believed that women's independence in spiritual matters led inevitably to heresy, limited as they were with weaker wills, intellectual frailty, and a troubling curiosity, and they had to look no farther than Ferrara, 40 kilometers to the north, to confirm their suspicions. Duchess Renée of Ferrara had turned her court into a refuge for Protestants for almost a decade and a half, and was soon (1554) to lose contact with her children and be sentenced for heresy as a result. Given a history of strong cultural ties between the two cities, Bologna's patrician women had no doubt enjoyed her hospitality, particularly those with the wealth, power, and influence of the Baraccano gentlewomen some of whom, like the Bentivoglio sisters, had close relatives there.

Wielding real power had made the Baraccano gentlewomen anomalous in Bologna, and that anomaly could not be sustained as broader political and religious forces coincided with the drive to get the Stretta to support the home more fully. The gentlewomen retained their responsibilities as intermediaries between the girls and male administrators, but lost their decisive role as the home's gatekeepers. This became the new local standard for involving women in charitable enclosures that might shelter poor women and children. A decade later, the men planning the operation of the Opera dei Poveri Mendicanti added a similar three-person team of gentlewoman auxiliaries to the Opera's thirty-four-person rotating team of voluntary officials.[92]

It was to be three decades before a new conservatory opened in Bologna. As we saw in chapter 2, S. Croce's founder the merchant Bonifacio dalle Balle first gathered needy girls off the street in the early 1580s and entrusted them to a widow, whom he subsidized. A decade of hard work and two larger houses later, he turned to a community of male and female Franciscan tertiaries for help, and another decade after that his precarious finances forced him to bring into the administration some high-born men who were determined to bend S. Croce to the local model. The statutes they forced on dalle Balle in 1609 followed the Baraccano example in most respects, though the ten or twelve women of the Congregation of Gentlewomen were not to be drawn from the existing confraternity (which would remain exclusively male), but from the city at large. The men aimed particularly for influential patrician women, whom they would appoint to life terms; those of lesser status could join on probationary annual appointments. S. Croce's men did not understand the real resource that these women represented, and assigned them duties on the level of a Ladies Auxiliary. Women reviewed applicants and visited the home to oversee staff and girls, but had no collective life, no voting powers, and no relations with the male company apart from oral reports between the women's *priora* and the S. Croce rector. Their special charge to take particular care of "the laundry and other things relating to women" shows the limits of the men's thinking here, and betrays an underlying class difference.

But these were women who did not do laundry. Administrative records suggest that they were many steps up the social ladder from the merchant Bonifacio dalle Balle who had started the home and the tertiaries who had staffed it. And indeed, the likes of Camilla Paleotti Gozzadini, Isabella Viggiani, and Hippolita Volta Boncompagni concerned themselves with more than just laundry, regardless of statutes. Yet for all their shine and status, they were coming into a home that had functioned for almost three decades without a Congregation of Gentlewomen. The resident tertiaries deeply resented their arrival and initially refused to obey the gentlewomen. The men never fully understood their potential and their indifference allowed the congregation to lapse into inactivity. It disappeared from the first statute review of 1647, but the women seem to have disappeared long before that. By 1630 Hippolita Volta Boncompagni moved over to the conservatory of S. Giuseppe, where she could be far more active.[93]

S. Giuseppe was quite different from either S. Croce or the Baraccano in that it was run solely by women. Twelve patrician women had established this conservatory in 1606, working with a Jesuit priest, Giorgio Giustiniani. Their methods were far closer to those of Florentine widows' communities, though they did not live together. Like Florence's Pietà, they had no elected executive of specialized officers beyond a prioress. Rather, all the women gathered for all the meetings and simply conducted business together. Like the Pietà, they had simple entrance requirements and procedures. Like the Pietà, they steered clear of the dowry business, refusing to offer these or even to arrange marriages at all. They seem to have seen themselves as best suited to offering emergency aid quickly to young women, eschewing the protracted and invasive review process of other male-administered conservatories in favor of immediate and always short-term shelter. Their most innovative strategy locally was a system of direct mentoring: each entering girl was paired with one of the twelve women, who would then take a personal interest in training her in domestic arts and preparing her for service as a maid in a Bolognese home. They did not operate at arm's length, and were willing to take on hard work. At the extreme end of this kind of direct and protracted involvement in the lives of the girls, one of the women, Margherita Angiosoli Fantuzzi, actually moved into the home as the resident *guardiana* for a short term when the existing *guardiana* quit suddenly.[94]

Another parallel with the Pietà is that S. Giuseppe had no statutes until 1641. By this point its character had already begun to change significantly. Six men had come into the company in 1631 at the insistence of Giustiniani, who drew the six from the Jesuits' local lay Congregation of Giesu Maria. By 1646 there were almost as many men as women in the company (ten to twelve).[95] The ostensible reason, as conveyed in the first set of statutes drawn up in 1641, was that women experienced difficulties with some of the details of administration. Yet the picture of the women as well-meaning but hapless doyens is unconvincing.[96] They were drawn from some of the best and most powerful families of Bologna, including Marchese Diamante Campeggi Pepoli, Marchese Giulia Paleotti, and Hippolita Boncompagni, and as such often had considerable experience tending family estates while their husbands were pursuing political and administrative careers elsewhere in the papal state.[97] In less than a decade from their origin in 1606, the women had accumulated sixteen rural properties and two city homes.[98] The account books demonstrate no signs of difficulty, and no complaints about it either. Yet the men took over the positions having to do with finance (*depositario*), provisioning (*provveditore*), and record keeping (*secretario*), and as they came into the home's administration, other changes followed. The system of direct mentorships that paired women and wards seems to have ended by April 1636.[99] Dowries and marriages were still avoided, but fundraising now shifted to the girls and their sponsors outside the home. Just as Florence's Pietà and Carità were gradually metamorphosing into convents, Bologna's S. Guiseppe was turning into a boarding school or a lay shelter offering something like *serbanza*. Families or guardians seeking admission for a girl had to pay monthly fees (in advance) for subsistence, and the male administrators carefully kept admissions to within the financial resources available. The *qualità* of girls began edging upward, judging from their family names, and the number who went into domestic service began edging down.[100]

Cultures of Governance

Men like Gian Galeazzo Bottrigari in Bologna and Francesco Rosati in Florence were fulfilling spiritual duties, charitable needs, and political ambitions when they undertook to start or run orphanages and conservatories. They worked with forms that were familiar to them, chiefly the confraternity and the *ospedale* as it had developed locally. In both cities they practiced a form of coordinated decentralization: what seem on the surface to be a number of entirely independent homes turn out on closer analysis to be a network linked together by a series of personal and official connections. Women like Lionarda Ginori and Marietta Gondi also aimed to meet spiritual, charitable, and political needs, and they too worked with forms that were familiar to them—in this case forms of community that Italian women had developed through the middle ages. Yet their distinct communities never lasted more than a few decades, if even that long, and their homes either disappeared, metamorphosed into convents or schools, or gradually adopted the local institutional administration.

Both cities' networks of confraternities evolved in symbiotic relation to local political culture. Bologna's tradition of subdividing charitable confraternities into a few semiautonomous groups that held together in a collegiate system and that sometimes allotted executive seats to particular social and occupational groups fit its evolving oligarchy. It was broadly representative and open to individual patronage networks, but it still preserved the ultimate authority of citizens, the well-born, and senators. As such, it was characteristic of early modern republicanism, with oligarchs preaching open participation and practicing closed control. They carefully divided up political, judicial, and economic power and fashioned formal and informal agreements to ensure the preservation of their rights, privileges, and spheres of control. What coordination there was existed largely through the efforts of those individuals who served as syndics, conservators, or *massari* in more than one confraternity, and also of those senators who became rector of one confraternity after another in turn.

At another level that we have not investigated here, the city's Monte di Pietà handled the finances of a growing number of charitable institutions and so imposed further coordination. Some confraternal charities tended to move over time toward administrations that were more congregational and bureaucratic. Yet even in them, having large memberships, representative executives, and a very active and public cultic life were critical elements in maintaining the broad popular support base that generated officers, donors, and advocates. A long membership list gave these institutions a degree of legitimacy as public institutions. Coordinated decentralization fit local political needs so well that when the jewel was finally fit into the crown in 1563 with the Opera dei Mendicanti workhouse and poor relief system, it took the same confraternal organizational model.

In Florence's form of coordinated decentralization more of the strings went back to Medici hands, which pulled and slackened them inconsistently and in pursuit of dynastic political goals. Florence's charitable confraternities reflected the historical and administrative trauma that came from having been frequently suppressed and co-opted. They had lost their broad memberships and turned into small congregations of directors who set policy and hired staff to carry it out. This was a step farther along the continuum toward early modern state bureaucracies, which goes a long way to explaining why the Medici found it excellently adapted to their purposes. Yet the grand dukes shied away from the logic of moving farther along that continuum until they could be sure of their own power and sure that powerful magistrates would buttress and not undermine it. This caution split care for boys from that for girls into the Bigallo and S. Maria Vergine confraternities, respectively, and ensured that neither confraternity would be able fully to realize the ambitions of its members. Yet too little coordination was at least as impolitic as too much. What emerged instead in Florence was a smaller set of congregationally run institutions with self-perpetuating patrician memberships and a modest overlap of members, coordinated informally through ducal management, patronage, and favorites. Few of these groups had the broad memberships or short-term rotating executives that lent popular legitimacy to Bolognese institutions; these were not broadly public institutions, but narrowly bureaucratic ones. Cultic life and public ritual were not a fundamental part of confraternal recruitment or collective life or, for that matter, of popular legitimacy. But finances were important, and Florence's compact administrations trimmed spending on food, clothing, and firewood so efficiently that they regularly recorded healthy surpluses (see Table A.2). Whether the Medici helped themselves to these funds, as they did with other Florentine charities, is not yet clear.

In both cities, conservatories opened by women initially ran by different models, but moved gradually toward local norms and into local networks. Women founding homes took their expectations from examples familiar to them, such as the communities of *pinzocchere* (which were decentralized and participatory) and the practice of *serbanza* (i.e., girls brought in to the religious community as a temporary *home*—and not just an institutional *shelter* as it was for the boys).[101] These existing forms legitimate our talking about women's particular approach to *governo* as arising from deliberate choice, and not just a practical response to legal or cultural restrictions.[102] In all cases, women typically relied more on group meetings than on the decisions of an executive. Their administration was more informal, apparently conducted without benefit of formal statutes and often without leaving minutes. Innovative forms of fundraising and governance brought women far more directly into the day-to-day life of the home and of its wards. All started with relatively open doors, avoiding protracted reviews of applicants, demonstrating fewer concerns for dowries and marriage (arguably more an issue for males concerned with lineage), and focusing on helping girls through an immediate period of difficulty and giving them some skill with which to fashion a life outside the home.

This kind of community could not survive Bologna's drive to a uniform model of civic institution that met social and economic needs. The spoiler in Florence was the particular and enduring politics of Savonarolism, which gradually turned these conservatories into convents. Though much diluted, Savonarolan values continued to resonate in spiritual songs, popular biographies, and the actions of laity and clergy whose memories stretched back to the middle of the sixteenth century. By century's end, Savonarolan lay women seem to have been a greater threat than Savonarolan clergy, whose loyalty to the regime was accepted. In both cities, the distinct characteristics of women's governance gradually disappeared as men took a larger role in administration. After this point, each institution adopted the administrative and financial conventions found locally. In each, the direct participation of a large number of women in the work declined, and in the Carità and Pietà even the confraternities themselves disappeared. More to the point, these latter two moved away from being conservatories offering emergency and temporary shelter to abandoned and orphaned girls, and directed their care instead to meet the concerns of patrilineage—either preparing girls for marriage (as in S. Giuseppe and initially the Carità), or removing this possibility from them (as in the Pietà, the Carità, and eventually S. Caterina). Meeting these concerns—which many patrician women shared—required tighter forms of administration and different notions of participation and accountability.[103]

We should not romanticize, or depict these women simply as victims. Although the Pietà's gradual transformation into a convent and S. Giuseppe's into a boarding school were processes that developed after men took a larger role in confraternal administration, some women supported the shift and cooperated in making it happen. Certainly both homes had in their confraternities patrician women who were not easily cowed, and neither seems to have repudiated the statutes or changes imposed on them by their Dominican or Jesuit spiritual guides. They knew too much about their fathers, brothers, and husbands, and were too experienced in gender restrictions to appeal to the law of unintended consequences. The broader shifts at work were generational. Change came when founders died and successors arrived with new inspirations, ambitions, and models.

Florence's congregational model was undeniably more efficient and rational. It was more recognizably modern in its move to a few specialized institutions, its division of labor between a small core of appointed (and often permanent) magistrates and a hired staff, and the distance it placed between magistrates and wards. Bolognese homes moved toward this congregational model by the early seventeenth century, but they never entirely abandoned the broad-based collegiate model that brought dozens of confraternity members into administration in regular rotation. Some of these changes came out of the drive to make the institutions economically self-sufficient, a self-sufficiency built not on accumulated endowments or ongoing pledges but on the children's own piecework. Some came in the shift of political accountability away from broad supporting communities and toward a single ruler or an oligarchy that wound itself ever more tightly together into a smaller and smaller knot by intermarriage. Did this more efficient bureaucracy have any effect on the care offered in the homes? We saw earlier that Florentine homes tended to invest less time and energy than Bolognese ones on the procedures for bringing children in. Did they do the same when letting children out?

CHAPTER SIX

Leaving Home

On a Sunday in June 1588, Pirrino Bettolo and twelve of his companions come to the end of their time at the S. Bartolomeo di Reno orphanage. After morning Mass in the church adjoining the orphanage, their *guardiano* Sebastiano Iacconi shepherds them out of a side door and up a stairway leading to an oratory on the third floor above the church, where the brothers of the Compagnia di S. Bartolomeo have heard their weekly private Mass. The boys don't enter the oratory—and unless some were daring or mischievous in the past few years, none have ever set foot there—but remain in the adjoining *audienzia*, or meeting room. Behind a table on a raised dais at one end of the room sit three men; another twenty-five fill the first few rows of benches facing them. In a corner sits a pile of bags and a kit of shoemaker's tools. Pirrino is familiar with most of these men, who have come by the home from time to time to see how things were going, or periodically visited the workshop in the years of his apprenticeship to see that he was being treated well. He may try to signal to one or two who were particularly friendly or helpful, but this is a formal occasion. *Guardiano* Iacconi keeps Pirrino and the others in line as one of the men in the pews rises with a sheet of paper in his hand and reads out the name of each boy in turn and tells the others where each is going, whether back to a mother, father, or other family member, or into a shop. This is likely Alessandro Stiatici who, together with Giulio Passi and Thomaso Rostighelli, has spent the past month checking through the orphanage to see which boys were old enough to leave, and then checking with family and shop masters to see whether there was a home for them to leave for. Stiatici took extensive notes through the course of his investigations, and then called the orphanage's highest council, the Twelve Conservators, to a meeting in his home to discuss whether the boys were ready to leave. They considered whether the boys' families had stabilized, or whether there was a good workshop ready to receive them as journeymen. The Twelve voted on each boy separately after discussing his prospects. These reviews, interviews, and deliberations resulted in the list of thirteen boys that Stiatici now reads. He also reads aloud what the boys will take with them beyond the clothes on their backs: Aurelio dal Ferro will have a shirt and another pair of shoes in his sack; Luccha Gallo will get a shirt and the goods that he entered the home with and that have been held in storage for him until this day; Ascano Dainese will get the set of shoemaker's tools; and Pirrino will get shoes, a pair of breeches (*bragoni*), and a set of heavier stockings (*scoffeni*) that he can wear once winter comes.

After Stiatico sits down and the boys have their belongings, the man sitting at the center of the raised table rises to speak. Senator Galeazzo Poeti is the confraternal rector and, as such, the institution's chief officer. He now reinforces the lessons that their teachers have given Pirrino and his companions over the past few years, telling them to be worthy men, "*huomini da Bene,*" and to carry themselves well in all they do. The teenage boys thank the men for having accepted, sheltered, and educated them, and then grab their bags and file back through the door, down the staircase, and back into S. Bartolomeo's courtyard for what is likely a more emotional leave-taking with the resident staff who have cooked their meals and sewed their clothes, and with the other boys they have eaten, worked, and slept beside for the past few years. Then they head out through the iron gates that S. Bartolomeo installed only a year ago. Some may find a relative waiting for them there; others may head down the street to a workshop or to a home they left five or ten years before. In the room three floors above, the *confratelli* turn to considering a sheaf of fifteen new applications.[1]

Across the city, in the fall of 1580, 23-year-old Serafina Bertaze prepares for the wedding that will open the doorway out of S. Maria del Baracano, her home for the past ten years. She has not seen her future husband, Vincenzo di Michele

Bonsi, nor he her. Their match was arranged by Giambattista Scotti and Signora Laura Malvezzi Lignana, the confraternal prior and *priora*, respectively, who may or may not have consulted Serafina's brother or her widowed mother. Scotti had certainly investigated Vincenzo as he was negotiating the dowry of 300 lire: 200 lire from the conservatory, 50 lire from Serafina's brother, and another 50 lire given in charity by Signora Faustina Malvasia. Vincenzo was decidedly the supplicant here, and in order to gain both Serafina and her dowry, he had to promise to invest half the dowry in something secure and give a pledge for the remainder. The conservatory wanted to be able to recover the dowry if either the bride or groom died before Serafina had given birth to an heir. Scotti reports to the Baraccano conservators on the results of his negotiations in early September, and they approve the terms and the notary who will put this into contract language. While Scotti has dealt with groom Vincenzo, Malvezzi Lignana has taken Serafina in hand and into her house for a few days to give her practical lessons in how a woman should run a household and care for husband and children.

On Sunday, 7 October, Malvezzi Lignana and Serafina return to S. Maria del Baraccano and head to the confraternal meeting room, where they meet Vincenzo, Scotti, and other men and women of the confraternity. In their frequent trips to the conservatory as visitors, these *confratelli* and *consorelle* had seen Serafina grow up. A few may even have had a hand in arranging her entry ten years before. Scotti puts Vincenzo's hand in Serafina's and says a few words about marriage before inviting the couple and guests to enjoy the food and drink that have been laid out on a table. After refreshments, the group walks a short distance to the parish church of S. Giuliano to solemnize their vows before the confraternity's priest and according to the new Tridentine regulations. Scotti and Malvezzi Lignana both attend as Serafina's surrogate parents. Having exchanged their vows, the couple pay a visit to the home of Serafina's mother in Mirasole, accompanied once again by the gentlemen and gentlewomen of S. Maria del Baraccano who have, for the past decade, acted *in loco parentis* to the girl. Two weeks later, Vincenzo signs the dowry contract and so frees the way for payment of the funds.[2]

Four years earlier, in 1576, 16-year-old Anna di Marco di Genova had left Florence's Casa della Pietà under contract as a domestic servant to Taddeo di Giovan Maria da Prato. For five years, Taddeo would put clothes on her back, shoes on her feet, and 10 lire annually on account for Anna's dowry, all the while looking out for a spouse for the orphaned girl. True to his word, Taddeo arranged a marriage and on 1 August 1581 passed Anna into the hand of Iacopo da Rovezano, a *battilano* (wool-dresser) whose productivity—or something else—was so great that he had the nickname "Battaglione" (literally a "battalion," but colloquially a "big clapper" or "big knocker"). Apart from its initial contract with Taddeo, the Pietà conservatory and its administrators played no part in arranging, paying for, or solemnizing the marriage. Arrangements like this were not always so straightforward. A decade earlier, Marietta di Domenico da Fiesole had left the S. Niccolò conservatory on a similar contract to be a domestic servant with the shoemaker Domenico di Piero and his wife Chamilla. Domenico also promised Marietta a dowry when she married, though it is not clear if he promised to find the husband. Marietta had other ideas though, and less than three weeks later, she ran away. She may have bolted if Domenico began suggesting that she ought to express her gratitude with more than words, but the fact that she didn't flee back to S. Niccolò suggests that she had planned this all along as a way to escape the tightly enclosed conservatory. The S. Niccolò governors began making inquiries and tracked her down in Pistoia, where she had fled to the home of Domenica Chantansantj and where, it appears, she stayed.[3]

Many decades later, 61-year-old Caterina di Cosimo di Firenze died in her bed in Florence's S. Caterina conservatory, the only home she had known since entering as a 14-year-old girl. Together with three sisters, Caterina had been left a true orphan on the death of her father and mother, possibly in the famines of the early 1590s. She watched other girls come and go, but never had the will or opportunity to leave herself, serving instead for eighteen years as a mistress of novices known for her skill in training newly admitted girls. Over these years, she saw the conservatory gradually metamorphose into a convent. In recognition of her years of service, the sisters buried Caterina in the conservatory church.[4]

Leaving a home was generally easier than entering, but not always. Some youths bypassed formalities and simply jumped out the window or ran out a door, hoping that the crowded streets would cover their traces. Others like Marietta di Domenico da Fiesole planned their exit more carefully, but with the same goal of being the masters of their own fate. But most found their way out of the home only through a set of bureaucratic formalities similar to the ones that had governed their entry five, eight, or a dozen years earlier. A team of confraternal or governmental officials acted as surrogate parents and cautiously balanced a child's personality and prospects with the home's resources or its need for space to take in new children. They had procedures to minimize self-interest or exploitation, and to ease children back into society as productive adults. Aware of their wards' vulnerability, they tracked those who had been sent to work in homes and workshops and frequently opened the door again for someone who hadn't made it. Acting *in loco parentis* meant acting cautiously, and like any parents of the time these confraternity members acted more cautiously with girls than with boys. Acting as citizens of Bologna or Florence brought its own demands: we once again see that the former city was more selective and protective than the latter, and that it worked harder at getting its wards back into local homes as mothers and artisans. And again, once statutes had been written, reality set in: convenience, laxness, and desperation shaped and hammered abstract procedures into manageable practices.

Boys

The most immediate barrier to understanding when and how boys left their orphanages is the lack of records. Even fewer records track boys' exits than mark their entrances. Of the four orphanages operating in Florence and Bologna, only S. Bartolomeo di Reno has any record of exits at all, and it would be generous to call these sporadic and sketchy.[5] The indifference in recording boys' destinations should make us skeptical of the complicated procedures set out in these same homes' statutes, but it suggests another side of boys' lives that the statutes could not predict. Most boys eased back into society gradually through apprenticeships that started years before their formal leave-taking, or returned to the care of relatives when either blood or surrogate parents thought best, regardless of careful procedures. Famine and economic downturns could also render procedures moot, and lead homes to plan—or at least threaten—to simply send the older boys back to the streets and leave them to their own devices.

S. Bartolomeo's officials actively sought out places for their boys, while others took a more passive approach and waited for opportunity to arise. Bologna's S. Onofrio and Florence's Abbandonati fall into the latter category. Neither institution's archive retains records of processing a boy's departure, though S. Onofrio's statutes set out some procedures for this and the Abbandonati established, if not procedures, at least a set of expectations on how these boys were to act as they moved back into society.

S. Onofrio didn't initially direct any of its officials to seek out opportunities for its boys, but assumed that a reserve pool of young and healthy workers would have its own attraction in the Bolognese labor market, and that masters would come knocking for able apprentices. That said, it would not send its boys into a workshop without a second thought. When a master came to the home seeking a boy, the resident *guardiano* would direct him to the confraternity's serving *massaro*, who explained the home's terms and expectations and checked around to get a better sense of the master's financial stability and reputation. S. Onofrio was prepared to send out boys "a vitta o per qualche tempo" (for life or for a specified time), but expected that the master would cover the cost of feeding him; boys sent out "for a time" would continue wearing the orphanage uniform at their workshop and return to the home at night to sleep. *Massaro* and master came to a verbal agreement on length of stay, salary, and training opportunities, which the *massaro* then took back to his fellow officials. They discussed the reliability and reputation of the master and the terms of the verbal agreement, and added further terms and conditions if it seemed to them that the state of the boy or the state of the master might require it. They wanted to be sure that the boy would not be exploited or set to menial low-skill work like a *sottoposto* day laborer, but that he would be well treated and trained in a craft. Understanding that their deliberations would be translated into contract language by the notary and then signed by the master, they took out their black and white beans and voted. The boy could go once the master signed the contract, and the *massaro* would drop by periodically to ensure that its terms were being kept and that the salary was being paid.[6]

Any father putting his son out to apprenticeship understood these procedures, and even the language used reflects this parallel: this was what the verb used (*allogare*) conveyed, and the *massaro* and officials were to do it diligently with ample consideration of the *qualità* and *condicione* of the person to whom they were giving and entrusting the boy ("darano e allogarano"), as though the boy were one of their own sons ("come se fosero soi figlioli"). It is also the language of fostering or adoption, as the prospect of the term *a vitta* indicates.

Fathers and guardians appreciated the security of a signed contract, but so too did masters. Florence's Abbandonati took a similarly passive approach to placing its boys, but reversed the emphasis in its statutes and set out a series of expectations as to how these boys should behave. Certainly the person taking the boy in had to be of highest reputation and quality, and legitimately married—the fear of Abbandonati boys ending up as male concubines hovers in the background—but the onus was on the boys to prove their worth and re-spectability. Swearing, thieving, and laziness would pitch a boy out onto the street: the master could dismiss him, and the Abbandonati would refuse to let him return. Bolognese homes typically took such boys in again, and the Abban-donati's more aggressive and punitory tone underscores the extent to which its captain-magistrates considered themselves less the boy's surrogate fathers than the duke's willing policemen. In their statutes, they do not take on any respon-sibility for finding a home or apprenticeship for their wards, and plan to be involved only as the ones approving these departures and disciplining boys who fail to live up to their part of the contractual bargain. The discipline they antic-ipated but had no authority to implement— expulsion, exile from Tuscany, or a term pulling the oars on the duke's Mediterranean galleys—seemed less oriented to shaping unruly teenagers than to handling enemies of the state.[7]

The contracts and expectations structure a leave-taking graduated over a period of years, and in the case of boys we have to put their departure at the end of a continuum that includes the work they had done while still wards of the home. Wearing the uniform by day in a city workshop, and returning at night to sleep in the orphanage dormitories was the first stage. At this point, the Ab-bandonati would be paying apprenticeship fees in regular installments, as it did in 1543 when placing a boy, Michelangelo, with Bastiano di Marcho the carpen-ter.[8] The Abbandonati additionally wanted masters to allow—and ensure—times through the day when the boy could pray for Duke Cosimo, his wife Eleonora, and their children, as though these were by virtue of state guardianship the boy's true parents and siblings. It is less easy to imagine a master stopping the work-day to allow this, than it is to see him sending the boy back to Via S. Gallo every couple of months in order to confess to the orphanage priest, a subtle but effec-tive way for the institution to keep tabs on the boy when he no longer slept under the Abbandonati roof. What marked a boy's formal leave-taking as much as anything was the day when the Abbandonati magistrates formally restored to him the goods and property that they had held in trust during his wardship. He reached this day and recovered his property when the magistrates decided that he had learned enough about proper deportment, money management, the will of God, and the pious life. This portion of the draft statutes demonstrates most clearly the hope of Savonarolan *piagnoni* and Catholic reformers more generally that the duchy's central orphanage could be a seminary for citizens, imparting that closely woven set of civic and religious values that made up a healthy social fabric in the eyes of its supporters and administrators.[9]

But reformers' dreams always had difficulty negotiating with immediate realities. The experience of Pirrino Bettolo laid out in the first account at the beginning of this chapter came out of the enthusiasm and drive of Alessandro Stiatici, the legal scholar who was S. Bartolomeo's oldest member, its eventual historian, and one of those behind a reform of procedures in 1588 that capped a decade of stability and expansion. S. Bartolomeo had steadily expanded its quarters through the 1580s, and an administrative stocktaking at the end of the decade resulted in appointment of a deliberative and governing body modeled on the city's senate (and also called the Quaranta), a new matriculation and new statutes for the Stretta company (1588), and the purchase of some blank books in which to begin writing the minutes of the revivified *corporale* and conservators, the deliberative and executive bodies, respectively, that oversaw the boys. For the first time in this company's history, we get running records of decisions taken to run a home.[10] Stiatici's name is at the head of the list of conservators, and his energy moves through at least the early pages of the record, when issues are described in detail and boys are mentioned by name when they come up for discussion. But as we saw in the previous chapter, these pages soon begin recording a string of disasters as the confraternity struggles through the dearth of 1589–94, threatening at one point to open the door and throw out all procedures and all boys so that at least they can beg for their bread rather than starve behind the newly installed gates.[11] By December 1588, the scribe saves his ink for descriptions of uncollected legacies and lawsuits, and deals telegraphically with the coming and going of boys, who are seldom named or described.

But this same necessity reinforces the more active process for releasing boys described at the opening of this chapter. S. Onofrio and the Abbandonati seem to send their boys out one by one as opportunity and maturity allow. S. Bartolomeo is more deliberate and proactive. It regularly appoints teams of *assonti* to go through the home looking for boys ready to leave, and through the city looking for shops ready to take them. Their instructions are clear: no placing the boys with spinners, rope-makers, dishonorable or low-earning craftsmen, or as day-laborers. These regulations aim to give the boys a good start in their work life. Another regulation—that they cannot be placed in the homes of the men of the company—forestalled any accusation that the men were exploiting the boys and limited the men's own liability. In tough times, high-born members of the company would be pressured to relieve the home by taking some boys into domestic service, but this would saddle them with costs while failing to provide the boys with much of a future. The blanket prohibition handled both eventualities, but we know that it was occasionally broken. By 1590, two officials proposed that each noble and citizen family in the city take one or more of the boys into their homes because of the great famine, arguing that since they left early in the morning for their workshops, and returned to the orphanage church for worship before dinner, this wouldn't be a great imposition, presumably nothing more than a bed for the night and breakfast in the morning. This kind of emergency plan formalized the practice found across Europe of families allowing beggars to stay the night, and it seemed to pop up in times of crisis. The Calvinist consistory in Nimes was drawing up a list matching local poor with wealthy families in this same period, and Bologna itself had contemplated the same approach in lieu of a general poorhouse more than forty years before. But what seemed good on paper and in the abstract usually generated considerable resistance before it could be put into general practice. The S. Bartolomeo *corporale* endorsed the plan enthusiastically, but few members seem to have opened their doors.[12]

The *assonti* appointed to "lift" (*levare*) the boys out of the home usually returned with some results within about a month, and triggered a general housecleaning when a dozen or more boys gained their release at once. This could represent 15 to 20 percent of the home's resident population, which helps explain the desire for some kind of formal leave-taking ceremony. The teams of *assonti* expanded as opportunity contracted, and what had been a roughly semiannual process picked up frequency. Three *assonti* went out in May 1588, three again in July 1590, and four in August 1592, but a year later six went out in June and seven in August. By September the confraternity threw up its hands at the lack of opportunity in the famine- and depression-bound city and voted simply to expel all boys who were of age, or even just physically mature, all who had mothers or fathers in the city, all who entered without formal review, all "foreigners," and, a bit opportunistically, all who were troublesome (*discoli*). The records preserve the results of the June 1593 purge, when sixteen boys were released. The formal and almost festive ceremony of five years before, when the boys came in a group to a meeting of all the confraternity brothers, had been abandoned. Now they came one by one to a meeting of the executive conservators to hear confirmed where they were heading and on what terms. There was no group ceremony, no formal speeches, and no involvement of the broader confraternity membership.

Of the 11 for whom ages are given, most are between ages 14 and 16, though 3 are in their mid-20s and the youngest is 11. Of the 16, 12 will be working in

artisinal workshops: 3 with a tailor, 3 with a shoemaker, 3 in the shop of a barber, 2 with pin-makers, and one with a painter. Wages for 12 have been negotiated, and of these most will be earning between 24 and 36 lire per year, though
one will have 16 and another 50 lire—respectable starting wages when the average master artisan earned between 200 and 300 lire annually. There is no immediate relation between age, occupation, and wage, but we can trace a rough
occupational wage scale that puts pin-makers at the top, followed by shoemakers, barber, tailors, domestic servant, and painter. This is a very imprecise
measure, since a worker's remuneration would include many elements "in kind"
that are not specified here.[13] Only one is headed into holy orders, joining the
friars of S. Salvatore through the intercession of Sig. Lattantio Fellicini, whose
name does not appear on any of the confraternity's matriculation lists of the
period. One is going to a home, most likely as a domestic servant; one has no
specified placement; and Andrea di Clementi, age 24, is being taken on staff at
S. Bartolomeo "to help in every thing" ("per aiuttar in ogni cosa"); Andrea may
be a particularly efficient young man, but it is more likely that he has some physical, mental, or psychological disability that has prevented successive teams of
assonti from finding him a suitable work opportunity in the city. Such boys might
go out on a trial basis, but would return if the master decided that they simply
couldn't do the job, like Giulio de Cochi, who returned after six months when
the printer who'd taken him complained that his eyesight was too poor to do the
job ("per essergli mancato la vista").[14]

On a couple of points, we can compare the sixteen Bartolomeo boys released
in June 1593 with the thirteen whose leave-taking five years earlier is described
at the head of the chapter. Of the latter, admitted in the generally prosperous
1580s and heading out into a city not yet choked with famine, twelve have
family names and only one a patronymic, underlining the fact that Bolognese
orphanages preferred to take the children of respectable citizens or residents. Of
the class of June 1593, six are identified by family names, four by a patronymic,
and six by only their own given names, suggesting that they were a distinctly
less-advantaged group. Many of these may have entered when that same famine
killed parents, strained households, and forced S. Bartolomeo to ease its entrance requirements. They were also the boys whom the *assonti* working in the
summer of 1590 and 1592 hadn't been able to place. And here is where we do
find a correlation with wages: the boys with family names tended to leave at
younger ages for jobs with higher wages, pointing to the stronger network or
better prospects that even a slightly higher social standing brought with it.

Beyond family name lies family survival. Only two of the 1593 group of boys have surviving relatives, one a mother and the other an aunt, both living in Bologna. While the 1588 record gives no family connections at all, the instructions given to the *assonti* in this earlier period assume that relatives are waiting outside the door. Stiatici and his *assonti* had discussed their wards' prospects in the first instance with "their fathers or mothers or relatives," and in releasing them, the company recorded that it "sends them to their homes" ("mandargli alle loro case").[15]

This was the eventual result of admitting so many boys who were not *veri orfani*. It is also the opposite of the passivity of Bologna's S. Onofrio, which in thirty-five years appears only once (in 1600) to have appointed a couple of *confratelli* to see who was old or large enough to be released from its care. Put most simply, it framed its entrance requirements such that it would not have to worry a great deal about its wards' prospects or its own open-ended liability. Its first statute reform demonstrates this quite clearly, scaling back the complicated process of making legal agreements with a master, and requiring simply that when boys turned 18, they had to be returned to their mothers if these were living, or to some other relatives, so that the boys would not go to ruin. These relatives received the 20 lire "deposit" collected upon the boys' entry to the home, and which was to help outfit them for their new lives. In Amsterdam's Burgerweeshuis orphanage for citizen children, this was taken very seriously; a boy on his way out the door needed to be dressed in the clothes appropriate to his middle-class station, and so each one was outfitted with a hat, the signal marker of class status. S. Onofrio was sufficiently attuned to this that it provided handkerchiefs and even silk shirts to the boys in its care. S. Bartolomeo enjoyed one legacy specifically dedicated to giving a full set of vestments to two boys who wanted to be secular priests. When one of the beneficiaries subsequently decided to become a friar instead, he lost the clothes to another of the boys who was ready to take on parish work.[16] Returning to family armed with a clothes allowance is a far cry from the image of late adolescent boys cast out on the street, and again underlines the reality that orphanages generally and Bolognese homes in particular served a "worthy" clientele more marked by temporary need than by dire indigence. It took a famine like that of 1589–94 to alter this situation, but S. Bartolomeo's threats of drastic action at this time showed another side of orphanage life. If beds were full and pantries were empty, administrators could open the door and send the more mature boys out to fend for themselves. Conservatories had no such freedom.

Table 6.1. Ages of Girls Leaving Conservatories

	Period	Sample	Average	Median	Mode	Minimum	Maximum
Florence							
S. Caterina	1594–1635	121/276	25.53	19	16	7	86
S. Maria Vergine	1552–56	30/95	14.44	14	13	12	17
Pietà	1554–59	283/361	16.99	16	16	3	69
Pietà	1559–68	86/165	17.84	15	13	5	74
Pietà	1569–1623	178/272	18.19	16	16	3	55
Bologna							
S. Giuseppe	1616–41	29/111	16.86	16	16	6	28
S. Maria del Baraccano	> 1570	128/161	24.36	25	26	8	44
S. Maria del Baraccano	1570–84	35/121	22.11	22	18	14	28
S. Maria del Baraccano	1584–99	0/143	n/a	n/a	n/a	n/a	n/a

Sources: Florence: ASF, S. Caterina, ms. 17; ASF, Ceppo mss. 59, 145; ASF, CRSF ms. 112/78, 79; Bologna: ASB, PIE, S. Giuseppe, ms. 23; ASB, PIE, S. Maria del Baraccano, mss. 6.1, 6.2, 7.

Girls

If a girl was going to leave a conservatory at all, she was generally gone within a decade. Some married, some returned to their families, some went into domestic service, some died. It is in their handling of girls' exits that we see the greatest differences between Bologna and Florence. Bolognese homes busied themselves in marrying their girls and restoring them to the pool of child-bearing citizens. Florentine homes passed their girls into the hands of others—largely employers or family—who would look after this. Girls who couldn't be passed on stayed in until they died or escaped or, in some instances, followed their home's metamorphosis into a convent by becoming tertiaries or nuns. We can first compare the lengths of time that girls typically stayed in one or another home, and their ages on exiting, before considering how or to what they exited. The stories at the beginning of this chapter represent the most common fates for conservatory girls: Serafina Bertaze left the Baraccano to marry and Marietta di Domenico da Fiesole left S. Niccolò to become a household servant, while Caterina di Cosimo di Firenze died while still a ward of S. Caterina. Since the conservatories of the Baraccano in Bologna and the Pietà in Florence both kept excellent records, we can look more closely at how patterns developed in those homes and how two very different approaches to a conservatory's purpose emerged—one more common in Florence, and the other in Bologna.

How old were girls when they left? Table 6.1 compares leaving ages at 3 homes in Florence and 2 in Bologna. The average leaving ages range from a low of just over 14 at S. Maria Vergine in the 1550s, to a high of 25 in S. Caterina's 1594 cohort and S. Maria del Baraccano's 1554 cohort. At the Pietà, the average age at which a girl left crept slowly upward, from 17 in the 1550s to 18 by century's end. Median leaving ages group more closely together in the mid-teens in Florence, and the early to mid-20s in Bologna (with the exception of S. Giuseppe). When we turn to age ranges, there is less consistency and a difference emerges between the two cities: girls in Florentine homes might leave at a somewhat younger age, but could end up staying into their 50s, 70s, or even 80s. Bolognese girls generally entered later and left far earlier.[17]

How much of their lives did they spend in the conservatory? Table 6.2 compares the duration of stay at this same range of homes, calculated in months. These statistics fluctuate far more widely, with an average stay at S. Maria Vergine or S. Giuseppe being slightly more than a year, while girls remained an

Table 6.2. Duration of Stay for Conservatory Girls
(months)

	Period	Sample	Average	Median	Mode	Minimum	Maximum
Florence							
S. Caterina	1594–1635	203/276	194.65	96	48	2	912
S. Maria Vergine	1552–56	27/95	13.15	10	10	0.5	40
Pietà	1554–59	285/361	53.94	21	1	0.5	696
Pietà	1559–68	86/165	90.16	43.5	9	0.5	713
Pietà	1569–1623	178/272	102.58	78.5	15	0.5	465
Bologna							
S. Giuseppe	1616–41	55/111	18.62	8	6	0.25	114
S. Maria del Baraccano	>1570	155/161	137.19	135	120	1	372
S. Maria del Baraccano	1570–84	113/121	93.48	96	96	0.42	326
S. Maria del Baraccano	1584–99	116/143	109.46	108	84	1	296

Sources: Bologna: ASB, PIE, S. Maria del Baraccano, mss. 6.2, 7; ASB, PIE, S. Giuseppe, ms. 23; Florence: ASF, Ceppo mss. 59, 145; ASF, CRSF mss. 112/78, 79; ASF, S. Caterina, ms. 17.

average of 12 years at S. Maria del Baraccano and 16 years at S. Caterina. The range between maximum and minimum also varies widely: girls might stay as short as a week at S. Giuseppe or as long as 75 years at S. Caterina. Pietà girls stayed on average far longer as the century progressed, from 4.5 years in the 1550s to almost 9 years by the early 1600s. The opposite happened at S. Maria del Baraccano, where average stays dropped from over 11 years in the 1550s to just over 9 years by the 1590s.

These statistics are compromised by sample size in a number of instances, particularly at S. Maria Vergine, which counts only one-third of the girls who left within the first four years, and so omits the majority who stayed on longer and left at older ages. S. Giuseppe's sample size for age is also quite small, but the sample for duration rises to 50 percent and confirms that girls left this home very quickly. In fact, the tables highlight the argument made by the Bolognese women who began S. Giuseppe, which was that something had to be done to address the city's need for short-term emergency shelter for girls. The flagship Baraccano home was simply too hard to get into or out of.

In a few instances where homes have successive record books, and where names early in the list are transferred from a prior book, and those later in the list disappear into another (possibly no longer extant) one (e.g., Pietà, S. Maria del Baraccano), the tables divide the groups into cohorts that isolate the groups of girls for which most statistics are available. This highlights changes in practice over time. Thus, the Pietà's first list, called the *Libro Segreto*, runs from its opening in 1554 until 1559 and totals 361 names. The second list begins in 1559, but repeats the entire cohort then resident: 171 girls, the oldest of whom had entered in 1555. This second book carries on to 1623, when the home started a third volume called the *Libro Nuovo*; 106 records were transferred over to this no longer extant volume. This gives us a sign of how many girls were in the home at that point, but it prevents us from learning what happened to them, since their fates were not recorded in the older volume where they had first been registered. In the tables given here, the girls first registered in the *Libro Segreto* are removed from the second register and that register is itself divided into two parts—one before and one after the home's move from Borgo Ognissanti to via Mandorlo in the city's north end (November 1568).

We saw at the beginning of the chapter that Serafina left the Baraccano with her Vincenzo and Anna left the Pietà with her "Big Clapper," while Caterina di Cosimo di Firenze left S. Caterina on a bier. Table 6.3 underscores the differences between individual homes and between the two cities that we saw in the

Table 6.3. Comparative Outcomes for Conservatory Girls

Home	Period	Total	Died	%	Married	%	Family	%	Service	%
Florence										
S. Caterina	1594–1635	276	159	58	23	8.33	43	15.57	14	5.07
S. Maria Vergine	1552–56	88	10	11.36	0	0	2	2.24	29	32.58
S. Niccolò	1570–79	94	6	6.38	8	8.51	13	13.82	39	41.48
S. Niccolò	1579–99	82/116	23	19.82	18	15.51	11	9.48	26	22.41
Pietà	1554–59	361	210	58.17	16	4.43	45	12.46	61	16.89
Pietà transferred from *Libro Segreto*										
Pietà	1558–59	171	90	52.63	18	10.52	13	7.6	27	15.78
Pietà	1559–68	165	114	69.09	10	6.06	18	10.09	32	19.39
Pietà	1569–1623	272	157	57.72	33	12.13	62	22.79	15	5.05
Bologna										
S. Giuseppe	1616–41	111	2	1.8	4	3.6	14	12.61	21	18.91
S. Maria del Baraccano	1554 cohort	76	10	13.15	42	55.26	5	6.57	0	0
S. Maria del Baraccano	1554–68	161	37	22.98	88	54.65	15	9.31	0	0
S. Maria del Baraccano	1570–84	121	14	11.57	69	57.02	23	19	4	3.31
S. Maria del Baraccano	1584–99	143	27	18.88	79	55.24	16	11.19	1	0.7

(continued)

Table 6.3. (continued)

Home	Period	Total	Convent	%	Fled	%	Remain	%	Unknown	%
Florence										
S. Caterina	1594–1635	276	0	0	10				27	9.78
S. Maria Vergine	1552–56	88	0	0			56	62.92	10	11.36
S. Niccolò	1570–79	94	1	1.06	4	4.25	22	23.4		
S. Niccolò	1579–99	82/116	3	2.58	1	0.8	34	29.31		
Pietà	1554–59	361	1	0.27	7	1.93	0	0	21	5.82
Pietà transferred from										
Libro Segreto	1556–50	171	0	0	0	0	0		23	13.45
Pietà	1559–68	165	1	.6	0	0	0	0	0	0
Pietà	1569–1623	272	6	2.2	2	0.46	0	0	0	0
Bologna										
S. Giuseppe	1616–41	111	4	3.6	3	2.7	0	0	63	32.43
S. Maria del Baraccano	1554 cohort	76	4	5.26	0	0	0	0	6	7.89
S. Maria del Baraccano	1553–68	161	11	6.83	1	0.62	0	0	9	5.59
S. Maria del Baraccano	1570–84	121	7	5.98	0	0	0	0	4	3.31
S. Maria del Baraccano	1584–99	143	5	3.49	0	0	0	0	15	10.49

Sources: Bologna: ASB, PIE, S. Maria del Baraccano, mss. 6.1, 6.2, 7; ASB, PIE, S. Giuseppe, ms. 23; Florence: ASF, Ceppo mss. 59, 145; ASF, CRSF mss. 112/78, 79; ASF, S. Caterina, ms. 17.

Table 6.4. Returns to Family for Conservatory Girls

	S. Niccolò	Pietà	S. Caterina	S. Maria del Baraccano, > 1570 Cohort	S. Maria del Baraccano, 1570–84 Cohort	S. Maria del Baraccano, 1584–99 Cohort	S. Giuseppe
Number	24/210	125/708	43/276	15/161	23/121	16/143	14/111
Mother	11	46	21	2	5	3	6
Father	4	13	4	2		2	2
Brother	2	18	4				3
Sister	3	10	3				1
Aunt/uncle	1	16	2	1	3	1	
Grandparent	1	2		1			
Other	2	20	9	9	15	10	2

Sources: ASF, Ceppo ms. 59, cc. 105v–128v, 135v–193r; ASF, CRSF ms. 112/78 (1554–56), 112/79 (1559–1623); ASF, S. Caterina, ms. 17 (np); Bologna: ASB, PIE, S. Maria del Baraccano, mss. 6.1, 6.2, 7; ASB, PIE, S. Giuseppe, cart. 24.

two tables above. Only a handful of girls transferred from conservatories to con-vents, though somewhat more made this transition in Bologna. The available Florentine records say nothing about the age at which girls made this move, while in Bologna it tended to be in the early 20s. In neither city is there a pattern to the convents chosen for the girls, which could be local or in another city; only a minority of the Baraccano girls became tertiaries.[18] Similarly, few girls in either city fled or simply left, a sign either of the security of their enclosures or of the girls' own realization that life outside did not offer much. One woman left S. Caterina at age 45 after twenty years in the home, and the scribe noted acer-bically, "She left by her will and to our satisfaction. She was never useful. Un-governable."[19] Domestic service offered a route out of the home for many girls in Florentine conservatories, though as we saw earlier, one-third or more re-turned in a few weeks, months, or even years if their masters turned against them. Those who returned generally remained in the conservatory until their deaths; those who wanted to avoid that fate fled from their new masters' homes.

In some instances, conservatories sheltered girls only until their families could once again care for them. This happened far more frequently in Florence, and on far different terms than in Bologna. Girls returned voluntarily to their families from Florentine conservatories to marry, but usually left Bolognese ones because they had been expelled. Roughly 10 to 20 percent of Florentine girls might leave to live with a family member, and as Table 6.4 demonstrates in almost half the cases or more they were returning to their mothers. Siblings also took their conservatory sisters back, but fathers seldom did; in most cases, of course, it was the father's death that had precipitated the girl's entry into the home. Conservatories often kept contact with the girls who had left, and some-times recorded in their books whether these had married; S. Caterina offered dowries to some of these girls, even though they were not marrying directly out of the conservatory.[20] In these Florentine instances, the conservatory was a tem-porary shelter that stood ready to assist families in difficulty: a mother over-whelmed by the number of mouths she had to feed, or a brother not yet old enough to assume responsibility for a sister. Once the family was back on its feet, the girl could return home.

In Bologna, a girl who left the conservatory to return to her family most often did so in shame or sickness. The ten who left from S. Maria del Baraccano's 1554 cohort are typical: three had contagious illnesses, four had been disobedient ("mal desposta and senza riforma"), and one was pregnant. Only two left for what we might call positive reasons—returning home to nurse sick relatives.[21] Ex-

Table 6.5. Length of Time in the Pietà, 1554–56 Cohort

Time (in months)	Number Dying	%	Number Not Dying	%
Less than 2	17	13.17	16	16.9
3–6	24	18.60	6	8.45
7–12	15	11.62	6	8.45
13–24	32	24.80	10	14.08
25–36	10	7.75	8	11.26
37–60	20	15.50	8	11.26
61+	8	6.20	8	11.26
Not stated	3		15	
Total	129		71	

Source: ASF, CRSF ms. 112/78.
Note: Comparison of those who die in home and those who leave home. Average time in Pietà: dying (22.36 months); not dying (27.33 months).

pelling girls for illness and insubordination was routine in many homes, but at least six times through the mid-1580s the Baraccano feared that the devil had slipped past the *portinara* and possessed a girl, who was then promptly sent home.[22] S. Maria del Baraccano even required that incoming girls have alternate guardians in place in the event that it would have to dismiss them. All of this suggests that the typical Bolognese home was not just a temporary shelter for families in crisis but a gateway to a new life for girls whose extended families were otherwise functioning relatively well. Any girl who threatened the integrity of that gateway had to be removed in order to preserve the others. The one exception to the Bolognese rule was S. Giuseppe, which deliberately offered only short-term custodial care, and so passed most of its girls back to families or on to employers.

Discussing "leaving time" and "leaving age" and comparing the young ages of those departing from conservatories like the Pietà and S. Caterina borders on euphemism. For most of these girls, it was not the conservatory they were leaving, but life itself. Both of these Florentine conservatories had staggering death rates that were many times worse than any home in either city and that were particularly severe in the famine and plague years of their opening. While most other conservatories lost far fewer than 20 percent of their girls to death, over half the girls living in the Pietà and S. Caterina died while they were still wards— and still adolescents. This mortality rate was not far from the rates at foundling homes, but in comparative terms it was far more catastrophic. The girls entering the Pietà and S. Caterina conservatories had survived their early years and so ought to have been safe from gastrointestinal and other illnesses that regularly killed one- to two-thirds of abandoned babies. Working with the cohort of 250 girls who entered the Pietà when it first opened, Table 6.5 compares the longevity of those who eventually died there as compared to those who left to return to family, to enter service, or to marry. Girls dying "left" the Pietà half a year earlier than the others; that is, they had lived in the Pietà an average of 22.4 months while their counterparts had lived there an average of 27.3. But this average is misleading, because as the table shows, a third of those who died (31.77%) lived barely half a year, and almost half (43.49%) were dead within twelve months.

The mortality rate held steady at the Pietà through the following decades, but conditions did improve slightly to the extent that girls were surviving more than twice as long in the home. Table 6.6 compares girls on the basis of the fates that eventually awaited them, and shows that those who died did so younger and after a shorter time in the home than either those who married or those who returned to family. Death was still the default. The Pietà was certainly crowded, but conditions in its damp work rooms and tight dormitories would not have been enough in themselves to cause so many deaths; thousands of Florentines worked and slept in similar if not worse conditions and lived decades longer. Clearly most Pietà girls were sick at the time they entered the home, and the grim conditions there led to rapidly deteriorating health and premature death. This helps explain why so few were able to find work or husbands outside the home, and why relatively few families wanted to welcome these girls back into the household. It may also explain the willingness of the women running it to turn to extreme medical remedies.

Syphilis may be one of the reasons why so many of the girls who entered this

Table 6.6. *Age, Time, and Fates at the Pietà, 1559–1624*
(months)

	Dying	Marrying	Service	Return to Family
Number with age/time	165 of 361	27 of 61	29 of 74	68 of 93
Age at exit—average	17.44	22.64	15.2	17.84
Age—median	15	22	14	16
Time in—average	53.5	148.95	52.75	85.3
Time in—median	93.24	133	35	60

Source: ASF, CRSF ms. 112/79.
Note: This table excludes the cohort that remained in the home after 1624.

home in the middle of Florence's red-light district died quickly and young. A few may have acquired it directly through sexual contact, but those whose mothers were prostitutes could have suffered from congenital syphilis. Most would die in infancy, but some girls would only begin showing symptoms between ages 6 and 17. Although congenital syphilis was not immediately or invariably fatal, serious cases could certainly hasten death. By the time she was 6, a girl's bones and joints could begin aching as a result of lesions, and she could suffer sharp pains in her eyes and dimming vision that might deteriorate until she was blind. Gummy patches would develop in the soft tissue of her nose and mouth, and could open into perforations in the mouth and the collapse of the nose. Tremors and headaches could follow after a few years, and degenerate into paralysis and deafness. In cases of neurosyphilis, she could become irritable, apathetic, or paranoid, and begin suffering seizures.

Many of these symptoms are temporary and treatable in modern medicine, and even Florence's syphilitics' hospital of S. Trinità degli Incurabili, established a few decades earlier, had significant success in restoring adult "incurables" to health.[23] But a sixteenth-century prostitute or widow, seeing symptoms multiply as her daughter reached age 10 or 12, might well abandon her to a home like the Pietà in fear, confusion, or desperation. The Pietà in turn attempted to medicate—and this may explain the recipes for eye ailments, joint troubles, and skin diseases in its *ricettario*—but with few resources and overcrowded wards, it could not offer much. At this early stage in the pox's development in Europe, the Pietà women likely had little idea what they were dealing with. Contemporaries believed that bad air, contaminated food, or infected clothes and bedsheets could transmit the disease, but congenital syphilis produced fewer of the skin lesions that pockmarked the body of those with acquired syphilis, so the impoverished girls deteriorating before their eyes would not readily have been identified as victims of the French pox. Without benefit even of the expensive treatments offered at S. Trinità degli Incurabili, they joined the great number of those dying in the Pietà's infirmary.[24]

Marriage provided a more positive way of leaving the home and building a new life. Table 6.3 shows that relatively few girls married out of Florentine conservatories. The first statutes for both the S. Maria Vergine and the S. Niccolò homes encouraged administrators to find places for the girls, but put marriage in fourth place after domestic service, textile trades, and other skilled crafts. Even then, it emphasized finding craftsmen in these trades who wanted to marry, as a way of killing two birds with one stone.[25] By contrast, most Bolognese girls in

S. Maria del Baraccano left by way of the altar—regularly four times as many as in Florence. Other evidence shows that the Baraccano's pattern was echoed in S. Marta's and S. Croce's statutes and practice, even if we do not have the statistics to demonstrate how successful they were. Financial need and the cost of providing dowries does not explain this difference since, as Table A.2 demonstrates, Florentine homes regularly accumulated surpluses while Bolognese homes barely broke even. Moreover, Bolognese homes found ways to encourage relatives and donors to subsidize girls' dowries. The difference between Florence and Bologna on this score seems to be one of policy or culture rather than finances.

With their more deliberate purpose of turning *fanciulle* into wives and mothers, Bolognese homes worked out three interlocking regulations aimed at reducing conflict between the girls in the race to exit the home by late adolescence. The first concerned seniority. S. Marta and S. Maria del Baraccano both adopted the principle of "first in = first out," with the former stating that this was the most prudent, just, honest, and conscientious procedure, and the latter arguing that it was necessary "to keep the equality and justice between the girls." S. Maria del Baraccano's scribes observed this order scrupulously, producing matriculation lists every six months from the latter half of the sixteenth century and always ranking the girls hierarchically according to the day they entered.[26] Confraternities had traditionally organized their internal hierarchies in the same way, though what they had done in service of spiritual egalitarianism was adopted in order to give the appearance of objective access to institutional dowry funds.

Should a 15-year-old girl who had been in the home for eight years take priority over a 20-year-old who had been in for only five? Theoretically yes, and perhaps in an effort to uphold that principle, S. Maria del Baraccano ceased recording its wards' ages in the main record book after 1578 even though it continued recording the length of time they had lived and worked in the home.[27] But could administrators hide their heads in the sand in this way, or coyly avoid questions raised by potential suitors? In a marriage market that favored the fertile late adolescent female, the 20-year-old would soon pass into unmarriageability and could become a permanent ward. This logic would not impress the 15-year-old, but it did focus administrators' attention. Confraternity brothers aimed to forestall such disputes by policing entrance ages more carefully, even if they did not record them. A more proactive policy was to allow jumping the line for a price, a policy that recognized that most lobbying for exceptions came not from the girls inside, but from relatives outside who had found a prospec-

tive spouse and wanted to seal the nuptial deal as quickly as possible. The Baraccano capitalized on this by allowing girls to marry before their turn only if family, friends, or sponsors would foot all or most of the dowry. It allowed Cornelia
di Simone di Cortolini to marry "ahead of her time" ("inanti al suo tempo") in
1576 because subsidies from three female relatives, a patrimony in trust, and
some furniture in storage made for an attractive dowry with very little contribution required from the conservatory. S. Marta more ambiguously promised a
lesser dowry for girls who, for "urgente et legitima causa" got married before
their turn, and it wanted those officials voting for either a late-age entry or a
queue-jumping departure to be willing to put up the dowry funds personally
rather than draw on confraternal resources.[28]

The second regulation followed by most Bolognese conservatories aimed to
preserve a rough equity between the girls. The homes adopted minimum dowries
that were standardized according to a girl's origins or destination. In the mid-
sixteenth century, S. Maria del Baraccano guaranteed citizen girls 100 lire and
at least 16 braccie of woolen cloth; rural girls and foreigners were promised only
50 lire and no cloth. A century later the confraternity readjusted the figures and
terms, now giving 700 lire in cash and 200 in goods to girls who were marrying,
and up to 1,000 lire for girls entering a convent. S. Croce followed this same distinction between wives and nuns, offering 300 lire to the former and 500 lire to
the latter in 1606.[29] By this point, demand for convent space was so great that
convent dowries could be double that charged to girls who married. Generous
patrons and family subsidies could take a girl beyond this minimum, and homes
would reduce their own contribution as outside funds increased, meaning that
the profits from a girl's years of piecework stayed with the conservatory.

What social class did dowries this size put a girl into? Serious dowry inflation
did not hit Bologna until the mid-sixteenth to early seventeenth centuries, a full
century after Florence and Venice. Bologna did not even have a formal dowry
fund like Florence's Monte delle Doti until 1583, and the Monte del Matrimonio that opened in that year operated more as a savings bank for the lower and
middling ranks than as a Florentine-style investment fund aimed at professional
and upper ranks. Significantly, it also attracted many employers who used it to
save the dowries that they would pass on to servant girls at the end of their contract. The median dowry for the first girls registered with Bologna's Monte del
Matrimonio when it opened was 173 lire; roughly 45 percent were between
100 and 500 lire and most of the rest were under 100. Through the seventeenth

century, the median fluctuated from 266 to 380 lire, while the percentage between 100 and 500 lire was consistently between 60 and 70 percent. The Baraccano and S. Croce dowries, which ranged from 100 lire in 1550 to 1,000 lire a
century later, put the conservatory girls solidly into the ranks of working and
modest artisinal families.[30]

The third common regulation in Bolognese conservatories concerned the
length of time a girl would have to stay in the home before being released, and
it arose directly from the second. The Baraccano stipulated a minimum stay of
seven years, and S. Croce eight. This might seem to be self-defeating when most
conservatories wanted to release their girls back into society as soon as possible,
but it, too, was tied to the dowry system. While homes referred to the dowries
that they "offered" to girls, in fact it was the girls' own labor that generated these
so-called gifts. Homes estimated that it took seven or eight years of income-
producing piecework for a girl to generate the funds for the dowry they would
be "giving" her. In late-sixteenth-century Bologna, a minor artisan or small shop-
keeper earned the equivalent of 200 to 300 lire annually, so in general terms, a
conservatory dowry was roughly equivalent to a minor artisan's annual pay.
Short-term stays increased dotal liabilities while reducing income. Rates paid for
girls' piecework were lower than for boys or men, and conservatory girls were
at an even greater disadvantage because their vulnerability and needs were well
known. We saw earlier that the girls might spin thread, embroider, make veils,
and finish cloth in conservatory workshops, but that sufficient piecework was not
always available and a girl might work no more than a week per month on average. Each conservatory mandated a ledger that would record each girl's earnings
so that they could be returned to her in dowry form, and some historians have
assumed that the ledgers—and the promise—were kept.[31]

Yet tracking the earnings of fifty, sixty, or seventy girls who might work a day
one month and two weeks the next was apparently too complicated for either
staff or volunteer administrators, and no home actually followed through with
these records in our period. Stipulating a seven- or eight-year stay as S. Croce
and the Baraccano avoided this accounting nightmare while achieving, in a
rough rule of thumb way, much the same result. And in fact, the Baraccano benefited from this because its girls actually stayed an average of over twelve years
in the mid-sixteenth century and nine years by century's end. The moral connection between work and dowry was clear to all concerned, even if the financial accounting was not. When Ortensia di Ser Giovanni Diola was expelled be-

cause of a contagious illness in 1581, she demanded a dowry that would allow her to enter a convent; the Baraccano gave her 200 lire plus goods in explicit recognition of the nine years she had worked in the home.[32]

We saw earlier that statute prescriptions were often ignored, and this certainly applies to the rules on seniority, standard dowries, and length of tenure. If we look at some statistics for Baraccano girls, we can see how skilled the administrators were at ignoring their own rules, even rules of thumb. Of the 89 girls in the first register (1554–68) who married from the home, 46 are recorded as leaving with dowries but the bulk of these (42) came from family or donors; only 20 clearly received some contribution from the Baraccano. Most were the 100 lire dowries standard at the time, though they ranged from a low of 25 lire to a high of 300. The length of time a girl had stayed and worked in the conservatory did not seem to affect the dowry she received from the Baraccano. Yet these records are fragmentary, and it is possible that the 43 girls for whom no records are given all received a 100 lire Baraccano dowry. Certainly when we move to the cohort that lived in the home when a third and more detailed register began in 1584, the conservatory seems more generous. Out of 89 girls 53 married, and at least 39 went to the altar with a Baraccano dowry; in 15 cases family or donors provided additional funds. The remaining cases are unclear, and only one girl out of the 53 definitely did not receive a dowry from the conservatory. By this point, the dowries had risen to 200 or 300 lire in cash or financial credits supplemented with another 150 lire of linens and household goods (*li apparati*). Girls received these standard amounts regardless of the time they had spent in the home, and they did not leave in the order that they came, as the statutes had stipulated.[33]

In practice, then, the Baraccano did not follow its own rules regarding seniority or the connection between a girl's productivity and the size of her dowry. It used its funds strategically in order to get girls out of the home and up to the altar. Most girls married, thanks to private or family dotal funds, and the Baraccano used its own money to even disparities or hasten difficult cases out the door. That said, there was indeed a concerted effort to get those girls out, and at this level private charity was part of public institutional strategy. We saw earlier that the Bolognese had established a dowry fund for conservatory girls by public subscription as early as 1535. This was still paying out dowries decades later: at least seven of the forty-nine girls marrying in the Baraccano's 1554–68 cohort received all or part of their dowries from it. Local confraternities distributed dowries here as elsewhere in Italy, with one of the city's leading brotherhoods, the Compagnia di S. Maria della Vita, staging elaborate evening processions on its feast day in which white-robed brides gripped hollow torches that held their 100 lire gifts. In an odd twist, the Vita *confratelli* had to double check the processants before the ceremony because some of those chosen actually exchanged—and possibly sold—their place in line to other young girls. Dowry charity grew in the century following. Mauro Carboni estimates that between confraternal, guild, and parish funds, private trusts, and larger financial institutions like the Monte della Pietà and the Monte del Matrimonio, half of all couples marrying in Bologna from the mid-seventeenth century to the end of the eighteenth were subsidized with charitable dowries.[34]

Private donors might supplement the dotal funds of individual girls at a conservatory like the Baraccano, but some made it a standing act of charity available to many, particularly if they were conservatory officers. Baraccano Conservator Alessandro Bono gave eleven dowries of 100 lire, while his colleague Sebastiano Lodi offered five dowries of 25 lire. Outside donors also brought funds in: the powerful Count Pepoli offered five of 100 lire and Signora Faustina Malvasia showed at least two other girls the same generosity she had demonstrated when supplementing Serafina Bertaza's dowry with a 50 lire gift.[35] Some offered pledges and others gave lump sums that had to be devoted to dowries until they were exhausted. Girls were aware of these funds, possibly tipped off by the visitors or staff. So, for instance, three years after Bologna's senator Francesco Maria Casali died in April 1586, the fourteen girls who had been in S. Maria del Baraccano the longest ("le pie anciane et le piu antiche") petitioned the conservatory's governors, drawing attention to the fact that they were not yet married, that Casali had left 1,400 lire "to the benefit of the girls of S. Maria del Baraccano" ("a favore delle Donzelle di S.ta Maria dil Barachano"), and that if the sum were divided equally between them, they would each get a 100 lire dowry. The governors agreed to this, and in short order twelve of the girls married and one entered a convent.[36]

Unusually for Florence, a similar fund developed there at the S. Caterina conservatory. One of its first administrators, Girolamo di Antonio Michelozzi, died within a few years of its opening, leaving 7,000 lire (scudi 1,041.8.5) and the instructions to his heirs to distribute the sum in one or two dowries of 100 lire annually. This would be small help to the more than eighty girls crowded into S. Caterina at a time, but the heirs complied with forty-eight such dowries over the next thirty-one years before trying to squeeze out of the obligation.[37]

By the end of the sixteenth century, the Baraccano was moving away from dowry charity and emphasizing instead the pledges, funds, and goods that a girl could bring in when she was admitted. The number of unrelated donors dropped steadily, while those from the extended family rose. Average dowries rose to 320 lire, and the range extended to include dowries of 1,000 lire, together with those of 50 lire, which were still the basic dowry given to rural girls. More tellingly, however, the entries for individual girls in the Baraccano's ledgers became longer and longer as scribes added lengthy inventories of the clothing, household goods and furniture, and rural and urban properties that girls brought in when they entered and that the conservatory administered on their behalf.[38] By the turn of the century, what had begun as a purely charitable home for poor girls was gradually expanding into a custodial shelter for those of means, and the dowries were being generated as much through the Baraccano's investment of pledges and properties as through the piecework done by the girls through their eight to twelve years of residence. Yet the Baraccano continued to be a portal through which vulnerable young women could be rescued from marginality and be "made normal," passing back into society as productive wives and mothers thanks to the active intervention of volunteers who assembled dowries and negotiated marriage contracts.[39]

Dowries were only half the challenge. How do you find a husband for an orphaned or abandoned girl? Bolognese conservatories developed procedures that were a coy blend of commerce and pious modesty, even for a time when marriage was more about the exchange of resources than about affection. Men in search of a spouse periodically came by the home to ask which girls were available. Allowing them to enter in order to see which girls pleased them would put the conservatory on a level with brothels, but there were more discrete alternatives. Homes used public religious processions as advertising opportunities, something that Rome's Santo Spirito in Sassia practiced from the 1470s and that Florence later picked up on.[40] Since the girls marched in order of seniority, the single men standing by the side of the road could see that those first in line behind the confraternal banner would be those first in line to the marriage altar, and make their calculations if a girl farther down the line attracted them more. Men would line the road out of simple curiosity or because a girl's relative or even a confraternity member had tipped them off as a particular girl moved up in seniority. They might even come to a series of processions in order to keep tabs on a girl's progress through the ranks. Other men might be mildly curious about a girl's looks (although they were veiled) and bearing, and more intensely interested in the size of her dowry.

Whatever the case, negotiations began once a man presented himself at the door as a prospective suitor. Confraternal visitors added his name to their list of people to investigate, and looked into his lifestyle and reputation, his health, his occupation and resources, his birth and age. Neighbors, workmates, and the parish priest all had their say, and the visitors had a face-to-face interview as well. Some mid-seventeenth-century Baraccano visitors reported on the state of a man's furniture, the stores in his cellar, and even the cleanliness of his home and clothing: "his personal grooming does not appear very healthy," they reported, when turning one down.[41] Yet it was a two-way interview in which the prospective groom aimed to fill in what he didn't already know about what funds, goods, and skills a girl would bring into a marriage, whether she was healthy and "whole," and what her family had been. A girl with artisinal skills had a better chance of marrying, though she did not necessarily marry into the same trade.[42] Mid-sixteenth-century Bolognese statutes treat these negotiations vaguely, but experience quickly shaped practice and rules in a process that was not far from what these men faced when they arranged their own daughters' marriages. When negotiating in 1561 with Domenigo di Andrea for the hand of Caterina di Simone del Miglio, the Baraccano visitor offered 250 lire, but Domenigo countered that he wanted 300. Caterina had no family, had no other resources, and was already 25 years old; Domenigo got his 300 lire.[43] As conservatories relied more on kin to subsidize dowries, they gave the relatives a greater say in approving or rejecting these marital negotiations by sending the visitors around to their doors as well. The visitors made arrangements to collect on the dowry pledges that these kin had promised years before, and clearly if they wanted their voice heard on the choice of spouse, they had to be ready to pay up at this time.[44]

Was the girl herself part of these negotiations? Not in any formal way, and given the numbers whose marriages might be under negotiation at any particular time, it is doubtful that the visitors would include the girl in their rounds. But neither could they ignore her. Staff and female visitors supplied the terse descriptions of a girl's personality that we sometimes find in the conservatory's written records: "works well," "good girl," or, more pungently, "possessed."[45] It certainly wasn't in a home's long-term interest for its girls to get a reputation as restless and unhappy wives, and the girl's anticipated reaction was one of the items that might be discussed when the visitors came back with their report. The Baraccano conservatory's executive discussed and voted on each girl's case, and the notary then drew up her official exit papers (to be signed by the *priore* and handed to the *guardiana*) and the legal instrument for the dowry that spelled out contributions in cash and goods from the home, relatives, and other sponsors, and the properties or guarantors that the groom had found to secure the sum.

The girl and her future spouse met for the first time in a conservatory office when it was time to sign this instrument, a ceremony that most often took place a few days, weeks, or even months before the exchange of vows. Baraccano statutes required that the girl be present, perhaps to nip the marriage in the bud if either youth could not stand the looks of the other—with no space for conversation, looks was all they had to go on, but popular custom had a whole set of sayings for how to interpret the shape of a nose, the look of an eye, or the set of a mouth.[46] If they had legal and financial obligations, the girl's kin would attend the signing as well. Yet once the documents were signed, it was the home's prior who put the man's hand on that of the girl ("fara toccare dal Sposo la Mano alla Sposa"), and then invited everyone present to enjoy the food and drink that the home had laid on. In a brief speech, he confirmed the home's satisfaction with the arrangements. The group then dispersed and the names of the couple were sent over to the local parish priest so that he could read the banns.

The prioress or another gentlewoman of the S. Maria del Baraccano confraternity invited the girl to her home for a few days or weeks to prepare her for what lay ahead, and then accompanied the girl when the day came for the exchange of vows. S. Marta allowed a marriage ceremony only if the gentlewoman sponsor paid for it herself, but S. Maria del Baraccano was more generous and festive. Before Trent, the party gathered in the confraternity's own church for vows solemnized by its own priest, but by the later sixteenth century the ceremony moved to the nearby parish church of S. Giuliano, with the prioress, some of the gentlewomen, and possibly the prior attending. It frequently married girls in pairs, perhaps to make it easier for these officials to attend. Vows exchanged, this group then made its way either to the home of the girl's closest kin or to the husband's home, where, by local custom, they sealed the vows with another feast.[47]

The gentlewomen took their leave and the girl began her new life, but the two sides kept up contact, with the dowry their common concern. It might be months before the home paid the dowry, and if it thought that the man's situation was a bit unsettled or that the young couple's lifestyle was not sufficiently sober, it could make this a small payment, or give only some goods, or even pass on only the interest generated by the dowry funds. Homes always insisted that the dowry be backed by a guarantor or invested in something "stable" like furniture, properties, or workshop tools (all of which could be redeemed, unlike consumables like food, clothing, or linens), but from 1576, the Baraccano went a step further and retained up to half of the dowry under its own management as securities in the city's funded debts.[48] Setting itself up as the couple's de facto financial administrator was a short and logical step from its earlier role as the girl's surrogate parent, because the home was always wary of a husband's mismanagement and, like any parent, demanded the return of the dowry if the girl died before having given birth to children.[49] But it also made the couple involuntary investors in those funds that benefited patricians and investors.

A Bolognese girl entered a convent in much the same way. The visitors looked around the city and region to see which convents might be willing to take her, sometimes choosing one where the girl already had an aunt or sister, and negotiated directly on terms. In most cases, the girl would go in as a servant sister, and spend the rest of her days doing the laundry, cleaning, and cooking for those patrician women with larger dowries who would have entered as contemplative or choir nuns. Both serving and contemplative nuns took vows primarily because husbands could not be found for them, but the financial dynamics were reversed. Private families generally paid less for monachation than for marriage, making it a cheaper alternative that many across the peninsula turned to by the end of the sixteenth century. By contrast, conservatories paid higher dowries to convents than to men in search of a spouse. This discouraged the overuse of an otherwise convenient option for releasing conservatory girls, but also points to how modest a conservatory dowry was, and how likely it was that some girls married below their station. Monachation was a reversible step and, unlike marriage, the girl had a larger say. A probationary period of a few months allowed the convent to decide if the girl was adaptable, allowed the girl to decide if the convent was acceptable, and allowed the conservatory to decide if she was being sufficiently fed and cared for. She remained essentially a boarder at this stage, with the conservatory paying for her upkeep for a couple of months until all sides had made their decision. The confraternity executive voted to approve arrangements, but unlike marriage there was no particular ceremony or celebration attending a girl's entry into the convent, and the prior and prioress seem not to have been there to lead her from one enclosure to the next.[50]

A handful of girls in Bologna left to join convents, and even fewer took this route in Florence—never even 3 percent. Yet this simple statistic obscures a more puzzling picture, for in Florence it was less a matter of conservatory girls entering convents than it was of conventual discipline entering conservatories. The Pietà and S. Caterina homes were the city's largest conservatories and served the lower range of population, while the Carità was the smallest and most exclusive. All three evolved slowly into convents through the first decades of the seventeenth century. The process usually began, as it had at the Pietà, when some women who had been in the home for decades and who had no prospects of ever leaving took the veil as tertiaries. This took them out of the ambiguous status of being legally children and wards when they might be in their 30s or 40s or beyond. Yet it simply imported another ambiguity into the conservatory, and in all cases the logic of the situation favored the home's gradual metamorphosis into a convent. But there was more than just logic here. Florence seemed resigned to enclosure as a fact of life in all its institutions for women and, unlike Bologna, seemed to have difficulty embracing the idea of a lay shelter that would deliberately work to restore orphaned and abandoned girls to the population of marriageable females. The S. Caterina home that opened in 1591 adopted this ethos on opening in 1593, ordering that marriages would have to be organized and paid for by families, but adding that this was an option only to be exercised if the girls wished it: those who wished to save their virginity for Christ could expect to have a home in the conservatory for life.[51] As Philip Gavitt has shown with the Innocenti, large numbers of girls who entered as foundlings lived out their lives within its walls or at least under its care: in 1579, 968 of its 1,220 residents were female; 733 (60%) of these were of marriageable age and 223 (18%) were over 40 years old. When the Innocenti could hold no more, increasing numbers of its girls were transferred over to the Orbatello home, formerly a shelter for destitute widows, and the process was repeated.[52]

When did they start to lose any hope or expectation of leaving? We saw in the previous chapter that the Carità home moved by stages toward conventual status; most of its girls simply remained resident as it passed through these stages and they went on to become nuns. At the Pietà, the situation was more complicated, with two cultures or sets of expectations coexisting until at least 1624, when a new register began. We can compare the ages and length of time in the home of two groups: first the 272 girls who passed in and out of the home from 1569 to 1623, and then the 106 girls of that register whose names transfer into

Table 6.7. Exits from the Pietà and Baraccano by Decade, 1558–1627

Time Period	Pietà	S. Maria del Baraccano
> 1558	134	34
1558–68	188	73
1569–79	91	77
1580–89	56	89
1590–99	43	57
1600–1609	29	84
1610–19	32	8*
1620–27	13	

Sources: ASF, CRSF ms. 112/79; ASB, PIE, S. Maria del Baraccano, mss. 6/1, 6/2, and 7 (with duplicate records removed).
*Of entrants to December 1599.

the *Libro Nuovo*, or new register, begun in 1624. Tables 6.1 and 6.2 showed that the girls who left before 1623 were, on average 18 years old, and that they had stayed in the home an average of 102 months; some of these girls had entered in the first decade of the seventeenth century, fully expecting to leave. By contrast, the cohort that was in the home and whose names headed the new 1624 list averaged 31 years old. These women had lived in the home an average of 281 months, or 23 years. Most had come into the Pietà after Fra Gherardo had first vested eighteen girls as tertiaries in 1595, and at least some had entered with the expectation that they would not live in the Pietà temporarily, as at a conservatory, but permanently, as at a convent.[53] We can hardly call this a process of self-selection, since these girls and women were not in control of their own destinies. Yet we can see that at the Pietà, as at the Innocenti, the Carità, and S. Caterina, the home gradually filled with women who would and could not leave. The number of women who left the home dropped steadily decade by decade, a phenomenon not found to the same extent in Bologna, as Table 6.7 demonstrates.[54]

Graph 6.1 paints the picture more graphically. Through the course of the later sixteenth century, more girls entered the Pietà than exited from it. The result over time was a gradual increase in the permanent population, and the consequent loss of the home's ability to function as a temporary shelter for girls in need.

Whether they were sick, maimed, lacking dowries, or burdened with some other impediment, the women who were slowly becoming the Pietà's permanent population were the victims of a peculiar culture that held sway in Florence.

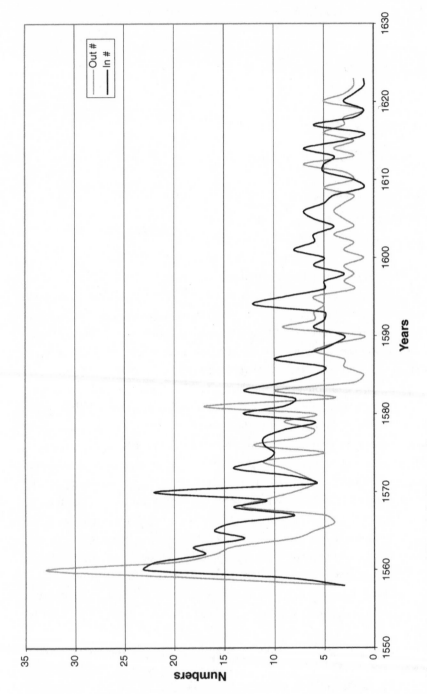

Graph 6.1. Entrances and Exits at the Pietà, 1558–1623
Source: ASF CRSF 112/79.

When confronted with women in need, few Florentines could imagine alternatives to the conventual model. A culture of enclosure was far more deeply rooted here, and its effects were felt by a wide range of women. By the mid-sixteenth century, Florence had 50 percent more convents than Bologna (forty-two to twenty-seven), and a higher percentage of the city's population was housed in them.[55] Its convents were expanding rapidly in number and size, but they were largely for the daughters of patrician and perhaps professional families and very few conservatory girls ever entered them. By the seventeenth century, almost half of patrician daughters were taking the veil rather than marrying. This was largely forced, and has usually been explained as a strategy adopted by wealthy families who could minimize dowry liabilities by marrying off only one or two daughters and removing the others from the marriage market by placing them in convents.

Yet what was happening at the Pietà, Carità, and S. Caterina was essentially the forced monachation of girls from poor and artisinal families. These conservatories were becoming lay convents for the lower classes, where poor families could deposit their surplus daughters, sisters, or nieces without having to pay a dowry to cover their maintenance (as wealthy families had to do when enrolling a girl in a convent). Florence's conservatories therefore allowed poorer families to ape the marriage strategies of their betters, keeping some adolescent females off the marriage market in order to increase the dowries available for others in the family. Bologna's alternative approach demonstrated that these girls could earn all or part of their dowries, and that if there were sufficient will on the part of administrators, and sufficient volunteers to do the negotiations, conservatory girls could indeed be married. Yet volunteers and funds were lacking in Florence—partly because it entrusted administration to small teams of five or six men, but equally because the public will to adopt an alternative approach was not there. Rather, in Florence forced enclosure took on a normativity that it did not have elsewhere. By means of shelters like the Innocenti foundling home and the conservatories, choked with unmarried women who worked hard and died young, it was extended to all classes of girls.

The Politics of Renaissance Orphanages

In the first half of the sixteenth century, Florence and Bologna both faced the challenge of sheltering increased numbers of orphaned and abandoned children. They decided to move beyond traditional *ospedale* shelters and ad hoc fostering arrangements, and experiment instead with institutional homes that would be dedicated solely to caring for these children. The scale and coordination of these experiments were unprecedented, and mark a historic step in the evolution of state-sponsored social welfare in Europe. Both cities developed networks of homes that were loosely connected to each other and that between themselves were able to shelter between three hundred and five hundred children by the end of the century. Other cities had shelters, but none could boast this kind of coordinated network. The charitable networks represented a radical shift in social policy based on the conviction that the whole community was responsible for taking care of the hundreds of children who were orphaned or abandoned through plague, famine, legal restrictions, or negligence.

More to the point, this responsibility was not simply one facet of the community's care for the poor generally. It was to be exercised deliberately, on a large scale, with policy and coordination, and with the government itself involved either directly or indirectly as the prime mover. This was also unprecedented, and a radical transfer of responsibilities that had once been assumed by the Church or private groups like guilds. Yet these were not purely secular bureaucracies. Both urban governments worked together with lay charitable religious agencies like hospitals and confraternities in order to realize the new social goal, and much of their motivation came from movements of religious reform that emphasized the Christian duty to exercise charity to the poor and dispossessed. The resulting hybrid of lay religious groups and institutions working together with governments became the pattern for the evolution of welfare bureaucracies across Europe through the course of the ancien régime. Finally, the networks of orphanages and conservatories also represented a significant shift in European perceptions about children, and adolescents in particular. The homes demonstrated a broad recognition that adolescence was a particularly vulnerable but also a particularly promising phase of life, and their rapid multiplication across Europe shows how many people were willing to translate this conviction into political and social action.

The networks in Florence and Bologna evolved over decades, with new homes generated by plague or famine, until each city had more than seven. Florentine homes tended to be larger and more institutional, while the Bolognese were generally smaller, though not so small as to fully bear out the pious fiction that they were families in themselves. And there were other nodes in each city's network. Both cities had a single large foundling home that sheltered hundreds of infants, children, and youths, most of them illegitimate and most abandoned anonymously. This was in sharp contrast to the orphanages and conservatories, which were more selective, where most of the children were legitimate, and where girls and boys were in separate buildings, not just in separate wards. Yet the greatest difference in the operation of the two urban networks lay outside of these homes altogether: Bologna opened a paupers' shelter in 1563, and it was this shelter outside the city that allowed the Bolognese homes to be so much smaller, more selective, and arguably more successful. The truly desperate cases were sent to the Ospedale dei Mendicanti beyond the city walls, allowing the shelters within the city to offer a higher standard of care to a better class of child. Until its own Ospedale dei Mendicanti opened in 1620, Florence's indigent and sick children were channeled into homes like the Pietà and S. Caterina, where populations shot up and where mortality rates quickly followed. Once Florence opened a paupers' shelter, it rapidly adjusted the rest of its network further. Both the Pietà and S. Caterina conservatories became convents, and the government opened a new institution for girls (the Ospedale delle Abbandonate) to run parallel to the long-standing Ospedale degli Abbandonati for boys, and under the care of the same state magistracy. Florence was following a certain bureaucratic logic here: one foundling home, one large orphanage for girls and one for boys, and one large paupers' workhouse. Bologna followed this logic on its upper and lower tiers, but preferred many smaller homes for adolescents in between. This may have recognized adolescence as a state requiring more personal attention. It certainly recognized that social rank had to be accommodated institutionally.

The homes for boys—one in Florence and eventually three in Bologna—operated similarly in both cities. They worked actively to educate the boys, to train them in a craft, and to return them to society. Some of the boys' work generated income for the homes themselves, but the emphasis was still on getting them out the door. Most did get out by late adolescence.

The ways girls were treated in Florence as compared to Bologna throws into sharper relief some otherwise hidden differences between the two cities' charitable cultures and between their political systems and social environment.

Bologna's conservatories worked deliberately and directly to ensure the passage of their wards out of the homes and into marriages. To this end, they recruited private dowries, offered institutional dowries (funded in part out of girls' own piecework), and arranged marriages directly using this combination of dotal funds. Conservatories were part of an active demographic strategy that was aimed at expanding the local population, and girls passed steadily through them on their way back to family life. In its first conservatory of S. Marta, Bologna experimented briefly with the idea of a lay convent, but it rejected this in favor of an aggressive marriage strategy. Florence's conservatories worked far more indirectly, and far less successfully, at getting their girls into marriages, to the point where one could legitimately question whether the demographic strategy at work was aimed at limiting rather than expanding the population. Few marriages were arranged, and few dowries were offered. Most marriage negotiations were devolved to families or employers. We can assume that families took this seriously, but the records we have suggest that many employers barely had a chance to get to know their girls, let alone marry them off, before the girls quit, fled, or were dismissed and returned to the conservatory. Those girls who did not marry or leave to sweep floors in a shop or home remained working, sleeping, and eating in the conservatory until they died. And many died.

Bolognese homes worked actively to pass their girls back into society, and this mirrored the active and highly selective way in which they admitted girls. Likewise, the passivity with which Florentine homes approached their girls' fates was a mirror of the passivity with which they opened the doors and let girls in. Part of what lay behind this was the presence or absence of people to do the work. Bologna's homes, some of them sheltering only a few dozen children, had a multitude of volunteer administrators working alongside hired staff, even through those periods when they complained of too few hands or too little money. Florentine homes, in spite of having larger numbers of children to shelter, had but a handful of administrators. This difference grew out of local charitable traditions, and particularly the nature of the confraternities that organized and ran the homes. Bologna's network framed the work of caring for orphaned and abandoned children as a charitable activity that was undertaken by large numbers of confraternity members whose brotherhoods were organized on a collegiate system to better balance spiritual and charitable concerns. This fostered more immediate personal links between children and the adults who had volunteered to care for them, sometimes out of religious conviction, sometimes out of political opportunity, and most often out of an indistinguishable mix of the two. Florence's system of purely managerial confraternities with a limited spiritual life turned care of these same children into a problem of welfare administration that was undertaken on government commission; there were few personal links between the children and the adults who oversaw their care. The exceptions were those homes run by women, and their quick suppression proves the rule.

Florence's system of congregational confraternities was just one part of its charitable tradition. The other was its closer ties to the ecclesiastical hierarchy, and the willingness of many Florentines to let clerics take the lead in charity. Priests and friars were among the prime movers in the Compagnia di S. Maria Vergine that figured in the operation of all its conservatories. They were directly involved in the start and operation of a number of homes, from the Carità home that arose out of the vision, resources, and connections of the priest Vittorio dell'Ancisa, to the magistracy of the Bigallo whose president was always a bishop. No Bolognese home had this level of clerical involvement, with the possible exception of S. Giuseppe. Bologna's traditionally more testy relations with the papacy had fostered a civic religion that was far more firmly in lay hands. Nowhere was this more clearly seen than in its charitable institutions, all of which were controlled by lay confraternities that aggressively countered clerical efforts to exercise influence.

These brotherhoods supervised some of the major shrines of the local cult, and incorporated their wards into the processions that were a regular part of its public ritual. Florence had a healthy civic religious life, but it had always shaped that life in a closer alliance with regular and secular clergy. The Savonarolan vision of Florence as a holy and charitable republic led by friars and laity together was but one key instance of this long tradition, but the fact that it resonated so broadly and so long testifies to the tradition's enduring popularity. Moreover, a good part of Florentine banking wealth, artistic patrimony, and political importance had been generated out of alliances between its leading families and the ecclesiastical hierarchy. These are critical factors for explaining both the passive acceptance in Florentine conservatories of a culture of enclosure that simply took girls in and housed them as though they were nuns until they died, and also the uncontroversial metamorphosis of three conservatories into convents. Either development would be unthinkable in Bologna.

Bolognese religious and charitable traditions emphasized the role of confraternity brothers and sisters as surrogate parents to needy citizen girls and boys. With girls, the preference for marriage over convent was not an abstract statement of policy: confraternity members found spouses, subsidized dowries, negotiated terms, attended and even paid for weddings, and accompanied their "daughters" to the homes where they would become wives and mothers. They pushed the girl's blood relatives to the side in these ceremonies even when their own kin relationship was both symbolic and collective. Depending on the terms of office, one prior or prioress might oversee the dowry-signing ceremony, another the exchange of vows, and yet another the disbursement of dowry funds. Girls who had been expelled or restored to the care of brothers, aunts, or grandparents could still return to claim a dowry and be married as other Baraccano girls were, with confraternity officers in attendance. Surrogate kinship that was at once so determined and yet potentially so detached underlines powerfully the extent to which Bologna's governing class saw its institutional charitable work as an exercise of parental authority over the city's poor. It closely guarded this authority against the papal governors, the religious orders, and a series of ambitious Tridentine bishops. Extending—and limiting—charity to citizens was fundamental to the republican ethos, and broad-based paternalistic control was fundamental to republican political practice.

Florentine conservatory and orphanage statute books employed some of the same paternalistic rhetoric, but in a grand duchy it was inevitably the grand dukes who were the real political fathers. They threw the doors open to needy children from across the duchy to highlight this symbolic and charitable kinship. The strategy was more generous than Bologna's tight focus on helping only local citizen children, but with more needy children and fewer adult volunteers in Florentine homes, it further watered down the possibility of any personal links between them. There was no room politically or culturally for Florence's home administrators to become active surrogate parents on the scale of their Bolognese counterparts. The women of the Pietà played the role for a generation, and quite deliberately adopted the rhetoric of being mothers to the girls. Yet they could not organize marriages. More critically, they were challenged and eventually outmaneuvered by Florence's Dominicans, who wrote the home's chronicle in order to assert just as deliberately that *they* were the genuine spiritual fathers to the girls, going so far as to insert a scene where the agitated girls cried for the protection of their holy fathers against the meddling of their lay mothers. The language of kinship was not empty rhetoric, but powerful, contested, and an inducement to action. The result, in the most basic terms, was that an orphaned or abandoned Bolognese girl could look on the conservatory as a temporary way station or portal to a new life, and count on her guardians to arrange a marriage for her. Her Florentine counterpart had to resign herself to the fact that the conservatory might become a permanent home unless her own kin, and possibly an employer, found her a way out.

Conservatories and orphanages multiplied rapidly across Italy and Europe in the sixteenth century. Brescia opened a conservatory in 1512 to shelter girls rendered homeless as a result of the Italian wars and particularly the sack of the city in that same year. Perugia's confraternity of S. Tommaso d'Aquino opened the Pia Casa delle Derelitte in 1539, and its confraternity of S. Girolamo opened the Pia Casa della Carità in 1563, thanks in part to civic authorization. *Confratelli* in both institutions reviewed applicants and raised alms for dowries. Rome's confraternity of S. Maria della Visitazione degli Orfani opened a hospice for legitimate girls ages 7 to 10 in 1542, and a year later the Compagnia delle Vergini Miserabili di S. Caterina opened its shelter for the daughters of prostitutes and other endangered girls; additional institutions followed through the next century. Ferrara's confraternity of S. Agnese opened a conservatory in 1554.[1] Many of these homes targeted particular social groups, and they became ever more specialized through the course of the sixteenth and seventeenth centuries as individual donors, confraternities, and civic governments responded to general concerns—chiefly the drive to prevent prostitutes' daughters from following in their mothers' footsteps—or particular local challenges. In 1578, Milan opened the Collegio delle Vergini Spagnole for the young girls fathered by Spanish soldiers, and four years later it followed with a companion institution, the Collegio di S. Giacomo for young boys.[2]

Similar developments occurred north of the Alps. In Paris, the confraternity of Saint Esprit had founded a hospice in 1363, which later came to shelter and educate orphans, deliberately excluding foundlings and just as deliberately focusing on legitimate local children. From the early sixteenth century it required relatives to swear to the fact that these were children born both locally and legitimately before they would be accepted. Paris's Hotel-Dieu hospital raised the children who were orphaned when the adults in its care died, and this developed in 1536 into a separate institution that, like Saint Esprit, took only local and legitimate children. In 1545, the Parlement of Paris ordered the long-standing pilgrims' hostel of the Trinité to turn to sheltering young male orphans. The keystone was Paris's Aumône générale, also authorized by the Parlement of Paris in 1544, and bringing lay and clerical leaders together to arrange the care and fostering of orphans as part of a general brief to oversee the city's poor relief.[3] London's Christ's Hospital opened in 1552 to shelter "fatherless children" and provide the kind of care and education that would let these orphans break the cycle of poverty that had claimed their parents' lives.[4] In 1572, the city fathers of Augsburg responded to economic collapse by opening an orphanage for local children abandoned when their parents fled the city; this was the first such home in Germany, and it gathered all legitimate children of both Catholic and Protestant families until 1649, when two confessionally specific homes succeeded it.[5] Amsterdam opened its first residence for a handful of burgher orphans in 1520, though the Burgerweeshuis remained a fairly small operation until 1578, when the city's adoption of the Reformation and consequent appropriation of Catholic institutions gave the home's regents both the capital assembled by their Catholic predecessors and a large convent in which to house their charges. Outrelief for poorer orphans would wait until 1613, and the Aalmoezeniersweeshuis orphanage would not open to shelter this class until 1664.[6]

Did Protestant and Catholic governments care differently for their orphaned and abandoned children? Some have argued that foundling homes (and municipal brothels, for that matter) point to a Catholic willingness to accommodate lesser evils in order to avoid greater ones. Better that an illegitimate infant should be abandoned and baptized rather than aborted or killed, even if the foundling home's presence might seem to condone and even encourage the generation of more illegitimates.[7] Yet once we move to the question of caring for older children, the dynamics shift and broad confessional differences wane. The cities just listed and many more besides shared many fundamental values regardless of religious confession. Care should be distinguished by gender and also by class. It should be protective and redemptive. The children should be educated, and that education should prepare them to return to society. They should work, and that work should support their own homes while also serving the needs of the local economy. The children admitted to the home should be legitimate or, if they were not, the home should be a means for them to recover social honor that their parents had lost. These were the obligations of parents to their children, and where blood parents had failed, social fathers and mothers must step in for the good of the children and of society itself.

Yet there were still differences that were as much cultural and political as religious. Catholic institutions were frequently started and administered by groups like confraternities that deliberately structured themselves around the model of symbolic kinship and in which many *confratelli* shared the work of administration—as much to share in the spiritual rewards as to divide up labor. Where *confratelli* remained active in this way, care was generally better. The language of kinship certainly resonated through homes in Protestant countries, directed there too at the administrators, the staff, and the civic rulers who stood behind the enterprise, but in practice these homes were more often run by the kinds of smaller administrations that we have seen in Florence. If they had more success than Florence did in passing girls back into public life, it was because they did not have to worry about providing dowries and because convents had disappeared from the cultural horizon.

Comparing the Florentine and Bolognese models demonstrates that differences are rooted less in one or another religious confession than in the local culture and traditions through which religious impulses are channeled, and in the political purposes that charity served. The results disrupt conventional paradigms. Bologna's mix of republican and papal government and its lay civic religion shaped a network of homes that preserved the forms of civil society and accountability of the medieval commune. Hundreds of citizens engaged in the task of sheltering orphaned and abandoned children and launching them back into society as young adults. But, apart from those who slipped through loopholes, they cared only for citizen children. Florence's absolutist ducal government and more ecclesiastically oriented civic creed generated a network that was more authoritarian in its methods and more economical in its use of volunteer and state resources. Yet its institutions were concerned only that children come from the Florentine state, and not necessarily from the citizen class. Bologna's network served the political needs of its oligarchy, while Florence's served the dynastic and territorial needs of its grand dukes. Bologna's administrators drew more frequently on religious language, observances, and groups to animate their own efforts and lend them popular legitimacy. Their Florentine counterparts left religion to the clerics and operated as secular administrators.

There can be little doubt that children were better cared for in Bologna's orphanages and conservatories. But there can equally be no doubt that Florence's institutions—larger, more efficient, and run by small and rational bureaucracies accountable chiefly to the head of state—provided the template for other European charities in the centuries that followed. Where Bologna held to a welfare bureaucracy rooted in the whole civic community but offering benefits only to *citizens*, Florence pioneered the rational bureaucracy of absolutism and extended care to the more broadly defined group of *subjects*. This resulted in very different approaches to care and very different outcomes for orphaned and abandoned children.

Institutional Finances

Conservatories and orphanages did not follow a single model when keeping their ledgers. As was frequently the case with charitable organizations, successive financial administrators might also use different rubrics when summarizing income and expense, if indeed they summarized them at all. Currency differences both within the cities (between the currency of account and currency in circulation) and also between them renders comparisons difficult.

Tables A.1 and A.2 aim to circumvent these difficulties by summarizing income and expense according to standard categories that are compared not in absolute terms but as a percentage of the total institutional budget. These percentages are calculated over periods of two to thirty-four years in order to smooth out the sharp jumps or drops that may result from either a temporary crisis or a change in record keeper. Table A.1 gives the high, low, and average annual budget totals for Bolognese institutions in the period. In four Florentine instances, the column marked "Total" records a figure given at the end of a particular ledger as the total for the years under review; this is then broken down to an annual average. Expense and income categories in Table A.2 have been simplified and grouped together, although this omits some of the other ways in which homes generated and spent money; the table indicates what percentage of total expense or income the categories listed represent. Figures in this column that exceed 100 percent may indicate either fraud, or simply imprecise or variable accounting from one year to the next. Similarly, figures under 100 percent indicate that often sums were frequently paid to or collected from individuals without a clearly designated purpose (this explains, for example, why some institutions have no salary figures in particular years).

The tables underscore some critical similarities and differences between the two cities. In their expenses, all homes spent roughly similar proportions of their budget on clothing, food, and accommodation. The chief difference lay in marriages, where Bolognese conservatories spent significantly more. In their income, Bolognese homes earned more than Florentine ones from investments and rents; this was particularly the case with older homes like S. Maria del Baraccano and S. Bartolomeo di Reno that had existed for a century or more as charitable hostels before sheltering children and that had assembled large legacies.[1] This left them less dependent on children's efforts at alms collecting or piecework. Since most also had a chapel on site, they spent more on cultic obligations (chiefly Masses), but also earned more from collections. Yet despite having fewer sources of income, it was Florentine conservatories that consistently generated annual surpluses. These surpluses usually exceeded the amount that Bolognese conservatories spent on marriages, underscoring the fact that it was policy rather than lack of funds that led Florentine conservatories to avoid arranging marriages for their wards.

Table A.1. Budget Totals in Monetary Terms in Conservatories and Orphanages

Institution	Years	High	Low	Annual Average	Balance over Period	Source
Bologna						
S. Bartolomeo di Reno	1577–81	9,771	2,869	6,677	[2,748]	ASB PIE S. Bartolomeo di Reno, ms. 137
	1582–91	15,998	7,254	10,535	0	ASB PIE S. Bartolomeo di Reno, ms. 138
	1595–97	9,198	7,640	8,755	[3,066]	ASB PIE S. Bartolomeo di Reno, ms. 139
S. Croce	1620–25	5,399	3,534	4,457	0	ASB PIE S. Croce, ms. 149
S. Maria del Baraccano	1575–85	12,700	6,597	8,693	263	ASB PIE S. Maria del Baraccano, ms. 264
	1592–99	15,733	10,905	12,648	0	ASB PIE S. Maria del Baraccano, ms. 265
Florence						
Pietà	1572–78	26,243	12,895	19,713	2,585	ASF Pietà, ms. 57
S. Caterina	1591–1625	487,891*		14,349	9,871	ASF S. Caterina, ms. 25
S. Niccolò	1560–74	160,230*		11,445	[35]	ASF Ceppo, ms. 147
S. Maria Vergine	1565–83	96,593*		5,366	3,138	ASF Ceppo, ms. 149
Pietà	1557–58	21,150*		10,575	975	ASF Pietà, ms. 55
	1566–71	69,104*		11,517	[1,161]	ASF Pietà, ms. 57

Note: All amounts are calculated in lire of Bologna and Florence, respectively.
* = Total.

Table A.2. Expense and Income by Percentage in Conservatories and Orphanages

EXPENSE

Institution	Years	Clothing	Cult	Facilities	Food	Marriage	Salaries	Miscellaneous	Total
Bologna									
S. Bartolomeo di Reno	1577–81	23	1	10.8	36			13.3	84.1
	1582–91	13.3	2.7	7.7	46.3		3.5	25.2	98.7
	1595–97	5.6	1.3	4.3	56.3		4	19.7	91.2
S. Croce	1620–25		5.5	3.7	61	1.3	1	10.7	83.2
S. Maria del Baraccano	1575–85	7	11.6	7.4	51.2	8.9	4.5	17.4	108
	1592–99	4.4	7.2	11.9	52.1	21.5	5.6	7.6	110.3
Florence									
S. Caterina	1591–1625	18.3	2	7	55.5			10.2	90.5
S. Niccolò	1560–74	13			62		0.3	13	95.3
S. Maria Vergine	1565–83	1.25	4.67	19.53	60.1			16	101.5
Pietà	1557–58	7		1	89		1	1.5	99.5
	1566–71	11		17	54	2	5	9.9	100
	1572–78	6.8	1	2.2	40.6	1.4	5.4	4.6	61

INCOME

Institution	Years	Alms	Rents	Work	Total
Bologna					
S. Bartolomeo di Reno	1577–81	76.3	15	10	101.3
	1582–91	58.4	14.8	6.2	80.3
	1595–97	44.8	16.3	7.4	68.5
S. Croce	1620–25	47.7	12.5	17.8	78
S. Maria del Baraccano	1575–85	77.1	11.5	15.1	103.7
	1592–99	38.2	46.4	19	103.6
Florence					
S. Caterina	1591–1625	71		29	100
S. Niccolò	1560–74	74.5		26	100.5
S. Maria Vergine	1565–83	69.9	9.5	20.6	100
Pietà	1557–58	67.2	0.5	26.9	94.6
	1566–71	59		40	99
	1572–78	31.1		44	75.1

Notes

Abbreviations

AAB   Archivio Arcivescovile di Bologna
AAF   Archivio Arcivescovile di Firenze
ASB   Archivio di Stato di Bologna
ASF   Archivio di Stato di Firenze
BCB   Biblioteca Comunale di Bologna
BNCF Biblioteca Nazionale Centrale di Firenze
BRM   Biblioteca Riccardiana—Moreniana (Florence)
CRSF Corporazione religiose soppresse dal governo Francese
Dem   Fondo Demaniale
PIE   Pii Istituti Educativi
OPM Opera dei Poveri Mendicanti (Bologna)
USL   Unità Sanitaria Locale (Bologna)

INTRODUCTION: Down and Out and *Off* the Streets

1. This long discussion began with Ariès, *Centuries of Childhood;* for a recent review of the debate, see Cunningham, *Children and Childhood.* For a spirited dismissal of Ariès focused on Renaissance Italy, see Haas, *Renaissance Man and His Children.*

2. Stiatici, *Narratione, overo cronicha*, 13.

3. Apart from miscarriages, those of Dati's children for whom ages can be determined died between three days and fourteen years after birth. Brucker, *Two Memoirs*, 126–28, 134–36. Cunningham, *Children and Childhood*, 97.

4. The bulk of Florentine statistics on death rates are taken from Herlihy and Klapisch-Zuber, *Tuscans and Their Families*, 260–79. Survey statistics from Cunningham, *Children and Childhood*, 90–91.

5. Brucker, *Two Memoirs*, 132. Herlihy and Klapisch-Zuber, *Tuscans and Their Families*, 78–80, 257–79.

6. Dati's first wife Bandecca died (1390) after nine months of constant illness following the miscarriage of her first child. Second wife Betta died (1402) five months after the birth of her eighth child in nine years, though Dati does not indicate the cause. Third wife Ginevra died (1419) in childbirth delivering her eleventh child in fifteen years of marriage, just a year after her oldest child with Dati, Manetto, died in Pisa (age 14) and a month after her seventh child Filippo (age 4) died in Val di Pesa. She was 36 years old. Brucker, *Two Memoirs*, 112, 115, 117, 132. Musacchio, *Art and Ritual of Childbirth*, 25–31.

7. Klapisch-Zuber, "Demographic Decline," 28–32. Ferraro, *Marriage Wars*, 62.

8. Klapisch-Zuber, "Cruel Mother," 120. But see *Tuscans and Their Families*, 221–23. Calvi, *Il contratto morale*, 33–34.

9. Only 2 percent of the wealthiest 472 Florentine households, themselves representing less than 5 percent of all Florentine households, were headed by a woman. Klapisch-Zuber, "Cruel Mother," 120–21.

10. Calvi, "Reconstructing the Family," 275–96.

11. Klapisch-Zuber, "Cruel Mother," 128.

12. Calvi, "Reconstructing the Family," 282–96.

13. Gavitt, *Charity and Children*, 208–9. Cunningham, *Children and Childhood*, 93–96.

14. Brucker, *Two Memoirs*, 126–27, 134–35. Hanawalt, *Ties That Bound*, 248. Coster, "From Fire and Water," 301–11. See now Coster's *Baptism and Spiritual Kinship*.

15. Park, "Healing the Poor," 31. ASB, PIE, S. Maria Maddalena, 2, ms. 3, cap. 18.

16. Marcello, "Andare a bottega," 232, 235, 242.

17. For this and what follows, see King, *Brunelleschi's Dome*, 46, 134–38, 154.

18. Chambers and Pullan, *Venice*, 310. Gaspar Loarte, *Avisi di sacerdoti et confessori* (Parma: 1584), as cited in Bell, *How to Do It*, 194, 338n. 37.

19. For more detail on the legal and practical circumstances of adoption, see Kuehn, "Adoption à Florence," 69–81. Idem, *Illegitimacy in Renaissance Florence*, 47–49, 168. Gavitt, *Charity and Children*, 243–58. Gager, *Blood Ties and Fictive Ties*, 37–70.

20. Calvi, "Widowhood and Remarriage," 280. Caroline Fisher, "A Family Affair? Guardianship in Late Fourteenth-Century Florence," paper presented at Sixteenth Century Studies Conference, Denver, Colo., October 2001. For Bologna's statutes of 1267 and 1389, see Archivio di Stato di Bologna, *Governo, Statuti*, vol. XIV (1389–1453), Libro IV, Rubric 84. ASB, *Archivio Notarile: Amministrazione di Beni di Pupilli*, #1 (1390–1454). See also ASB, Inventory VI/3a, pp. 1–2.

21. Brucker, *Renaissance Florence*, 60–61.

22. Calvi, "Widowhood and Remarriage," 280–82. See also idem, *Il contratto morale*.

23. Strocchia, "Taken into Custody," 179–80.

24. Ibid., 181, 184–85, 188–89, 194–98.

25. Gill, "*Scandala*," 177–203. Terpstra, "Mothers, Sisters, and Daughters," 204–9.

26. Boswell, *Kindness of Strangers*, 228–35, 296–321.

27. In Florence, S. Maria della Scala had 151 children in 1428, S. Gallo had 150 in 1448, while the Innocenti admitted 62 in 1445; that number rose to 193 by 1466. Gavitt, *Charity and Children*, 209. Sandri, "Modalità dell'abbandono dei fanciulli," 993–1015. Takahasi, "I bambini abbandonati," 59–79. For Venice and the Veneto, see Grandi, ed., "*Benedetto chi ti porta, maledetto chi ti manda.*"

28. Gavitt, *Charity and Children*, 13.

29. Ibid., 21. Gavitt, "Charity and State Building," 238–39, 246. Kerzer, *Sacrificed for Honor*, 138–44.

30. Formal challenges came in 1695, 1777, and 1786, and Carboni notes that later administrators were sufficiently perplexed by their legal status that they commissioned a report in 1725 to clarify it. Carboni, *Le doti della "povertà*," 69–70. By contrast, the Monte di Pietà was a *luogo pio* under ecclesiastical oversight, and was used by Archbishop Gabrielle Paleotti and the senate to advance an ambitious reform of charitable institutions and services. Fornasari, *Il "thesoro" della città*, 169–92.

31. Vives, *On Assistance to the Poor.* Terpstra, "Confraternities and Public Charity," 97–121. Jütte, *Poverty and Deviance,* 100–142.

ONE: Opening a Home

1. Ghirardacci, *Historia di Bologna,* 338.
2. Ferrante, "Il sostegno alle giovani declassate," 207–9. Guidicini, *Cose notabili,* V, 231, 251–52. Fanti, *Confraternite e città,* 451–67.
3. It is unclear how long this transfer was in the works. According to one source, the five Poor Clares of Corpus Domini had been in the convent of S. Maria delle Pugliole from 23 March 1521, yet the Augustinian nuns who had held title to it, the nuns of S. Mauro di Mantova, were not officially removed until Lorenzo Campeggi's reform in 1526. Farné, *Opere pie a Bologna,* 108–9.
4. Signatories to the agreement were Carlo Antonio Rubini (S. Marta), Carlo Antonio Fantuzzi (Poveri Vergognosi) and Canon Carlo de Poeti (S. Giobbe), and Marc Antonio Marsigli (rector of S. Maria della Castità). S. Maria della Castità paid 2,250 lire. An agreement of 20 May 1530 assigns legacies given before 21 March 1526 to the *abbandonate,* suggesting that this was the date when the thirty-two left to form their convent. Farné, *Opere pie a Bologna,* 109–11.
5. ASB, PIE, S. Maria del Baraccano, busta 43, #39/2.
6. Terpstra, *Lay Confraternities and Civic Religion,* 16–17, 33, 190–93.
7. Members of the 1528 commission were Ottavio Rubini, Carlo de Poeta, Silvio Guidotti, notary Bartholomeus Arnolfini, and cardinal legate Innocenti Cibo. ASB, PIE, S. Maria del Baraccano, busta 4, Libro I, #11. Poeta and Guidotti were both sindics with the Ospedale degli Esposti and the Ospedale di S. Giobbe.
8. Clement VII's first *breve* authorizing the five-person commission to tax confraternities and *ospedali* was issued 16 April 1528, expanded 7 February 1530, and modified 26 August 1530. One of the issues was the problem of a lay commission taxing monasteries; this was addressed with a *breve* of 28 December 1530 authorizing the legate alone to tax monasteries and *luoghi pii.* ASB, PIE, S. Maria del Baraccano, ms. 546, cc. 37v, 60r–v; busta 4, Libro I, ##11, 12, 13.
9. Stiatici, *Narratione overo chronica,* 12–13. Stiatici claims this occurred in Guastivillani's term in 1534, but Guastavillani was *gonfaloniere* in November and December 1530. Alidosi, *I signori Anziani,* 75.
10. ASB, PIE, S. Bartolomeo di Reno, ms. 63, 2. ASB, Dem, S. Bartolomeo di Reno, ms. 2/7651, 13, 14.
11. The list was formalized 4 April 1535. S. Marta is referred to as "S. Maria de Castitate," after the confraternity that had assumed control in 1526. Ten of its 12 donors are identified as widows and one as a single woman (identified as an unmarried daughter); 5 are wives or widows of guild masters. There are 2 widows, 4 single women, and 5 guild connections among donors to S. Maria del Baraccano, and 7 widows, 3 single women, and 3 guild connections at S. Gregorio. ASB, PIE, S. Maria del Baraccano, busta 43, #41/2. This fund predates those discussed in the recent volume by Chabot and Fornasari, *L'economia della carità,* 17–42.
12. Antonelli et al., eds., *Cronaca di Giacomo Rinieri,* 29.
13. Terpstra, "Frati, confratelli, e famiglie dirigenti," 105–14. See also Fanti, *Confraternite e città,* 515–50, *I Bastardini,* and the special issue of *Sanità, scienze e storia* 2 (1989).

14. The Bolognese corba measured 78 liters, and would have fed one person for three to four months. *Cronaca di G. Rinieri*, 7, 65–89, 302.

15. The published plans: *Provisione elemosinaria per li poveri di qualunque sorte della città di Bologna* (Bologna: 1548). *Modo et ordine per li poveri mendicanti fatto nuovamente nella citta di Bologna* (Bologna: 1550). See also Terpstra, "Apprenticeship in Social Welfare," and Calori, *Una iniziativa sociale*, 33–34.

16. ASB, PIE, S. Maria Maddalena/S. Onofrio, ms. 103, pp. 24–25, 29, 31. Calzoni, *Storia della Chiesa parrochiale*, 82–84. Fornasini, *La Chiesa priorale*, 230. Terpstra, *Lay Confraternities and Civic Religion*, 89–90.

17. ASB, PIE, S. Maria Maddalena/S. Onofrio, busta 13, B, #43. busta 3, #5, 5/2, 6. busta 2, ms. 2., cc. IV, 26v.

18. The annotated draft statutes are found in ASB, PIE, S. Bartolomeo di Reno, ms. 78, fasc. 1 and 2. For unions (1552) and gifts, see ASB, PIE, S. Bartolomeo di Reno, ms. 279, c. 24v ff; 234 (np). ASB, Dem, S. Bartolomeo di Reno, ms. 2/7651, #15.

19. ASB, PIE, S. Maria del Baraccano, cart. 1, ms. 2 (1553); the confraternity had adopted regulations governing its Congregation of Gentlewomen and their work with the girls in 1548: busta 44, 46/1, 46/2. BCB, ms. B3633, pp. 135–85 (S. Marta, 1554).

20. ASB, PIE, S. Maria Maddalena/S. Onofrio, busta 3, #6. Calzoni, *Storia della Chiesa*, 84. The first statutes for S. Maria Maddalena had similarly been adapted from those of the confraternity of Ss. Sebastiano e Rocco, see Terpstra, *Lay Confraternities and Civic Religion*, 90.

21. For more on this process, see Terpstra, *Lay Confraternities and Civic Religion*, 124–25, 139–44, 172–205. Idem, "Confraternal Prison Charity," 217–48.

22. *Statuti dell'Opera de Poveri Mendicanti* (Bologna: 1574), 34. Terpstra, "Apprenticeship in Social Welfare," 101–20.

23. Calori, *Iniziativa sociale*, 17, 26.

24. Vittori, "La pietà di un mercante bolognese," 327–50. Idem, "Bonifacio dalle Balle."

25. ASB, PIE, S. Croce, ms. 2, fasc. 3, pp. 1–14. Dalle Balle dowered the servant Lucrezia Fanti in 1573 and also Anna herself when she entered the convent in 1591. Vittori, "Bonifacio dalle Balle," 67–69.

26. For dalle Balle's spiritual and autobiographical writings, see ASB, PIE, S. Croce, 2, fasc. 2, fasc. 3, pp. 1–30. Vittori, "Bonifacio dalle Balle," 123.

27. ASB, PIE, S. Croce, ms. 2, fasc. 3, pp. 5–7, 9–14.

28. ASB, PIE, S. Croce, ms. 2, fasc. 2, fasc. 3, pp. 23–30. Vittori, "Pietà di un mercante bolognese," 340–43; idem, "Bonifacio dalle Balle," 123–37.

29. ASB, PIE, S. Croce, ms. 2, fasc. 4, fasc. 5. Vittori, "Bonifacio dalle Balle," 162–82. Faggioli, "Origine ed appunti storici," ASB, PIE, S. Croce, cart. 1, pp. 3–5.

30. ASB, PIE, S. Croce, ms. 2, fasc. 3, pp. 31–32. Vittori, "Bonifacio dalle Balle," 183–91. Faggioli, "Origine," 6–7.

31. ASB, PIE, S. Croce, cart. 1, ms. 2 (supplement). Faggioli, "Origine," 9–10.

32. ASB, PIE, 1, ms. 1 (17 January 1609), ms. 2 (26 April 1609). Faggioli, "Origine," 11–15.

33. A 1589 census counted 129 boys at S. Bartolomeo and 64 at S. Onofrio, 79 girls at S. Maria del Baraccano and 53 at S. Marta, and 194 children of both genders at the Ospedale dei Mendicanti. B. Carrati, "Miscellanea storica Bolognese," BCB, ms. B695, 127–28.

34. ASB, Dem, S. Giacomo, ms. 12/6470, pt. 2, cc. 1r–v, pt. 3 (unpaginated chronicle).

35. ASB, PIE, S. Giuseppe, cart. 1, Libro +, pp. 22–25.

36. ASB, PIE, S. Giuseppe, cart. 1, Libro +, pp. 1–3. Cart. 19, ms. 1, 16 February 1631 (np). The houses were purchased in 1628, using income from a legacy of 11,000 lire left by Giulio Antonio Ercolani in 1621. BCB, ms. B3598, 587–97.

37. ASB, PIE, S. Giuseppe, cart. 23, ms. 1, cc. 5r–22v, 39v–41v, 52r–v.

38. Park and Henderson, "'The First Hospital among Christians,'" 165, 176. d'Addario, "Noti di storia," 121. For a review of the hospitals and their patrons, see Passerini, *Storia degli stabilmenti*, 107–8.

39. Park, "Healing the Poor," 26–45. Henderson, "Hospitals of Late Medieval and Renaissance Florence," 63–92. d'Addario, "Noti della religiosità e della carità," 118–19.

40. Terpstra, "Confraternities and Public Charity," 110–21. Idem, "Competing Visions of the State and Social Welfare," 1319–55.

41. From 1531 to 1539, abandonments at the Innocenti were equivalent to 21.9 percent of Florentine baptisms. Gavitt, "Charity and State Building," 238–39, 246. Henderson, "Epidemics in Renaissance Florence," 167.

42. Cochrane, *Florence in the Forgotten Centuries*, 88–89.

43. Strocchia, "Taken into Custody," 177–79.

44. Manno Tolu, "'Ricordanze' delle abbandonate fiorentine," 1008. For expanded treatment, see Terpstra, "Mothers, Sisters, and Daughters," 204–9.

45. A Johannes Leonardi di Barduccis was elected to the six-person Bigallo captainate in 1539–40, and again in 1540–41. ASF, Bigallo ms. 20, IV c. 4v: V c. 1r.

46. The connection between the two is underscored by the orphanage's first account book. Giovanni del Giunta, one of the magistrates appointed by Cosimo I on 17 March 1542, begins keeping the accounts on 5 March 1542, and carries on to the end of the volume in 1545. ASF, Bigallo ms. 1679, c. 57r.

47. The Bigallo was suppressed 17 November 1542: ASF, Senato dei Quarantotto, ms. 5, cc. 13v–15v. For a broader discussion and archival references, see Terpstra, "Confraternities and Public Charity," 110–18. Lombardi, "Poveri a Firenze," 165–72.

48. Niccolò di Pietro Gerini and Ambrogio di Baldese completed the fresco in 1386. Kiel, *Il museo del Bigallo*, cat. no. 42, 43, 120–21. Levin, "Advertising Charity in the Trecento," 215–309. Richard Trexler believes that these were primarily children entrusted temporarily to the safekeeping of the Misericordia captains until their families could reestablish themselves and reclaim their children: *Public Life in Renaissance Florence*, 369.

49. ASF, Bigallo ms. 22, II, cc. 36v, 47v. ASF, Bigallo ms. 155, c. 46r.

50. Passerini, *Storia degli stabilmenti*, 201.

51. This small act of charity could mount incredibly: in its first two months, the Abbandonati bought 27 pairs of shoes, but in 1589–90 it purchased 654 pairs of shoes, and paid for repairs to another 1,169. ASF, Bigallo ms. 768, cc. 37, 50, 57, 70. ASF, Bigallo ms. 1679, cc. 33r–36r.

52. Preparations for this feast included the purchase of extra drinking cups and 39 *mezette* (one-pint wine measures) and 36 *fondelli* (small rings laid under dishes in order to keep the tablecloths clean). ASF, Bigallo ms. 1679, cc. 35r, 37v.

53. Trexler, *Public Life in Renaissance Florence*, 215–24. Chretien, *The Festival of San Giovanni*, 31–99.

54. ASF, Bigallo ms. 1679, cc. 35r, 37v.

55. ASF, Bigallo ms. 1679, cc. 1v–2v.

56. ASF, Senato dei Quarantotto, ms. 5, cc. 8v–9v (law on blasphemy: 7 July 1542), 13v–15v (Bigallo suppression: 17 November 1542). From 1543 to 1546, the Bigallo's income accounts become largely a record of these fines, with few entries from the almsboxes, suggesting either a significant shift in the source of its income or, more likely, a degeneration in record keeping: ASF, Bigallo ms. 1679, cc. 8v–13r.

57. The Bigallo's first draft statutes anticipated making provision for abandoned girls and female beggars, but did not frame details, assuming perhaps that these would be worked out with Ginori's *Abbandonate:* ASF, Bigallo ms. 1669/II, cc. 5r–6v, 9r–26v. ASF, Bigallo ms. 1679, cc. 6r–10r, 38r, 41r, 44r–v, 45v, 46r, 47r–v, 48v, 49r, 50r, 51r, 52r, 54r, 56r. From June 1542 through December 1543, the gifts totaled lire 792.6.4, or 12.8 percent of the Bigallo's income of lire 6,235.17.03.

58. Manno Tolu, "'Ricordanze' delle abbandonate fiorentine," 1008, citing ASF, Bigallo ms. 154, nn. 91 and 233, *suppliche* of 22 May 1550.

59. Admissions to the Innocenti went from 417 in 1547 to 884 in 1551, dropping to 607 in 1552. Abandonments of foundlings from 1548 to 1552 ranged from 20.9 to 37.3 percent of baptisms in Florence. Gavitt, "Charity and State Building," 239n. 29.

60. ASF, Bigallo ms. 154, cc. 52r, 68r, 72r, 91r, 161r. The latter requests are undated. Passerini notes that Francesco I granted the Abbandonate's home of S. Niccolò dei Fantoni to a group of friars in 1587. Passerini, *Storia degli stabilmenti,* 107.

61. Arnaldo d'Addario asserts that the two were one institution, but provides no documentation: "Noti di storia," 101.

62. ASF, Ceppo ms. 69, cc. 1r–2r.; ms. 145, cc. 1r, 171r–72v.

63. The first donations were registered on 3 January 1542: ASF, Ceppo ms. 145, cc. 2, 4, 8, 12, 161–66. The Florentine staio measured 24 liters or 0.68 bushel. Burr Litchfield, *Emergence of a Bureaucracy,* xiii.

64. ASF, Ceppo ms. 145, cc. 11, 26. Manno Tolu, "Abbandonate fiorentine," 1008–11nn. 22 and 24.

65. Manno Tolu, "Abbandonate fiorentine," 1012–13.

66. d'Addario, "Noti di storia," 101.

67. S. Maria dell'Umiltà was founded by Simone di Piero Vespucci, and put under control of the Compagnia di S. Maria del Bigallo in 1400: Richa, *Notizie istoriche,* vol. 7, pt. 3, 263–64. According to a 1561 memorial, rent was 80 scudi annually. "Cronicha delle Suore della Pietà," BRM, Acquisiti Diversi, ms. 93, p. 5.

68. Gavitt, "Charity and State Building," 260–70. Burr Litchfield, *Emergence of a Bureaucracy,* 100–101. Menning, *Charity and State in Late Renaissance Italy,* 175–232. Parigino, *Il tesoro del principe.*

69. Two accounts vary in dating. The "Registro delle donne di detta Compagnia" (ASF, CRSF ms. 112/97) registers Pietà members and their pledges on cc. 1r–83r. The first member is registered on 28 December 1554, and the last in this volume (#320) is on 17 December 1558 (c. 73r). Another volume of miscellanea (ASF, CRSF ms. 112/81) records the first pledge as being that of Marietta de Gondi, given on 10 September 1554 (c. 42v), and lists pledges by 59 women in place by the time the home opens on 23 December 1554. Of these 59, 30 are married, 25 widowed, and 4 single or in a convent. Gondi's servant, Lucrezia di Francesco da Signa, gave 7.10 annually 1555–56 (c. 58v).

70. ASF, CRSF ms. 112/97, cc. 235r–v: account from 28 December 1554 through 31 December 1555. Of total expenses of lire 6,062.18.04, food accounted for 4,827.07 (79.62%), furnishings and repairs 729.08.08 (12.03%), and clothing 296.03.04 (4.88%).

Of total income of lire 6,061.08, general alms accounted for 3,533.14 (58.3%), pledges for 1,572 (25.93%), and the girls' work for 590.14 (9.74%). See also cc. 154–55 for a special gift of 365 lire given by 5 members on 5 July 1555.

71. ASF, CRSF ms. 112/97. Manno Tolu, "Echi Savonaroliani," 218–23. But see Terpstra, "Mothers, Sisters, and Daughters," 210–21.

72. Passerini, *Storia degli stabilimenti*, 892–95. Manno Tolu, "Echi Savonaroliani," 210. "Croniche delle Suore della Pietà," 1–3, cc. 188–90. Though the Pietà remained in these quarters for about fifteen years, a recent history of the hospital (later renamed the Ospedale di S. Giovanni di Dio) does not mention it: Diana, *San Matteo e San Giovanni di Dio*.

73. ASF, CRSF ms. 112/78, cc. 1–37 (through 29 December 1555).

74. ASF, CRSF ms. 112/78, cc. 29r–v, 31r–v. "Croniche delle Suore della Pietà," 1–4. Andrea di Benedetto Biliotti had joined the Compagnia di S. Maria Vergine only a year before (8 March 1554): ASF, Ceppo ms. 145, c. 165. On Capocchi's Savonarolan mission, see Manno Tolu, "Echi Savonaroliani," 213.

75. d'Addario, "Note di storia," 101. Terpstra, 'Mothers, Sisters, and Daughters," 213–15.

76. Brackett, *Criminal Justice and Crime*, 110.

77. ASF, Ceppo ms. 69, c. 2r; 145, cc. 4, 163. Manno Tolu, "Abbandonate fiorentine," 1007–8. None of the members of the Otto in 1556 were members of S. Maria Vergine: Brackett, *Criminal Justice and Crime*, 144–45.

78. ASF, Ceppo ms. 69, cc. 1r–3r, 12r–14r,17r–19v.; ms. 59, cc. 105v–118v, 129v–135r. Manno Tolu, "Abbandonate fiorentine," 1007–15, 1017–18. Lombardi, "Poveri a Firenze," 167–70.

79. "Regolamenti sopra Deputazione dei Poveri Bisognosi dal 1647 al 1677," ASF, *Pratica Segreta* ms. 184, cc. 10–11 (untitled/undated proposal for a Florentine Ospedale dei Mendicanti that draws direct relation to Bologna's Ospedale dei Mendicanti), cc. 41–48 (handwritten 1573 draft of revised statutes that Bologna's Ospedale dei Mendicanti published in 1574), cc. 51–53 (11 March 1576 request to duke for permission to license beggars, together with example of a printed license).

80. Aranci, *Vittorio dell'Ancisa*, 12–32. For expanded treatment, see Terpstra, "Mothers, Sisters, and Daughters," 221–25.

81. Aranci, *Vittorio dell'Ancisa*, 44–56.

82. Strocchia, "Taken into Custody," 177–200.

83. Aranci, *Vittorio dell'Ancisa*, 56–68. Cionacci, "Notizie di Messer Vettorio dell'Ancisa," cc. 88v–89v. See also d'Addario, "Noti di storia," 102.

84. Aranci, *Vittorio dell'Ancisa*, 83–91. Cionacci, "Notizie di Messer Vettorio dell'Ancisa," cc. 84v–88r, 89v.

85. ASF, Ceppo ms. 69, c. 2r. ASF, S. Caterina, ms. 17, c. 1r. Lombardi, "Poveri a Firenze," 169–72. The S. Onofrio *ospedale* was established by the Dyers Guild in 1339, and funded by various endowments and a tax on guild members; some beds were reserved for aged and sick Dyers, and others for the poor generally. After the girls left, it was restored to the Dyers Guild. Passerini, *Storia degli stabilmenti*, 100–101.

86. ASF, Bigallo ms. 157, #22.

87. On S. Maria Vergine and S. Caterina, see ASF, Ceppo ms. 237, cc. 26v–27r. Lombardi, "Poveri a Firenze," 168n. 12.

88. The first month's expenses totaled fiorini 644.8.2, of which 479.10 (74.5%) went

to grain, 58.19.04 (9.2%) to other food purchases, 75.07.10 (11.7%) to repairs, 15.01.06 (2.3%) to furnishings, and 15.09.06 (2.3%) to firewood. Income in this period came from two large donations: 600 fiorini came from Botti, and 200 from Averardo and Antonio Salviati. The first income from alms boxes (fiorini 52.6) was recorded 31 October 1591. ASF, S. Caterina, ms. 36, cc. 2r, 49r–52v.

89. Richa, "Notizie istoriche," vol. 7, pt. 3, pp. 274–76.

90. Trexler, *Public Life in Renaissance Florence*, 51.

91. ASF, S. Caterina, ms. 7, cap. I/1–3, 5–7; ms. 17, c. IV–2r. Manno Tolu, "Abbandonate fiorentine," 1012. Lombardi, "Poveri a Firenze," 167–68. Gavitt, "Charity and State Building," 267–68.

92. ASF, Bigallo ms. 1669/IV, cc. 46r–v. d'Addario, "Religiosità e carità," 131–32.

93. Antonia di Matteo Bechato was 46 years old and had lived at the Pietà for 34 years. Maddalena di Giovanni tessitore was 36, and had lived there for 23 years. ASF, CRSF ms. 112/79, #495, 572.

94. Gavitt notes that the Innocenti boys wore brown uniforms at a funeral in 1574. "Charity and State Building," 258.

95. ASF, Bigallo ms. 155, c. 6r. Lombardi, "Poveri a Firenze," 169. Modern art historians have identified the two children as orphans, but seem unaware that the girl represents an appeal rather than a reality. Kiel, *Il museo del Bigallo*, 124 (cat. 26 and 27). Levin, "Confraternal Self-Imaging," 3–14.

96. Lombardi, "Poveri a Firenze," 169, 172–78. Idem, *Povertà maschile, povertà femminile*.

97. Gavitt, "Charity and State Building," 241.

TWO: Entering a Home

1. ASF, CRSF ms. 112/79, c. 30v (#179). BRM, Bigazzi ms. 61, cc. 45r–48v.

2. ASF, Bigallo ms. 1459, #281. ASF, Bigallo ms. 22/II, 78v.

3. ASF, Ceppo ms. 141, c. 2r.

4. ASB, PIE, S. Croce, ms. 3, cc. 1r–2v. Ibid., 1, ms. 2, cap. 10. Ibid., 2, fasc. 2, #2.

5. This section is based primarily on a review of all extant statutes. Dates of statutes and complete archival references for the short references that follow: *Bologna:* S. Bartolomeo di Reno (1550): ASB, PIE, S. Bartolomeo di Reno, ms. 78. S. Croce (ca. 1605): ASB, PIE, S. Croce, 1, ms. 2 b. (17 January 1609): 1, ms. 1. (26 April 1609): ibid., 1, ms. 2. (1653): ibid., 1, ms. 3. S. Giuseppe (1641): ASB, PIE, S. Giuseppe, 1, Libro +. S. Maria del Baraccano (1548): ASB, PIE, S. Maria del Baraccano, ms. 44, #46/1; (1553) ibid., 1, ms. 2; (1647) ibid., 1, ms. 3. S. Marta (1554 capitoli): BCB, ms. B3633, pp. 135–85. S. Onofrio (1560): ASB, PIE, S. Maria Maddalena, 2, ms. 2. (1664): ibid., 2, ms. 3. *Florence:* Abbandonati (1542): ASF, Bigallo ms. 1669/II, cc. 9r–25r. Carità (>1598): BNCF, ms. II.I.410, cc. 84v–88v. S. Caterina (ca. 1590): ASF, S. Caterina, ms. 7. S. Maria Vergine and S. Niccolò (1551/1598): ASF, Ceppo ms. 69. Ibid., ms. 1 bis. Pietà (1570): BRM, Bigazzi ms. 61.

6. ASB, PIE, S. Bartolomeo, ms. 78, c. 13r; ASB, PIE, S. Maria Maddalena, 2, ms. 2, c. 13v; ibid., 2, ms. 3, cap. XVIII. ASB, S. Bartolomeo di Reno, 7, #2, cc. 5r–15r.

7. ASF, Bigallo ms. 1669/IV, c. 4r. Bando of 16 October 1542: ASF, Bigallo ms. 1671, cc. 15r–v.

8. ASF, Bigallo ms. 155, c. 64r. ASF, Bigallo ms. 157, #130.

9. 280 of 308 fathers, and 135 of 203 mothers had died. ASF, Bigallo ms. 1459.

10. ASF, Bigallo ms. 22/II, cc. 36v, 47v, 62r, 78v. Saalman, *The Bigallo*, 9–25.

11. "pigliando tutti questi Putti che sono lasciati si farebbe un altro Sped/le de Nocenti." This was Francesco's reply when his secretary Carlo Pitti discussed with him the Bigallo's request for additional funds and powers to handle an upsurge in abandonments. ASF, Bigallo ms. 1669/IV, cc. 33r–v.

12. Ferdinand I granted this during the famine of 1591: ASF, Bigallo ms. 1669/IV, c. 44v (27 November 1591).

13. ASF, Ceppo ms. 69, cc. 12v–13v. ASF, S. Caterina, ms. 7, cap. 1/7. Isidore of Seville had set age 28 as the end of *adulescens* and the beginning of *iuventus;* by contrast, Florentine law extended rights and obligations progressively to young men at ages 18, 25, and 30. Taddei, *Fanciulli e giovani*, 40–63.

14. Of 54 girls recorded in a 1571 census of girls in S. Niccolo, only 21 (38.88%) had no father or mother; 16 (29.62%) had no father, one had no mother, and another 16 had no information on parentage. Of 133 girls enrolled from 1571 through 1598, 35 (26.31%) had no father or mother, 18 (13.53%) had no father, 2 no mother, and 78 (58.66%) had no information on parentage. ASF, Ceppo ms. 59, 105v–118v, 120v–182r. Among the first 100 girls registered when S. Caterina began its registry (ca. 1594), 55 had no father or mother. ASF, S. Caterina, ms. 17 (np, nd).

15. ASB, PIE, S. Maria del Baraccano, 1, ms. 3, p. 77.

16. BCB, ms. B3633, pp. 173, 175; ASB, PIE, S. Giuseppe, 1, Libro +, p. 2; ASB, PIE, S. Croce, 1, ms. 2b, cap. 9; 1, ms. 1, cap. 12; 1, ms. 2, cap. 10; 1, ms. 3, cap. 9.

17. "figlie di donne di non buona vita, et in pericolo evidentiss.o di perdere li honesta, di modo che non accetandole si conoschi manifestamente essere per perdere l'honore et capitare mal." ASB, PIE, S. Croce, 1, ms. 2, cap. 10.

18. "un bello, o almeno gratioso Aspetto della Facia, & percio non sicuro dalli pericoli dell'Honesta." ASB, PIE, S. Maria del Baraccano, 1, ms. 3, ##8, 9, 12.

19. ASF, Bigallo ms. 1669/II, c. 10v; ms. 1669/IV, c. 4r; ASF, Bigallo ms. 155, c. 51r. On ages, see ASF, Bigallo ms. 1459. Ninety-eight of these 110 children were between ages 4 and 8.

20. ASB, PIE, S. Maria Maddalena, 2, ms. 2, c 13v; ibid., 2, ms. 3, cap. 18.

21. ASB, PIE, S. Maria del Baraccano, 1, ms. 2, c. 7r; 1, ms. 3, #12. ASB, PIE, S. Giuseppe, 1, Libro +, p. 23; S. Croce varied the age with each statute revision: 12 (ca. 1605), 10–16 (January 1609); 10–13 (April 1609); 11–14: (1653). ASB, PIE, S. Croce, 1, ms. 2b, cap. 9; ms. 1, cap. 12; ms. 2, cap. 10; ms. 3, cap. 9.

22. BCB, ms. B3633, p. 173. S. Marta's restriction to ages 11–15 came in reforms of 1580 and 1647: pp. 176, 180.

23. ASF, Ceppo ms. 69, c. 12r; ASF, S. Caterina, ms. 7, cap. 1/7. Of the 165 S. Caterina girls for whom ages are given, 63 (38.18%) were between 6 and 10 while 14 (8.48%) were younger and 88 (53.33%) were older. ASF, S. Caterina, ms. 17.

24. Thirty-nine of the 54 girls (72%) in S. Niccolò's 1571 census were from families whose roots were clearly outside the city, as were 83 of the 133 girls (62.4%) enrolled from 1571 to 1598: ASF, Ceppo ms. 59, cc. 105v–118v, 120v–182r. The same was true of S. Caterina, where 184 of the 270 girls enrolled to 1635 left traces of origin, and where 137 (74.46%) of these were from outside the city. ASF, S. Caterina, ms. 17 (np). Of 361 entrants to the Pietà from 1554 to 1559, 224 (62%) had roots outside the city. ASF, CRSF ms. 112/78. Of 316 children nominated for the Abbandonati from 1574 to 1590, only 125 (39.55%) were clearly from Florence. ASF, Bigallo ms. 1459.

25. Of 284 girls enrolled in S. Maria del Baraccano from 1554 to 1584, 25 (8.8%) had patronymics indicating that their families had come from outside Bologna. ASB, PIE, S. Maria del Baraccano, mss. 6.1, 6.2.

26. ASB, PIE, S. Maria Maddalena 2, ms. 3, cap. 18.

27. Niccoli, *Il seme della violenza*, 141–91.

28. ASF, Ceppo ms. 69, c. 12v. ASB, PIE, S. Giuseppe, 1, Libro +, p. 23.

29. ASF, S. Caterina, ms. 7, I/7. ASB, PIE, S. Giuseppe, 1, Libro +, p. 24. ASB, PIE, S. Maria del Baraccano, 1, ms. 3, #12.

30. ASB, PIE, S. Maria del Baraccano, 1, ms. 2, c. 7r; 1, ms. 3, #12. ASB, PIE, S. Giuseppe, 1, Libro +, p. 23.

31. ASF, Ceppo ms. 69, cc. 12v–13r.

32. ASF, Ceppo ms. 69, c. 13r. BCB, ms. B3633, p. 140. ASB, PIE, S. Giuseppe, 1, Libro +, pp. 22–23. ASB, PIE, S. Croce, 1, ms. 1, cap. 12.

33. ASB, PIE, S. Bartolomeo di Reno, ms. 79, #7.

34. ASF, Bigallo mss. 1459 and 1460. *Fede* had been required earlier, and individual examples exist in the records, but these two volumes, marked on their covers as "Filza prima" and "Filza a/2," are the first of a forty-three-volume series of *fede* continuing to 1775.

35. ASF, Bigallo ms. 1459. The file contains 348 *fede*, but 33 of these are duplicates or death notices. Differences between successful and unsuccessful *fede* were statistically insignificant. Eighty-six percent of successful applicants recorded locality, and of these 49 percent were from Florence; 88 percent of nonsuccessful applicants recorded locality, and 43 percent were from Florence. On parentage, all successful applicants recorded the father's fate, as did 96 percent of unsuccessful applicants; 92 percent of the former had died, as had 90 percent of the latter. Only 58 percent of successful applicants recorded the mother's fate, and 69 percent of unsuccessful; 65 percent of the former had died, and 67 percent of the latter. On siblings, 44 percent of successful and 40 percent of unsuccessful applicants had brothers or sisters.

36. ASF, Bigallo ms. 1459, ##314, 327. The number of signatories begins increasing from 1586.

37. Sponsorship was recorded from June 1566, and of 396 girls registered in the balance of the entry register (ASF, CRSF ms. 112/79), 372 had sponsors. The Grand Duchesses Eleonora and Cristina nominated four (##317, 335, 455, 588), priests at least fourteen (314, 331, 336, 381, 385, 397, 402, 404, 413, 418, 429, 441, 451, 527, 546, 637), and the Buonomini di S. Martino and the Pupilli two each (406, 410, 466, 535).

38. ASB, PIE, S. Croce, ms. 3, 5v–6v.

39. Of 425 girls registered on the Baraccano's three extant lists (ASB, PIE, S. Maria del Baraccano, mss. 6.1, 6.2, 7), 121 had sponsors.

40. ASB, PIE, S. Bartolomeo di Reno, ms. 79 #7. Item #16 is a 1569 *memoriale* for a child. ASB, PIE, S. Croce, ms. 2, fasc. 2, #2. Items ##4 and 5 in this *fascicolo* are undated *memoriale* of the 1590s for two children.

41. BCB, ms. B3633, pp. 173, 179, 181. Ferrante, "Il sostegno alle giovani declassate," 212–18. An inventory of the Poveri Vergognosi's archive has been published in preparation for its eventual opening: Accarrino and Aquilano, *L'Archivio dell'Opera Pia dei Poveri Vergognosi*.

42. Graph 2.2 is based on 17 cohorts investigated between 1563 and 1601; of 348 girls investigated, 173 were accepted (49.7%). ASB, PIE, S. Maria del Baraccano, busta 12, ms.

1, cc. 4rv, 8v–9v, 17v–18r, 18v, 43r, 1570 (np), 1575 (np), 1578 (np); ms. 2, 1590 (np); ms. 3, cc. 11v–13r, 26v–27r, 33v, 39v, 42v, 47v–48r, 51r, 52v. S. Onofrio: ASB, PIE, S. Maria Maddalene, ms. 5/IX.

43. ASB, PIE, S. Bartolomeo di Reno, busta 7, #2, cc. 2v–3v, 5r–6v, 9r–12r, 15r, 16r, 19v–23v, 27r–30r, 35r, 39r, 42v.

44. A *confratello* was deputed to keep track of her, and Faccari could return if she regained health. ASB, PIE, S. Croce, ms. 3, c. 1r. Through this same year (1609), *confratelli* released three girls into the custody of their families due to illness, including one described as being in the early stages of *hidrocesia*, or hydrocephalus; they also appointed a *medico* for the home: c. 4r.

45. BCB, ms. B3633, pp. 177–79. ASB, PIE, S. Maria del Baraccano 1, ms. 3, #10.

46. Length of stay is recorded for 54 of the 112 girls registered from 1616 to 1620 and 1628–41. Of these, 8 stayed for less than 2 months, 15 for 3 to 6 months, 9 from 7 to 12 months, 11 for 13 to 24 months, and 11 for more than 25 months. ASB, PIE, S. Giuseppe, cart. 23.

47. ASB, PIE, S. Croce, ms. 3, cc. 37v, 40r. ASB, PIE, S. Giuseppe, cart. 23. Accepting fee-paying girls, and collecting those fees more consistently occurred after men took over the conservatory's administration. Some Florentine homes took in fee-paying girls, but they did not write this into their statutes. An example was the Casa della Pietà, which accepted a girl for 40 lire per year and the promise of a 100 lire dowry. ASF, CRSF ms. 112/88, c. 2v.

48. ASB, PIE, S. Maria del Baraccano, ms. 7. *Confratelli* approved large numbers of girls on single days, in meetings that tended to occur either in December–January or May–July (corresponding to semestral turn-overs in administration) : 17 (17 May 1594, c. 43r), 22 (20 April 1606, c. 82v), 34 (8 December 1608, c. 90v), 22 (9 May 1613, c. 101v), 22 (31 May 1617, c. 109r), 28 (2 July 1621, c. 119r), 28 (9 January 1626, c. 129r), 24 (10 December 1628, c. 137v), 17 (15 July 1637, c. 162v), 10 (2 December 1638, c. 171r). Smaller groups and individual girls were also approved throughout the year.

49. ASB, PIE, S. Maria del Baraccano, ms. 44, #46/1; ibid., 1, ms. 3, pp. 67–77.

50. ASB, PIE, S. Croce, 1, ms. 2 (supplement), cap. 9. These undated statutes are bound together with those adopted in April 1609 (see below). They follow after the home's transfer to Via S. Mamolo and make note of involvement by the Franciscan tertiaries, but give the latter no particular role. I take these to be the statutes that Archbishop Alfonso Paleotti ordered dalle Balle to draw up in 1605: Faggioli, "Origine," 9–10.

51. "In conclusione si potria dire a queli che fanno la domanda che la faciano con quelo che ha a avuto li dinari Contanti in suo mani." ASB, PIE, S. Croce, 2, fasc. 3, pp. 33–35.

52. The conservatory hung a portrait of dalle Balle, surrounded by S. Croce *zitelle* in the home's oratory, but balked at mounting his coat of arms. Written minutes of meetings, with notice of applications, visitations, and votes began 20 August 1609: ASB, PIE, S. Croce, ms. 3, and those attended by dalle Balle cover cc. 1r–15v. On the coat of arms, see c. 20v.

53. After announcing openings in November 1627, S. Croce put all applications in a large urn and then pulled out 17 for formal visits. The competition for 1676 was launched with a decree on 17 February, and determined in a vote of 30 April, when 212 girls were considered and 31 accepted. Nominations and acceptances by Quarter: Porta Piera 11 of 66; Porta Stiera 5 of 47; Porta Procula 9 of 55; Porta Ravegnana 6 of 44. The competition of 1691 was launched 15 March and concluded 17 May, accepting 34 of 224 applica-

tions: Porta Piera 9 of 57; Stiera 6 of 58; Procula 10 of 54, Ravegnana 9 of 55. ASB, PIE, S. Croce, ms. 3, cc. 68v–70r; ms. 83.

THREE: Making a Home with Girls

1. ASB, PIE, S. Maria del Baraccano, 6, ms. 2, cc. 97v–98r.
2. Twenty-three girls had been accepted on 13 January 1570, the most recent large influx: ASB, PIE, S. Maria del Baraccano, 12, ms. 2, c. 43r.
3. ASB, PIE, S. Maria del Baraccano, 12, ms. 1, np (23 March 1575).
4. ASB, PIE, S. Maria del Baraccano, 6, ms. 2, cc. 91v–99r.
5. Two girls had been accepted on 14 May 1573, the only new entrants since a group of four had been accepted on 7 November 1572. ASB, PIE, S. Maria del Baraccano, 6, ms. 2, cc. 84v–91r.
6. ASB, PIE, S. Maria del Baraccano, ms. 7, c. 3rv. Musacchio, "The Rape of the Sabine Women," 66–82.
7. BCB, ms. B3633, pp. 145–46. The statutes were written fifty years after the conservatory opened.
8. In a printed circular of the 1590s, S. Croce required its girls to bring two chests with 12 shirts, 12 smocks, 12 kerchiefs (half of each of these could be used, but half had to be new), 12 silk *voleselle*, 6 napkins, one set of winter clothing and one of summer, a comb, a *gendinarola*, 3 yards of tafeta or some other material with which to make veils, shoes, and slippers, a copy of the Office of the Madonna, and a booklet of Christian Doctrine. ASB, PIE, S. Croce, cart. 2, fasc. 2 (np).
9. ASB, PIE, S. Maria del Baraccano, 1, ms. 2, cc. 9v–10r.
10. The revised statutes of 1648 also noted that the girls were not to keep their out-of-season clothes with them (presumably in their chest or *casone*), but that these were to be put in a central storage area. ASB, PIE, S. Maria del Baraccano, 1, ms. 3, 61–62.
11. Aranci, *Vittorio Dell'Ancisa*, 70–72.
12. Even before formally adopting uniforms for all its girls, S. Maria del Baraccano bought uniforms for those who went in procession or gathering alms. ASB, S. Maria del Baraccano, ms. 264, c. 138. On S. Caterina, see ASF, Ceppo ms. 237, cc. 26v–27r.
13. For what follows: ASB, PIE, S. Giuseppe, ms. 1, Libro +, pp. 28–31. ASB, PIE, S. Croce, 1, ms. 1 (January 1609), cap. 21 and ms. 2 (April 1609), cap. 21. Though these two sets of statutes differ on a number of points (see chap. 2, above), the outline of the day's spiritual exercises is virtually the same in both.
14. Ferrante, "Il sostegno alle giovane declassate," 210.
15. Zarri, "The Third Status," 181–99. Casagrande, *Religiosità penitenziale*, 211–314. Esposito, "St. Francesca," 197–218.
16. S. Marta's tertiaries retained their own communal life, deciding many of their activities jointly in congregation, and electing one of their number as the *guardiana* or prioress who would head daily administration and conduct their relations with the confraternity's financial officials and visitors. BCB, ms. B3633, pp. 161–69.
17. ASF, S. Caterina, ms. 17, np (#43). Conservatories whose statutes included chapters on the duties of a mistress of novices: S. Croce, ASB, PIE, S. Croce, 1, ms. 1; Pietà, BRM, Bigazzi ms. 61, cc. 31v–33r; S. Caterina had both a mistress of novices and a mistress of the young, ASF, S. Caterina, ms. 7, III/5–6. Other conservatories left it to the prioress or *guardiana* to oversee the initiation of new girls.

18. On the *portinara*, see *Bologna*. S. Marta BCB, ms. B3633, p. 164. ASB, PIE, S. Giuseppe, 1, Libro +, p. 35. ASB, PIE, S. Croce, 1, ms. 2, cap. 18. *Florence* ASF, Ceppo, ms. 69, cc. 14v. BRM, Bigazzi ms. 61, cc. 30r–32r. ASF, S. Caterina, ms. 7, cap. III/11. S. Maria del Baraccano's Lena de Fiore served 1573–76, and was paid 14 lire (+ residency) annually. ASB, PIE, S. Maria del Baraccano, ms. 264, c. 32v.

19. ASB, PIE, S. Giuseppe, 23, ms. "Ingresso e ussita delle Putte," cc. 17v–21v; 35v.

20. In 1634–35, *hortolano* Pirino Gavignano had a monthly salary of 5 corbe of *frumento*, one castellate of grapes, 2 carra of wood and 2 of kindling, and 6 lire. Ibid, cc. 32r–v, 34v.

21. On the female resident head and the terms used, see *Bologna* S. Marta (1553 statutes—*priora*), BCB, ms. B3633, pp. 163–69. S. Maria del Baraccano (1553 statutes—*guardiana*), ASB, PIE, S. Maria del Baracanno, 1, ms. 2, cc. 11v–12r. (1647 statutes), ibid., 1, ms. 3, pp. 51–54. S. Giuseppe (1641 statutes—*maestra*), ASB, PIE, S. Giuseppe, 1, Libro +, p. 35. S. Croce (April 1609—*guardiana/priora*), ASB, PIE, S. Croce, 1, ms. 2, cap. 17. (1653 statutes—*governatrice*), ibid., 1, ms. 3, cap. 17. *Florence* S. Maria Vergine/S. Niccolò (1551/1598 statutes—*madre priora*), ASF, Ceppo ms. 69, cc. 15r–16r. Pietà (1570 statutes—*madre generale*), BRM, Bigazzi ms. 61, cc. 25r–27r. S. Caterina (1590+ statutes—*priora*), ASF, S. Caterina, ms. 7, cap. III/1–3. cc. 31r–v.

22. Lutia served 1572–76, and was paid 30 lire (+ residency) annually: ASB, PIE, S. Maria del Baraccano, ms. 264, c. 33r. For two widow-*guardiane* hired in 1589 and 1590, see ASB, PIE, S. Maria del Baraccano, 7, cc. 31r–v. For appointment at S. Maria Vergine in 1599, see ASF, Ceppo, ms. 237, c. 2r.

23. ASF, Ceppo ms. 237, c. 1r–v. ASF, S. Caterina, ms. 17 (np), #5. See also ASF, CRSF ms. 112/79 #39 for Caterina di Piero Legnaiuolo, a *fanciulla* who becomes *priora* of the Pietà.

24. The Baraccano also employed a *guardiano*, though the statutes make no reference to the office or his duties, suggesting that he may have been in charge of the public shrine that was part of the larger Baraccano complex. A contemporary plan shows that he also had a garden. ASB, PIE, S. Maria del Baraccano, ms. 264, c. 136r; 265, c. 180v.

25. ASB, PIE, S. Giuseppe, 23, ms. "Ingresso e ussita delle putte," p. 52.

26. *Guardiana* Lucretia di Fini had six girls expelled during her term from November 1587 to March 1589 (##15, 64, 66, 71, 78, 81), and when she was fired her daughter Girolama also lost her place in the Baraccano home and with it any rights to a Baraccano dowry. ASB, PIE, S. Maria del Baraccano, ms. 7, cc. 4r, 16r–22v.

27. "sia detta Priora sollecita, et vigilante, ricordandosi che tutte le altre dormono sotto gli occhi suoi, et pero non si fidi di alcuna Persona, senon di se medisima." ASF, Ceppo ms. 69, 15v–16r.

28. BRM, Bigazzi ms. 61, c. 46r. ASF, S. Caterina, ms. 7, III/5. Grendler, "Schools of Christian Doctrine," 305–32.

29. ASF, S. Caterina, ms. 7, III/5 and 6.

30. See chap. 5, below, for the circumstances under which the Pietà statutes were written. BRM, Bigazzi ms. 61, c. 31v–33r. ASF, S. Caterina, ms. 7, III/5.

31. ASF, Bigallo ms. 1669/II, c. 11r. ASB, PIE, S. Croce, cart. 1, ms. 3, cap. 11.

32. "si guardi non avezzarle troppo delicate, accio non le paia poi strano il servire." ASB, PIE, S. Giuseppe, cart. 1, Libro +, p. 15.

33. Manno Tolu, "'Ricordanze' delle abbandonate fiorentine," 1014. On professional alms collectors, see ASB, PIE, S. Maria del Baraccano, 43, #39/2 (1534 permit for S. Gre-

gorio); 10, #1, c. 19v (requirement in 1598 apostolic visitation that *confratelli* get a license from the archbishop before collecting alms for the *abbandonate* dressed in their flagellants' capes); 264, c. 130.

34. BRM, Bigazzi ms. 61, cc. 24v–25r., 42v–45r. For receipts 1577–79, see ASF, CRSF ms. 112/81, [np—volume index, letters P, S, T, Z].

35. See ASF, S. Caterina, ms. 7, III/5 for very similar guidelines on alms collecting, including the note that the girls were not to sleep on the job.

36. ASF, S. Caterina, ms. 7, III/5, III/14. BCB, ms. B3633, pp. 164–65.

37. She gave all her *mobili*, and made S. Croce the residual heir if a long-lost brother failed to claim his 300 lire share within ten years: Faggioli, "Origini . . .," ASB, PIE, S. Croce, cart. 1, p. 58.

38. Polecritti, *Preaching Peace in Renaissance Italy*, 140–63.

39. S. Caterina sent out twenty-three girls with an additional fourteen as backup ("per supplemento"). ASF, S. Caterina, ms. 17, np (9 July 1595). See notes following for Pietà and S. Maria Vergine.

40. The number of days Pietà girls gathered alms from April 1578 through June 1579, and their monthly receipts in lire/soldi/denari: April (13 days: 155.1.8), May (15 days: 300.4.4), June (16 days: 157.9.4), July (16 days: 147.12.0), August (15 days: 212.17.4), September (13 days: 147.14.0), October (15 days: 142.17.4), November (13 days: 230.6.0), December (14 days: 241.0.8), January (14 days: 181.19.0), February (11 days: 158.18.0), March (14 days: 401.17.8), April (18 days: 244.01), May (16 days: 340.6.4), June (14 days: 215.6.4). ASF, CRSF ms. 112/81, [np—index P–Z], cc. 1r–2v. For buying power in food, see ibid., 70r.

41. S. Maria Vergine: alms were lire 2,800.19.4 of total income of lire 3,264.06.06 (girls collected lire 195.17.4): ASF, Ceppo, 145, cc. 70. Pietà: 1556 income was lire 9,034.15.00, with alms totaling 6,518.11.08. ASF, CRSF ms. 112/96, c. 82. Rounding off S. Giuseppe's income to the lire: 1629: 286 of 1,208 (25.67%). 1631: 4,839 of 5,698 (77.02%). 1632: 1,932 of 3,069 (62.95%). 1633: 4,386 of 5,915 (74.15%). 1634: 1,275 of 3,087 (41.3%). 1636: 1,537 of 3,899 (39.12%). 1637: 470 of 3,054 (15.38%). 1639: 1,231 of 2,889 (42.6%). ASB, PIE, S. Giuseppe, 19/2.

42. ASB, PIE, S. Giuseppe 1, Libro +, pp. 18–21, 32. ASB, PIE, S. Croce, 1, ms. 2, cap. 21; ms. 3, cap. 11.

43. For food purchases, see ASB, PIE, S. Giuseppe, ms. 19, 1, a; cart. 23, ms. 1, c. 41v (see cc. 2r–4v for instructions to sharecroppers).

44. Italians in this period generally ate 20 to 40 kilograms of meat annually. Bread consumption rose from 500 to 900 grams daily between the fifteenth and seventeenth centuries. Molinari, *The Culture of Food*, 104–7.

45. On measures, see Burr Litchfield, *Emergence of a Bureaucracy*, xiii. Meats were itemized inconsistently, but beef usually cost roughly half the price of mutton (*castrone*). Table 3.2 does not include costs for wine or for the barrels of oil purchased between January and March. Bulk purchases registered as *spese di camangiare* include 7 staia of chestnuts (lire 11.4), 10 staia of *faggioli* (lire 34.5), 1,300 onions (lire 8.13) purchased between November 1578 and February 1579: ASF, CRSF ms. 112/81, cc. 88v–94r.

46. ASF, S. Caterina, ms. 7, III/5–16. On bread baking, see III/15. The Pietà merged some of these duties so that the *sarta, refectorara, cuoca*, and *infirmiera* with their assistants (eight girls in all) carried out all the domestic work: BRM, Bigazzi ms. 61, cc. 36r–39r. The Pietà brought in flour, but had its bread baked outside by a *fornaio* Bartolomeo,

whose deliveries every two weeks through 1577–79 earned him 15 lire per month, paid on or around the 24th: ASF, CRSF ms. 112/81, cc. 68v, 70v, 73r, 75v, etc. For domestic work in other homes, see BCB, ms. B3633, pp. 157, 164–65, 168. ASB, PIE, S. Croce, cart. 2, fasc. 3, pp. 31–32, 39–40.

47. ASF, S. Caterina, ms. 7, III/12.

48. ASF, S. Caterina, ms. 7, III/16. On Pietà's *infermiera*, BRM, Bigazzi ms. 61, cc. 39v–40v.

49. ASF, S. Caterina, ms. 7, III/10. The Pietà gave the laundry and storage duties to the *sarta* and her two assistants who along with washing clothes had to air them out periodically in order to dispel plague contagion that may have settled on them. BRM, Bigazzi ms. 61, cc. 36r–37r.

50. The underlying fragility of both city's textile industries was demonstrated by their collapse in the following century: Poni, "Per la storia del distretto industriale serico," 93–167. Malamina, "L'Industria fiorentina," and Rolova, "La manifattura nell'industria tessile," 295–308, 309–25.

51. Mola, *The Silk Industry*, 203, 268, 291, 403–8.

52. BRM, Bigazzi ms. 61, cc. 39–41. ASF, S. Caterina, 7, cap. III/7, 8, 8 (*sic*). ASB, PIE, S. Croce, 1, ms. 2. ASB, PIE, S. Giuseppe, 1, Libro +, pp. 18–19.

53. ASF, CRSF ms. 112/78, cc. 29–31 (##115, 123, 124).

54. BRM, Bigazzi ms. 61, cc. 42v–44v. ASF, CRSF ms. III/7–8.

55. The *madre di casa* could appoint new mistresses semiannually, and the girls and staff participated in formal installation ceremonies in May and November. The ceremonies aimed to put the mistresses' authority and the girls' obedience on a spiritual foundation, judged more secure and open to a wider range of punishments than a purely practical or skill-based foundation would be. BRM, Bigazzi ms. 61, cc. 25v–27r.

56. Ciammitti, "Fanciulle monache madre," 461–520. Foschi, "La Compagnia e il Conservatorio del Baraccano," 25–27.

57. These included "seta nostrale [i.e., Florentine] per filare, seta di lombardia per adoppiare," or "per filare, seta di bologna a incanare, seta di messina, seta di mantova, seta di Ferara per filare, seta cruda, seta rosa, seta nera per rasi, seta gialla, seta seminara, seta verde per cordoni." ASF, Ceppo ms. 245, *Libro di Lavori A (1589–1627)*, cc. 26rv, 36rv. On the Pietà's brocades, see Sandri, "L'attività di banco," 166. Mola, *The Silk Industry*, 3–19, 406–7.

58. ASB, PIE, S. Maria del Baraccano, 1, ms. 2, cc. 8v, 11v–12r. ASB, PIE, S. Giuseppe, 1, Libro +, 18–19. BCB, ms. B3633, pp. 142, 150, 157.

59. "tutti li lavorieri sieno a benefficio della casa." ASB, PIE, S. Croce, 1, ms. 2, cap. 19.

60. On visitors, see ASB, PIE, S. Maria del Baraccano: ms. 44, #46/1, cc. 6r, 8r–v; ibid., 1, ms. 2; BCB, ms. B3633, cap. 3. S. Giuseppe encouraged all female members of its governing congregation to visit frequently, and required the prioress to visit at least weekly—ASB, PIE, S. Giuseppe, 1, Libro +, pp. 11, 14. ASB, PIE, S. Croce, 1, ms. 1, cap. 23; 1, ms. 2, cap. 9, 16. *Florence* ASF, Ceppo ms. 69, c. 15r; ASF, S. Caterina, ms. 7, I/2, III/1.

61. "discreta in far differenza nel conversare con una gentildonna o con una vile artiera." ASF, S. Caterina, ms. 7, III/7.

62. From 1620 to 1623, all silk work was channeled through Paris Grimaldi, whose relatives Vespasiano, Grimaldo, and Carlo all served on the executive. After his death, Alessandro Zaniboni, who had been prior in 1622, served as silk broker from 1624 to

1629. ASB, PIE, S. Croce, ms. 3, cc. 5r, 9r, 10r, 11r, 28r–38r; ms. 149, cc. 6, 44v–45v, 118. The statutes, and the *confratelli*'s conviction that "havendo il luoco maggiore numero di zittelle che tessono, habbia anco l'utile maggiore," are in ASB, PIE, S. Croce, 1, ms. 1; ms. 2.

63. ASF, Ceppo ms. 245, *Libro di Lavori A (1589–1627)*.

64. ASB, PIE, S. Maria del Baraccano, ms. 7, cc. 42r–61v.

65. ASF, CRSF ms. 112/96, c. 82; ms. 112/97, c. 235. The absolute figures and percentages for 1572–78 at the Pietà: 1572: 15,633 lire (64% of total income); 1573: 4,807 lire (18%); 1574: 10,289 lire (48%), 1577: 6,173 lire (48%), 1578: 5,398 lire (33%). ASF 112/57, cc. 182r, 208r, 264r, 307r, 330r.

66. "Et perche il lavoro apporta afflictione, e maninconia, le faccia alle volte cantare lauda, o, l'Avemaris stella, o, La Salve Regina, ne permetta che si canti rispetti del'mondo." ASF, S. Caterina, ms. 7, cap. III/7. BRM, Bigazzi ms. 61, cc. 42v–44v. ASB, S. Croce, 1, ms. 2, cap. 21. Dalle Balle's concerns were expressed in a 1607 list of complaints: ASB, PIE, S. Croce, 2, fasc. 3, pp. 39–40.

67. ASF, PIE, S. Croce 1, ms. 2, cap. 9. BRM, Bigazzi ms. 61, c. 46v. ASB, PIE, S. Maria del Baraccano, ms. 6, cc. 149v–150r; 7, 15v–16r.

68. ASB, PIE, S. Croce, 1, ms. 3, cap. 11. ASB, PIE, S. Giuseppe, cart. 1, Libro +, p. 32.

69. ASB, PIE, S. Croce, ms. 2, fasc. 3, pp. 39–40. Dalle Balle responded that "non e verita alcuno di questo."

70. ASB, PIE, S. Giuseppe, ms. 1, Libro +, pp. 33–34. For the rules for the Carità, see BNCF, ms. II.I.410, 87v–88r. S. Maria del Baraccano limited disobedient girls to bread and water for a period determined by the gentlewoman visitors. ASB, PIE, S. Maria del Baraccano, 1, ms. 2, c. 12r.

71. BRM, Bigazzi ms. 61, cc. 45v–48v. S. Maria del Baraccano also had a *pregione* (ASB, PIE, S. Maria del Baraccano, 1, ms. 2, c. 12r.), as did S. Caterina (ASF, S. Caterina, ms. 7, cap. III/9).

72. This is phrased obliquely as "chi nominassi di marito per la casa o, di cose di matrimonio." BRF, Bigazzi ms. 61, c. 46r.

73. "si licentij dal luogo, e tra altro stij rinchiusa in prigione." ASB, PIE, S. Giuseppe, 1, Libro +, p. 34. Carità: BNCF, ms. II.I.410, 85r. S. Croce also wanted girls keeping to their own beds: ASB, PIE, S. Croce, 1, ms. 3, cap. 11. Brown, *Immodest Acts*.

74. A later hand superscripts "Casale" in the various records relating to Laura di Francesco il Bologna until after she marries, when she is consistently referred to as Laura Casale or even "La Casale." She entered April 1578, was expelled October 1584, and married Domenico Cevenini in November 1586. Widow Caterina Castelani received 4 lire per month, the standard rate when the Baraccano boarded out girls. Laura's dowry of lire 636.6.4 included 200 lire from the Baraccano and the balance from Senator Casale, who put 100 lire on deposit when she first entered, purchased some goods from Laura's mother with the money designated for Laura's use, and gave a direct gift of 100 lire when she married. ASB, PIE, S. Maria del Baraccano, ms. 6.2, cc. 136r–137v; ms. 7, c. 11rv; ms. 264, cc. 152rv, 275r, 283r; ms. 265, cc. 23rv, 40rv, 42r, 57r.

75. ASB, PIE, S. Maria del Baraccano, 6, ms. 1, cc. 81v–82r, 145v–146r. ASB, PIE, S. Croce, 3, c. 11r. ASF, Ceppo ms. 59, c. 12r. ASF, S. Caterina, ms. 17 (np), #6, 7, 16, 18, 27. ASF, CRSF ms. 112/78, c. 64, #249.

76. ASB, PIE, S. Giuseppe, 1, Libro +, pp. 17–18, 26–27; ASB, PIE, S. Croce, 1, ms. 2, cap. 15, 21. BRM, Bigazzi ms. 61, cc. 18r–v. ASF, S. Caterina, ms. 7, cap. II/1–4, III/9.

77. ASB, PIE, S. Giuseppe, 1, Libro +, pp. 17–18. ASF, S. Caterina, ms. 7, cap. II/10–11, III/9.

78. BCB, ms. B3633, pp. 151–52. ASB, PIE, S. Maria del Baraccano, 1, ms. 2, c. 7v. ASB, PIE, S. Croce, 1, ms. 2b; 1, ms. 1, cap. 9; 1, ms. 2, cap. 12. ASF, Ceppo ms. 69, cc. 16r–v. BRM, Bigazzi ms. 61, cc. 19r–21r. ASF, S. Caterina, ms. 7, cap. I/13. Dalle Balle's sermons and exhortations are found in ASB, PIE, S. Croce, 2, fasc. 2 (np). They include, for example, a piece headed "p matutino," which opens, "Carissime surele qui noi siamo tutte Congregata." S. Marta required that the *padre confessore* be an Observant Franciscan from the Annunziata.

79. On medical care, see BCB, ms. B3633, p. 144. ASB, PIE, S. Maria del Baraccano, 1, ms. 2, c. 9r. ASB, PIE, S. Croce, 1, ms. 1, cap. 10, 19; 1, ms. 2, cap. 13; BRM, Bigazzi ms. 61, cc. 36v–39v. BNCF, ms. II.I.410, cc. 87v–88r. ASF, S. Caterina, ms. 7, cap. II/9.

80. The nine-page *ricettario* of unguents and plasters is unnumbered and unpaginated. The fifteen recipes contain fifty-three distinct ingredients, of which ten can only be obtained through the brokers (*sensali*) licensed by the Arte dei Medici e Speziali. The recipes are written in two and possibly three distinct hands, and the tenth is headed with the date 1567; by 1577, the manuscript volume was being used to record alms receipts and food payments. ASF, CRSF ms. 112/81 (np; recipes on cc. 61v–66r). ASF, Arte dei Medici e Speziali, ms. 4, 41v–45v.

81. Gentilcore, *Healers and Healing*, 56–95. The Pietà's *ricettario* had eleven unguents or ointments, two flour plasters, and two *diachylons*, which were medicated elixers.

82. ASF, CRSF ms. 112/81 (np), [#4]. Soranus, *Gynecology*, 62–68. Soranus is not mentioned in the Pietà *ricettario*, but two recipes are attributed to Avicenna, three to Mesue, one to "Gian di Vico," and one to "Guido": Riddle, *Conception and Abortion*, 133–57.

83. Cohen, *The Evolution of Women's Asylums*, 55–60.

84. The day book for 1566–79 (ASF, CRSF ms. 112/3) and the account book for 1564–74 (ASF, CRSF ms. 112/29) note amounts spent as *spese d'infermeria* but seldom specify what is bought beyond sugar and a remedy known as *acqua borra*.

85. Baraccano *Medico* Domenico da M. Santo served 1572–81 and received 20 lire annually for being on call. ASB, PIE, S. Maria del Baraccano, ms. 264, c. 32v. From 1571 through 1579, the Pietà paid doctor Jacopo Soldani a 21 lire retainer annually. ASF, CRSF ms. 112/29 cc. 198r, 205r, 211r, 236r; ms. 112/3 cc. 145r–182r. The Pietà sometimes also retained a surgeon on similar terms, or simply paid a fee (one lire in 1579) to have a girl bled: ASF, CRSF ms. 112/81, c. 97v.

86. ASB, PIE, S. Croce, ms. 3, cc. 1r–4r . The only girl whose condition was described was in the early stages of *hidrocesia*, or hydrocephalus: c. 4r.

87. ASF, S. Caterina, ms. 17, ##21, 33, 40, 46, 50, 61, 67, 73, 80, 90, 91, 94, 96. ASF, CRSF ms. 112/78, cc. 1–63. S. Niccolò also transferred terminally ill girls to S. Maria Nuova: ASF, Ceppo ms. 59, c. 114v; ms. 141, c. 5r.

88. For provisions and guidelines, see BCB, ms. B3633, pp. 143–44. ASB, PIE, S. Maria del Baraccano, 1, ms. 1, c. 9r. ASB, PIE, S. Giuseppe, 1, Libro +, pp. 1, 6, 11. ASB, PIE, S. Croce, 1, ms. 1, cap. 6, 22; 1, ms. 2, cap. 11. ASF Ceppo ms. 69, cc. 14r, 19r. ASF, S. Caterina, ms. 7, cap. I/5. Homes that forbade or made no provision: S. Marta, Carità, Pietà.

89. ASB, PIE, S. Maria del Baraccano, ms. 6, #1, ms. 7, cc. 94v–95r, 120v–121r, 124v–125r, 131v–132r, 136v–137r. The register periodically noted how many girls were outside the home, but this was seldom very many: 7 of 67 in 1589 (32r–33v), 2 of 80 in 1596 (52v).

90. ASF, Ceppo ms. 145, cc. 171–87.

91. Seventeen of 57 girls (29.82%) left this way. Ten of the employers were women and 7 men. *Age of leavers:* 6 (1), 13 (1), 14 (3), 15 (2), 16 (3), 17 (1), 18 (1), 20+ (3). *Time in S. Giuseppe* 1–12 months (4); 13–24 months (9); 25–36 months (2), 36+ months (2). ASB, S. Giuseppe, 23, cc. 8r–36v. Murphy, "'In Praise of the Ladies of Bologna,'" 440–54.

92. ASB, PIE, S. Giuseppe, 1, Libro +, pp. 1, 6, 11. ASF, Ceppo ms. 69, cc. 14r, 19r.

93. ASF, Ceppo ms. 59, cc. 1r–16v.

94. Ibid. Girls leaving: 1558 (1), 1559 (2), 1560 (4), 1561 (6), 1562 (6), 1564 (2), 1565 (8), 1566 (12). Annual payments in lire: 7 (1), 10 (14), 12 (1), 14 (3), 25 (1). Length of contract: 4 years (1), 5 years (3), 7 years (1), 10 years (4). Occupations of male employers: *tessitore* (5), *mercante* (2), *lanaiuolo* (1), *sarto* (1), *calzolaio* (1), *calzolaro* (1), *matterasaro* (1).

95. ASF, Ceppo ms. 59, cc. 5r, 6r, 11v–12r.

96. Ibid. Ages: 4 (1), 7 (2), 8 (2), 9 (2), 10 (3), 11 (1), 12 (3), 13 (2), 15 (2), 16 (2), 17 (2), 19 (2), 20+ (3). Twenty-four came from non-Florentine families; origins of the remaining fifteen are unclear.

97. ASF, Ceppo ms. 59, cc. 105v–118v, 129v–182r.

98. ASF, S. Caterina, 17, ##10, 12, 13, 20, 32, 39, 55, 59, 69, 142, 153, 156, 161, 175. Nine had no surviving parent, 2 had been abandoned by a father and 2 by a mother after the death of the other parent. Of the 14, 6 left within 2 years, 4 after 6 to 10 years, and 4 after 10 to 15 years. The last contract was signed in 1626.

99. Of those for whom statistics are available: *Time in Pietà:* > 1 month (3); 2–12 months (10); 13–24 months (11); 25–60 months (16); 61+ months (14). *Age of leavers:* 10 (1), 13 (7), 14 (3), 15 (4), 16 (6), 17 (10), 18 (5), 19 (3), 20 (2), 21 (5), 22 (2), 23 (2), 24 (1), 30+ (3). ASF, CRSF ms. 112/78, cc. 1–93.

100. Nine girls (14.75%) returned, and 4 died soon after; of the 8, time in service before return is recorded for 4 (in months: 8, 9, 14, 23). Baker's daughter (#216). "Ungovernable" girl (#132). ASF, CRSF ms. 112/78, cc. 1–64.

101. ASF, CRSF ms. 112/78 and ms. 112/79. 112/79 records 708 names from 1558 to 1623. Table 3.4 covers only those registered to 1601 because from this point the records are increasingly incomplete as girls' names and destinations were transferred over to a third (no longer extant) volume that began in 1624.

FOUR: Making a Home with Boys

1. ASF, Bigallo ms. 1459. Girolamo Honesti's *fede* for Ruggiero di Lorenzo is #75. The others noted here are ##70, 74, 76. Forty-eight children were nominated from 1 January 1576 through 17 December 1577, and only three (##75, 80, 116) were clearly accepted.

2. ASB, PIE, S. Bartolomeo di Reno, ms. 7, #1, c. 3r. The opposite message comes in a nomination of 1588, where the legal guardians proposing a boy in 1588 promised to give the orphanage the profits generated by his assets during his time he was resident; the boy was accepted: ms. 7, #2, c. 4v. On his exit in June 1588, Ascanio Dainese received the

shoemaking tools he had brought with him. Only one other boy of the thirteen sent away that day took old goods, in this case some cloth, with him; the others took only a set of clothes provided by the orphanage: ms. 7, #2, c. 6r. In August 1590, trustees were appointed to administer a house inherited by one of the boys: ms. 7, #2, c. 24v. Florence's Abbandonati required a full record of each boy, but this was either never kept or it did not survive: ASF, Bigallo ms. 1669/II, c. 12v.

3. What follows will be based in part on the following orphanage statutes, many of them drafts: *Florence:* Abbandonati (1542 statutes): ASF, Bigallo ms. 1669/II, cc. 9r–24r. These are draft statutes approved at the first meeting (1 September 1542) of the expanded board of poor relief commissioners appointed to deal with beggars and orphans in Florence; they include provisions for dealing with beggars (cc. 4r–8v) that were never implemented. The commission did not subsequently revise its statutes in order to reflect its more restricted mandate. *Bologna:* S. Bartolomeo di Reno (1550 statutes): ASB, PIE, S. Bartolomeo di Reno, 78. S. Onofrio (1560 statutes): ASB, PIE, S. Maria Maddalena, 2, ms. 2. S. Onofrio (1664 statutes): ASB, PIE, S. Maria Maddalena, 2, ms. 3. On maintaining registers of boys, see Abbandonati (1542 statutes), c. 12v. S. Bartolomeo di Reno (1550 statutes), 12v–13r, 29r–31v. S. Onofrio (1560 statutes), 9v.

4. Antoniano, *Dell'educazione cristiana.* Logan, "Counter-Reformatory Theories," 275–84.

5. In the entry blessing, the official made the sign of the cross on the boy, invoking the name of the Father (placing three fingers on the boy's head in honor of the Trinity), the Son (placing a hand on his abdomen because Christ was nine months in his mother's womb), and the Holy Spirit (a hand on the left shoulder and then on the right in view of support the Spirit gives in tribulation). On the "amen," he touched the mouth as a sign of submission to the will of God. ASF, Bigallo ms. 1669/II, c. 13r. Sebregondi, "Clothes and Teenagers," 27–50.

6. ASB, PIE, S. Maria Maddalena/S. Onofrio, ms. 4/VII, c. 7r. There were also 15 pairs of sheets and 5 tablecloths. In its first 3 months, the Abbandonati bought 27 pairs of shoes, 55 braccia of cloth for shirts (*chamice*), 93 braccia of local russett-colored cloth for smocks, 18 braccia of local cloth for underclothes and collars (*soppannare e chollarinj*), and 16 braccia of lombard cloth for robes (*camiciotti*) that may have been worn in procession. It also paid a tailor to sew 24 vests. These are the only specific entries regarding clothing in a volume covering 1542–45; by July 1542, entries are far less specific. ASF, Bigallo ms. 1679, cc. 33r–37r.

7. In 1574, S. Onofrio bought 15 handkerchiefs, 31 caps, 30 pairs of breeches, 46 pairs of shoes, and other clothing for its boys. ASB, PIE, S. Maria Maddalena/S. Onofrio, ms. 78, cc. 4v, 5v, 46v, 48v, 49r, 50r. On clothes bought for boys in masters' service, see cc. 48r–v. In 1589–90, the Bigallo bought 654 pairs of shoes at 5 soldi per pair, suggesting that they were being distributed to more than just the boys in the home. ASF, Bigallo ms. 768. Costs of shoes and clothing escalated steadily through this period: 1588–89: 22.2.3.8 (Bigallo 768,c. 28r); 1589–90: 36.4.12.0 (c. 71r); 1590–91: 32.2.3.8 (c. 102r). 1591–92: 52.1.6.0 (Bigallo 769, c. 32r); 1592–93: 62.2.6.8 (c.79r); 1593–94 58.0.3.0 (c. 140r). All amounts recorded in florins.

8. "per esser conosciuti": ASB, PIE, S. Bartolomeo di Reno, 7/1, c. 1r (1575). In 1576, S. Onofrio spent 12 lire, equivalent to two months' salary, to outfit its priest. ASB, PIE, S. Maria Maddalena/S. Onofrio, 78, c. 45v. On Abbandonati robes, which bore a cross on

the chest as a time-honored symbol of the Christian beggar, see ASF Bigallo ms. 1669/II, cc. 19r–20r and n. 2, above.

9. ASF, Bigallo ms. 52, #34. AAB Miscellanea Vecchia 622, "S. Onofrio Orfanotrofio."

10. ASB, PIE, S. Bartolomeo di Reno, ms. 234, "Beni stabili in Bologna" [np]. This description dates from 1748; sixteenth-century sources note the construction of the archive room and administrative offices in 1547, the school room and sacristy in 1550, further rooms in 1577, an infirmary in 1578, the internal *loggia* in 1581, the new dormitory in 1583: ms. 7, #1a, cc. 1–10r. Terpstra, "The *Qualità* of Mercy," 126–28. For Florentine hospital design, including that of institutions beside the Abbandonati's home in the old Ospedale Broccardi, see Goldthwaite and Rearick, "Michelozzo and the Ospedale di San Paulo," 275–80.

11. The home had been purchased in 1568. For an inventory of its furniture, see ASB, PIE, S. Maria Maddalena/S. Onofrio, 78, cc. 2v–4v; for the locks in the dormitory doors, see 49r.

12. In August 1562, S. Onofrio appointed Giovanno Liardi as *guardiano*. Piero Giovano replaced him by July 1563, was replaced in turn by Filippo di Sarti and his wife in March 1565, but returned to the position three months later. Another hung vote stalled a second effort to remove him in 1567, but a new *guardiano* was hired again in 1576 and in 1580 ASB, PIE, S. Maria Maddalena/S. Onofrio, ms. 4/VII, cc. 6v–18r, 28r; 4/VIII (2 September 1576); 5/IX (18 October 1580, 6 November 1580, 18 June 1601).

13. ASB, PIE, S. Bartolomeo di Reno, ms. 7, #2, cc. 12r, 14r, 16v, 33v–35r, 37v.

14. ASF, Bigallo ms. 154, c. 32r.

15. ASF, Bigallo ms. 1669/II, c. 10v.

16. S. Onofrio paid its *guardiano* slightly more than its priest, 83 lire annually versus 75 lire for the priest, but neither was as well paid as the professional alms collector, who in this same sample year (1576) earned at least lire 138.0.6; this latter agent was paid a percentage of his receipts: ASB, PIE, S. Maria Maddalena/S. Onofrio, 78, c. 48r, 53v–56r.

17. On teachers, see ASF, Bigallo ms. 1669/II, c. 17r. ASB, PIE, S. Maria Maddalena/S. Onofrio, 2, ms. 2, cc. 14v–15r; 2, ms. 3, cap. XVI.

18. Grendler estimates that about 28 percent of boys in 1480s Florence and 26 percent of boys in 1587 Venice attended formal day schools. With others attending propietorial or charity schools, the basic literacy rate rose to something around 33 percent. Grendler, *Schooling in Renaissance Italy*, 46, 78.

19. On a Christian Doctrine catechism printed and used in Bologna, see Ledesima, *Dottrina christiana breve*, 29. Broadsheet: *Avertimenti, et brievi ricordi circa il vivere christiano. Regola de' costumi christiani alli fanciulli:* all these found in AAB, Miscellanea Vecchie 798, fasc. 2.

20. Grendler, *Schooling in Renaissance Italy*, 278–81.

21. Ibid., 289–305.

22. Ibid., 323–29.

23. Examples and further background given in ibid., 22–23, 306–19.

24. This "pseudo-Donatus" was known as the *Ianua:* ibid., 162–82.

25. Ibid., 391, 336–37, 381–99. The staged curriculum of these schools, beginning with religious and moral materials in the vernacular and expanding gradually to the *studia humanitatis* in Latin closely duplicated that of the larger orphanage schools like the Abbandonati, which themselves resembled the schools for Veneto orphans opened by Somaschans from 1534.

26. Construction of school rooms had been among the first expansions to the S. Bartolomeo quarters in 1550. ASB, PIE, S. Bartolomeo di Reno 7, ms. 1a (looseleaf sheet): 1r, 4v, 10v–11v. Grendler, *Schooling in Renaissance Italy*, 40.

27. Pannolini wrote his will in 1584. Toniolo, "'Per il mezzo delle scienze prestissimo si sorge," 77–88.

28. ASB, PIE, S. Maria Maddalena/S. Onofrio, 2, ms. 2, cc. 11v–12r, 14v–16r.

29. ASF, Bigallo ms. 1669/II, cc. 10r, 12v, 21r. ASB, PIE, S. Maria Maddalena, 5, ms. 9 (22 February 1587). ASB, Dem, S. Giacomo 12/6470, ms. 2, c. 3r. For legacies to S. Bartolomeo di Reno, see ASB, PIE, S. Bartolomeo di Reno, ms. 234, 279.

30. The most extensive description is in ASB, PIE, S. Maria Maddalena/S. Onofrio, 2, ms. 2, 10v–13v.

31. The *fratelli* voted 31 to 2 to fire the *guardiano*, and took two months to find a replacement. ASB, PIE, S. Bartolomeo di Reno ms. 7, #1, cc. 6v–7r. ms. 7, #2, 12r, 14r. On visitors' reports, see ms. 7, #2, cc. 3v, 8r, 33r, 41v.

32. In the early 1580s, S. Bartolomeo di Reno had a "stancia da caneppe," where it finished or stored hemp brought in from its own farms in S. Giovanni in Persiceto, though it is not clear if the boys participated in this work. ASB, PIE, S. Bartolomeo di Reno, ms. 138, c. 62.

33. ASF, Bigallo ms. 1669/II, c. 19r.

34. The Abbandonati's alms boxes and keys were delivered on 14–15 April 1542. ASF, Bigallo ms. 1679, c. 35r. S. Onofrio had twenty-five small alms boxes and one large one. In 1576, the SS. Sacramento confraternity of S. Martin's parish paid the home lire 1.3.0 for the services of a boy who had collected alms through the parish on its feast day: ASB, PIE, S. Maria Maddalena/S. Onofrio, ms. 78, cc. 3v–5r, 42–58; ms. 2, #2, c. 12v.

35. "e li giorni di pesse, pesse per le pescarie." *Istitutione, provisione, e capitoli dello Hospitale*, 27.

36. These gatherers included *confratelli* appointed due to the increasing dearth of food. ASB, PIE, S. Bartolomeo di Reno 7, #1, c. 3v. ASB, PIE, S. Maria Maddalena/S. Onofrio, 2, ms. 2, 12v, 18r.

37. The statutes forbade "alchuna gincolaria, ciurmaria, ni baratteria, ni alchuna cosa brutta, ne anche dire alchuna bestemia parole . . . ne ragionamenti vitiosi." ASF, Bigallo ms. 1669/II, c. 19r.

38. Niccoli, "I 'fanciulli' del Savonarola," 107–8, 110–11.

39. ASB, PIE, S. Bartolomeo di Reno, ms. 7, #1, c. 45r; ms. 138, cc. 242, 295; for alms-collecting permits and efforts to settle territorial disputes in the 1550s, see ms. 279, cc. 25r, 26r–27v, 31r–33r, 38r, 44r. Niccoli, *Il seme della violenza*, 159–93.

40. Niccoli, "I bambini del Savonarola," 278–88. Idem, "I 'fanciulli' del Savonarola," 105–20. Sardi, "Fanciulli e angeli fanciulli," 159–84. Trexler, "Ritual in Florence," 247–64. Glixon, *Honoring God and the City*, 200. On youth confraternities, see Eisenbichler, *The Boys of the Archangel Raphael*. Polizzotto, *Children of the Promise*, 107–68. Taddei, *Fanciulli e giovani*. Terpstra, *Lay Confraternities and Civic Religion*, 21–23, 182–83.

41. Onuphrius lived in the desert for sixty years, receiving the Eucharist from an angel. When he died, two lions came and dug his grave; these lions were frequently shown with Onuphrius, who was portrayed covered only by long and unkempt hair and a garland of leaves. Ferguson, *Signs and Symbols*, 137.

42. S. Maria Maddalena's organ also attracted legacies stipulating anniversary requiems from its own members: ASB, PIE, S. Maria Maddalena/S. Onofrio, 5/IX (23 Sep-

tember 1586), (22 November 1587), (16 June 1591). For aggregations and indulgences, see cart. 3, ##1–13, 15–17. For the costs of a confraternity funeral and the role of singers in it, see Glixon, *Honouring God and the City*, 72–75, 126–29.

43. Strocchia, *Death and Ritual*, 91–104. Terpstra, *Lay Confraternities and Civic Religion*, 68–82. See also Banker, *Death in the Community*.

44. Niccoli, "I 'fanciulli' del Savonarola," 108–9. Idem, *Il seme della violenza*, 25–48. Muir, *Mad Blood Stirring*.

45. From 3 January through 22 May 1574, the boys collected 1,203.5 loaves of so-called *pane del sepoltura* from 35 funerals, recorded as having a total value of lire 144.8.4. ASB, PIE, S. Maddalena/S.Onofrio, ms. 79, c. 2v.

46. ASB, PIE, S. Bartolomeo di Reno, ms. 7/II, cc. 17rv. The *corporale* balance sheet employs different categories than those found in the company's *libro mastro* and used in Tables 4.1. A.1, and A.2. Of a total income of lire 2,675.3.8 reported to the *corporale*, "sepultura de morti" generated 312.1.2 (11.74%), alms collection 580.7.8 (21.68%), legacies 423.15.8 (15.81%), and a subsidy from the Reggimento 200 (7.48%).

47. The confraternity of S. Giacomo attracted legacies worth lire 88,272.03.02 from the opening of its new orphanage chapel to 1654. ASB, Dem, S. Giacomo, ms. 12/6470, pt. 2, cc. 3r–19r. Although a priest would clearly be the main celebrant of the funerary and requiem rituals, a number of the legacies stipulate that it is the children who will say, for example, a daily "De Profundis" for the soul of the testator (ibid., c. 2r, 3r, 11r–13r). For balance sheets of 1612, 1646, 1652, see AAB, Miscellanea Vecchie, G, cart. 158; Miscelleana Vecchie, G, Visite Pastorali, "Poveri Orphanelli di S.to Giacomo" [1646–47]; and "Ospetal di S. Giacomo" [1652].

48. ASB, PIE, S. Bartolomeo di Reno, ms. 7, #2, c. 30r.

49. ASB, PIE, S. Maria Maddalena/S. Onofrio, ms. 5/IX (24 June 1590); cart. 3, #14. Parochial *cura animarum* was not conducted by secular clergy, but by the *frati Gesuati*, members of a Hieronymite congregation based in the local parish church. The confraternity and orphanage could continue to display the host and carry it in procession, and could conduct burials during Holy Week. They were not allowed to have preaching in their church or ring their bells while the friars were preaching in the parish church. On celebration of the Magdalen's feast day, see ms. 78, c. 49r. In 1586, S. Bartolomeo's chaplain was ordered to cease confessing the boys, and leave this up to the chaplain of the local parish: ASB, PIE, S. Bartolomeo di Reno, ms. 7, #1a, c. 11r.

50. ASF, Bigallo ms. 142, #656.

51. Memmo, *Dialogo*, 121.

52. ASF, Bigallo ms. 1669/II, cc. 9v–11r. ASB, PIE, S. Maria Maddalena/S. Onofrio, 2, ms. 2, cc. 23rv.

53. "Ne si vergognino i padri, ancora che non habbiano bisogno, di metter lor figliuoli in casa altrui ad imparare tali arti: perche essendo nelle altrui mani, & mancando di quella ombra paterna, nè havendo quello ardire in casa altrui, che nella propria, piglieranno miglior creanza; & si faranno parimente migliori maestri. Ben voglio, che i padri usino ogni diligenza in quardare a cui danno i lor figliuoli: accio che in vece d'un arte honesta, non apparassino molti vitij & arti dishoneste . . . Veggano medesimamente, che a quelli, à quali danno i figliuoli, siano huomini humani, & non fiere crudeli: come sono molti, che si satiano in battere si acerbamente quelli, che sono dati al loro governo, che molte fiate li fanno morire, over infermare, & divenire stupidi & insensati." Memmo, *Dialogo*, 122.

54. "non gli esercitij vili, et pocco proficui et giorevoli": ASB, PIE, S. Bartolomeo di Reno, busta 7, #1, c. IV. For similar concerns in Amsterdam, see McCants, *Civic Charity in a Golden Age*, 73–82.

55. So, for example, in January 1593, the S. Bartolomeo *massaro* was instructed to visit all the houses and shops where boys were working, and prepare a list of names, wages, and masters' recommendations on the individual boys. He submitted his list of sixteen boys in June of that year: ASB, PIE, S. Bartolomeo di Reno, ms. 7, #1, cc. 45, 50r.

56. ASF, Bigallo ms. 1669/II, 9v, 22r–v.

57. "di qui, per fuggir al tutto l'ocio di ogni male cagione, vorrei che le feste, benche sieno instituite solo per attendere al culto divino, nelle quali a tempi di hoggi si attende all'ocio, & ad ogni altra lascivia; vorrei, dico, che andando prima la mattina alla Chiesa." Memmo, *Dialogo*, 122.

58. Ibid., 122–23.

59. The *Quaderno di Casa*, for 1588–92 and 1592–94, notes the majority of boys working with *tessitori*, followed by *calzolari* and *legniaiole*. ASF, Bigallo mss. 768 and 769.

60. ASB, PIE, S. Bartolomeo di Reno, ms. 7/1, c. 50r. Marcello, "Andare a bottega," 244–46.

61. Income from boys' wages in local currency (lire in Bologna and florins in Florence) and as percentage of total income: S. Bartolomeo di Reno: 1582: 402 lire (4% of income); 1583–84: 786 (4%); 1586: 796 (5%); 1588: 753 (7%); 1589: 585 (5%); 1590: 804 (12%); 1595: 680 (9%); 1596: 555 (7.3%); 1597: 454 (6%); 1598: 345 (6%) ASB, PIE, S. Bartolomeo di Reno, ms. 138, cc. 40rv, 190rv, 242rv, 295rv, 314rv; ms. 138, cc. 172rv, 235rv, 254rv. For Ospedale degli Abbandonati: 1588–89: 171 florins (4.14%). 1589–90: 181 (4.46%). 1590–91: 120 (2.59%). 1591–92: 233 (3.25%). 1592–93: 270 (4.64%). 1593–94: 318 (5.35%). ASF, Bigallo ms. 768, cc. 34v, 67v, 113v; ASF, Bigallo ms. 769, cc. 35v, 81r, 139r. ASF, Bigallo ms. 675 36v, 72r, 102v, 138r, 302r, 370v. The undated list is in ASF, Bigallo ms. 52, #34: the boys earn 680 florins and generate a further 1,670 in other revenues against a total of 4,400 florins.

62. Payments of one lire per week were made every two weeks to four individuals, three of them women and at least one a widow, for keeping boys: ASF, Bigallo ms. 769, cc. 80v–81r. For the Bigallo's March and August 1591 appeals to the duke, see ASF, Bigallo ms. 157, ##114, 115. For the November request that parents who abandoned their boys on its steps be liable to punishment in the galleys, see ASF, Bigallo ms. 1669/IV, c. 44v.

63. ASB, PIE, S. Bartolomeo di Reno, ms. 279, c. 68v. ASB, Dem, S. Giacomo, 12/6470, pt. 2, cc. 11–13r. The boys reciprocated by saying the seven penitential psalms for the soul of the testator of the first Sunday of every month. On sharecropping and the efforts of charitable institutions to use it in order to become more self-sufficient in food, see Sneider, "Charity and Property."

64. ASB, PIE, S. Maria Maddalena/S. Onofrio, ms. 79, cc. 6r–17v, 21r–v. On donations by officials and appeals to the guilds of *notarii, sallaroli*, 4 *marzari, sarti*, 4 *arti, spiciali, muraduri, strazaroli, calzolari, perlacani, fabri*, see ms. 4/VII, cc. 20r, 22r, 25v, 36r–v. For Laura Bentivoglio's nomination of an orphan, see ms. 4/VIII (22 June 1578). This boy was accepted without further investigation or review. Senator Ercole Bentivoglio served as rector in the second semester of 1564, the first semester of 1565, and the second semester of 1591, and was nominated in 1569: ms. 4/VII, cc., 12r, 14v, 40v. 5/IX (16 June 1591).

65. Grieco, "The Social Politics," 131–49. Molinari, *Culture of Food,* 82–91.

66. McCants, *Civic Charity in a Golden Age,* 147–50.

67. In a rare exception, the undated Abbandonati account referred to earlier notes that of total expenses of 4,390 scudi, 3,350 went to feeding and clothing the 187 children. ASF, Bigallo ms. 52, #34. In the eighteen months from July 1589 through December 1590, when the Abbandonati was seriously overcrowded and likely housing even greater numbers, it purchased 353 staia of grain for 247 scudi, lire 4.7.8, and 173 barilli of wine for 142 scudi, lire 1.16.8. This was less than 10 percent of the income generated in 1589 alone (4,057 scudi, lire 5.2.5). ASF, Bigallo ms. 619, cc. 26v–27; 675 c. 72r. M. Sneider notes that Bologna's main hospitals of S. Maria della Morte and S. Maria della Vita followed the common practice of using a fictitious price (called the "common price") when setting an value on sharecroppers' rents-in-kind, with the result that the accounting figures became increasingly unreliable as inflation progressed through the sixteenth century. Sneider, "Charity and Property," chap. 3, section 1, n. 290. Landi, "Per una storia dei falsi in bilancio," 41–62.

68. ASB, PIE, S. Bartolomeo di Reno, ms. 7, #2cc. 17r–v; ms. 138, cc. 242r–v, 295r–v. In local measures, the boys collected 2,369 bolognese libbre of bread, and ate 33,533 (one libbre = 361 grams). They collected 64 corbe of wine, and drank 205 (one corba = 78 liters). Rinieri, *Cronaca 1535–1549,* 302, 305.

69. The 52 *biolche* bought from Bonaparte Zani on 23 November 1587 cost lire 8,311.16.4, and S. Bartolomeo sold one of its urban properties for 4,775 lire in order to fund the purchase; land purchases from 1564 had totaled 3,025 lire (this figure omits the value of lands donated). Fibbie made his private agreement to purchase the property in 1588, and gained title to it on 5 May 1591, having paid at least 1,300 lire in food. ASB, PIE, S. Bartolomeo di Reno, ms. 234, #1; ms. 279, cc. 67r–68r. He was a close neighbor to S. Bartolomeo, owning a palace across the canal from the orphanage, and served as conservator from at least 1588, and prior in 1593: ms. 7, #1, cc. 1r, 33v. On the purchases of October 1591, including instructions regarding the "pallio da morto per li putti, ma, che sia honorevole," see ms. 7, #1, c. 39r. Among his other duties with S. Onofrio, Fibbie had been part of a delegation of eight appointed in May 1567 to counter Cardinal Gabrielle Paleotti's suggestion that it merge with S. Bartolomeo di Reno, and among the five who reviewed and updated the statutes in 1596: ASB, PIE, S. Maria Maddalena/ S. Onofrio, ms. 4/VII, c. 27v; 5/IX (15 September 1596; 31 August 1597).

70. ASB, PIE, S. Bartolomeo di Reno, ms. 7, #2, cc. 23v–25r, 39v, 42r. Terpstra, *Lay Confraternities and Civic Religion,* 179–205.

71. ASB, PIE, S. Maria Maddalena/S.Onofrio, ms. 5/IX (17 January 1587). McCants, *Civic Charity in a Golden Age,* 136–42.

72. Sneider, "Charity and Property," 131–51. Sneider notes that impressive property registers were produced by the two largest institutional landholders, the *ospedali* of S. Maria della Vita (1601) and S. Maria della Morte (1606), as they redeemed these mortgaged properties. The registers celebrated the restoration of the properties and aimed to "immortalize" them. Ibid., n. 288. For an expanded discussion, see ibid.

73. ASB, PIE, S. Maria Maddalena/S. Onofrio, ms. 5/IX (17 January 1597).

74. ASB, PIE, S. Bartolomeo di Reno, ms. 7, #1a (*sommario*), cc. 1r, 5r; 7, #2, cc. 16v–18r. Guardiano di Bianchi died in June 1593: ibid., 33v–35r. Stiatici, *Narratione overo chronicha,* 27–28. ASB, PIE, S. Maria del Baraccano, ms. 7, cc. 31r, 32v, 34r.

75. ASB, PIE, S. Bartolomeo di Reno, ms. 7, #1a, c. 12v (gate at main entrance); 7 #2,

c. 21v (for acceptance a second time of a boy who had run away) and 37v (for keeping the boys locked in at night). ASF, Bigallo ms. 1669/II, c. 10v.

76. Niccoli, *Seme della violenza*, 101–5.

77. Venetian statistics cover the period 1406–1500, and Genevan 1444–1500. Rocke, *Forbidden Friendships*, 47, 191. Idem, "Il fanciullo e il sodomita," 211–12.

78. The session dealing with these two pieces of legislation was the senate's only meeting between 28 June and 23 August, and these items were the senate's only item of business. ASF, Senato dei Quarantotto, ms. 5, cc. 7v–8v (sodomy law), 8v–9v (blasphemy law), 13v–15v (portion of blasphemy fines to Bigallo magistracy). Rocke, *Forbidden Friendships*, 51, 232–35, 243.

79. Rocke, *Forbidden Friendships*, 162–64, 183. Marcello, "Andare a bottega," 246–48.

80. ASF Bigallo ms. 1669/II c. 23v. ASB, PIE, S. Bartolomeo, ms. 78 cc. 13v, 19r, 33r–v. On dormitory and beds, see ms. 7, #1a, c. 10r. Grendler, *Schooling in Renaissance Italy*, 40.

81. 478 of 687 (69.57%) condemnations from 1478 to 1502 involved actives ages 18 to 30. Rocke, *Forbidden Friendships*, 245, Table B7; pp. 97–98, on mutual penetration on the part of young boys.

82. ASB, PIE, S. Maria Maddalena/S. Ofrio, 2, ms. 2, cc. 16r, 21r. ASF, Bigallo ms. 1669/II, cc. 9r–11r.

83. ASF, Bigallo ms. 1669/II, cc. 22r–24v.

FIVE: Running a Home

1. In 1564, Giovanni Galeazzo Bottrigari became *principe* of S. Maria della Morte, the confraternity that operated one of Bologna's major hospitals (AAB, Aula 2a—C-VII-3), and in 1597 he joined that confraternity's subgroup in charge of charity to prisoners, the Compagnia dei Poveri Prigionieri (BUSL, 29 Lib 1–2 #44). In 1584, he also served on the board of the Monte di Pietà, which operated as the financial arm of a number of key charitable institutions. Maragi, *Monte di Pietà*.

2. ASB, PIE, S. Maria Maddalena, 2 ms. 2, cc. 2r–v, 19r, 21v–24v, 26v; ms. 4/VII, cc. 2r–8v.

3. ASF, Ceppo ms. 69, c. 2r. Francesco Rosati enrolled one of his servant girls, Margherita da Prato, in S. Maria Vergine on 1 December 1555. ASF, Ceppo ms. 145, c. 187.

4. This is based on statutes from both cities: *Bologna:* S. Marta (BCB, ms. B3633, pp. 135–85—statutes of 1554, with additions of 1580 and 1641), S. Maria del Baraccano (ASB, PIE, S. Maria del Baraccano, cart. 1, #2 [1553], #1 [1647]); S. Croce (ASB, PIE, S. Croce, cart. 1, #1, 2 [January 1609]). *Florence:* S. Maria Vergine (ASF, Ceppo ms. 69— 1551 statutes with reforms of 1598 and 1616) and S. Caterina (ASF, S. Caterina, ms. 7— nd, ca. 1590)

5. These six were known formally as the "Illustri e Molto Magnificenti Signore Operari delle Fanciulle di S.ta Caterina." ASF, S. Caterina, ms. 7, 1/1–13. The first two *provveditori* were Francesco Covoni and Girolamo Renzi, the first *priora* was Alessandra Dragnonari, a widow, and the first *governatore* was a friar of S. Marco, Domenico Portigiani: ASF, S. Caterina, ms. 17, cc. 1r–v.

6. Beginning at 30 members in March 1552, it lost 2 by the end of that year, leaving it with 28 through 1553. Three new members were recruited in 1554, but 3 also died and

one retired, leaving S. Maria Vergine with 27 by year's end. Two joined the following year, but 2 left and one died, dropping it to 26. Five were added between March and May 1556, but by the end of the year 2 more had died, leaving the total at 29. By 1556 it had lost 11 members, or over one-third of its original strength, 7 through death and 4 through resignation. ASF, Ceppo ms. 145, cc. 161–66.

7. Muzzarelli, *Il denaro e la salvezza*, 234–44. Carboni, *Le doti della "povertà,"* 70–85. ASB, Assunteria dei Magistrati, Affari diversi cittadinanze, ms. 121/1, cc. 14r–17v.

8. Park and Henderson, "'The First Hospital among Christians,'" 176. Terpstra, "Competing Views of the State and Social Welfare," 1319–55.

9. For a broader discussion of the origins and development of this phenomenon, see Terpstra, *Lay Confraternities and Civic Religion*, 28–30, 63–65, 86–87, 24–25, 139–44.

10. De Benedictis, *Repubblica per contratto*, 86–105.

11. Terpstra, "Piety and Punishment," 679–94; idem, "Confraternal Prison Charity," 217–48. Fanti, *Confraternite e città*, 61–174.

12. The committee appointed to handle the sale in 1534 included Alessandro Stiatici, Francisco di Nigrelli (merchant), Ludovico di Luco del Jacco (butcher), Alfonso de Benincha, and Alessandro de Giovanni Fontana (architect): ASB, PIE, S. Bartolomeo di Reno, ms. 63, #2. See also ASB, Dem, S. Bartolomeo di Reno, ms. 2/7651 (5 January 1534). The *processo* against Fellicini was launched 12 December 1556. ASB, PIE, S. Bartolomeo di Reno, ms. 279, c. 30v.

13. Stiatici, *Narratione overo chronica*, 20–22.

14. ASB, Dem, S. Bartolomeo di Reno, ms. 2/7651, ##13, 14. Stiatici, *Narratione overo chronica*, 21–25. The Stretta's lease on life was, in any event, short-lived; revised statutes of 1588 refer to members wearing the flagellant's cloak in procession, but make no reference to the practice of flagellation itself. A matriculation list appended to the statutes notes fifty-nine members, four of them senators and the rest guild masters. BCB, Gozz, 210, cc. 64r–v, 68v, 73r. For an expanded treatment, see Terpstra, "The *Qualità* of Mercy," 126–28.

15. De Benedictis, *Repubblica per contratto*, 222–24; S. Verardi Ventura, "L'ordinamento Bolognese," 279–80, 295. The silk fair lasted from 30 May through 1 August.

16. The Monte del Matrimonio originated in 1583 with a broad *corporale*, and an executive *congregazione* with seats allotted to artisans (3), merchants (3), gentlemen (3), doctors (1), ecclesiastics (1), and senators (1). Carboni, *Le doti della "povertà,"* 70–85.

17. Francesco Sampieri served on the senate 19 May 1590 through 2 January 1610, renewing a position enjoyed by ancestors Lodovico (1478–94) and Hieronimo (1514–16). He was also Gonfaloniere di Giustizia in 1592, 1602, and 1609. Guidicini, *I Riformatori*, vol. 3, 92. Maragi, *Monte di Pietà*. ASB, PIE, S. Bartolomeo di Reno, ms. 7/2, cc. 26r, 28r. ASB, PIE, S. Maria Maddalena, ms. 5/IX (22 June 1597; 13 December 1601). His relatives at S. Maria Maddalena included Astorre (joined 1577), who became very active as a frequent official and rector (1593, 1604), and who may have engineered the entry of Pier, Alessandro, and Hieronimo in the large influxes of 1580.

18. AAB, Aula 2a—C (July 3). USL 29, Lib 1–2 #44. Maragi, *Monte di Pietà*.

19. Yeo, *Religion and Voluntary Organizations*.

20. ASB, PIE, S. Bartolomeo di Reno, ms. 7/2. BBA, Gozz, 210, cc. 63–80 (1588 Stretta statutes). For S. Maria Maddalena meetings, see ASB, PIE, S. Maria Maddalena, mss. 4/VII, 4/VIII, 5/IX.

21. Three members had joined 27 December 1588, and three on 30 June 1591. A

matriculation of 3 June 1593 recorded forty-seven members, and ninety-eight members were enrolled at the next meeting on 30 August 1593. ASB, PIE, S. Bartolomeo di Reno, ms. 7/2, cc. 15v, 26v, 33v–36r.

22. This matches attendance at confraternity meetings in the fifteenth and sixteenth centuries. Very few members attended all meetings, but most attended at least a couple of times in the year. Terpstra, *Lay Confraternities and Civic Religion,* 106–8.

23. "e meglio il numero de pochi e boni, che la confusion de molti." ASB, PIE, S. Maria Maddalena, ms. 2, 2, c. 25r.

24. Stretta membership ranged from 14 to 32 in the 1560s, while the entire membership in December 1562 numbered 52: ASB, PIE, S. Maria Maddalena, ms. 4/II, cc. 1v, 2v, 9r, 17v, 61r–v. On later additions, see ibid., ms. 4/VIII (25 March 1580; 29 May 1580); 5/IX (29 October 1595; 19 November 1600).

25. The house was located next to S. Onofrio; in November 1581, Scargi's heirs abandoned a lawsuit and renounced their claim in return for a 100 lire credit deposited in the Monte di Pietà. ASB, PIE, S. Maria Maddalena, busta 14, # 41, 44. On tax exemptions, see ibid., #42 (1581); busta 13, #43 (1559). On lobbying generally, see ibid., ms. 4/VII, cc. 25v, 27v, 36r–v, 38v.

26. De Benedictis, *Repubblica per contratto,* 86–105. Robertson, *Tyranny under the Mantle of St. Peter,* 66–79. Carboni, *Il debito della città.*

27. Murphy, "'In Praise of the Ladies of Bologna," 440–54. Carboni, "La formazione di una elite di governo," 9–46.

28. The confraternity received indulgences from Paul IV (1588) and Gregory XIII (1579), and negotiated aggregations with the Augustinians (1579), Franciscans (1585, 1608), and S. Spirito in Sassia (1580, 1606, 1608). ASB, PIE, S. Maria Maddalena, 3, #5/2, 7–13.

29. Terpstra, "Showing the Poor a Good Time," 19–34.

30. The image was also known as the Madonna del Reno. For expanded treatment, see Terpstra, "The *Qualità* of Mercy," 126–28. Idem, "Confraternities and Local Cults," 143–74.

31. The home spent over 200 lire, equivalent to an artisan's annual earnings, on twenty-four flagellants' capes in 1584 and 1588, and frequently marched in public processions. ASB, S. Bartolomeo di Reno, ms. 138, c. 160r–v; ms. 282, "B." BBA, Gozz, 210, cc. 73r–v.

32. Stiatici was S. Maria del Baraccano *massaro* in 1549, *procuratore* in 1556, sindic in 1557, and supernumary in 1534, 1553, and 1566. ASB, PIE, S. Maria del Baraccano, 1, ms. 1, pt. 4; ms. 2, c. 3v; ms. 11, cc. vi–viii, 4v–7v, 11r, 20v, and was one of the eight men who wrote the new statutes in 1554 (BBA, Gozz, 209 #1, 39). Fantuzzi, *Notizie degli scrittori bolognesi,* vol. 7, 55. Stiatici, *Narratione overo chronicha.*

33. The best study of Florentine confraternal life in its neighborhood context is Eckstein, *The District of the Green Dragon.*

34. Henderson, *Piety and Charity,* 57–65. Polizzotto, *Elect Nation,* 210, 266, 399, 420, 424. Idem, *Children of the Promise,* 149–50, 176–80.

35. Polizzotto, *Elect Nation,* 29–38. Cosimo Il Vecchio contributed up to half of the Buonomini's annual income during his lifetime: Kent, "The Buonomini di San Martino," 50. Spicciani, "The 'Poveri Vergognosi,'" 119–82.

36. Polizzotto, *Elect Nation,* 38.

37. Ibid., 322, 334–86.

38. Lorenzo Polizzotto offers an excellent discussion of the effect of repeated bans on officers and confraternity members in *Children of the Promise*, 169–81.

39. "di disponer provedere et ordinare in benefitio commodo et sublevamento deli detti poveri." ASF, Magistrato Supremo, ms. 5, fol. 62r–v (13 March 1540).

40. BNCF, Poligrafo Gargani 539, #164 (Francesco di Giovanni Cavalcanti); 1068 #91 (Francesco di Girolamo Inghirami).

41. ASF Pratica Segreta 184 (F). I am grateful to John K. Brackett for the reference: "Who were the deserving poor in late Renaissance Florence?" Renaissance Society of America, Florence, Italy, 22 March 2000, 5.

42. ASF, Bigallo ms. 1669/II, fol. 27v. IV, fols. 4r, 5v.

43. Cosimo I's plan, laid out in a *patente* of 19 March 1542, was approved by Cardinal Penitentiary Antonio Pucci (27 June 1542), Archbishop Buondelmonti (17 October 1542), and Pope Paul III (18 July 1543). For transcriptions of the texts, see Passerini, *Storia degli stabilmenti*, 800–812.

44. d'Addario, "Noti di storia," 126–35. Lombardi, "Poveri a Firenze," 28–34.

45. ASF, Bigallo ms. 157, ##201, 202, 203 lay out the process of three-way consultation from 15 December 1595 through 26 March 1596 under which Bishop Alessandro Marzi Medici was nominated by the archbishop of Florence and appointed by Duke Ferdinand I. The boundaries of the diocese of Fiesole reached into central Florence, and the bishop's palace was not far from the Bigallo's headquarters on Piazza S. Giovanni. Comerford, *Ordaining the Catholic Reformation*, 27–37.

46. For Table 5.2, see ASF, Bigallo ms. 1669/IV, cc. 199r–203v. ASF, Tratte ms. 725. Gamurrini, *Istoria delle famiglie nobili*. Mecatti, *Della nobiltà*. Burr Litchfield, *Emergence of a Bureaucracy*, 339–82.

47. Promotion to the senate sometimes came after appointment to the Bigallo: 9 of Cosimo I's 16 (56.25%), 2 of Franceso I's 8 (25%), 11 of Ferdinando I's 22 (50%). A significant minority were the first senatorial appointments in their families: 5 of 16 appointed by Cosimo I, none of Francesco I's appointments, and 6 of 22 appointments by Ferdinando I. On patricians, the 200, and the senate, see Berner, *The Florentine Patriciate*, 148–58, 170–84.

48. On the court and the Order of Santo Stefano, see Berner, *The Florentine Patriciate*, 232–38.

49. ASF, Bigallo ms. 1669/IV, c. 200v. ASF, Tratte ms. 725, c. 55r. Gamurrini, *Istoria delle famiglie nobili*, vol. III, 292–302. Mecatti, *Della nobiltà*, 131, 163–64.

50. ASF, Bigallo ms. 1669/IV, c. 200v. ASF, Tratte ms. 725, c. 83r. Mecatti, *Della nobiltà*, 132, 224. Gamurrini, *Istoria delle famiglie nobili*, vol. II, 61, 64.

51. ASF, Bigallo ms. 1669/IV, fol. 201r. Mecatti, *Della nobilità*, 133, 161. Gamurrini, *Istoria delle famiglie nobili*, vol. I, 492–94.

52. Terpstra, "Competing Visions of the State and Social Welfare," 1328–34, 1338–47.

53. Fasano Guarini, *Lo stato mediceo di Cosimo I*, 19–62. Brackett, *Criminal Justice and Crime*, 20–21. Burr Litchfield, *Emergence of a Bureaucracy*, 67–82.

54. Beyond Michelozzi, Zanchini, and Botti, Flaminio Flamini and Lottieri Gherardi joined the first council; Gherardi oversaw renovations to the building and the writing of statutes in 1613. Both Flamini and Gherardi were still governors when Vergine *fratello* Antonio Maria Bartolomei joined the council on 26 September 1632. ASF, Ceppo ms. 237, cc. 26v–27r. Manno Tolu, "'Ricordanze' delle abbandonate fiorentine," 1007–13. Cionacci, "Vettorio dell'Ancisa," c. 77r. "Croniche delle Suore della Pietà," 2.

55. Corsini was among the first appointments of senators on 27 April 1532; he was also the first member of S. Maria Vergine to die, on 5 November 1552. The next senator in the brotherhood was Simone di Jacopo Corsi, elected to it 30 March 1555, and to the senate 12 March 1557 (ns). Senators in the ranks in 1600 were Luigi Capponi, Girolamo Morelli, and Altobianco Buondelmonti (into the senate in 1605). ASF, Ceppo ms. 145, cc. 163, 165; ms. 237, cc. 1r–2r. Mecatti, *Della nobiltà*, vol. 1, 125, 128, 130, 134. Eighteen of the initial forty members and sixteen of twenty-six members noted in three matriculations of 1600 were of what Mecatti would in the eighteenth century identify as *famiglie nobili*: ibid., 12–15.

56. ASF, Ceppo ms. 145, cc. 161–66. Members with Piagnone family connections: Tommaso di Lodovico Bonsi, Donato di Bartolomeo Cambini, Sapiano di Ansaldo Canigiani, Antonio di Donato Cioni, Alisandro di Gerardo Corsini, Zanobi di Bartolomeo Pandolfini, Carlo di Francesco Portinari, Giovanni de Rossi. Aranci, *Formazione religiosa*, 335–39. Polizzotto, *Elect Nation*, 446–60. AAF, Visite Pastorale 5 (Altoviti) and 6 (de Medici).

57. ASF, Bigallo ms. 154, c. 162r.

58. "possino accetare questa e non più." Entries in the Abbandonati's first account book note frequent payments to the Abbandonate. ASF, Bigallo ms. 1679, c. 57r. On Giovanni Leonardo Barducci, see ASF, Bigallo ms. 20, IV, c. 4v; V, c. 1r. ASF, Bigallo ms. 154, c. 91r, 233r. The three patrician women who sponsored the young girl were Lena Arrighi (wife of Antonio), Margherita Buoninsegni (widow of Lionardo), and Alessandra Mazzinghi (wife of Paradiso); the girl was the unnamed daughter of Antonio di Ser Niccolò da Romena. Ibid., c. 161r. For other appeals, see ibid., cc. 12, 28, 33, 44, 45, 50, 52, 69, 70, 72, 73, 74, 75, 95, 156, 161.

59. "poi che l'Eccelenza Vostra e resoluta di non voler più la cura delle fanciulle abbandonate." ASF, Bigallo ms. 154, c. 233. Torelli left the decision up to the Bigallo captains, who decided to sell the farm in order to generate funds to place the girls in other settings.

60. BRM, Acquisti Diversi, ms. 93, p. 2.

61. Two sources note memberships: ASF, CRSF ms. 112/97, cc. 1r–83r (memberships recorded from 28 December 1554 through 17 December 1558). See also ASF, CRSF ms. 112/81, where recording begins with Marietta Gondi on 10 September 1554. Pledges were usually only a few florins; only 18 of the first 270 donors gave more than a scudo, and most of the rest gave lire 1.5 or 2.10. In 1557 the *limosine dalle donne* generated lire 803.15 (7.6% total income) and in 1558, lire 589.16.08 (5.4%): ASF, CRSF ms. 112/55, cc. 25r, 108r. See also Manno Tolu, "Abbandonate Fiorentine," and idem, "Echi Savonaroliani," 218–23. The only male member was Fra Giovan Maria, a Fransciscan from S. Croce.

62. On 5 July 1555, five women (Marietta Gondi, Margerita Bonsi, Alessandra Mazzinosi, Marietta Strozzi, Maria del Pugliase) intervened with alms of 70 to 75 lire, and one man (Niccolo Doni) with 35 lire to meet an urgent but unspecified need. ASF, CRSF ms. 112/97, cc. 154r–55v. Macey, *"Infiamma il mio cor,"* 164. The Pietà received a small government subsidy, in the form of alms of salt, from 1557. Manno Tolu, "Echi Savonaroliani," 210.

63. For a broader discussion of the chronicle's authorship and misrepresentation, see Terpstra, "Mothers, Sisters, and Daughters," 211–21. Four authors contributed materials to the chronicle, which exists in a copy transcribed by Sister Maria Teresa Petruccia,

prioress of the Pietà from 1738. "Cronicha delle Suore della Pietà." BRM, Acquisti Diversi, ms. 93.

64. Manno Tolu, "Echi Savonaroliani," 218–22. Polizzotto, *Elect Nation,* 366, 385. Guasti, ed., *Le lettere di S. Caterina de' Ricci,* 301. ASF, Bigallo ms. 1669/IV, c. 200r; ASF, Tratte ms. 725, c. 59r. For Marietta Gondi's will, see ASF, CRSF ms. 112/92 (25 February 1569).

65. Terpstra, "Confraternities and Mendicant Orders," 10–13, 15–21.

66. On efforts by the friars of S. Marco to exert control over four other convents, efforts that escalated through the sixteenth century, see Polizzotto, "When Saints Fall Out," 522–23.

67. d'Addario, "Noti di storia," 100–101. Marchi, *Vita di Alessandro Capocchi.* Polizzotto, *Elect Nation,* 438–45.

68. The Dominican chronicle obscures the connection to the Jesuits by describing the removed cleric as one of the "preti of S. Giovannino," neglecting to add that at that point the Jesuits were based in the church of S. Giovannino, their first home in Florence. "Cronicha delle Suore della Pietà," cc. 193r–194v. Aranci, *Formazione religiose,* 140–45.

69. "Cronicha delle Suore della Pietà," 4–10, 13. Manno Tolu believes that the Compagnia della Pietà had statutes from its inception, but (as she also acknowledges) there is no record of these remaining. "Echi Savonaroliani," 215. Representation by quarters was a traditional communal/confraternal practice that the *piagnoni* had emphasized as fundamental to representative republican government. The donor of the land on Via Palazzuolo was Girolamo da Sommaia (Francesco da Sommaia was on the 1497 petition to Pope Alexander VI). ASF, CRSF ms. 112/88, cc. 1v, 4v.

70. Macey, *"Infiamma il mio core,"* 164–65.

71. "Cronicha delle Suore della Pietà," 10–17, 197r–197v.

72. "siera partito dal Governo di esse Abbandonate per che non haveva potuto ottenere un suo intento circa di esse." "Cronicha delle Suore della Pietà," 12, cc. 192r–v, 194v.

73. ASF, CRSF ms. 112/88, c. 4v. "Cronicha delle Suore della Pietà," 13–14. Capocchi became *padre spirituale* at S. Maria Vergine in 1580, and died a year later: d'Addario, "Noti di storia religiosa," 101.

74. In its worst year (1574–75), the conjunction of collapsing alms and increased costs gave the Pietà a deficit of 16,584 lire in an annual budget of 26,243. By slashing costs for food, clothing, and wood, and doubling receipts from alms and work, it ended the following year with a surplus of 2,600 lire. ASF, CRSF ms. 112/57, cc. 208rv, 264rv.

75. AAF, *Visite Pastorale,* 5. Aranci, *Formazione religiosa,* 39–43. Two of the Pietà chronicle's authors differ in their accounts. The earlier one claims that Altoviti ordered the move to the Dominicans after the Camaldolese friar Franceschini quit, while the later one claims that the women and girls dismissed Franceschini a day after receiving assurances from Capocchi and the Dominican provincial that San Marco would be willing to provide a *padre confessore.* "Cronicha delle Suore della Pietà," 15, c. 194v.

76. Gondi left the Pietà as her universal heir, with the sole provision that her two female servants receive 4 gold florins annually for as long as they remained with the conservatory: ASF, CRSF ms. 112/92 (25 February 1569 sf). "Cronicha delle Suore della Pietà," c. 193r. The friars of S. Marco followed a strikingly similar process from 1507, when they took over the spiritual direction of the youth confraternity of the Purification and reshaped it into a Savonarolan group. Polizzotto, *Children of the Promise,* 137–46.

77. Between 1554 and 1564, the Pietà purchased ten matching vellum-bound volumes for various accounts, identified these alphabetically (A = CRSF ms. 112/97; B = 112/96; C = 112/55; E = 112/95, H = 112/2), and kept them systematically: ASF, CRSF 112/95, c. 160r–v. By the mid-1570s, some accounts were being kept on the spare pages of books initially dedicated to other purposes (e.g., 112/81, which begins as a record of cloth piecework and ends up as a miscellaneous record book). The day books (*Giornali*) run from before 1565 to 1579 (112/1–3) but are not extant from 1579 to 1605; the account books (*Entrate/Uscite*) run from 1557 to 1577 (112/27–31) but are not extant from 1577 to 1609; the records of creditors and debtors (*Debitori/Creditori*) run from 1557 to 1579 (112/55–57) but are not extant from 1579 to 1604. Sets of accounts from the 1580s and 1590s can be found as sets of looseleaf sheets bundled together in no particular order (e.g., 112/103–4). The gaps may be due to flood, fire, or theft of records, although the progressive deterioration of all record keeping, the parallel gaps in three separate records, and the presence of sporadic and unorganized looseleaf records suggests that there were other problems in the home or with its scribe Giovanni Bencini.

78. Some examples: ASF, CRSF mss. 112/88, c. 1r [1566]; 112/95 and 96 [1562–65 and 1556–63]; 112/97 c. 1r (the first matriculation and pledge book of the "donne della società dello hospitale della pietà"). "Cronicha delle Suore della Pietà," 6–9.

79. "Cronicha delle Suore della Pietà," 199r–201r

80. The *Libro Nuovo* is no longer extant, but ASF, CRSF ms. 112/79 notes which names were transferred. "Cronicha delle Suore della Pietà," 27–28. The chronicle fails to mention the election of a *priora generale* after 1625 (Signora Maria Biffoli), and last notes a *priora generale* in 1633 (Signora Maria Maddalena Nobili). The building was later restructured, and currently serves as the Kunsthistorisches Institut. Micali and Roselli, *Le soppressioni dei conventi a Firenze*, 83–84.

81. These regulations are contained in Dell'Ancisa's first will of 17 March 1592: Cionacci, "Vittorio dell'Ancisa," cc. 88v–89r. For a broader discussion, see Terpstra, "Mothers, Sisters, and Daughters," 221–25.

82. Cionacci, "Vettorio dell'Ancisa," cc. 88r–89v.

83. Aranci, *Vittorio dell'Ancisa*, 56–68. Cionacci, "Vettorio dell'Ancisa," cc. 88v–89v. See also d'Addario, "Noti di storia," 102.

84. Dell'Ancisa's 1598 testament was dictated 5 May, the day before he died: Cionacci, "Vettorio dell'Ancisa," 47r–49v, 63r–v, 85r–88r. Aranci, *Vittorio Dell'Ancisa*, 64–65.

85. Cionacci, "Vettorio dell'Ancisa," cc. 10v–14r. Aranci, *Vittorio dell'Ancisa*, 84–89.

86. Cionacci, "Vettorio dell'Ancisa," 85r–88r. For the 1644 conventual statutes, see 3r–35v.

87. For the 1644 statutes, see Cionacci, "Vettorio dell'Ancisa," cc. 3r–35v. Servant sisters were decidedly subordinate: "non permettendo che tra di loro si diano del Tu," c. 28v.

88. Murphy, "'In Praise of the Ladies of Bologna," 440–54. Carboni, "La formazione di una elite di governo," 9–46.

89. ASB, PIE, S. Maria del Baraccano, ms. 44, #46/1, 46/2; ms. 110, cc. 26rv.

90. Statutes that reduced women's early role were adopted 25 March 1553. The agreements between the Stretta and the Larga occurred 2 July 1553 and 14 October 1554, though they continued fighting into the eighteenth century: BBA, Gozz, 209, #1, pp. 3–18, 39. On male values in the Stretta, see Terpstra, *Lay Confraternities and Civic Religion*, 116–32.

91. Terpstra, "Women in the Brotherhood," 193–212. Dall'Olio, *Eretici e Inquisitori,* 202.

92. Terpstra, "Showing the Poor a Good Time." The three women worked together closely and the men governing the Opera were unwilling to leave their election to chance. Every three years, the prioress would draw up a list of women fit for office. She passed this to the male officials, who divided them into groups of three, writing the three names on a single ballot and determining which of the three would be prioress. If any one of the trio could not serve when drawn, the entire slate was set aside and a second group was drawn. Though the reasons for this procedure were not stated, it allowed the men to ensure that the gradations of rank that they guarded in the election of their own executive could be recognized in the election of the women's executive as well; it also allowed them to take political alliances and enmities into account. Election of the women's officers always followed a few weeks after the male officials had been drawn and confirmed. ASB, OPM, ms. 2, no. 2, 27–28. AAB, Raccolta degli statuti, cart. 26, fasc. 29, no. 1 (5; 29).

93. ASB, PIE, S. Croce, ms. 3, c. 3r, 5v; ASB, PIE, S. Giuseppe, ms. 23, pp. 19, 22, 29, 39.

94. ASB, PIE, S. Giuseppe, cart. 1, Libro +, pp. 22–25; cart. 23, cc. 5r–22v, 39–41v, 52rv.

95. ASB, PIE, S. Giuseppe, cart. 1, Libro +, pp. 1–4, 7–9, 16–17. AAB, 619, #31 (28 January 1646)

96. ASB, PIE, S. Giuseppe, cart. 1, Libro +, pp. 1–3. Cart. 19, ms. 1, 16 February 1631 (np).

97. Murphy, "'In Praise of the Ladies of Bologna,'" 440–54.

98. ASB, PIE, S. Giuseppe, cart. 23, "MDCXIII. Patti, conventioni, accordi, et oblighi con nostri lavoratori fuori in villa, da osservarsi."

99. ASB, PIE, S. Giuseppe, cart. 23, p. 39.

100. Regulations on entry now required a quorum of two-thirds of the Company members and approval of 75 percent for an individual girl to win entrance; this essentially put control on entrants into the hands of a minority. ASB, PIE, S. Giuseppe, cart. 1, Libro +, pp. 22–25.

101. Gill, "*Scandala,*" 177–203.

102. But see Strocchia, "Sisters in Spirit," 735–67, for an illustration of how women of the sixteenth-century Miracolo consorority adopted the conventions of confraternal governance.

103. One factor that allowed the Pietà and Carità to get out of short-term help for vulnerable young women was the opening in 1619–20 of Florence's Ospedale dei Mendicanti, a beggars' hostel that served primarily women. On these transitions, see Gavitt, "Charity and State Building." Lombardi, *Povertà maschile, povertà femminile.*

s i x : Leaving Home

1. ASB, PIE, S. Bartolomeo di Reno, ms. 7/1, c. 1r–v, 20r. Rostighelli was also a conservator and, in the first semester of 1588, a sindic. Passi was a once and future prior. ms. 7/2, cc. 4r, 6r.

2. ASB, PIE, S. Maria del Baraccano, ms. 6/2, cc. 75v–76r. Serafina's father Martino had been a master builder (*muratore*). She entered 27 January 1570, her departure was

approved 3 September 1580, with the ceremony on the 7th, and signing of the dotal agreement on the 23rd; this last step usually preceded the exchange of vows.

3. Anna had entered the conservatory 9 December 1570 at age 10. Her father was a weaver of velvet cloth. ASF, CRSF ms. 112/79, c. 62. Marietta left S. Niccolò in January 1565. ASF, Ceppo ms. 59, c. 12r.

4. ASF, S. Caterina, ms. 17, #43. Caterina entered S. Caterina in 1594, and died 5 August 1641.

5. The minute books for S. Bartolomeo's Conservatori note in June 1593 that the lists of boys will henceforth be kept in a separate volume, but no such volume remains. ASB, PIE, S. Bartolomeo di Reno, ms. 7/1, c. 50r .

6. ASB, PIE, S. Maria Maddalena/S. Onofrio, ms. 2/2, c. 23r. By 1664, S. Onofrio expected the *massaro* (now called the *camerlengo*) to be more active in seeking out opportunities for those boys whom the *guardiano* thinks are ready to work. Ibid., 2/3, cap. XIX.

7. ASF, Bigallo ms. 1669/II, cc. 9r–10r.

8. The Bigallo made two payments of 7 lire each. ASF, Bigallo ms. 1679, cc. 49v, 50r.

9. ASF, Bigallo ms. 1669/II, cc. 10r–22v.

10. For Stretta statutes and matriculation, see BCB, Gozz, 210, cc. 63–80. The Stretta matriculation recorded members by seniority, and had Stiatici at the head of the list (c. 64r). S. Bartolomeo's administrative records evolved from the generic *Scritture di Cassa* (1527–42; ASB, PIE, S. Bartolomeo di Reno, ms. 282) and miscellaneous financial and legal records to a system of daily ledgers (*Libri Giornale*) and account books (*Libri Mastri*) begun in 1546 (ibid., mss. 136, 154), before adding the minutes of its governing councils in 1588 (ibid., mss. 7/1, 7/2).

11. The company made the threat in 1590, and described it as a way to alleviate (*allecxtiare*) the boys' suffering: ASB, PIE, S. Bartolomeo di Reno, ms. 7/2, cc. 23v.

12. *Provisione elemosinaria per li poveri di qualunque sorte della città di Bologna* (Bologna: 1548). Mentzer, "Organizational Endeavour and Charitable Impulse," 25. In the 1593 list discussed below, only one of the sixteen boys is in this situation, staying in the home of Count Battista Bentivoglio. ASB, PIE, S. Bartolomeo di Reno, ms. 7/1, c. 50r.

13. The boys placed with pin-makers earned the most (50 and 33 lire), followed by those with shoemakers (36, 36, 30 lire), barbers (31, 30, 30 lire), tailors (24, 16 lire), the domestic servant (27 lire), and the painter (18 lire).

14. ASB, PIE, S. Bartolomeo di Reno, mss. 7/1, c. 50r; 7/2, cc. 24v.

15. ASB, PIE, S. Bartolomeo di Reno, ms. 7/2, cc. 4r, 6r.

16. ASB, PIE, S. Bartolomeo di Reno, ms. 7/2, 25v, 26r. Another legacy of 1,000 lire directed to feeding, teaching, and outfitting two boys preparing for the priesthood was given by the widow Vinceza Paselli Lodi in 1558, and registered by the notary Alessandro Stiatici: ASB, PIE, S. Maria del Baraccano, ms. 546, c. 131r. ASB, PIE, S. Maria Maddalena, ms. 2/3, cap. XVIII. Though the statute reform was not published until 1664, it seems to enshrine a long-standing practice. The only *assonti* on leave-taking in records stretching from 1562 to 1569, and from 1576 to 1603, are two members appointed 14 May 1600: ibid., 5/9 (np).

17. In 1692, S. Maria del Baraccano set a maximum age of 25 for girls with relatives in the city and 30 for those without, but it is not clear if this rule was ever followed. ASB, Dem, S. Maria del Baraccano, 8/7646, "G."

18. Of twenty-three girls who take orders in the three Baraccano lists, further information is given for seventeen. Only five become tertiaries, and the rest go to convents in

Bologna, Florence, Torino, and Faenza. ASB, PIE, S. Maria del Baraccano, mss. 6/1 cc. 28, 57, 61, 63, 64, 73, 83, 99, 104; 6/2 cc. 82, 98, 100, 115, 128, 143; 7 cc. 21, 27, 39, 46, 49, 56 (all references recto and verso).

19. ASF, S. Caterina, ms. 17, #7.

20. ASF, S. Caterina, ms. 17 (np), ##20, 24, 25, 31, 38, 42, 45, 53, 60, 87.

21. ASB, PIE, S. Maria del Baraccano, ms. 6/1, cc. 37r, 54r, 56r, 72r, 73r, 79r, 84r, 96v. In the 1570 cohort, three were returned to mothers due to contagious illness, and one went to a family member because of *indisposicioni*. She later went to the Mendicanti workhouse and died there. Ibid., ms. 6/2, cc. 17r, 26r, 53r, 56r.

22. The expulsions for demon possession occurred between 1583 and 1588: ASB, PIE, S. Maria del Baraccano, ms. 6/2, cc. 91v, 136v, 142v, 145v, 147v, 150v.

23. Arrizabalaga et al., *Great Pox*, 145–68, 187–201.

24. I am grateful to Dr. Anne Dillon for suggesting this hypothesis and for sources on the epidemiology of late congenital syphilis. See McMillan et al., *Clinical Practice in Sexually Transmissible Infections*, 429–32; Hutchinson and Hook, "Syphilis in Adults," 1389–1416; Holmes et al., *Sexually Transmitted Diseases*, 363–67. See also Quétel, *History of Syphilis*; Arrizabalaga et al., *Great Pox*, 234–51.

25. ASF, Ceppo ms. 69, 18r, 19r.

26. Some examples: ASB, PIE, S. Maria del Baraccano, ms. 7, cc. 32r (January 1589), 38v (January 1592), 61r (July 1599), 61v (January 1600). The Baraccano's emphasis on seniority can also be seen in the overlap on matriculation lists. When Florentine homes began a new list, they registered the existing cohort alphabetically. Bolognese homes registered this cohort by date of entry.

27. Ages are recorded until March 1575 (90v), after which they are omitted save for the ages of fourteen girls admitted in April 1578 (119r–138v): ASB, PIE, S. Maria del Baraccano, ms. 6/2.

28. BCB, ms. B3633, 147, 176. ASB, PIE, S. Maria del Baraccano, ms. 1/2, c. 10r. Cornelia had a legacy of 300 lire, two subsidies of 100 lire and one of 50 from three aunts, and 50 lire from the Baraccano: it noted, "li suoi la maritano del loro per la maggior parte": ibid., ms. 6/2, cc. 63v–64r.

29. ASB, PIE, S. Croce, ms. 1/2 (supplementary), cap. 17. Both dowries were in cash and goods. ASB, PIE, S. Maria del Baraccano, ms. 1/2, c. 10v; 1/3, p. 64. Dowries given to the 51 girls of the 1554 cohort who married or entered a convent averaged 258 lire (median = 200 lire). For the 39 girls in the 1570 cohort who married, the average dowry was 219 lire and the median was 200. ASB, PIE, S. Maria del Baraccano, mss. 6/1, 6/2.

30. Carboni, *Le doti della "povertà,"* 16–17, 30–42, 56, 184–94. Alessandro Pastore has found that artisans' dowries in the first half of the seventeenth century ranged between 200 and 1,600 lire in the city, and 80 and 1,000 lire in the *contado*. Pastore, "Rapporti familiari e pratica testamentaria," 163–64.

31. In 1548, the Baraccano described its girls' dowries as "denari di lavori e per l'elemosine." ASB, PIE, S. Maria del Baraccano, ms. 110, c. 26r. Ciammitti, "Quanta costa," 482–84.

32. ASB, PIE, S. Maria del Baraccano, ms. 6/2, cc. 52v–53r. Ortensia returned to her widowed mother 17 March 1581, and subsequently entered a convent.

33. ASB, PIE, S. Maria del Baraccano, mss. 6/1; 7, cc. 1v–20v. Dowry amounts in lire: 100 (1), 200 (33), 300 (7). Those receiving 200 lire had been in an average of 115 months (range: 30–161), and those receiving 300 an average of 125 months (range: 72–180). The

single dowry of 100 lire went to a girl resident for 161 months (c. 9v). The 1570–84 matriculation (ms. 6.2) overlaps with both of these: of seventy-three girls marrying, the Baraccano clearly dowers thirty-four, all of whom also received funds from family or donors.

34. Bologna avoided the centralized funds found in Rome, Florence, and Venice, and distributed dotal charity though a host of semiautonomous social groups. Carboni notes, among mid-sixteenth-century groups, the Monte di Pietà (20 dowries annually), guilds (10), confraternities (20), Poveri Vergognosi (9), parishes (80), and religious orders (20). Carboni, *Le doti della "povertà,"* 17, 40–49. See also Chabot and Fornasari, *L'economia della carità*. On the Vita dowry processions, see Ciammitti, "Quanto costa," 486–87.

35. ASB, PIE, S. Maria del Baraccano, mss. 6/1, cc. 12r, 13r, 15r, 21r, 22r, 24r, 27r, 33r, 35v–r, 45r, 48r, 58r, 78r, 113r, 122r, 126r; 6/2, cc. 8r–41r. Bono served on the 12 Conservatori seven times from 1534 to 1556, and was prior in 1555. Lodi was a member of the 12 Conservatori in 1554, and the prior of the supernumaries in 1558. ASB, PIE, S. Maria del Baraccano, 11, cc. iv– vii, 4r–7r, 13r, 38r–39v. Signora Faustina Malvasia offered three dowries of 50 lire to the 1570–84 cohort: ms. 6/2, cc. 65r, 73r, 76r.

36. The fourteenth girl died before she could opt for either. In the end, two others died soon after, and so all three dowries returned to the conservatory and three more were chosen. ASB, PIE, S. Maria del Baraccano, ms. 7, 33r–34v.

37. Michelozzi's legacy was given 10 March 1593 and the first dowry was awarded a day later. The last recorded dowry was awarded in 1625, and in 1628 administrators calculated the heirs' obligation to be fiorini 269.4.2, yet no further dowries are recorded. ASF, S. Caterina, ms. 17 (np).

38. The record notes 87 dowries for the 122 girls who either marry or enter a convent. These range from 40 to 3,500 lire, with 5 at 1,000 lire and above. The average dowry was lire 319.19, while the median was still 200 lire. ASB, PIE, S. Maria del Baraccano, mss. 6/2 and 7. For examples of property inventories: ms. 7, cc. 32r, 35v, 59r.

39. Ciammitti, "Quanto costa," 469–97.

40. Sixtus IV began the Roman practice with processions on the Monday following Pentecost. In these Roman processions, girls could be picked out by bystanders, married at the conclusion of the procession, and be on their way to their new marital home by nightfall. Howe, "Appropriating Space," 248–49.

41. "non mostra nella sua persona molta sanità," cited in Ciammitti, "Quanto costa," 484.

42. Thirty-five of the 161 girls in the Baraccano's 1554–68 cohort had skills or artisinal training, usually in the textile trade. Of these, 26 married (79.41%), or over twice the rate of 31.05 percent for the group as a whole. The men they married came from a range of occupations including and beyond textiles. ASB, PIE, S. Maria del Baraccano, ms. 6/1. The first statutes for Florence's S. Maria Vergine and S. Niccolò both emphasized finding artisans who could benefit from a girl's skills.

43. ASB, PIE, S. Maria del Baraccano, ms. 6/1, cc. 66v–67r.

44. This became the norm from the mid-seventeenth century, when families contributed more of the dowry and played a larger role in chosing a groom. Ciammitti, "Quanto costa," 471, 482–84.

45. ASB, PIE, S. Maria del Baraccano, ms. 6.2, cc. 99r, 105r, 109r, 137r, 143r.

46. Bell, *How to Do It*, 200–202.

47. BCB, ms. B3633, pp. 144–45. ASB, PIE, S. Maria del Baraccano, mss. 1/2, cc. 9r–

10v; 1/3, pp. 62–67. From 1559 to 1569, there were seven instances when two girls married in a single day, and from 1585 to 1601 there were eight. ASB, PIE, S. Maria del Baracanno, 7, cc. 3r, 5–12r, 17r, 20r, 25r, 30r, 32r, 40r. ASB, PIE, S. Croce, ms. 1/1, cap. 6, 22; 1/2, cap. 7, 11.

48. The Baraccano paid 6 percent interest on dowry accounts. ASB, PIE, S. Maria del Baraccano, ms. 6.2, cc. 57v–58r. On later forms of security and social control, see Ciammitti, "Quanto costa," 472–82.

49. The Baraccano demanded return of half the dowry, and requiring that half be invested in Monte credits under the conservatory's management was aimed at least in part at avoiding lawsuits. ASB, PIE, S. Maria del Baraccano, ms. 110, cc. 26r, 87v, 98r, 137r. Ciammitti, "Quanto costa," 472–82.

50. In a 1641 addition, S. Marta required a larger vote for monachation (75%) than for marriage (66%), likely an indication that dowry inflation for the former required more caution. Of four documents between 1582 and 1604 where convents acknowledge that dowries had been paid in full by S. Maria del Baraccano, two are from a single convent in Faenza (SS. Trinità), one from Forlì, and one from Bologna. Two of the girls are recorded as entering as *conversa* and two as *monaca*. ASB, PIE, S. Maria del Baraccano, ms. 547, cc. 85v–89v.

51. For Pietà, see BRM, Acquisti Diversi, 93. For Carità, see Cionacci, "Vettorio dell'Ancisa," ASF, S. Caterina, ms. 7, I/5.

52. Gavitt, "Charity and State Building," 241. Trexler, "A Widows' Asylum," 444–48.

53. "Cronicha delle Suore della Pietà," 20–22.

54. At S. Caterina, exits also dropped dramatically. Exits by decade for the group enrolled 1591–1635: 1590s (64), 1600s (40), 1610s (22), 1620s (25), 1630s (10), 1640s (5). ASF, S. Caterina, ms. 17 (np). S. Caterina formally became a convent in 1734. ASF, Inventory N407, iv.

55. Florence had 42 convents in 1545, and between 63 and 69 by the end of the seventeenth century. Though equal numbers of men and women had entered orders in the early fifteenth century, by the mid-sixteenth century four times as many women as men were taking this step. Cohen, *Evolution of Women's Asylums*, 28–30, 187. Bologna had 27 convents in 1550, rising to 33 by 1634. The monachation rate was similar in Venice: see Sperling, *Convents and the Body Politic*, 18–29. Gabriella Zarri estimates that the 2,198 nuns resident in Bologna in 1570 represented 5.4 percent of the total population; the percentage rose to 7.4 percent by 1631. Zarri, "I monasteri femminili a Bologna," 144–45.

CONCLUSION: The Politics of Renaissance Orphanages

1. Black, *Italian Confraternties*, 206–11. Camerano, "Assistenza richiesta ed assistenza imposta," 227–60. Sonnino, "Between the Home and the Hospice," 94–116. Lazar, "'E faucibus deamonis,'" 259–79.

2. Falciola, "Assistenza a Milano," 169–98.

3. Gager, *Blood Ties and Fictive Ties*, 105–12.

4. Manzione, *Christ's Hospital of London*.

5. Safley, *Charity and Economy*, 1–3.

6. McCants, *Civic Charity in a Golden Age*, 22–24.

7. Pullan, "Orphans and Foundlings in Early Modern Europe."

APPENDIX: Institutional Finances

1. In a 1572 inventory, S. Bartolomeo di Reno recorded 8.5 houses, 2 shops, one farm, one vineyard, 2 rooms, and a grain storehouse, which collectively generated almost 1,000 lire annually. ASB, S. Bartolomeo di Reno, ms. 137, c. 293.

Bibliography

ARCHIVAL SOURCES

Bologna

Archivio Arcivescovile di Bologna (AAB)
Miscellanea vecchie 158G, 619G, 619/31, 621 (K 251 33 D), 622
Raccolta degli statuti, cart 26.

Archivio di Stato di Bologna (ASB)

    Archivio Notarile: Amministrazione di Beni di Pupilli, #1 (1390–1454)

    Assunteria dei Magistrati: Affari diversi cittadinanze 121, fasc. 1

    Fondo Demaniale (Dem)
    Compagna de S. Bartolomeo de Reno, ms. 2/7651
    Compagnia ed Ospitale de Putti di S. Giacomo, mss. 5/6463, 12/6470

    Governo, Statuti
    Vol. XIV (1389–1453), Libro IV, Rubric 84

    Pii Istituti Educativi (PIE)
    Conservatorio di S. Croce, mss. 1/1–4, 2/1–5, 3, 4, 19, 26, 83, 149
    Conservatorio di S. Giuseppe, mss. 1/1–2, 19, 23
    Conservatorio di S. Maria del Baraccano, mss. 1/1–4, 1b, 4, 6/I-II, 7, 11, 12, 35, 43,
        44, 110, 264, 265, 274, 275, 297, 298, 546, 547
    Orfanotrofio di S. Bartolomeo di Reno, mss. 7/1, 7/1a, 7/2, 78, 138, 139, 234, 279,
        282
    Orfanotrofio di S. Maria Maddalena o di S. Onofrio, mss. 1, 2/1–5, 3, 4/2–8, 5/9–13,
        13, 14, 78, 79

Biblioteca Comunale di Bologna (BCB)
ms. B1829, B3633, B3598

    Fondo Gozzadini (Gozz), 210

Unità Sanitaria Locale (USL)
#29

Florence

Archivio Arcivescovile di Firenze (AAF)
VP 07 Pastoral visits of Antonio Altoviti (1568)
VP 08 Pastoral visits of Alessandro de'Medici (1589)

Archivio di Stato di Firenze (ASF)
Compagnia poi Magistrato del Bigallo (Inventory N145), mss. 22, 23, 24, 52, 54, 143,
    154, 155, 157, 234, 619, 768, 769, 1360, 1459, 1460, 1669, 1671, 1679, 1687
Conservatorio di Domenicani denominato La Pietà di Firenze, Corporazione religiose
    soppresse dal governo Francese, #112 (CRSF 112) (Inventory N137A), mss. 2, 3, 4,
    31, 78, 79, 80, 81, 85, 86, 87, 88, 90, 96, 97
Fanciulle Abbandonate di S. Maria e di S. Niccolò dette 'del Ceppo' (Inventory N409),
    mss. 1bis, 59, 69, 141, 145, 237, 245
Fanciulle di Santa Caterina (Inventory N407), mss. 1, 7, 17, 25, 36
Tratte, ms. 725

Biblioteca Nazionale Centrale di Firenze (BNCF)
ms. II.I.410
Poligrafo Gargani

Biblioteca Riccardiana Moreniana (BRM)
Fondo Bigazzi ms. 61
Bibl. Moreniana, Acquisiti Diversi, ms. 93
Cod. Moreni 57

MANUSCRIPTS AND PRINTED PRIMARY SOURCES

Antoniano, S. *Dell'educazione cristiana de figliuoli.* Verona: 1584.
Avertimenti, et brievi ricordi circa il vivere christiano. Bologna: 1563.
Brucker, G., ed., *Two Memoirs of Renaissance Florence.* New York: Harper & Row, 1967.
Calzoni, F. *Storia della chiesa parrochiale di S. Maria in via Mascarella.* Bologna: 1785.
Carrati, B. "Miscellanea storica Bolognese." BCB 695.
Caterina de'Ricci. *Le lettere di S. Caterina de'Ricci.* Ed. C. Guasti. Florence: 1890.
Cionacci, F. "Notizie di Messer Vettorio dell'Ancisa Fondatore dell fanciulle Stabilite di
    Firenze." BNCF ms. II.I.410.
"Cronicha delle Suore della Pietà." Bibl. Moreniana, Acquisiti Diversi, ms. 93.
Faggioli, C. "Origine ed appunti storici del Conservatorio delle zitelle di S. Croce ..."
    Unnumbered mss. in ASB, PIE, S. Croce, cart. 1.
Fantuzzi, G. *Notizie degli scrittori bolognesi.* 8 vols. Bologna: 1789.
Gamurrini. E. *Istoria delle famiglie nobili Toscane et Umbre.* Florence: 1668–73.
Ghirardacci, C. *Historia di Bologna.* Bologna: 1657.
*Istitutione, provisione, e capitoli dello Hospitale, e governo delli Poveri Mendicanti della Città de
    Bologna.* Bologna: 1564.
Ledesima, D. *Dottrina christiana breve per insegnar in pochi giorni per interrogatione, a modo
    di Dialogo, fra'l Maestro e Discepolo.* Bologna: 1569.

Marchi, F. *Vita di Alessandro Capocchi*. Firenze: 1583.

Mecatti, G. M. *Della nobiltà, e cittadinanza di Firenze*. Naples: 1754.

Memmo, G. M. *Dialogo del Magn. Cavaliere M. Gio Maria Memmo, nel quale dopo alcune filosofiche dispute, si forma un perfetto Prencipe, & una perfetta Republica, e parimente un SENATORE, un Cittadino, un Soldato, & un Mercatante. Diviso in tre libri*. Venice: 1563.

Modo et ordine per li poveri mendicanti fatto nuovamente nella citta di Bologna. Bologna: 1550.

Provisione elemosinaria per li poveri di qualunque sorte della città di Bologna. Bologna: 1548.

Regola de'costumi christiani alli fanciulli desidere di vivere in gratia di Dio, de suoi maggiori, & d'ogni buon Christiano. Bologna: nd

Regolamenti sopra Deputazione dei Poveri Bisognosi dal 1647 al 1677. ASF *Pratica Segreta* 184.

Richa, G. *Notizie istoriche delle chiese fiorentine*. 8 vols. Firenze: 1758.

Rinieri, G. *Cronaca 1535–1549*. Ed. A. Antonelli and R. Pedrini. Bologna: Costa editore, 1998.

Soranus, *Gynecology*. Ed. and trans. O. Temkin. Baltimore: Johns Hopkins Press, 1956. 62–68.

Stiatici, A. *Narratione overo chronicha del principio, & fundatione, & successo dell'Hospitale di Santo Bartolomeo*. Bologna: 1590.

Vives, J. L. *On Assistance to the Poor*. Ed. A. Tobriner. Toronto: University of Toronto Press, 1999.

SECONDARY SOURCES

Accarrino, Anna, and Lia Aquilano, eds. *L'Archivio dell'Opera Pia dei Poveri Vergognosi in Bologna*. Bologna: Istituto per la storia di Bologna, 1999.

Aranci, Gilberto. *Formazione religiosa e santità laicale a Firenze tra cinque e seicento*. Florence: Giampiero Pagnini, 1997.

———. *Vittorio Dell'Ancisa: Un prete fiorentino del Cinquecento e l'origine delle "Stabilite nella Carità."* Firenze: Giampiero Pagnini, 1997.

Ariès, Philippe. *Centuries of Childhood: A Social History of Family Life*. New York: Knopf, 1962.

Arrizabalaga, J. J. Henderson, and R. French. *The Great Pox: The French Disease in Renaissance Europe*. New Haven: Yale University Press, 1997.

Balestracci, Duccio. *The Renaissance in the Fields: Family Memoirs of a Fifteenth-Century Tuscan Peasant*. Trans. P. Squariti and B. Merideth. University Park: Pennsylvania State University Press, 1999.

Banker, James. *Death in the Community: Memorialization and Confraternities in an Italian Commune in the Late Middle Ages*. Athens: University of Georgia Press, 1988.

I Bastardini: Patrimonio e memoria di un ospedale bolognese. Bologna: Edizioni A.G.E., 1990.

Bell, Rudolph. *How to Do It: Guides to Good Living for Renaissance Italians*. Chicago: University of Chicago Press, 1999.

Berner, Samuel Joseph. "The Florentine Patriciate in the Transition from Republic to Principato, 1530–1610." Ph.D. diss., University of California at Berkeley, 1969.

Black, Christopher. *Italian Confraternities in the Sixteenth Century*. Cambridge: Cambridge University Press, 1989.

Boswell, John. *The Kindness of Strangers: The Abandonment of Children in Western Europe from Late Antiquity to the Renaissance*. New York: Pantheon Books, 1988.

Brackett, John K. *Criminal Justice and Crime in Late Renaissance Florence, 1537–1609.* Cambridge: Cambridge University Press, 1992.

———. "Who Were the Deserving Poor in Late Renaissance Florence?" Renaissance Society of America, Florence, Italy, 22 March 2000.

Brown, Judith. *Immodest Acts: The Life of a Lesbian Nun in Renaissance Italy.* New York: 1986.

Brucker, Gene. *The Society of Renaissance Florence.* New York: Harper & Row, 1971.

Calori, Giovanni. *Una iniziativa sociale nella Bologna del '500: L'opera dei Mendicanti.* Bologna: Azzoguidi, 1972.

Calvi, Giulia. *Il contratto morale: Madri e figli nella Toscana moderna.* Rome: Laterza, 1994.

———. "Reconstructing the Family: Widowhood and Remarriage in Tuscany in the Early Modern Period." In *Marriage in Italy, 1300–1650,* ed. T. Dean and K.J.P. Lowe. Cambridge: Cambridge University Press, 1998. 275–96.

Carboni, Mauro. *Il debito della città: Mercato del credito fisco e società a Bologna fra Cinque e Seicento.* Bologna: il Mulino, 1995.

———. *Le doti della "povertà": Famiglia, risparmio, previdenza: il Monte del Matrimonio di Bologna (1583–1796).* Bologna: il Mulino, 1999.

———. "La formazione di una elite di governo: le alleanze matrimoniali dei senatori bolognesi (1506–1796)." *Studi storici Luigi Simeoni* 52 (2002): 9–46.

Casagrande, Giovanna. *Religiosità penitenziale e città al tempo dei comuni.* Rome: Istituto storico dei Cappuccini, 1995.

Chabot, Isabelle, and Massimo Fornasari. *L'economia della carità: Le doti del Monte di Pietà di Bologna (secoli XVI–XX).* Bologna: il Mulino, 1997.

Chambers, David, and Brian Pullan. *Venice: A Documentary History, 1450–1630.* Oxford: Blackwell, 1992.

Chretien, Heidi L. *The Festival of San Giovanni: Imagery and Political Power in Renaissance Florence.* New York: Peter Lang, 1994.

Ciammitti, Luisa. "Quanto costa essere normali, La dote nel conservatorio femminile di Santa Maria del Baraccano (1630–1680)." *Quaderni storici* 53 (1983): 469–97.

———. "Fanciulle monache madre. Povertà femminile e previdenza a Bologna nei secoli XVI–XVIII." In *Arte e pieta: I patrimoni culturali delle Opere Pie.* Bologna: 1980. 461–520.

Cochrane, Eric. *Florence in the Forgotten Centuries, 1527–1800.* Chicago: University of Chicago Press, 1973.

Cohen, Sherrill. *The Evolution of Women's Asylums Since 1500.* New York: Oxford University Press, 1992.

Comerford, Kathleen. *Ordaining the Catholic Reformation: Priests and Seminary Pedagogy in Fiesole, 1575–1675.* Florence: L. S. Olschki, 2001.

Coster, William. *Baptism and Spiritual Kinship in Early Modern England.* Aldershot: Ashgate, 2002.

———. "'From Fire and Water': The Responsibilities of Godparents in Early Modern England." In *The Church and Childhood,* Studies in Church History, vol. 31, ed. D. Wood. Oxford: Blackwell, 1994. 301–11.

Cunningham, Hugh. *Children and Childhood in Western Society since 1500.* London: Longman, 1995.

d'Addario, Arnaldo. "Noti di storia della religiosità e della carità dei Fiorentini nel secolo XVI." *Archivio storico italiano* 126 (1968): 61–147.

Dall'Olio, Guido. *Eretici e Inquisitori nella Bologna del Cinquecento.* Bologna: Istituto per la storia di Bologna, 1999.

De Benedictis, Angela. *Repubblica per contratto. Bologna: una città europea nello Stato della Chiesa.* Bologna: il Mulino, 1995.

Diana, Esther. *San Matteo e San Giovanni di Dio: Due ospedali nella storia fiorentina.* Florence: Le Lettere, 1999.

Eckstein, Nicholas. *The District of the Green Dragon: Neighbourhood Life and Social Change in Renaissance Florence.* Florence: L. S. Olschki, 1995.

Eisenbichler, Konrad. *The Boys of the Archangel Raphael: A Youth Confraternity in Florence, 1411–1785.* Toronto: University of Toronto Press, 1998.

Esposito, Anna. "St. Francesca and the Female Religious Communities of Fifteenth Century Rome." In *Women and Religion in Medieval and Renaissance Italy,* ed. D. Bornstein and R. Rusconi. Chicago: University of Chicago Press, 1996. 197–218.

Falciola, Enrica. "Per una storia dell'assistenza a Milano: il Collegio di San Giacomo per gli orfani dei militari spagnoli (1582–1781)." *Archivio storico Lombardo,* series 11, vol. II, anno CXI (1985): 169–98.

Fanti, M. *Confraternite e città a Bologna nel medioevo e nell'età moderna.* Rome: Herder Editrice, 2001.

Farné, Andrea. *Opere pie a Bologna: Ruolo e storia della Compagnia de'Poveri Vergognosi.* Bologna: Le Coq, 1989.

Fasano Guarini, Elena. *Lo stato mediceo di Cosimo I.* Firenze: Sansoni, 1973.

Ferguson, George. *Signs and Symbols in Christian Art.* New York: Oxford University Press, 1961.

Ferrante, Lucia. "Il sostegno alle giovane declassate: L'Opera Pia dei Poveri Vergognosi di Bologna e il Conservatorio di Santa Marta." In *Povertà e innovazioni istituzionali in Italia,* ed. V. Zamagni. Bologna: il Mulino, 2000. 207–24.

Ferraro, Joanne M., *Marriage Wars in Late Renaissance Venice.* New York: Oxford University Press, 2001.

Fisher, Caroline. "A Family Affair? Guardianship in Late Fourteenth-Century Florence." Paper presented at Sixteenth Century Studies Conference, Denver, Colo., October 2001.

Fornasari, Massimo. *Il "thesoro" della città: Il Monte di Pietà e l'economia bolognese nei secoli XV e XVI.* Bologna: il Mulino, 1993.

Fornasini, Giovanni. *La chiesa priorale e parrochiale di S. Maria e S. Domenica detta della Mascarella in Bologna.* Bologna: La Grafica Emilia, 1943.

Foschi, Paola. "La Compagnia e il Conservatorio del Baraccano nella storia Bolognese." In *Il Conservatorio del Baraccano. La storia e i restauri,* ed. P. Foschi and F. Giordano. Bologna: Costa Editore, 2002. 25–27.

Gager, Kristin. *Blood Ties and Fictive Ties: Adoption and Family Life in Early Modern France.* Princeton: Princeton University Press, 1996.

Gavitt, Phillip. *Charity and Children in Renaissance Florence: The Ospedale degli Innocenti, 1410–1536.* Ann Arbor: University of Michigan Press, 1990.

———. "Charity and State Building in Cinquecento Florence: Vincenzo Borghini as Administrator of the Ospedale degli Innocenti." *Journal of Modern History* 69 (1997): 230–70.

Gentilcore, David. *Healers and Healing in Early Modern Italy.* Manchester: Manchester University Press, 1998.

Gill, Katherine. "*Scandala:* Controversies concerning *Clausura* and Women's Religious Communities in Late Medieval Italy." In *Christendom and Its Discontents: Exclusion, Persecution, and Rebellion, 1000–1500,* ed. S. L. Waugh and P. D. Diehl. Cambridge: Cambridge University Press, 1996. 177–203.

Glixon, Jonathan. *Honoring God and the City: Music at the Venetian Confraternities, 1260–1807.* Oxford: Oxford University Press, 2003.

Goldthwaite, Richard W., and William R. Rearick. "Michelozzo and the Ospedale di San Paulo in Florence." *Mittelungen des Kunsthistoriches Institutes in Florenz* 21 (1977): 275–80.

Grandi, C., ed. *"Benedetto chi ti porta, maledetto chi ti manda": L'infanzia abbandonata nel Triveneto (secoli XV–XIX).* Treviso: Edizioni Fondazione Bennetton Studi Ricerche, 1997.

Grendler, Paul. *Schooling in Renaissance Italy: Literacy and Learning, 1300–1600.* Baltimore: Johns Hopkins University Press, 1989.

Grieco, Allen J. "The Social Politics of Pre-Linnean Botanical Classification." *I Tatti Studies* 4 (1991): 131–49.

Guidicini, Giuseppe. *Cose notabili della storia di Bologna.* 5 vols. Bologna: Giacomo Monti, 1868–73.

———. *I Riformatori dello stato di libertà della città di Bologna dal 1394 al 1797.* 3 vols. Bologna: Regio Tipografia, 1876.

Haas, Louis. *The Renaissance Man and His Children.* New York: St. Martins, 1998.

Hanawalt, Barbara. *The Ties That Bound: Peasant Families in Medieval England.* Oxford: Oxford University Press, 1986.

Henderson, John. "Epidemics in Renaissance Florence: Medical Theory and Government Response." In *Maladie et Société (XIIe–XVIIIe siecles),* ed. N. Bulst and R. Delort. Paris: Editions de C.N.R.S., 1989. 165–86.

———. "The Hospitals of Late Medieval and Renaissance Florence: A Preliminary Survey." In *The Hospital in History,* ed. L. Granshaw and R. Porter. London: Routledge, 1989. 63–92.

———. *Piety and Charity in Late Medieval Florence.* Oxford: Oxford University Press, 1994.

Herlihy, David, and Christiane Klapsich-Zuber. *Tuscans and Their Families: A Study of the Florentine Catasto of 1427.* New Haven: Yale University Press, 1985.

Holmes, K. K., et al. *Sexually Transmitted Diseases.* New York: McGraw-Hill, 1984.

Howe, Eunice D. "Appropriating Space: Women's Place in Confraternal Life at Santo Spirito in Sassia, Rome." In *Confraternities and the Visual Arts in Italy,* ed. B. Wisch and D. C. Ahl. Cambridge: Cambridge University Press, 2000. 235–58.

Hutchinson, C. M., and E. W. Hook. "Syphilis in Adults." *Medical Clinics of North America* 74, no. 6 (1990): 1389–1416.

Jütte, Robert. *Poverty and Deviance in Early Modern Europe.* Cambridge: Cambridge University Press, 1994.

Kent, Dale. "The Buonomini di San Martino: Charity for 'the Glory of God, the Honour of the City, and the Commemoration of Myself.'" In *Cosimo "il Vecchio" de'Medici, 1389–1464,* ed. R. Ames-Lewis. Oxford: Oxford University Press, 1992. 49–67.

King, Ross. *Brunelleschi's Dome: The Story of the Great Cathedral in Florence.* London: Pimlico, 2001.

Klapisch-Zuber, Christiane. "The 'Cruel Mother': Maternity, Widowhood, and Dowry in Florence in the Fourteenth and Fifteenth Centuries." In *Women, Family, and Ritual in Renaissance Italy*. Chicago: University of Chicago Press, 1985. 117–31.

———. "Demographic Decline and Household Structure: The Example of Prato, Late Fourteenth to Late Fifteenth Centuries." In *Women, Family, and Ritual in Renaissance Italy*. Chicago: University of Chicago Press, 1985. 23–35.

Kuehn, Thomas. "Adoption à Florence à la fin du Moyen Age." *Médiévales* 35 (1998): 69–81.

———. *Illegitimacy in Renaissance Florence*. Ann Arbor: University of Michigan Press, 2002.

Landi, Fiorenzo. "Per una storia dei falsi in bilancio: le contabilità pubbliche dei conventi e dei luoghi pii." In *L'uso del denaro. Patrimoni e amministrazione nei luoghi pii in Italia (secoli XV–XVIII)*, ed. A. Pastore and M. Garbellotti. Bologna: il Mulino, 2001. 41–62.

Levin, William R. "Advertising Charity in the Trecento: The Public Decorations of the Misericordia in Florence." *Studies in Iconography* 17 (1996): 215–309.

———. "Confraternal Self-Imaging in Marian Art at the Museo del Bigallo in Florence." *Confraternitas* 10 (1999): 3–14.

Litchfield, R. Burr. *Emergence of a Bureaucracy: The Florentine Patricians, 1530–1790*. Princeton: Princeton University Press, 1986.

Logan, Oliver. "Counter-Reformatory Theories of Upbringing in Italy." *The Church and Childhood: Studies in Church History* 31 (1994): 275–84.

Lombardi, Daniela. *Povertà maschile, povertà femminile: L'ospedale dei Mendicanti nella Firenze dei Medici*. Bologna: il Mulino, 1988.

———. "Poveri a Firenze. Programmi e realizzazioni della politica assistenziale dei Medici tra cinque e seicento." In *Timore e carità: I poveri nell'Italia moderna*, ed. Giorgio Politi et al. Cremona: Biblioteca Statale, 1982. 164–84.

Macey, Patrick. *"Infiamma il mio cor:* Savonarolan *Laude* by and for Dominican Nuns in Tuscany." In *The Crannied Wall: Women, Religion, and the Arts in Early Modern Europe*, ed. C. A. Monson. Ann Arbor: University of Michigan Press, 1992.

Malamina, P. "L'Industria fiorentina in declino fra Cinque e Seicento: Linee per un'analisi comparata." In *Firenze e la Toscana dei Medici nell'Europa del '500*. Firenze: L. S. Olschki, 1983. 295–308.

Manno Tolu, Rosalia. "Echi Savonaroliani nella Compagnia e nel conservatorio della Pietà." In *Savonarola e la politica*, ed. G. C. Garfagnini. Firenze: Edizioni del Galluzzo, 1997. 209–24.

———. "'Ricordanze' delle abbandonate fiorentine di Santa Maria e San Niccolò del Ceppo nei secoli XVII–XVIII." In *Studi in onore di Arnaldo D'Addario*, ed. L. Borgia et al. Lecce: Conti, 1995.

Manzione, C. K. *Christ's Hospital of London, 1552–1598: A Passing Deed of Pity*. Selinsgrove: Susquehanna University Press, 1995.

Maragi, Mario. *I cinquecento anni del monte di Bologna*. Bologna: Banca del Monte, 1973.

Marcello, L. "Andare a bottega: Adolescenza e apprendistato nelle arti (Sec. XVI–XVII)." In *Infanzie*, ed. O. Niccoli. Florence: Ponte alle Grazie, 1993.

McCants, Anne E. C. *Civic Charity in a Golden Age: Orphanage Care in Early Modern Amsterdam*. Urbana: University of Illinois Press, 1997.

McMillan, A., et al. *Clinical Practice in Sexually Transmissible Infections*. London: Saunders, 2002.

Menning, Carol B. *Charity and State in Late Renaissance Italy: The Monte di Pietà of Florence.* Ithaca: Cornell University Press, 1993.

Mentzer, Raymond. "Organizational Endeavour and Charitable Impulse in Sixteenth Century France: The Care of Protestant Nimes." *French History* 5 (1991).

Micali, O. F., and P. Roselli. *Le soppressioni dei conventi a Firenze. Riuso e trasformazione dal sec. XVIII in poi.* Florence: L. S. Olschki, 1980.

Mola, Luca. *The Silk Industry of Renaissance Venice.* Baltimore: Johns Hopkins University Press, 2000.

Molinari, Massimo. *The Culture of Food.* Oxford: Blackwell, 1994.

Muir, Edward. *Mad Blood Stirring: Vendetta and Factions in Friuli during the Renaissance.* Baltimore: Johns Hopkins University Press, 1993.

Murphy, Caroline P. "'In Praise of the Ladies of Bologna': The Image and Identity of the Sixteenth-Century Bolognese Female Patriciate." *Renaissance Studies* 31, no. 4 (1999): 440–54.

Musacchio, Jacqueline M. *The Art and Ritual of Childbirth in Renaissance Italy.* New Haven: Yale University Press, 1999.

———. "The Rape of the Sabine Women on Quattrocento Marriage-Panels." In *Marriage in Italy, 1300–1650,* ed. Trevor Dean and Katherine Lowe. Cambridge: Cambridge University Press, 1998. 66–82.

Muzzarelli, Maria Giuseppina. *Il denaro e la salvezza: L'invenzione del Monte di Pietà.* Bologna: il Mulino, 2001.

Niccoli, Ottavia. "I bambini del Savonarola." In *Studi Savonaroliani: Verso il V centenario,* ed. G. C. Garfagnini. Florence: Edizioni del Galluzzo, 1996. 278–88.

———. "I 'fanciulli' del Savonarola: Usi religiosi e politici dell'infanzia nell'Italia del Rinascimento." In *Savonarole: Enjeux, Débats, Questions,* ed. A. Fontes et al. Paris: Université de la Sorbonne Nouvelle, 1997. 105–20.

———. *Il seme della violenza: Putti, fanciulli e mammoli nell'Italia tra Cinque e Seicento.* Bari: Laterza, 1995.

Parigino, Giuseppe V. *Il tesoro del principe: funzione pubblica e privata del patrimonio della famiglia Medici nel Cinquecento.* Firenze: L. S. Olschki, 1999.

Park, Katherine. "Healing the Poor: Hospitals and Medical Assistance in Renaissance Florence." In *Medicine and Charity before the Welfare State,* ed. J. Barry and C. Jones. London: Routledge, 1991. 26–45.

Park, Katherine, and John Henderson, "'The First Hospital among Christians': The Ospedale di S. Maria Nuova in Early Sixteenth-Century Florence." *Medical History* 35 (1991): 164–88.

Passerini, Luigi. *Storia degli stabilmenti di benificenza e d'istruzione elementare gratuita della città di Firenze.* Florence: Le Monnier, 1853.

Pastore, Alessandro. "Rapporti familiari e pratica testamentaria nella Bologna del Seicento." *Studi Storici* 25 (1984): 153–68.

Polecritti, Catherine L. *Preaching Peace in Renaissance Italy: Bernardino of Siena and His Audience.* Washington: Catholic University of America Press, 2000.

Polizzotto, Lorenzo. *Children of the Promise: The Confraternity of the Purification and the Socialization of Youths in Florence, 1427–1785.* Oxford: Oxford University Press, 2004.

———. "When Saints Fall Out: Women and Savonarolan Reform in Early Sixteenth-Century Florence." *Renaissance Quarterly* 46 (1993): 486–525.

————. *The Elect Nation: The Savonarolan Movement in Florence 1494–1545.* Oxford: Oxford University Press, 1994.

Poni, Carlo. "Per la storia del distretto industriale serico di Bologna (secoli XVI–XIX)." *Quaderni Storici* 73 (1990): 93–167.

Pullan, Brian. "Orphans and Foundlings in Early Modern Europe." In *Poverty and Charity: Europe, Italy, Venice, 1400–1700.* Aldershot: Variorum, 1994. III.

Quétel, C. *History of Syphilis.* Baltimore: Johns Hopkins University Press, 1990.

Riddle, John. *Conception and Abortion from the Ancient World to the Renaissance.* Cambridge, Mass.: Harvard University Press, 1992.

Robertson, Ian. *Tyranny under the Mantle of St. Peter: Pope Paul II and Bologna.* Turnhout: Brepols, 2002.

Rocke, Michael. *Forbidden Friendships: Homosexuality and Male Culture in Renaissance Florence.* New York: Oxford University Press, 1996.

Rolova, A. "La manifattura nell'industria tessile di Firenze del Cinquecento." In *Firenze e la Toscana dei Medici nell'Europa del '500.* Firenze: Olschki, 1983. 309–25.

Saalman, Howard. *The Bigallo: The Oratory and Residence of the Compagnia del Bigallo e della Misericordia in Florence.* New York: New York University Press, 1969.

Safley, Thomas M. *Charity and Economy in the Orphanages of Early Modern Augsburg.* Atlantic Highlands: Humanities Press, 1996.

Sandri, Lucia. "L'attività di banco di deposito dell'Ospedale degli Innocenti di Firenze: Don Vincenzo Borghini e la 'bancarotta' del 157." In *L'uso del denaro: Patrimoni e amministrazione nei luoghi pii e negli enti ecclesiastici in Italia (secoli XV–XVIII).* Bologna: il Mulino, 2001.

————. "Modalità dell'abbandono dei fanciulli in area urbana: gli esposti dell'ospedale di San Gallo di Firenze nella prima metà del XV secolo." In *Enfance abandonnée et société en Europe, XIVe–XXe siècle.* Rome: Ecole Francaise de Rome, 1991. 993–1015.

Sardi, D. "Fanciulli e angeli fanciulli." In *Infanzie,* ed. O. Niccoli. Florence: Ponte alle Grazie, 1993. 159–84.

Sebregondi, Ludovica. "Clothes and Teenagers: What Young Men Wore in Fifteenth Century Florence." In *The Premodern Teenager: Youth in Society, 1150–1650,* ed. K. Eisenbichler. Toronto: Centre for Renaissance and Reformation Studies, 2002. 27–50.

Sneider, Matthew. "Charity and Property: The Patrimonies of Bolognese *Opere Pie.*" Ph.D. diss., Brown University, 2004.

————. "Charity and Property: The Wealth of *Opere Pie* in Renaissance Bologna." In *Forme di povertà e innovazioni istituzionali,* ed. V. Negri Zamagni. Bologna: il Molino, 2000. 131–52.

Spicciani, Ameletto. "The 'Poveri Vergognosi' in Fifteenth Century Florence." In *Aspects of Poverty in Early Modern Europe,* ed. Thomas Riis. Florence: Le Monnier, 1981. 119–82.

Strocchia, Sharon. *Death and Ritual in Renaissance Florence.* Baltimore: Johns Hopkins University Press, 1992.

————. "Sisters in Spirit: The Nuns of S. Ambrogio and Their Consorority in Early Sixteenth-Century Florence." *Sixteenth Century Journal* 33, no. 3 (2002): 735–67.

————. "Taken into Custody: Girls and Convent Guardianship in Renaissance Florence." *Renaissance Studies* 17, no. 2 (2003): 177–200.

Taddei, Ilaria. *Fanciulli e giovani: Crescere a Firenze nel rinascimento.* Florence: L. S. Olschki, 2001.

Takahasi, Tomoko. "I bambini abbandonati presso lo Spedale di Santa Maria a San Gallo di Firenze nel tardo medioevo (1395–1463)." *Annuario dell'Istituto giapponese di cultura in Roma* 24 (1990–91): 59–79.

Terpstra, Nicholas. "Competing Views of the State and Social Welfare: The Medici Dukes, the Bigallo Magistrates, and Local Hospitals in Sixteenth Century Tuscany." *Renaissance Quarterly* 54, no. 4 (2001): 1319–55.

————. "Confraternal Prison Charity and Political Consolidation in Sixteenth Century Bologna." *Journal of Modern History* 66 (1994): 217–48.

————. "Confraternities and Local Cults: Civic Religion between Class and Politics in Renaissance Bologna." In *Civic Ritual and Drama in Late Medieval and Renaissance Europe*, ed. Alexandra Johnson and Wim Hüsken. Amsterdam: Rodopi, 1997. 143–74.

————. "Confraternities and Mendicant Orders: The Dynamics of Lay and Clerical Brotherhood." *Catholic Historical Review* 79 (1996): 1–22.

————. "Frati, confratelli, e famiglie dirigenti: fanciulli esposti tra carità e politica nella Bologna del Rinascimento." In *Confraternite, chiesa e società: Aspetti e problemi dell'associazionismo laicale europeo in età moderna e contemporanea*, ed. Liana Bertoldi Lenoci. Bari: 1994. 105–14.

————. *Lay Confraternities and Civic Religion in Renaissance Bologna*. Cambridge: Cambridge University Press, 1995.

————. "Making a Living, Making a Life: Work in the Orphanages of Florence and Bologna." *Sixteenth Century Journal* 31, no. 4 (2000): 1063–79.

————. "Mothers, Sisters, and Daughters: Girls and Conservatory Guardianship in Late Renaissance Florence." *Renaissance Studies* 17, no. 2 (2003): 201–29.

————. "Piety and Punishment: The Lay *Conforteria* and Civic Justice in Sixteenth Century Bologna." *Sixteenth Century Journal* 22 (1991): 679–94.

————. "Showing the Poor a Good Time: Caring for Body and Spirit in Bologna's Civic Charities." *Journal of Religious History* 28, no. 1 (2004): 19–34.

————. "The *Qualità* of Mercy: (Re)building Confraternal Charities in Renaissance Bologna." In *Confraternities and the Visual Arts in Renaissance Italy: Ritual, Spectacle, Image*, ed. Barbara Wisch and Diane C. Ahl. Cambridge: Cambridge University Press, 2000.

————. "Women in the Brotherhood: Gender, Class, and Politics in Renaissance Bolognese Confraternities." *Renaissance and Reformation* 24 (1990): 193–212.

Toniolo, Alberta. "'Per il mezzo delle scienze prestissimo si sorge . . .': L'esperimento sociale del collegio Pannolini (1617–1745)." In *I Bastardini: Patrimonio e memoria di un ospedale Bolognese*. Bologna: Edizioni A.G.E., 1990. 77–88.

Trexler, Richard. *Public Life in Renaissance Florence*. New York: Academic Press, 1980.

————. "Ritual in Florence: Adolescence and Salvation in the Renaissance." In *The Pursuit of Holiness in Late Medieval and Renaissance Religion*, ed. C. Trinkaus and H. Oberman. Leiden: Brill, 1974. 247–64.

————. "A Widows' Asylum of the Renaissance: The Orbatello of Florence." In *Dependence in Context in Renaissance Florence*. Binghamton: MRTS, 1994. 415–48.

Trkulja, Silvia Meloni, ed. *I Fiorentini nel 1562: Descritione delle Bocche della Città et stato di Fiorenza fatta l'anno 1562*. Firenze: Alberto Bruschi, 1991.

Una farmacia preindustriale in valdelsa: La Spezieria e lo spedale di Santa Fina nella città di San Gimignano Secc. XIV–VIII. S. Gimignano, Città di S. Gimignano, 1983.

Verardi Ventura, Sandra. "L'ordinamento bolognese dei secoli XVI–XVII." *L'Archiginnasio* 76 (1981).

Vittori, Ridolfo. "Bonifacio dalle Balle e le Putte di Santa Croce (1547?-1612)." Tesi di Laurea, Università di Bologna, 1985.

———. "La pietà di un mercante bolognese del tardo Cinquecento. Bonifacio dalle Balle e le putte di Santa Croce." *Il Carrobbio* 12 (1986): 327–50.

Yeo, Stephen. *Religion and Voluntary Organizations in Crisis*. London: Croom Helm, 1981.

Zarri, Gabriella. "I monasteri femminili a Bologna tra il XII e il XVII secolo." *Atti e memorie della deputazione di storia patria per le province di Romagna*, new series 24 (1973): 133–224.

———. "The Third Status." In *Time, Space, and Women's Lives in Early Modern Europe*, ed. Anne J. Schutte, Thomas Kuehn, and Silvana Seidel Menchi. Kirksville: Truman State University Press, 2001. 181–99.

Index